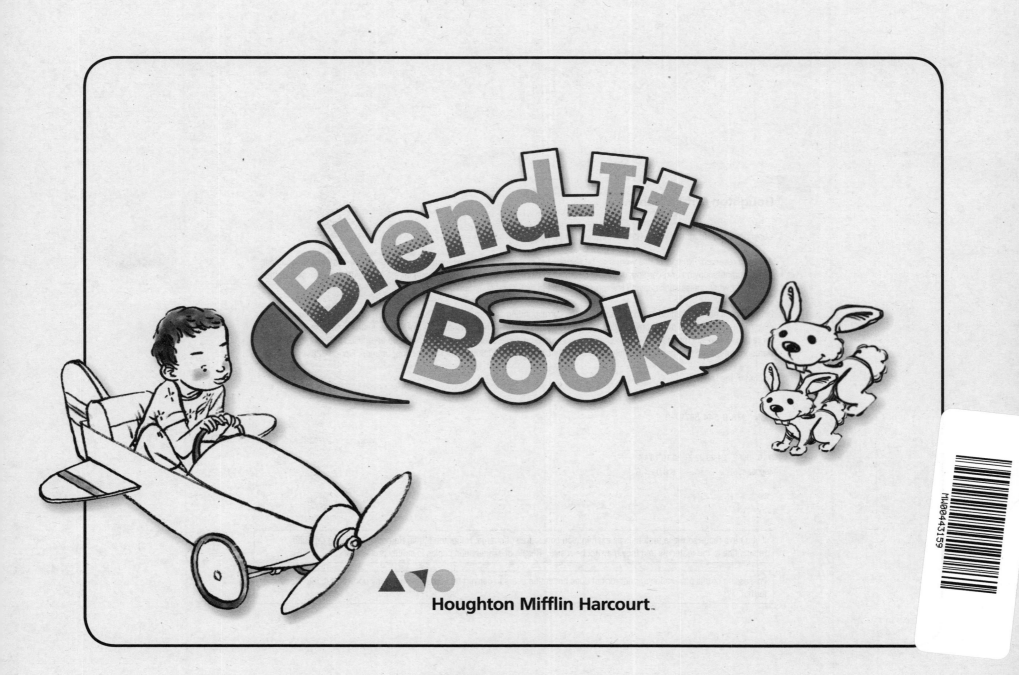

Blend-It Books

Houghton Mifflin Harcourt

Houghton Mifflin Harcourt

ISBN   978-0-544-58721-2

9 10   0982   24 23 22 21 20 19 18 17
4500654367   B C D E F G

What is the purpose of the **Blend-It Books?**

The **Blend-It Books** provide engaging, highly decodable texts (75% or more decodable words) for independent blending and reading practice, to promote decoding automaticity and fluency. For each sound-spelling reviewed or introduced in Grade 2 of the Houghton Mifflin Harcourt *Journeys* program, two four-page books feature the skill within connected text. For sounds with multiple spellings, two sound-spellings are sometimes paired in the same books for comparison. For example, there are two books for the short *o* sound. For the long *o* sound, there are two books for the *o_e* spelling, and two for the *oa* and *ow* spellings. Later in the year, two more books feature all those known spellings in longer words.

In addition, the **Blend-It Books** provide practice for key structural analysis skills. For example, for the -*ed* inflection there are two books for *each* pronunciation: /ĕd/, /d/, and /t/. Later in the year, four more books feature -*ed*, this time using words with spelling changes (dropped final *e*, doubled final consonant) before the inflection.

The text for each book also includes a smaller number (25% or fewer) of high-frequency words taught previously in *Journeys*. Those words were drawn from research studies on the most commonly used words in English, and words were chosen only when they received high scores on multiple lists.

For reference, the back of each book lists all the decodable words, decoding skills, and high-frequency words featured in that selection. A summary list inside the back cover shows all the decoding skills and high-frequency words taught to date in *Journeys*.

How are the **Blend-It Books** organized?

The **Blend-It Books** are numbered sequentially and reflect the order of the decoding skills taught in each unit of *Journeys*. The chart on the following pages lists all the books for Grade 2.

Volume 1: Books 1–92 for the skills in Units 1–2
Volume 2: Books 93–188 for the skills in Units 3–6

When do I use the **Blend-It Books?**

- Users of *Journeys* will find references to corresponding **Blend-It Books** in the phonics lessons in the Teacher's Editions.
- The books are also an excellent resource any time a child needs extra practice reading words with a specific sound/spelling.

How can I use the **Blend-It Books** to meet specific needs?

- Help children differentiate between two or more similar sound/spellings by reading and comparing books that feature them.
- Have English learners focus on sounds and spellings they find difficult in English by reading books chorally with an adult.
- Informally assess children's understanding of a new skill by having them read a book aloud to you.

What are the options for setting up the **Blend-It Books?**

- The books are available as blackline masters for copying, or in digital files that can be read onscreen or downloaded.
- Provide children with the books only as they need them, or set up the numbered books for children to access on their own all year.
- Make copies for children to read and color in class or take home, or prepare a laminated set for use at school.
- Set up a chart for children to track their own progress as they read.

This chart lists all the Grade 2 **Blend-It Books** (both volumes) and identifies books that correspond to the *Journeys* Sound/Spelling Cards.

Book	Skill	Sound/Spelling Cards
Book 1	short *a*	Apple
Book 2	short *a*	Apple
Book 3	short *i*	Igloo
Book 4	short *i*	Igloo
Book 5	closed syllables (CVC: short *a, i*)	Apple, Igloo
Book 6	closed syllables (CVC: short *a, i*)	Apple, Igloo
Book 7	short *o*	Ostrich
Book 8	short *o*	Ostrich
Book 9	short *u*	Umbrella
Book 10	short *u*	Umbrella
Book 11	short *e*	Elephant
Book 12	short *e*	Elephant
Book 13	closed syllables (CVC: short *o, u, e*)	Ostrich, Umbrella, Elephant
Book 14	closed syllables (CVC: short *o, u, e*)	Ostrich, Umbrella, Elephant
Book 15	long *a* (CVC*e*)	Acorn
Book 16	long *a* (CVC*e*)	Acorn
Book 17	long *i* (CVC*e*)	Ice Cream
Book 18	long *i* (CVC*e*)	Ice Cream
Book 19	/k/ spelled *c*	Cat
Book 20	/k/ spelled *c*	Cat
Book 21	/s/ spelled *c*	Seal
Book 22	/s/ spelled *c*	Seal
Book 23	long *o* (CVC*e*)	Ocean
Book 24	long *o* (CVC*e*)	Ocean
Book 25	long *u* /yo͞o/ (CVC*e*)	Uniform

Book	Skill	Sound/Spelling Cards
Book 26	long *u* /yo͞o/ (CVC*e*)	Uniform
Book 27	long *u* /o͞o/ (CVC*e*)	Moon
Book 28	long *u* /o͞o/ (CVC*e*)	Moon
Book 29	long *e* (CVC*e*)	Eagle
Book 30	long *e* (CVC*e*)	Eagle
Book 31	consonant *g* (hard *g*)	Goose
Book 32	consonant *g* (hard *g*)	Goose
Book 33	/j/ spelled *g, dge*	Jump
Book 34	/j/ spelled *g, dge*	Jump
Book 35	blends with *r*	
Book 36	blends with *r*	
Book 37	blends with *l*	
Book 38	blends with *l*	
Book 39	blends with *s*	
Book 40	blends with *s*	
Book 41	final blend *nd*	
Book 42	final blend *nd*	
Book 43	final blend *ng*	Ring
Book 44	final blend *ng*	Ring
Book 45	final blend *nk*	
Book 46	final blend *nk*	
Book 47	final blend *nt*	
Book 48	final blend *nt*	
Book 49	double final consonants: *ll*	Lion
Book 50	double final consonants: *ll*	Lion

Book	Skill	Sound/Spelling Cards
Book 51	double final consonants: *ss*	Seal
Book 52	double final consonants: *ss*	Seal
Book 53	double final consonants: *zz*	Zebra
Book 54	double final consonants: *zz*	Zebra
Book 55	double final consonants: *ff*	Fish
Book 56	double final consonants: *ff*	Fish
Book 57	consonants *ck*	Kangaroo
Book 58	consonants *ck*	Kangaroo
Book 59	double consonants (closed syllables)	
Book 60	double consonants (closed syllables)	
Book 61	digraph *th*	Thumb
Book 62	digraph *th*	Thumb
Book 63	digraph *sh*	Sheep
Book 64	digraph *sh*	Sheep
Book 65	digraph *wh*	Whale
Book 66	digraph *wh*	Whale
Book 67	digraphs *ch, _tch*	Chick
Book 68	digraphs *ch, _tch*	Chick
Book 69	digraph *ph*	Fish
Book 70	digraph *ph*	Fish
Book 71	ending *-s*	
Book 72	ending *-s*	
Book 73	ending *-ed* /ēd/	
Book 74	ending *-ed* /ēd/	
Book 75	ending *-ed* /d/	Duck

Book	Skill	Sound/Spelling Cards
Book 76	ending *-ed* /d/	Duck
Book 77	ending *-ed* /t/	Tiger
Book 78	ending *-ed* /t/	Tiger
Book 79	ending *-ing*	
Book 80	ending *-ing*	
Book 81	ending *-ed*: drop *e*	
Book 82	ending *-ed*: drop *e*	
Book 83	ending *-ing*: drop *e*	
Book 84	ending *-ing*: drop *e*	
Book 85	open syllables (CV)	Acorn, Eagle, Ice Cream, Ocean, Uniform
Book 86	open syllables (CV)	Acorn, Eagle, Ice Cream, Ocean, Uniform
Book 87	contractions *'s, n't*	
Book 88	contractions *'s, n't*	
Book 89	contractions *'ll, 'd*	
Book 90	contractions *'ll, 'd*	
Book 91	contractions *'ve, 're*	
Book 92	contractions *'ve, 're*	
Book 93	endings *-s, -es*	
Book 94	endings *-s, -es*	
Book 95	vowel digraphs *ai, ay*	Acorn
Book 96	vowel digraphs *ai, ay*	Acorn
Book 97	vowel digraphs *ee, ea*	Eagle
Book 98	vowel digraphs *ee, ea*	Eagle
Book 99	vowel digraphs *oa, ow*	Ocean
Book 100	vowel digraphs *oa, ow*	Ocean

Book	Skill	Sound/Spelling Cards
Book 101	compound words	
Book 102	compound words	
Book 103	schwa sound spelled *e, a*	
Book 104	schwa sound spelled *e, a*	
Book 105	schwa sound spelled *o, u*	
Book 106	schwa sound spelled *o, u*	
Book 107	schwa sound spelled *a, e, i, o, u*	
Book 108	schwa sound spelled *a, e, i, o, u*	
Book 109	ending *-ed*: double consonant	
Book 110	ending *-ed*: double consonant	
Book 111	ending *-ing*: double consonant	
Book 112	ending *-ing*: double consonant	
Book 113	long *i* spelled *igh, ie*	Ice Cream
Book 114	long *i* spelled *igh, ie*	Ice Cream
Book 115	long *i* spelled *i, y*	Ice Cream
Book 116	long *i* spelled *i, y*	Ice Cream
Book 117	long *e* spelled *y*	Eagle
Book 118	long *e* spelled *y*	Eagle
Book 119	ending *-es*: change *y* to *i*	
Book 120	ending *-es*: change *y* to *i*	
Book 121	*r*-controlled *ar*	Artist
Book 122	*r*-controlled *ar*	Artist
Book 123	*r*-controlled *or, ore*	Orange
Book 124	*r*-controlled *or, ore*	Orange
Book 125	*r*-controlled *er*	Bird
Book 126	*r*-controlled *er*	Bird
Book 127	*r*-controlled *ir, ur*	Bird
Book 128	*r*-controlled *ir, ur*	Bird
Book 129	homophones	
Book 130	homophones	
Book 131	ending *-er*: double consonant	
Book 132	ending *-er*: double consonant	
Book 133	ending *-est*: double consonant	
Book 134	ending *-est*: double consonant	
Book 135	suffix *-y*	Eagle
Book 136	suffix *-y*	Eagle
Book 137	suffix *-ly*	
Book 138	suffix *-ly*	
Book 139	suffix *-ful*	
Book 140	suffix *-ful*	
Book 141	syllable *-tion*	
Book 142	syllable *-tion*	
Book 143	syllable *-ture*	
Book 144	syllable *-ture*	
Book 145	prefix *un-*	
Book 146	prefix *un-*	
Book 147	prefix *re-*	
Book 148	prefix *re-*	
Book 149	prefix *over-*	
Book 150	prefix *over-*	

Book	Skill	Sound/Spelling Cards
Book 151	prefix *pre-*	
Book 152	prefix *pre-*	
Book 153	prefix *mis-*	
Book 154	prefix *mis-*	
Book 155	silent consonants: *kn, gn*	Noodles
Book 156	silent consonants: *kn, gn*	Noodles
Book 157	silent consonants: *mb*	Mouse
Book 158	silent consonants: *mb*	Mouse
Book 159	silent consonants: *wr*	Rooster
Book 160	silent consonants: *wr*	Rooster
Book 161	/ô/ spelled *au, aw*	Saw
Book 162	/ô/ spelled *au, aw*	Saw
Book 163	/ô/ spelled *al, a*	Saw
Book 164	/ô/ spelled *al, a*	Saw
Book 165	/ô/ spelled *o*	Saw
Book 166	/ô/ spelled *o*	Saw
Book 167	/o͞o/ spelled *oo, ou*	Moon
Book 168	/o͞o/ spelled *oo, ou*	Moon
Book 169	/o͞o/ spelled *ew, ue*	Moon
Book 170	/o͞o/ spelled *ew, ue*	Moon
Book 171	/o͝o/ spelled *oo*	Cook
Book 172	/o͝o/ spelled *oo*	Cook
Book 173	possessives with *'s, s'*	
Book 174	possessives with *'s, s'*	
Book 175	/ou/ spelled *ou, ow*	Owl

Book	Skill	Sound/Spelling Cards
Book 176	/ou/ spelled *ou, ow*	Owl
Book 177	long *a* in longer words	Acorn
Book 178	long *a* in longer words	Acorn
Book 179	long *i* in longer words	Ice Cream
Book 180	long *i* in longer words	Ice Cream
Book 181	/oi/ spelled *oy, oi*	Boy
Book 182	/oi/ spelled *oy, oi*	Boy
Book 183	long *o* in longer words	Ocean
Book 184	long *o* in longer words	Ocean
Book 185	long *e* in longer words	Eagle
Book 186	long *e* in longer words	Eagle
Book 187	syllable *_le*	Table
Book 188	syllable *_le*	Table

Max Reaches

© Houghton Mifflin Harcourt Publishing Company

DECODABLE WORDS

BOOK 93

Target Skill: **base words and endings -s, -es**

catches	gives	licks	peaches	saves
dishes	glasses	likes	pitches	tells
eats	hands	passes	plates	tosses
gets	kisses	Patches	reaches	

Previously Taught Skills

and	fine	is	nice	this
at	full	it	on	will
ball	game	job	pass	with
Bea	he	Max	peach	yet
dad	has	mom	so	
dog	his	next	that	

SKILLS APPLIED IN WORDS IN STORY: short *a*; short *i*; short *o*; short *e*; long *a* (CVC*e*); long *i* (CVC*e*); /s/ spelled *c*; /g/ spelled *g*; blends with *l*; final blend *nd*; double final consonants *ll, ss*; consonants *ck*; double consonant (CVC, closed syllables); consonant digraph *th*; consonant digraph *sh*; consonant digraphs *ch, tch*; base words and ending -*s* (no spelling changes); CV syllable pattern (open syllables); base words and endings -*s* and -*es* **From Grade 1:** consonants; short vowels; long *e* spelled *ea*

HIGH-FREQUENCY WORDS

a	good	play(s)
does	help	the
for	her	to

Houghton Mifflin Harcourt.

Max Reaches

High-Frequency Words Taught to Date

Grade 1						
a	brown	far	here	myself	right	those	would
about	buy	father	high	near	said	thought	write
above	by	few	hold	never	school	three	years
across	call	field	house	new	second	to	yellow
after	car	find	how	night	see	today	you
again	carry	first	I	no	seven	together	young
all	caught	five	idea	noise	shall	too	your
almost	city	fly	into	nothing	she	took	
along	cold	follow	is	now	should	toward	**Grade 2**
always	come	food	kinds	of	show	try	afraid
and	could	for	know	off	sing	two	air
animal	country	four	large	old	small	under	another
are	covers	friend	laugh	once	soil	until	better
around	cried	friendship	learning	one	some	use	cheer
away	different	full	light	only	sometimes	very	children
baby	do	funny	like	open	soon	walk	dark
ball	does	give	listen	or	sorry	want	hard
be	done	go	little	our	starts	warms	hello
bear	don't	goes	live	out	stories	was	hundred
beautiful	door	good	long	over	story	wash	kept
because	down	great	look	own	studied	watch	might
been	draw	green	loudly	paper	sure	water	mind
before	earth	ground	loved	party	surprised	we	next
began	eat	grow	make	people	take	were	other
begins	eight	happy	many	pictures	talk	what	pretty
bird	enough	have	maybe	play	teacher	where	really
blue	even	he	me	please	the	who	says
both	every	head	minute	pull	their	why	sleep
boy	everyone	hear	more	pushed	there	window	table
bring	eyes	heard	most	put	these	with	this
brothers	fall	help	mother	read	they	work	told
	family	her	my	ready	think	world	

Decoding skills taught to date: short *a*; short *i*; CVC syllable pattern (closed); short *o*, short *u*; short *e*; long *a* (CVC*e*); long *i* (CVC*e*); /k/ spelled *c*; /s/ spelled *c*; long *o* (CVC*e*); long *u* /yōō/ (CVC*e*); long *u* /ōō/ (CVC*e*); long *e* (CVC*e*); /g/ spelled *g*; /j/ spelled *g*, *dge*; blends with *r*; blends with *l*; blends with *s*; final blend *nd*; final blend *ng*; final blend *nk*; final blend *nt*; double final consonants *ll, ss, ff, zz*; consonants *ck*; double consonant (CVC, closed syllables); consonant digraph *th*; consonant digraph *sh*; consonant digraph *wh*; consonant digraphs *ch, tch*; consonant digraph *ph*; base words and ending -*s* (no spelling changes); base words and ending -*ed* /ed/ (no spelling changes); base words and ending -*ed* /d/ (no spelling changes); base words and ending -*ed* /t/ (no spelling changes); base words and ending -*ing* (no spelling changes); base words and ending -*ed* (drop *e* before ending); base words and ending -*ing* (drop *e* before ending); CV syllable pattern (open syllables); contractions with *'s* and *n't*; contractions with *'ll* and *'d*; contractions with *'ve* and *'re*; base words and endings -*s* and -*es* **From Grade 1:** consonants; short vowels; long *e* spelled *ea*

Max reaches for his dog, Patches. Patches licks Max. Patches likes to play with Max. He gives Max dog kisses. Max likes this.

4

BOOK 93

Max Reaches

Max reaches for the dishes. He passes the plates to his mom. Next, he will pass the glasses. He likes to help, yet he has his hands full. Mom tells Max that he does a fine job.

1

Max plays ball with his dad. Dad pitches, and Max catches. Max is good at this game. Play on, Max!

Max reaches for peaches. He gets a peach and tosses it to Bea. Max eats his peach. It is so nice. Bea saves her peach.

Cass Rushes

DECODABLE WORDS

Target Skill: **base words and endings -s and -es**

brushes	dashes	jumps	rushes	washes
catches	dishes	peaches	snatches	
clocks	drinks	puts	socks	
cuts	eats	runs	splashes	

Previously Taught Skills

and	clock	is	rush	time
bag	did	late	set	toast
bed	dressed	milk	she	up
bus	face	Mom	sink	wake
buzz	get	next	so	will
can	glass	not	teeth	
Cass	in	on	then	

SKILLS APPLIED IN WORDS IN STORY: short *a*; short *i*; CVC syllable pattern (closed); short *o*; short *u*; short *e*; long *a* (CVC*e*); long *i* (CVC*e*); /s/ spelled *c*; /g/ spelled *g*; blends with *r*; blends with *l*; blends with *s*; final blend *nd*; final blend *mp*; double final consonants *ll, ss, zz*; consonants *ck*; consonant digraph *th*; consonant digraph *sh*; consonant digraphs *ch, tch*; base words and ending -*s* (no spelling changes); base words and ending -*ed* /t/ (no spelling changes); CV syllable pattern (open syllables); base words and endings -*s* and -*es* **From Grade 1:** consonants; short vowels; long *e* (*ee, ea*); long *o* (*oa*)

HIGH-FREQUENCY WORDS

a	of	to	water
for	out	too	
her	the	two	

© Houghton Mifflin Harcourt Publishing Company

Cass Rushes

High-Frequency Words Taught to Date

Grade 1							would
a	brown	far	here	myself	right	those	write
about	buy	father	high	near	said	thought	years
above	by	few	hold	never	school	three	yellow
across	call	field	house	new	second	to	you
after	car	find	how	night	see	today	young
again	carry	first	I	no	seven	together	your
all	caught	five	idea	noise	shall	too	
almost	city	fly	into	nothing	she	took	
along	cold	follow	is	now	should	toward	*Grade 2*
always	come	food	kinds	of	show	try	afraid
and	could	for	know	off	sing	two	air
animal	country	four	large	old	small	under	another
are	covers	friend	laugh	once	soil	until	better
around	cried	friendship	learning	one	some	use	cheer
away	different	full	light	only	sometimes	very	children
baby	do	funny	like	open	soon	walk	dark
ball	does	give	listen	or	sorry	want	hard
be	done	go	little	our	starts	warms	hello
bear	don't	goes	live	out	stories	was	hundred
beautiful	door	good	long	over	story	wash	kept
because	down	great	look	own	studied	watch	might
been	draw	green	loudly	paper	sure	water	mind
before	earth	ground	loved	party	surprised	we	next
began	eat	grow	make	people	take	were	other
begins	eight	happy	many	pictures	talk	what	pretty
bird	enough	have	maybe	play	teacher	where	really
blue	even	he	me	please	the	who	says
both	every	head	minute	pull	their	why	sleep
boy	everyone	hear	more	pushed	there	window	table
bring	eyes	heard	most	put	these	with	this
brothers	fall	help	mother	read	they	work	told
	family	her	my	ready	think	world	

Decoding skills taught to date: short *a*; short *i*; CVC syllable pattern (closed); short *o*; short *u*; short *e*; long *a* (CVC*e*); long *i* (CVC*e*); /k/ spelled *c*; /s/ spelled *c*; long *o* (CVC*e*); long *u* /yōō/ (CVC*e*); long *u* /ōō/ (CVC*e*); long *e* (CVC*e*), /g/ spelled *g*; /j/ spelled *g*, *dge*; blends with *r*; blends with *l*; blends with *s*; final blend *nd*; final blend *ng*; final blend *nk*; final blend *nt*; double final consonants *ll, ss, ff, zz*; consonants *ck*; double consonant (CVC, closed syllables); consonant digraph *th*; consonant digraph *sh*; consonant digraph *wh*; consonant digraphs *ch, tch*; consonant digraph *ph*; base words and ending -*s* (no spelling changes); base words and ending -*ed* /ed/ (no spelling changes); base words and ending -*ed* /d/ (no spelling changes); base words and ending -*ed* /t/ (no spelling changes); base words and ending -*ing* (no spelling changes); base words and ending -*ed* (drop *e* before ending); base words and ending -*ing* (drop *e* before ending); CV syllable pattern (open syllables); contractions with *'s* and *n't*; contractions with *'ll* and *'d*; contractions with *'ve* and *'re*; base words and endings -*s* and -*es*

Cass snatches her bag and rushes to the bus. Cass catches the bus. Next time, she will set two clocks so she can get up on time and not rush.

Cass Rushes

Cass is late! Her clock did not buzz to wake her up. Cass jumps out of bed. She dashes to get dressed. She puts on her socks, too.

Cass runs water in the sink. She splashes water on her face. She brushes her teeth.

Mom cuts peaches for Cass. Then Cass eats toast and peaches. She drinks a glass of milk. Then she washes her dishes.

Sunday Trip

DECODABLE WORDS

Target Skill: **vowel digraphs** *ai, ay*

Blains	jay	played	stay	yay
day	may	rail	tail	
gray	May	rain	wait	
hay	pain	Ray	way	

Previously Taught Skills

and	car	his	Mom	swishing
asked	Dad	hope	next	that
at	drive	in	nice	they
back	drove	it	no	time
barn	farm	its	not	trip
be	fell	it's	on	used
but	go	last	see	we
came	got	long	stack	will
can	had	map	Sunday	yelled

SKILLS APPLIED IN WORDS IN STORY: short *a*; short *i*; CVC syllable pattern (closed); short *o*; short *u*; short *e*; long *a* (CVCe); long *i* (CVCe); /s/ spelled *c*; long *o* (CVCe); /g/ spelled *g*; blends with *r*; blends with *l*; blends with *s*; final blend *nd*; double final consonants *ll*; consonants *ck*; consonant digraph *th*; consonant digraph *sh*; base words and ending *-ed* /d/ (no spelling changes); base words and ending *-ed* /t/ (no spelling changes); base words and ending *-ing* (no spelling changes); CV syllable pattern (open syllables); contractions with *'s*; vowel digraphs *ai, ay*   **From Grade 1:** consonants; short vowels; compound words; long *e* (*e, ee*); *r*-controlled vowel *ar*

HIGH-FREQUENCY WORDS

a	I	the	was
animal	of	their	would
could	said	to	

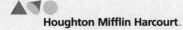
Houghton Mifflin Harcourt.

Sunday Trip

High-Frequency Words Taught to Date

Grade 1							Grade 2
a	buy	few	house	night	seven	too	afraid
about	by	field	how	no	shall	took	against
above	call	find	I	noise	she	toward	air
across	car	first	idea	nothing	should	try	another
after	carry	five	into	now	show	two	better
again	caught	fly	is	of	sing	under	cheer
all	city	follow	kinds	off	small	until	children
almost	cold	food	know	old	soil	use	dark
along	come	for	large	once	some	very	girl
always	could	four	laugh	one	sometimes	walk	hard
and	country	friend	learning	only	soon	want	hello
animal	covers	friendship	light	open	sorry	warms	hundred
are	cried	full	like	or	starts	was	kept
around	different	funny	listen	our	stories	wash	might
away	do	give	little	out	story	watch	mind
baby	does	go	live	over	studied	water	morning
ball	done	goes	long	own	sure	we	next
be	don't	good	look	paper	surprised	were	other
bear	door	great	loudly	party	take	what	pretty
beautiful	down	green	loved	people	talk	where	really
because	draw	ground	make	pictures	teacher	who	says
been	earth	grow	many	play	the	why	sleep
before	eat	happy	maybe	please	their	window	someone
began	eight	have	me	pull	there	with	table
begins	enough	he	minute	pushed	these	work	this
bird	even	head	more	put	they	world	told
blue	every	hear	most	read	think	would	
both	everyone	heard	mother	ready	those	write	
boy	eyes	help	my	right	thought	years	
bring	fall	her	myself	said	three	yellow	
brothers	family	here	near	school	to	you	
brown	far	high	never	second	today	young	
	father	hold	new	see	together	your	

Decoding skills taught to date: short *a*; short *i*; CVC syllable pattern (closed); short *o*; short *u*; short *e*; long *a* (CVC*e*); long *i* (CVC*e*); /k/ spelled *c*; /s/ spelled *c*; long *o* (CVC*e*); long *u* /yōō/ (CVC*e*); long *u* /ōō/ (CVC*e*); long *e* (CVC*e*); /g/ spelled *g*; /j/ spelled *g, dge*; blends with *r*; blends with *l*; blends with *s*; final blend *nd*; final blend *ng*; final blend *nk*; final blend *nt*; double final consonants *ll, ss, ff, zz*; consonants *ck*; double consonant (CVC, closed syllables); consonant digraph *th*; consonant digraph *sh*; consonant digraph *wh*; consonant digraphs *ch, tch*; consonant digraph *ph*; base words and ending -*s* (no spelling changes); base words and ending -*ed* /ed/ (no spelling changes); base words and ending -*ed* /d/ (no spelling changes); base words and ending -*ed* /t/ (no spelling changes); base words and ending -*ing* (no spelling changes); base words and ending -*ed* (drop *e* before ending); base words and ending -*ing* (drop *e* before ending); CV syllable pattern (open syllables); contractions with '*s* and *n't*; contractions with '*ll* and '*d*; contractions with '*ve* and '*re*; base words and endings -*s*, -*es*; vowel digraphs *ai, ay* **From Grade 1:** consonants; short vowels; compound words; long *e* (*e, ee*); r-controlled vowel *ar*

Sunday Trip

It was a nice Sunday in May. No rain fell. The Blains said they would go on a farm trip. Ray could not wait!

The Blains had a nice day. Ray played in the hay, but it came time to go.

"Can we stay?" asked Ray.

"We may be back next Sunday," said Mom.

"Yay!" yelled Ray. "I hope it will not be a pain to wait that long!"

4

1

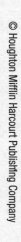

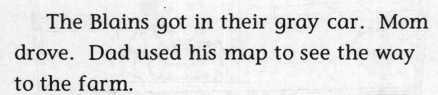

The Blains got in their gray car. Mom
drove. Dad used his map to see the way
to the farm.

"It will be a long drive," said Dad.

At last, the Blains got to the farm.

"See that barn and stack of hay?"
said Ray.

"See that jay on the hay?" said Dad.

"See the animal at the rail? It's
swishing its tail!" said Mom.

Snail's Mail Trail

DECODABLE WORDS

Target Skill: vowel digraphs *ai, ay*

day	mail	Snail	strain	way
fail	Quail	Snail's	trail	
gray	rain	stayed	wailed	

Previously Taught Skills

and	glad	is	on	this
came	go	it	see	up
did	got	job	she	went
drip	had	long	steep	wet
drop	he	mud	stop	
fell	him	nice	sun	
get	his	not	take	

SKILLS APPLIED IN WORDS IN STORY: short *a*; short *i*; CVC syllable pattern (closed); short *o*; short *u*; short *e*; long *a* (CVC*e*); long *i* (CVC*e*); /s/ spelled *c*; /g/ spelled *g*; blends with *r*; blends with *l*; blends with *s*; final blend *nd*; double final consonants *ll*; consonant digraph *th*; consonant digraph *sh*; base words and ending *-ed* /d/ (no spelling changes); CV syllable pattern (open syllables); vowel digraphs *ai, ay* **From Grade 1:** consonants; short vowels; possessives with *'s*; long *e* (*e, ee*)

HIGH-FREQUENCY WORDS

a	the	too
now	to	was

Snail's Mail Trail

High-Frequency Words Taught to Date

Grade 1							Grade 2
a	buy	few	house	night	seven	too	afraid
about	by	field	how	no	shall	took	against
above	call	find	I	noise	she	toward	air
across	car	first	idea	nothing	should	try	another
after	carry	five	into	now	show	two	better
again	caught	fly	is	of	sing	under	cheer
all	city	follow	kinds	off	small	until	children
almost	cold	food	know	old	soil	use	dark
along	come	for	large	once	some	very	girl
always	could	four	laugh	one	sometimes	walk	hard
and	country	friend	learning	only	soon	want	hello
animal	covers	friendship	light	open	sorry	warms	hundred
are	cried	full	like	or	starts	was	kept
around	different	funny	listen	our	stories	wash	might
away	do	give	little	out	story	watch	mind
baby	does	go	live	over	studied	water	morning
ball	done	goes	long	own	sure	we	next
be	don't	good	look	paper	surprised	were	other
bear	door	great	loudly	party	take	what	pretty
beautiful	down	green	loved	people	talk	where	really
because	draw	ground	make	pictures	teacher	who	says
been	earth	grow	many	play	the	why	sleep
before	eat	happy	maybe	please	their	window	someone
began	eight	have	me	pull	there	with	table
begins	enough	he	minute	pushed	these	work	this
bird	even	head	more	put	they	world	told
blue	every	hear	most	read	think	would	
both	everyone	heard	mother	ready	those	write	
boy	eyes	help	my	right	thought	years	
bring	fall	her	myself	said	three	yellow	
brothers	family	here	near	school	to	you	
brown	far	high	never	second	today	young	
	father	hold	new	see	together	your	

Decoding skills taught to date: short *a*; short *i*; CVC syllable pattern (closed); short *o*; short *u*; short *e*; long *a* (CVC*e*); long *i* (CVC*e*); /k/ spelled *c*; /s/ spelled *c*; long *o* (CVC*e*); long *u* /yo͞o/ (CVC*e*); long *u* /o͞o/ (CVC*e*); long *e* (CVC*e*); /g/ spelled *g*; /j/ spelled *g, dge*; blends with *r*; blends with *l*; blends with *s*; final blend *nd*; final blend *ng*; final blend *nk*; final blend *nt*; double final consonants *ll, ss, ff, zz*; consonants *ck*; double consonant (CVC, closed syllables); consonant digraph *th*; consonant digraph *sh*; consonant digraph *wh*; consonant digraphs *ch, tch*; consonant digraph *ph*; base words and ending -*s* (no spelling changes); base words and ending -*ed* /ed/ (no spelling changes); base words and ending -*ed* /d/ (no spelling changes); base words and ending -*ed* /t/ (no spelling changes); base words and ending -*ing* (no spelling changes); base words and ending -*ed* (drop *e* before ending); base words and ending -*ing* (drop *e* before ending); CV syllable pattern (open syllables); contractions with '*s* and *n't*; contractions with '*ll* and '*d*; contractions with '*ve* and '*re*; base words and endings -*s*, -*es*; vowel digraphs *ai, ay*
From Grade 1: consonants; short vowels; possessives with '*s*; long *e* (*e, ee*)

Snail stayed on the trail. The rain and wet mud did not stop him. He did not fail.

Snail got the mail to Quail. Quail was glad to see him. She was glad to get mail.

Snail's Mail Trail

The sun came up. Snail went to his job. He had mail to take to Quail. Snail was glad it was a nice day.

Snail went up the Mail Trail. It was a steep trail and a long way to go. Snail had to strain.

Rain fell on the Mail Trail. Drip, drip, drop.

"Rain, rain, rain!" wailed Snail. "This day is now gray. The trail is wet!" Snail got wet, too.

Lee's Tree

DECODABLE WORDS

Target Skill: **vowel digraphs *ee, ea***

clean	leaf	near	seeds	tree
each	leans	neat	sees	weeds
eats	Lee	peek	sleep	week
Green	Lee's	peeks	speeds	
keeps	meet	see	Street	

Previously Taught Skills

an	but	he	not	that
and	can	his	on	then
at	close	is	picks	up
before	glad	it	plants	
best	go	likes	play	
big	goes	next	Sam	
bike	has	nice	such	

SKILLS APPLIED IN WORDS IN STORY: short *a*; short *i*; short *o*; short *u*; short *e*; closed syllable (CVC); long *i* (CVC*e*); /k/ spelled *c*; /s/ spelled *c*; long *o* (CVC*e*); /g/ spelled *g*; blends with *r*; blends with *l*; blends with *s*; final blend *nd*; final blend *nt*; double final consonants *ll*; consonants *ck*; consonant digraph *th*; consonant digraph *ch*; ending *-s*; open syllables (CV); vowel digraph *ay*; vowel digraphs *ee, ea* **From Grade 1:** consonants; short vowels; /z/ spelled *s*; inflection *-s*; blends with *s*; final blend *st*; possessives with *'s*

HIGH-FREQUENCY WORDS

a	every	live(s)	to
animal	fall(s)	now	under
around	friend	pull	window
by	grow	pull(s)	
does	have	the	

Houghton Mifflin Harcourt

vowel digraphs *ee, ea*

BOOK 97

Lee's Tree

High-Frequency Words Taught to Date

Grade 1	buy	few	house	night	see	together	your
a	by	field	how	no	seven	too	
about	call	find	I	noise	shall	took	Grade 2
above	car	first	idea	nothing	she	toward	afraid
across	carry	five	into	now	should	try	against
after	caught	fly	is	of	show	two	air
again	city	follow	kinds	off	sing	under	another
all	cold	food	know	old	small	until	better
almost	come	for	large	once	soil	use	cheer
along	could	four	laugh	one	some	very	children
always	country	friend	learning	only	sometimes	walk	dark
and	covers	friendship	light	open	soon	want	everything
animal	cried	full	like	or	sorry	warms	girl
are	different	funny	listen	our	starts	was	hard
around	do	give	little	out	stories	wash	hello
away	does	go	live	over	story	watch	hundred
baby	done	goes	long	own	studied	water	kept
ball	don't	good	look	paper	sure	we	might
be	door	great	loudly	party	surprised	were	mind
bear	down	green	loved	people	take	what	morning
beautiful	draw	ground	make	picture	talk	where	next
because	earth	grow	many	pictures	teacher	who	other
been	eat	happy	maybe	play	the	why	part
before	eight	have	me	please	their	window	pretty
began	enough	he	minute	pull	there	with	really
begins	even	head	more	pushed	these	work	says
bird	every	hear	most	put	they	world	sleep
blue	everyone	heard	mother	read	think	would	slowly
both	eyes	help	my	ready	those	write	someone
boy	fall	her	myself	right	thought	years	store
bring	family	here	near	said	three	yellow	table
brothers	far	high	never	school	to	you	this
brown	father	hold	new	second	today	young	told

Decoding skills taught to date: short *a*; short *i*; short *o*; short *u*; short *e*; closed syllable (CVC); long *a* (CVC*e*); long *i* (CVC*e*); /k/ spelled *c*; /s/ spelled *c*; long *o* (CVC*e*); long *u* /yōō/ (CVC*e*); long *u* /ōō/ (CVC*e*); long *e* (CVC*e*); /g/ spelled *g*; /j/ spelled *g, dge*; blends with *r*; blends with *l*; blends with *s*; final blend *nd*; final blend *ng*; final blend *nk*; final blend *nt*; double final consonants *ll, ss, ff, zz*; consonants *ck*; double consonants (closed syllables); consonant digraph *th*; consonant digraph *sh*; consonant digraph *wh*; consonant digraphs *ch, tch*; consonant digraph *ph*; ending -*s*; ending -*ed* /ed/; ending -*ed* /d/; ending -*ed* /t/; ending -*ing*; ending -*ed*: drop *e*; ending -*ing*: drop *e*; open syllables (CV); contractions '*s* and *n't*; contractions '*ll* and '*d*; contractions '*ve* and '*re*; endings -*s*, -*es*; vowel digraphs *ai, ay*; vowel digraphs *ee, ea*   **From Grade 1:** consonants; short vowels; /z/ spelled *s*; inflection -*s*; blends with *s*; final blend *st*; possessives with '*s*

Lee's Tree

Lee's best friend, Sam, speeds up to the tree on his bike. Sam leans his bike on the tree. Then Lee and Sam play under the tree. Lee is glad that he has such a nice tree.

Meet Lee. He lives on Green Street. Lee can see a big tree by his window. Lee likes to peek at his tree before he goes to sleep.

Every week, Lee keeps his tree neat and clean. Lee pulls up weeds around the tree. He picks up each leaf that falls. Lee plants seeds under the tree.

Lee sees an animal near his tree. Lee peeks at it, but he does not go close to it. The animal eats the weeds that grow under the tree. Now Lee does not have to pull up weeds next week!

Seals and Seagulls

DECODABLE WORDS

Target Skill: vowel digraphs *ee, ea*

beach	eat	reach	seal	steep
beaks	feast	reaches	seals	year
beat	keep	sea	seek	
deep	meal	seagull	sees	
each	meals	seagulls	steal	

Previously Taught Skills

and	get	off	rock	that
at	go	on	rocks	these
barks	here	play	same	this
big	is	pup	sand	turn
bits	it	pups	she	use
catch	its	pup's	snap	waves
fish	mom	quite	swim	will

SKILLS APPLIED IN WORDS IN STORY: short *a*; short *i*; short *o*; short *u*; closed syllable (CVCe); long *a* (CVCe); long *i* (CVCe); /k/ spelled *c*; long *u* /yōo/ (CVCe); long *e* (CVCe), /g/ spelled *g*; blends with *l*; blends with *s*; final blend *nd*; double final consonants *ll*, *ff*; consonants *ck*; consonant digraph *th*; consonant digraph *sh*; consonant digraphs *ch*, *tch*; ending -*s*; open syllables (CV); endings -*s*, -*es*; vowel digraph *ay*; vowel digraphs *ee, ea*
From Grade 1: consonants; short vowels; /z/ spelled *s*; inflection *s*; final blend *st*; possessives with *'s*; *r*-controlled vowel *ar*; *r*-controlled *ur*; compound words

HIGH-FREQUENCY WORDS

a	for	live	their
are	have	sometimes	to
baby	into	the	too

Houghton Mifflin Harcourt.

vowel digraphs *ee, ea*

BOOK 98

Seals and Seagulls

High-Frequency Words Taught to Date

Grade 1							
a	buy	few	house	night	see	together	your
about	by	field	how	no	seven	too	
above	call	find	I	noise	shall	took	Grade 2
across	car	first	idea	nothing	she	toward	afraid
after	carry	five	into	now	should	try	against
again	caught	fly	is	of	show	two	air
all	city	follow	kinds	off	sing	under	another
almost	cold	food	know	old	small	until	better
along	come	for	large	once	soil	use	cheer
always	could	four	laugh	one	some	very	children
and	country	friend	learning	only	sometimes	walk	dark
animal	covers	friendship	light	open	soon	want	everything
are	cried	full	like	or	sorry	warms	girl
around	different	funny	listen	our	starts	was	hard
away	do	give	little	out	stories	wash	hello
baby	does	go	live	over	story	watch	hundred
ball	done	goes	long	own	studied	water	kept
be	don't	good	look	paper	sure	we	might
bear	door	great	loudly	party	surprised	were	mind
beautiful	down	green	loved	people	take	what	morning
because	draw	ground	make	picture	talk	where	next
been	earth	grow	many	pictures	teacher	who	other
before	eat	happy	maybe	play	the	why	part
began	eight	have	me	please	their	window	pretty
begins	enough	he	minute	pull	there	with	really
bird	even	head	more	pushed	these	work	says
blue	every	hear	most	put	they	world	sleep
both	everyone	heard	mother	read	think	would	slowly
boy	eyes	help	my	ready	those	write	someone
bring	fall	her	myself	right	thought	years	store
brothers	family	here	near	said	three	yellow	table
brown	far	high	never	school	to	you	this
	father	hold	new	second	today	young	told

Decoding skills taught to date: short *a*; short *i*; short *o*; short *u*; short *e*; closed syllable (CVC); long *a* (CVC*e*); long *i* (CVC*e*); /k/ spelled *c*; /s/ spelled *c*; long *o* (CVC*e*); long *u* /yo͞o/ (CVC*e*); long *u* /o͞o/ (CVC*e*); long *e* (CVC*e*); /g/ spelled *g*; /j/ spelled *g, dge*; blends with *r*; blends with *l*; blends with *s*; final blend *nd*; final blend *ng*; final blend *nk*; final blend *nt*; double final consonants *ll, ss, ff, zz*; consonants *ck*; double consonants (closed syllables); consonant digraph *th*; consonant digraph *sh*; consonant digraph *wh*; consonant digraphs *ch, tch*; consonant digraph *ph*; ending *-s*; ending *-ed* /ed/; ending *-ed* /d/; ending *-ed* /t/; ending *-ing*; ending *-ed*: drop *e*; ending *-ing*: drop *e*; open syllables (CV); contractions *'s* and *n't*; contractions *'ll* and *'d*; contractions *'ve* and *'re*; endings *-s, -es*; vowel digraphs *ai, ay*; vowel digraphs *ee, ea*   ***From Grade 1:*** consonants; short vowels; /z/ spelled *s*; inflection *s*; final blend *st*; possessives with *'s*; r-controlled vowel *ar*; r-controlled *ur*; compound words

Seals and Seagulls

This is the deep sea. Seals live here. Each year, these seals swim to the same beach. Seals go to this beach and have their pups. Pups are baby seals.

Seals eat fish, too. Sometimes seagulls seek to steal fish that seals get.

This seagull reaches for the seal pup's meal. The mom seal sees it reach. She barks. The pup will keep its meal!

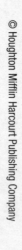

Waves beat on steep rocks at the beach. The waves snap bits off the rocks. These rock bits turn into beach sand. Seal pups play on rocks and beach sand.

Seagulls live at the beach, too. Seagulls use their beaks to catch their meals. A big fish is quite a feast! Seagulls eat this feast on the beach.

Joan's Boat

DECODABLE WORDS

Target Skill: vowel digraphs *oa*, *ow*

boat	Joan	road	stows
coast	Joan's	rows	Woodrow
coats	loads	slow	
float	low	soap	
Flow	Low	stowed	

Previously Taught Skills

at	gets	it	sets	up
back	had	man	she	will
boxes	has	named	shipping	with
bring	he	not	take	
brings	helps	on	takes	
called	his	places	that	
dock	in	pole	them	
from	is	rope	truck	

SKILLS APPLIED IN WORDS IN STORY: short *a*; short *i*; short *o*; short *u*; short *e*; /s/ spelled *c*; long *a* (CVC*e*); closed syllables (CVC); long *o* (CVC*e*); /k/ spelled *c*; /g/ spelled *g*; blends with *r*; blends with *l*; blends with *s*; final blend *ng*; double final consonants *ll*; consonants *ck*; consonant digraph *th*; consonant digraph *sh*; ending -*s*; ending -*ing*; ending -*ed* /d/; open syllables (CV); endings -*s*, -*es*; vowel digraph *ay*; vowel digraphs *oa*, *ow* **From Grade 1:** consonants; short vowels; /z/ spelled *s*; inflection -*s*; possessives with *'s*; final blend *st*; compound words; /o͞o/ spelled *oo*; ending -*ing*: double consonant; ending -*ed*: drop *e*

HIGH-FREQUENCY WORDS

a	her	onto	the	was
away	now	people	to	
call(ed)	of	puts	want(ed)	

Houghton Mifflin Harcourt

Joan's Boat

High-Frequency Words Taught to Date

Grade 1

a	by	find	idea	now	sing	until	cheer
about	call	first	into	of	small	use	children
above	car	five	is	off	soil	very	dark
across	carry	fly	kinds	old	some	walk	everything
after	caught	follow	know	once	sometimes	want	front
again	city	food	large	one	soon	warms	girl
all	cold	for	laugh	only	sorry	was	hair
almost	come	four	learning	open	starts	wash	hard
along	could	friend	light	or	stories	watch	hello
always	country	friendship	like	our	story	water	hundred
and	covers	full	listen	out	studied	we	kept
animal	cried	funny	little	over	sure	were	might
are	different	give	live	own	surprised	what	mind
around	do	go	long	paper	take	where	morning
away	does	goes	look	party	talk	who	next
baby	done	good	loudly	people	teacher	why	other
ball	don't	great	loved	pictures	the	window	part
be	door	green	make	play	their	with	pretty
bear	down	ground	many	please	there	work	really
beautiful	draw	grow	maybe	pull	these	world	says
because	earth	happy	me	pushed	they	would	sky
been	eat	have	minute	put	think	write	sleep
before	eight	he	more	read	those	years	slowly
began	enough	head	most	ready	thought	yellow	someone
begins	even	hear	mother	right	three	you	store
bird	every	heard	my	said	to	young	table
blue	everyone	help	myself	school	today	your	this
both	eyes	her	near	second	together		told
boy	fall	here	never	see	too	**Grade 2**	
bring	family	high	new	seven	took	afraid	
brothers	far	hold	night	shall	toward	against	
brown	father	house	no	she	try	air	
buy	few	how	noise	should	two	another	
	field	I	nothing	show	under	better	

Decoding skills taught to date: short *a*; short *i*; short *o*; short *u*; short *e*; closed syllables (CVC); long *a* (CVC*e*); long *i* (CVC*e*); /k/ spelled *c*; /s/ spelled *c*; long *o* (CVC*e*); long *u* /yo͞o/ (CVC*e*); long *o* (CVC*e*) /o͞o/; long *e* (CVC*e*); /g/ spelled *g*; /j/ spelled *g*, *dge*; blends with *r*; blends with *l*; blends with *s*; final blend *nd*; final blend *ng*; final blend *nk*; final blend *nt*; double final consonants *ll*, *ss*, *ff*, *zz*; consonants *ck*; double consonants (closed syllables); consonant digraph *th*; consonant digraph *sh*; consonant digraph *wh*; consonant digraphs *ch*, *tch*; consonant digraph *ph*; ending -*s*; ending -*ed* /ed/; ending -*ed* /d/; ending -*ed* /t/; ending -*ing*; ending -*ed*: drop *e*; ending -*ing*: drop *e*; open syllables (CV); contractions '*s* and *n't*; contractions '*ll* and '*d*; contractions '*ve* and '*re*; endings -*s*, -*es*; vowel digraphs *ai*, *ay*; vowel digraphs *ee*, *ea* **From Grade 1:** consonants; short vowels; /z/ spelled *s*; inflection -*s*; possessives with '*s*; final blend *st*; compound words; /o͞o/ spelled *oo*; ending -*ing*: double consonant; ending -*ed*: drop *e*

Bowie has a truck. He loads the
boxes of soap onto his truck. He sets
them in rows. He will take the soap on
the road to the man.

Joan gets back on Flow. She has
boxes of coats on her boat. Joan will
take them up the coast.

Joan's Boat

Joan has a shipping boat. Joan
named her boat Flow. Joan brings boxes
to people on the coast. She stows the
boxes on Flow. She stows them in rows
on Flow.

Woodrow Low helps Joan at the dock. Woodrow is not slow. He takes a rope from Joan's boat. He puts it on a pole. Now Flow will not float away.

Joan gets boxes that she stowed on Flow. A man had called Joan. He was low on soap. He wanted Joan to bring soap. Joan places the boxes in rows on the dock.

Everything Grows

DECODABLE WORDS

Target Skill: vowel digraphs *oa, ow*

bowl	glows	Joan	oats	stow
coat	goats	loads	Owen	tow
coats	grow	mow	rows	yellow
crows	grows	oak	snow	

Previously Taught Skills

and	hay	man	shoos	until
big	he	melts	sled	we
bin	helps	on	spring	wheat
can	him	place	stay	will
Dad	in	plants	summer	with
dog	is	play	sun	
eat	it	safe	then	
get	it's	see	time	
hat	like	sell	top	
hats	make	shoo	trees	

SKILLS APPLIED IN WORDS IN STORY: short *a*; short *i*; short *o*; short *u*; short *e*; closed syllables (CVC); long *a* (CVC*e*); long *i* (CVC*e*); /k/ spelled *c*; /s/ spelled *c*; /g/ spelled *g*; blends with *r*; blends with *l*; blends with *s*; final blend *nd*; final blend *ng*; final blend *nt*; double final consonants *ll*; double consonants (closed syllables); consonant digraph *th*; consonant digraph *sh*; consonant digraph *wh*; ending -*s*; open syllables (CV); contraction '*s*; endings -*s, -es*; vowel digraph *ay*; vowel digraphs *ee, ea*; vowel digraphs *oa, ow*
From Grade 1: consonants; short vowels; /z/ spelled *s*; inflection *s*; /o͞o/ spelled *oo*; compound words; *r*-controlled *er*

HIGH-FREQUENCY WORDS

a	away	of	the	too
also	cold	see	they	want
animals	everything	tall	to	

Houghton Mifflin Harcourt

Everything Grows

High-Frequency Words Taught to Date

Grade 1						
a	by	find	idea	now	sing	until	cheer
about	call	first	into	of	small	use	children
above	car	five	is	off	soil	very	dark
across	carry	fly	kinds	old	some	walk	everything
after	caught	follow	know	once	sometimes	want	front
again	city	food	large	one	soon	warms	girl
all	cold	for	laugh	only	sorry	was	hair
almost	come	four	learning	open	starts	wash	hard
along	could	friend	light	or	stories	watch	hello
always	country	friendship	like	our	story	water	hundred
and	covers	full	listen	out	studied	we	kept
animal	cried	funny	little	over	sure	were	might
are	different	give	live	own	surprised	what	mind
around	do	go	long	paper	take	where	morning
away	does	goes	look	party	talk	who	next
baby	done	good	loudly	people	teacher	why	other
ball	don't	great	loved	pictures	the	window	part
be	door	green	make	play	their	with	pretty
bear	down	ground	many	please	there	work	really
beautiful	draw	grow	maybe	pull	these	world	says
because	earth	happy	me	pushed	they	would	sky
been	eat	have	minute	put	think	write	sleep
before	eight	he	more	read	those	years	slowly
began	enough	head	most	ready	thought	yellow	someone
begins	even	hear	mother	right	three	you	store
begins	every	heard	my	said	to	young	table
bird	everyone	help	myself	school	today	your	this
blue	eyes	her	near	second	together		told
both	fall	here	never	see	too	**Grade 2**	
boy	family	high	new	seven	took	afraid	
bring	far	hold	night	shall	toward	against	
brothers	father	house	no	she	try	air	
brown	few	how	noise	should	two	another	
buy	field	I	nothing	show	under	better	

Decoding skills taught to date: short *a*; short *i*; short *o*; short *u*; short *e*; closed syllables (CVC); long *a* (CVC*e*); long *i* (CVC*e*); /k/ spelled *c*; /s/ spelled *c*; long *o* (CVC*e*); long *u* /yōō/ (CVC*e*); long *o* (CVC*e*) /ōō/; long *e* (CVC*e*); /g/ spelled *g*; /j/ spelled *g*, *dge*; blends with *r*; blends with *l*; blends with *s*; final blend *nd*; final blend *ng*; final blend *nk*; final blend *nt*; double final consonants *ll, ss, ff, zz*; consonants *ck*; double consonants (closed syllables); consonant digraph *th*; consonant digraph *sh*; consonant digraph *wh*; consonant digraphs *ch, tch*; consonant digraph *ph*; ending -*s*; ending -*ed* /ed/; ending -*ed* /d/; ending -*ed* /t/; ending -*ing*; ending -*ed*: drop *e*; ending -*ing*: drop *e*; open syllables (CV); contractions *'s* and *n't*; contractions *'ll* and *'d*; contractions *'ve* and *'re*; endings -*s*, -*es*; vowel digraphs *ai, ay*; vowel digraphs *ee, ea*; vowel digraphs *oa, ow*   **From Grade 1:** consonants; short vowels; /z/ spelled *s*; inflection *s*; /ōō/ spelled *oo*; compound words; *r*-controlled *er*

It is spring. The yellow sun glows. It melts the snow away. Dad plants wheat and oats. We can see them grow!

We make a man with hay. The man will shoo the crows away. We get him a coat and hat. Owen likes him!

4

© Houghton Mifflin Harcourt Publishing Company

Everything Grows

It is summer. The yellow sun glows. Plants grow big and tall. Rows of oats and wheat grow. Oak trees grow.

Animals also grow. Goats grow. Owen the dog grows, too.

1

It is fall. Time to mow the wheat and oats. Dad loads them in a bin. He will stow them until it's time to sell them. They will stay safe.

The crows want to eat the wheat and oats. We shoo them away. Owen shoos them, too!

It is cold. Time to get coats and hats. Time to play in the snow.

We make a man of snow. We get a bowl and place it on top. We tow Joan on a sled. Owen likes snow, too!

Rainbow
DECODABLE WORDS

Target Skill: compound words

inside	rainbow	sunshine	weekend

Previously Taught Skills

am	grass	must	red	wet
and	green	need	sad	when
Ben	has	nice	Sam	while
best	he	no	see	will
but	in	pass	stay	yard
can	is	play	stop	yelled
day	it	playing	tells	yellow
fast	jumped	rain	this	
game	leaped	rained	time	
games	leaping	raining	up	
glad	let's	rains	us	
go	long	ran	we	

SKILLS APPLIED IN WORDS IN STORY: short *a*; short *i*; short *o*; short *u*; short *e*; closed syllables (CVC); long *a* (CVC*e*); long *i* (CVC*e*); /k/ spelled *c*; /s/ spelled *c*; /g/ spelled *g*; blends with *r*; blends with *l*; blends with *s*; final blend *nd*; final blend *ng*; double final consonants *ll*, *ss*; double consonants (closed syllables); consonant digraph *th*; consonant digraph *sh*; consonant digraph *wh*; ending -*s*; ending -*ed* /d/; ending -*ed* /t/; ending -*ing*; open syllables (CV); contractions *'s*; ending -*s*; vowel digraphs *ai*, *ay*; vowel digraphs *ee*, *ea*; vowel digraph *ow*; compound words **From Grade 1:** consonants; short vowels; /z/ spelled *s*; final blend *st*; final blend -*mp*; r-controlled *ar*

HIGH-FREQUENCY WORDS

a	I	said	to
blue	laugh(ed)	the	
have	look	they	

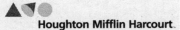
Houghton Mifflin Harcourt.

Rainbow

High-Frequency Words Taught to Date

Grade 1							
a	call	five	kinds	once	soon	was	front
about	car	fly	know	one	sorry	wash	girl
above	carry	follow	large	only	starts	watch	hair
across	caught	food	laugh	open	stories	water	hard
after	city	for	learning	or	story	we	hello
again	cold	four	light	our	studied	were	hundred
all	come	friend	like	out	sure	what	kept
almost	could	friendship	listen	over	surprised	where	might
along	country	full	little	own	take	who	mind
always	covers	funny	live	paper	talk	why	morning
and	cried	give	long	party	teacher	window	next
animal	different	go	look	people	the	with	other
are	do	goes	loudly	pictures	their	work	part
around	does	good	loved	play	there	world	pretty
away	done	great	make	please	these	would	really
baby	don't	green	many	pull	they	write	says
ball	door	ground	maybe	pushed	think	years	sky
be	down	grow	me	put	those	yellow	sleep
bear	draw	happy	minute	read	thought	you	slowly
beautiful	earth	have	more	ready	three	young	someone
because	eat	he	most	right	to	your	store
been	eight	head	mother	said	today		table
before	enough	hear	my	school	together	*Grade 2*	this
began	even	heard	myself	second	too	afraid	told
begins	every	help	near	see	took	against	
bird	everyone	her	never	seven	toward	air	
blue	eyes	here	new	shall	try	another	
both	fall	high	night	she	two	better	
boy	family	hold	no	should	under	book	
bring	far	house	noise	show	until	care	
brothers	father	how	nothing	sing	use	cheer	
brown	few	I	now	small	very	children	
buy	field	idea	of	soil	walk	dark	
by	find	into	off	some	want	ever	
	first	is	old	sometimes	warms	everything	

Decoding skills taught to date: short *a*; short *i*; short *o*; short *u*; short *e*; closed syllables (CVC); long *a* (CVC*e*); long *i* (CVC*e*); /k/ spelled *c*; /s/ spelled *c*; long *o* (CVC*e*); long *u* /yo͞o/ (CVC*e*); long *u* /o͞o/ (CVC*e*); long *e* (CVC*e*); /g/ spelled *g*; /j/ spelled *g*, *dge*; blends with *r*; blends with *l*; blends with *s*; final blend *nd*; final blend *ng*; final blend *nk*; final blend *nt*; double final consonants *ll*, *ss*, *ff*, *zz*; consonants *ck*; double consonants (closed syllables); consonant digraph *th*; consonant digraph *sh*; consonant digraph *wh*; consonant digraphs *ch*, *tch*; consonant digraph *ph*; ending *-s*; ending *-ed* /ed/; ending *-ed* /d/; ending *-ed* /t/; ending *-ing*; open syllables (CV); contractions *'s* and *n't*; contractions *'ll* and *'d*; contractions *'ve* and *'re*; endings *-s*, *-es*; vowel digraphs *ai*, *ay*; vowel digraphs *ee*, *ea*; vowel digraphs *oa*, *ow*; compound words   **From Grade 1:** consonants; short vowels; /z/ spelled *s*; final blend *st*; final blend *-mp*; r-controlled *ar*

"Look! A rainbow!" yelled Sam.

"I see red and blue," said Ben.

"I see yellow and green," said Sam.

"A rainbow tells us we will have a
nice day. I am glad we can play games
in the sunshine," laughed Ben.

Rainbow

"It has rained a long time," said sad
Ben. "When will it stop?"

"This is the weekend. We need to play
in sunshine," said sad Sam.

"We must stay inside while it rains," said Ben. "We can play games to pass the time."

"No. The best game is leaping and playing in the grass," said Sam. "But the grass is wet, and it is raining."

"Look! No rain! I can see sunshine. Let's go!" yelled Ben. He jumped up fast.

Sam and Ben ran to the yard. They ran and leaped.

Snowflake's Coat

DECODABLE WORDS

Target Skill: compound words

handmade	inside	sheepskin	Snowflake's
hillside	lifetime	Snowflake	springtime

Previously Taught Skills

am	from	it's	not	stuck
and	go	last	on	that
best	got	let's	play	then
big	groaned	like	Rabbit	thing
box	grow	lots	see	things
can't	had	mine	she	this
coat	he	moaned	showed	up
cute	held	Mom	sniffed	will
den	hole	much	snow	with
dug	in	need	so	yet
feet	is	no	soft	
fits	it	nose	stayed	

SKILLS APPLIED IN WORDS IN STORY: short *a*; short *i*; short *o*; short *u*; short *e*; closed syllables (CVC*e*); /k/ spelled *c*; long *a* (CVC*e*); long *i* (CVC*e*); long *o* (CVC*e*); long *u* /yoo/ (CVC*e*); /g/ spelled *g*; blends with *r*; blends with *l*; blends with *s*; final blend *nd*; final blend *ft*; final blend *ng*; double final consonants *ll*, *ff*; consonants *ck*; consonant digraph *th*; consonant digraph *sh*; consonant digraph *ch*; ending *-s*; ending *-ed* /d/; open syllables (CV); contractions *'s, n't*; vowel digraph *ay*; vowel digraph *ee*; vowel digraphs *oa, ow*; compound words
From Grade 1: consonants; short vowels; /z/ spelled *s*; final blend *st*; possessive *'s*

HIGH-FREQUENCY WORDS

a	I	the	was
cold	of	to	you
could	one	too	your
have	said	walk	yours

Houghton Mifflin Harcourt.

Snowflake's Coat

Snowflake's Coat

High-Frequency Words Taught to Date

Grade 1	by	find	idea	now	sing	until	book
a	call	first	into	of	small	use	care
about	car	five	is	off	soil	very	cheer
above	carry	fly	kinds	old	some	walk	children
across	caught	follow	know	once	sometimes	want	dark
after	city	food	large	one	soon	warms	ever
again	cold	for	laugh	only	sorry	was	everything
all	come	four	learning	open	starts	wash	front
almost	could	friend	light	or	stories	watch	girl
along	country	friendship	like	our	story	water	hair
always	covers	full	listen	out	studied	we	hard
and	cried	funny	little	over	sure	were	hello
animal	different	give	live	own	surprised	what	hundred
are	do	go	long	paper	take	where	kept
around	does	goes	look	party	talk	who	might
away	done	good	loudly	people	teacher	why	mind
baby	don't	great	loved	pictures	the	window	morning
ball	door	green	make	play	their	with	next
be	down	ground	many	please	there	work	other
bear	draw	grow	maybe	pull	these	world	part
beautiful	earth	happy	me	pushed	they	would	pretty
because	eat	have	minute	put	think	write	really
been	eight	he	more	read	those	years	says
before	enough	head	most	ready	thought	yellow	sky
began	even	hear	mother	right	three	you	sleep
begins	every	heard	my	said	to	young	slowly
bird	everyone	help	myself	school	today	your	someone
blue	eyes	her	near	second	together		store
both	fall	here	never	see	too	*Grade 2*	table
boy	family	high	new	seven	took	afraid	this
bring	far	hold	night	shall	toward	against	told
brothers	father	house	no	she	try	air	
brown	few	how	noise	should	two	another	
buy	field	I	nothing	show	under	better	

Decoding skills taught to date: short *a*; short *i*; short *o*; short *u*; short *e*; closed syllables (CVC); long *a* (CVC*e*); long *i* (CVC*e*); /k/ spelled *c*; /s/ spelled *c*; long *o* (CVC*e*); long *u* /yōō/ (CVC*e*); long *u* /ōō/ (CVC*e*); long *e* (CVC*e*); /g/ spelled *g*; /j/ spelled *g*, *dge*; blends with *r*; blends with *l*; blends with *s*; final blend *nd*; final blend *ng*; final blend *nk*; final blend *nt*; double final consonants *ll*, *ss*, *ff*, *zz*, consonants *ck*; double consonants (closed syllables); consonant digraph *th*; consonant digraph *sh*; consonant digraph *wh*; consonant digraphs *ch*, *tch*; consonant digraph *ph*; ending -*s*; ending -*ed* /ed/; ending -*ed* /d/; ending -*ed* /t/; ending -*ing*; open syllables (CV); contractions *'s* and *n't*; contractions *'ll* and *'d*; contractions *'ve* and *'re*; endings -*s*, -*es*; vowel digraphs *ai*, *ay*; vowel digraphs *ee*, *ea*; vowel digraphs *oa*, *ow*; compound words **From Grade 1:** consonants; short vowels; /z/ spelled *s*; final blend *st*; possessives with *'s*

Snowflake's Coat

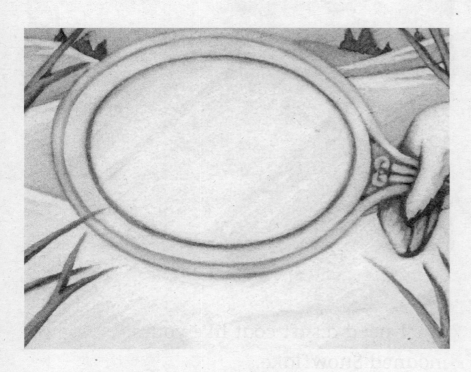

"See? You have the best coat. It's like mine. It fits you from your cute nose to your feet. It will grow with you and will last a lifetime!" Mom said.

Mom Rabbit dug a hole in the den. Snowflake could see snow. He sniffed. It was not yet springtime.

"Let's go and play," said Mom.

4

1

"No, it's cold on this hillside,"
Snowflake groaned. "I need a coat."
So he stayed inside.

Then Mom got a big coat. It was a
handmade sheepskin coat.

"This is too much coat," Snowflake
said. "I am stuck and can't walk."

"I need a soft coat like yours,"
moaned Snowflake.

So Mom got a box that had lots of
things inside it. She held up one thing
and showed Snowflake.

Book Sale

DECODABLE WORDS

Target Skill: schwa spelled *e, a*

animals	hundreds	never	Roland	travel
dozens	Japan	present	seven	

Previously Taught Skills

a	can	he	likes	read	way
am	carry	her	lots	replied	we
as	chimed	him	maybe	ride	well
asked	Chip	home	me	sale	who'd
at	Cole	I'd	Molly	smell	will
bags	dad	I'll	mom	so	with
be	exclaimed	in	most	soon	you
begins	for	is	much	them	Zack
bikes	fun	it	my	think	
book	get	it's	need	Tom	
books	go	Jan	noon	trucks	
but	going	like	on	used	

SKILLS APPLIED IN WORDS IN STORY: short *a*; short *i*; closed syllables (CVC); short *o*; short *u*; short *e*; long *a* (CVCe); long *i* (CVCe); /k/ spelled *c*; long *o* (CVCe); /g/ spelled *g*; blends with *r*; blends with *l*; blends with *s*; final blend *nd*; final blend *nk*; final blend *nt*; double final consonants *ll*; consonants -*ck*; consonant digraph *th*; consonant digraph *wh*; consonant digraph *ch*; ending -*s*; ending -*ed* /d/; ending -*ed*: drop e; open syllables (CV); contractions *'ll*, *'d*; vowel digraphs *ai*, *ay*; vowel digraphs *ee*, *ea*; schwa spelled *e, a*
From Grade 1: consonants; short vowels; /z/ spelled *s*; r-controlled *or*; r-controlled *er*; vowel digraph *oo* /o͞o/; /oo/ spelled *oo*; long *e* spelled *y*

HIGH-FREQUENCY WORDS

a	have	of	there	too
brother	I	said	they	
enough	new	the	to	

Houghton Mifflin Harcourt

Book Sale

High-Frequency Words Taught to Date

Grade 1	by	find	idea	now	sing	until	book
a	call	first	into	of	small	use	care
about	car	five	is	off	soil	very	cheer
above	carry	fly	kinds	old	some	walk	children
across	caught	follow	know	once	sometimes	want	dark
after	city	food	large	one	soon	warms	ever
again	cold	for	laugh	only	sorry	was	everything
all	come	four	learning	open	starts	wash	front
almost	could	friend	light	or	stories	watch	girl
along	country	friendship	like	our	story	water	hair
always	covers	full	listen	out	studied	we	hard
and	cried	funny	little	over	sure	were	hello
animal	different	give	live	own	surprised	what	hundred
are	do	go	long	paper	take	where	kept
around	does	goes	look	party	talk	who	might
away	done	good	loudly	people	teacher	why	mind
baby	don't	great	loved	pictures	the	window	morning
ball	door	green	make	play	their	with	next
be	down	ground	many	please	there	work	other
bear	draw	grow	maybe	pull	these	world	part
beautiful	earth	happy	me	pushed	they	would	pretty
because	eat	have	minute	put	think	write	really
been	eight	he	more	read	those	years	says
before	enough	head	most	ready	thought	yellow	sky
began	even	hear	mother	right	three	you	sleep
begins	every	heard	my	said	to	young	slowly
bird	everyone	help	myself	school	today	your	someone
blue	eyes	her	near	second	together		store
both	fall	here	never	see	too	Grade 2	table
boy	family	high	new	seven	took	afraid	this
bring	far	hold	night	shall	toward	against	told
brothers	father	house	no	she	try	air	
brown	few	how	noise	should	two	another	
buy	field	I	nothing	show	under	better	

Decoding skills taught to date: short *a*; short *i*; closed syllables (CVC); short *o*; short *u*; short *e*; long *a* (CVC*e*); long *i* (CVC*e*); /k/ spelled *c*; /s/ spelled *c*; long *o* (CVC*e*); long *u* /yo͞o/ (CVC*e*); long *u* /o͞o/ (CVC*e*); long *e* (CVC*e*); /g/ spelled *g*; /j/ spelled *g*, *dge*; blends with *r*; blends with *l*; blends with *s*; final blend *nd*; final blend *ng*; final blend *nk*; final blend *nt*; double final consonants *ll*; double final consonants *ss*; double final consonants *zz*; double final consonants *ff*; consonants *-ck*; double consonants (closed syllables); consonant digraph *th*; consonant digraph *sh*; consonant digraph *wh*; consonant digraphs *ch*, *tch*; consonant digraph *ph*; ending *-s*; ending *-ed* /ed/; ending *-ed* /d/; ending *-ed*: drop *e*; ending *-ing*: drop *e*; open syllables (CV); contractions *'ll*, *'d*; contractions *'ve*, *'re*; endings *-s*, *-es*; vowel digraphs *ai*, *ay*; vowel digraphs *ee*, *ea*; vowel digraphs *oa*, *ow*; compound words; schwa spelled *e*, *a*

"The sale begins at noon," Roland said. "We can ride bikes."

"We will need lots of bags to carry the books home," said Zack.

"Lots of bags for lots of books!" Roland exclaimed.

4

Book Sale

"I am going to a book sale," said Roland. "Who'd like to go with me?"

"I'd like to go," said Chip. "My mom is going to Japan. I'd like to get her a travel book."

"I'll go, too," Jan chimed in. "My dad likes animals. I'd like to get him a book on animals."

1

"I need a book," said Zack. "It's a present for my brother, Tom. He will be seven soon. He likes books with trucks in them."

"Will there be lots of books?" asked Molly. "I like new books. I like the way they smell."

"Most books will be used," replied Roland. "But I think there will be new books, as well. Maybe hundreds of them."

"You can never have enough books!" exclaimed Cole. "I have dozens of books at home. I like to read. It is so much fun!"

The Yellow Elephant

DECODABLE WORDS

Target Skill: schwa spelled *e, a*

about	around	elephant	Helen	sofa
above	asleep	elephants	opened	village
animals	chicken	forest	pajamas	

Previously Taught Skills

am	dream	inside	reading	up
an	dreamed	it	room	wallpaper
and	fell	looked	rug	whispered
big	flew	lucky	sat	woke
book	fly	most	she	yellow
box	had	mule	sky	
but	he	now	so	
cat	her	on	soon	
day	hills	own	thud	
dog	in	owned	trees	

SKILLS APPLIED IN WORDS IN STORY: long *o* (CVC*e*); long *u* (CVC*e*); closed syllables (CVC); /g/ spelled *g*; blends with *r, l, s*; final blends *nd, nt*; double final consonants *ll*; consonants -*ck*; double consonants (closed syllables); consonant digraphs *th, sh, wh*; endings -*s*, -*ed* /d/, -*ing*; open syllables (CV); vowel digraphs *ay, ee, ea*; vowel digraph *ow*; compound words; schwa spelled *e, a*   **From Grade 1:** consonants; short vowels; /z/ spelled *s*; r-controlled *or, er*; /o͞o/ spelled *oo, ew*; *ou* spelled *ou, ow*; long *e* spelled *y*

HIGH-FREQUENCY WORDS

a	eyes	lived	said	was
again	from	many	the	what
could	I	one	wanted	

Houghton Mifflin Harcourt.

The Yellow Elephant

High-Frequency Words Taught to Date

Grade 1							
a	by	find	idea	now	sing	until	book
about	call	first	into	of	small	use	care
above	car	five	is	off	soil	very	cheer
across	carry	fly	kinds	old	some	walk	children
after	caught	follow	know	once	sometimes	want	dark
again	city	food	large	one	soon	warms	ever
all	cold	for	laugh	only	sorry	was	everything
almost	come	four	learning	open	starts	wash	front
along	could	friend	light	or	stories	watch	girl
always	country	friendship	like	our	story	water	hair
and	covers	full	listen	out	studied	we	hard
animal	cried	funny	little	over	sure	were	hello
are	different	give	live	own	surprised	what	hundred
around	do	go	long	paper	take	where	kept
away	does	goes	look	party	talk	who	might
baby	done	good	loudly	people	teacher	why	mind
ball	don't	great	loved	pictures	the	window	morning
be	door	green	make	play	their	with	next
bear	down	ground	many	please	there	work	other
beautiful	draw	grow	maybe	pull	these	world	part
because	earth	happy	me	pushed	they	would	pretty
been	eat	have	minute	put	think	write	really
before	eight	he	more	read	those	years	says
began	enough	head	most	ready	thought	yellow	sky
begins	even	hear	mother	right	three	you	sleep
bird	every	heard	my	said	to	young	slowly
blue	everyone	help	myself	school	today	your	someone
both	eyes	her	near	second	together		store
boy	fall	here	never	see	too	*Grade 2*	table
bring	family	high	new	seven	took	afraid	this
brothers	far	hold	night	shall	toward	against	told
brown	father	house	no	she	try	air	
buy	few	how	noise	should	two	another	
	field	I	nothing	show	under	better	

Decoding skills taught to date: short *a*; short *i*; closed syllables (CVC); short *o*; short *u*; short *e*; long *a* (CVC*e*); long *i* (CVC*e*); /k/ spelled *c*; /s/ spelled *c*; long *o* (CVC*e*); long *u* /yoo/ (CVC*e*); long *u* /oo/ (CVC*e*); long *e* (CVC*e*); /g/ spelled *g*; /j/ spelled *g*, *dge*; blends with *r*; blends with *l*; blends with *s*; final blend *nd*; final blend *ng*; final blend *nk*; final blend *nt*; double final consonants *ll*; double final consonants *ss*; double final consonants *zz*; double final consonants *ff*; consonants -*ck*; double consonants (closed syllables); consonant digraph *th*; consonant digraph *sh*; consonant digraph *wh*; consonant digraphs *ch*, *tch*; consonant digraph *ph*; ending -*s*; ending -*ed* /ed/; ending -*ed* /d/; ending -*ed*: drop *e*; ending -*ing*: drop *e*; open syllables (CV); contractions '*ll*, '*d*; contractions '*ve*, '*re*; endings -*s*, -*es*; vowel digraphs *ai*, *ay*; vowel digraphs *ee*, *ea*; vowel digraphs *oa*, *ow*; compound words; schwa spelled *e*, *a*

The Yellow Elephant

Helen lived in a village in the hills. Helen had many animals. She had a cat and a dog. She had a mule and a chicken. But what Helen wanted most was an elephant.

A thud woke Helen from her dream. She opened her eyes and looked around. A big box sat on the rug. Helen opened it up. Inside was an elephant—a yellow elephant.

"Now I own a yellow elephant!" Helen said. "I am so lucky!"

"I am the lucky one," whispered the yellow elephant.

4

1

Helen had elephant pajamas. She had elephants on the wallpaper in her room.

One day, Helen sat on the sofa reading. The book was about a yellow elephant. Soon she fell asleep. Helen had a dream. She dreamed she owned a yellow elephant.

In her dream, the elephant could fly. He flew her up in the sky. He flew her above the trees in the forest. Again and again Helen and the elephant flew.

Lunch

DECODABLE WORDS

Target Skill: **schwa spelled** *o, u*

aprons	cotton	Melody	potato	second
bottom	gallon	minutes	season	tomato

Previously Taught Skills

add	first	kitchen	peeled	up
and	for	look	please	washed
asked	get	lot	pot	we
big	got	lunch	pretty	will
bring	great	made	sink	with
butter	he	make	sixty	you
came	help	me	sliced	
cook	helped	meat	smelled	
Dad	her	mix	soon	
exclaimed	home	Mom	spices	
fills	in	next	thank	
finds	it	package	then	

SKILLS APPLIED IN WORDS IN STORY: closed syllables (CVC); long *a* (CVC*e*); long *i* (CVC*e*); /k/ spelled *c*; /s/ spelled *c*; long *o* (CVC*e*); /g/ spelled *g*; blends with *r, l, s*; final blends *nd, nk*; double final consonants *ll*; consonants *-ck*; double consonants (CVC); consonant digraphs *th, sh, ch, tch*; endings *-s, -es, -ed* /d/; vowel digraphs *ai, ee, ea*; schwa spelled *a*; schwa spelled *o, u* **From Grade 1:** consonants; short vowels; /z/ spelled *s*; *r*-controlled *er, ir*; /o͞o/ spelled *oo*; /o͞o/ spelled *oo, ew*; long *e* spelled *y*

HIGH-FREQUENCY WORDS

a	I	said	to	wanted
finds	of	should	too	
her	put	the	two	

Lunch

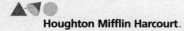
Houghton Mifflin Harcourt

High-Frequency Words Taught to Date

Grade 1	by	find	idea	now	sing	until	book
a	call	first	into	of	small	use	care
about	car	five	is	off	soil	very	cheer
above	carry	fly	kinds	old	some	walk	children
across	caught	follow	know	once	sometimes	want	dark
after	city	food	large	one	soon	warms	ever
again	cold	for	laugh	only	sorry	was	everything
all	come	four	learning	open	starts	wash	front
almost	could	friend	light	or	stories	watch	girl
along	country	friendship	like	our	story	water	hair
always	covers	full	listen	out	studied	we	hard
and	cried	funny	little	over	sure	were	hello
animal	different	give	live	own	surprised	what	hundred
are	do	go	long	paper	take	where	kept
around	does	goes	look	party	talk	who	might
away	done	good	loudly	people	teacher	why	mind
baby	don't	great	loved	pictures	the	window	morning
ball	door	green	make	play	their	with	next
be	down	ground	many	please	there	work	other
bear	draw	grow	maybe	pull	these	world	part
beautiful	earth	happy	me	pushed	they	would	pretty
because	eat	have	minute	put	think	write	really
been	eight	he	more	read	those	years	says
before	enough	head	most	ready	thought	yellow	sky
began	even	hear	mother	right	three	you	sleep
begins	every	heard	my	said	to	young	slowly
bird	everyone	help	myself	school	today	your	someone
blue	eyes	her	near	second	together		store
both	fall	here	never	see	too	Grade 2	table
boy	family	high	new	seven	took	afraid	this
bring	far	hold	night	shall	toward	against	told
brothers	father	house	no	she	try	air	
brown	few	how	noise	should	two	another	
buy	field	I	nothing	show	under	better	

Decoding skills taught to date: short *a*; short *i*; closed syllables (CVC); short *o*; short *u*; short *e*; long *a* (CVC*e*); long *i* (CVC*e*); /k/ spelled *c*; /s/ spelled *c*; long *o* (CVC*e*); long *u* /yōō/ (CVC*e*); long *u* /ōō/ (CVC*e*); long *e* (CVC*e*); /g/ spelled *g*; /j/ spelled *g*, *dge*; blends with *r*; blends with *l*; blends with *s*; final blend *nd*; final blend *ng*; final blend *nk*; final blend *nt*; double final consonants *ll*; double final consonants *ss*; double final consonants *zz*; double final consonants *ff*; consonants -*ck*; double consonants (closed syllables); consonant digraph *th*; consonant digraph *sh*; consonant digraph *wh*; consonant digraphs *ch*, *tch*; consonant digraph *ph*; ending -*s*; ending -*ed* /ed/; ending -*ed* /d/; ending -*ed*: drop *e*; ending -*ing*: drop *e*; open syllables (CV); contractions *'ll*, *'d*; contractions *'ve*, *'re*; endings -*s*, -*es*; vowel digraphs *ai*, *ay*; vowel digraphs *ee*, *ea*; vowel digraphs *oa*, *ow*; compound words; schwa spelled *e*, *a*; schwa spelled *o*, *u*

Soon Mom came home. The kitchen
smelled great. "Look, Mom!" Melody
exclaimed. "I made you lunch!"

"Thank you, Melody," Mom said.

"You should thank Dad, too, Mom.
He helped a lot!"

4

© Houghton Mifflin Harcourt Publishing Company

Lunch

Melody wanted to make lunch for
her mom. Dad said he will help her.
Melody got two cotton aprons.

"Melody, will you bring me a tomato,
please?" Dad asked. Melody got the
tomato. Then Dad washed it in the sink.

1

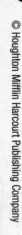

"Please get me a potato, Melody," said Dad. Melody got a potato. Then Dad peeled and sliced it.

"Will you get me a big pot, Melody?" asked Dad. Melody got a gallon pot. Dad put butter in it.

"Please bring me the package of meat, Melody," said Dad. Melody got the meat.

"First we put the meat in the bottom of the pot," said Dad. "Second, we add the potato and the tomato. Then we season it with spices and mix it up. Next we cook it for sixty minutes."

2

3

Circus Time

DECODABLE WORDS

Target Skill: schwa spelled *o, u*

circus	minutes	opposite	reason	suppose
Devon	occur	peanuts	suggest	

Previously Taught Skills

about	if	me	smiled	when
asked	I'll	must	so	why
can	in	my	sounds	will
can't	is	need	started	with
Dad	it	never	take	write
didn't	it's	not	teased	yelled
don't	June	notebook	that	yet
down	just	now	think	you
few	know	please	tickets	you'd
for	let's	quite	time	
go	like	seen	today	
going	liked	smells	town	

SKILLS APPLIED IN WORDS IN STORY: closed syllables (CVC); long *i* (CVCe); /k/ spelled *c*; /s/ spelled *c*; long *o* (CVCe); /g/ spelled *g*; blends with *r, l, s*; final blends *nd, nk*; double final consonants *ll*; consonants *-ck*; consonant digraphs *th, wh*; endings *-s, -ed* /d/, *-ing*; contractions *'s, n't, 'll, 'd*; vowel digraphs *ee, ea, ow*; compound words; schwa spelled *o, u*
From Grade 1: consonants; short vowels; /z/ spelled *s*; /kw/ spelled *qu*; digraph *kn*; *r*-controlled *or, ir*; digraph *ay*; /ou/ spelled *ou, ow*; long *i* spelled *y*

HIGH-FREQUENCY WORDS

a	give	love	the	want
do	have	said	to	what
find	I	someone	too	who

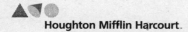
Houghton Mifflin Harcourt.

Circus Time

High-Frequency Words Taught to Date

Grade 1							
a	by	find	idea	now	sing	until	book
about	call	first	into	of	small	use	care
above	car	five	is	off	soil	very	cheer
across	carry	fly	kinds	old	some	walk	children
after	caught	follow	know	once	sometimes	want	dark
again	city	food	large	one	soon	warms	ever
all	cold	for	laugh	only	sorry	was	everything
almost	come	four	learning	open	starts	wash	front
along	could	friend	light	or	stories	watch	girl
always	country	friendship	like	our	story	water	hair
and	covers	full	listen	out	studied	we	hard
animal	cried	funny	little	over	sure	were	hello
are	different	give	live	own	surprised	what	hundred
around	do	go	long	paper	take	where	kept
away	does	goes	look	party	talk	who	might
baby	done	good	loudly	people	teacher	why	mind
ball	don't	great	loved	pictures	the	window	morning
be	door	green	make	play	their	with	next
bear	down	ground	many	please	there	work	other
beautiful	draw	grow	maybe	pull	these	world	part
because	earth	happy	me	pushed	they	would	pretty
been	eat	have	minute	put	think	write	really
before	eight	head	more	read	those	years	says
began	enough	hear	most	ready	thought	yellow	sky
begins	even	heard	mother	right	three	you	sleep
bird	every	help	my	said	to	young	slowly
blue	everyone	her	myself	school	today	your	someone
both	eyes	here	near	second	together		store
boy	fall	high	never	see	too	Grade 2	table
bring	family	hold	new	seven	took	afraid	this
brothers	far	house	night	shall	toward	against	told
brown	father	how	no	she	try	air	
buy	few	I	noise	should	two	another	
	field		nothing	show	under	better	

Decoding skills taught to date: short *a*; short *i*; closed syllables (CVC); short *o*; short *u*; short *e*; long *a* (CVC*e*); long *i* (CVC*e*); /k/ spelled *c*; /s/ spelled *c*; long *o* (CVC*e*); long *u* /yōō/ (CVC*e*); long *u* /ōō/ (CVC*e*); long *e* (CVC*e*); /g/ spelled *g*; /j/ spelled *g*, *dge*; blends with *r*; blends with *l*; blends with *s*; final blend *nd*; final blend *ng*; final blend *nk*; final blend *nt*; double final consonants *ll*; double final consonants *ss*; double final consonants *zz*; double final consonants *ff*; consonants -*ck*; double consonants (closed syllables); consonant digraph *th*; consonant digraph *sh*; consonant digraph *wh*; consonant digraphs *ch*, *tch*; consonant digraph *ph*; ending -*s*; ending -*ed* /ed/; ending -*ed* /d/; ending -*ed*: drop *e*; ending -*ing*: drop *e*; open syllables (CV); contractions '*ll*, '*d*; contractions '*ve*, '*re*; endings -*s*, -*es*; vowel digraphs *ai*, *ay*; vowel digraphs *ee*, *ea*; vowel digraphs *oa*, *ow*; compound words; schwa spelled *e*, *a*; schwa spelled *o*, *u*

"I like the circus, Dad!" yelled Devon.
"I want to go! Please take me with you."
Dad smiled. "Let's go now!"

Circus Time

"Devon, have you seen my notebook?"
Dad asked. "I can't find it. I need to
write down when the circus is in town."

"The circus?" Devon asked. "The
circus is in town in June, Dad. It's June
now! The circus started today. Why?
Will you need tickets?"

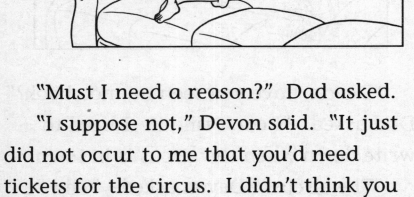

"Must I need a reason?" Dad asked.

"I suppose not," Devon said. "It just did not occur to me that you'd need tickets for the circus. I didn't think you liked going."

"Quite the opposite, Devon," Dad said. "I like the circus. I like the sounds and smells. I love the peanuts!"

"Who will you take to the circus?" Devon asked.

"I don't know yet," teased Dad. "Can you suggest someone? I'll give you a few minutes if you need to think about it."

The Article

© Houghton Mifflin Harcourt Publishing Company

DECODABLE WORDS

Target Skill: schwa spelled *a, e, i, o, u*

about	April's	lessons	sofa	suggested
animal	article	mother	subject	supportive
appealed	asleep	pencil	subjects	
April	dozen	poison	suggest	

Previously Taught Skills

an	dad	ivy	mind	that
and	did	knew	music	them
asked	didn't	laid	needed	think
at	down	like	no	those
bit	family	list	not	time
but	fell	little	on	up
can't	got	made	out	when
choices	had	make	she	woke
choose	happy	maybe	she'd	write
closed	her	might	so	you

SKILLS APPLIED IN WORDS IN STORY: closed syllables (CVC); long *a* (CVCe); long *i* (CVCe); /k/ spelled *c*; /s/ spelled *c*; long *o* (CVCe); /g/ spelled *g*; /j/ spelled *g*; blends with *r*, *l*, *s*; final blends *nd*, *nk*; double final consonants *ll*; double consonants (closed syllables); consonant digraphs *th*, *sh*, *wh*, *ch*; endings -*s*, -*ed* /ed/, -*ed* /d/; open syllables (CV); contractions '*s*, *n't*, '*d*; vowel digraphs *ai*, *ay*, *ee*; schwa spelled *a, e, i, o, u*
From Grade 1: consonants; short vowels; digraphs *kn*, *wr*; r-controlled *ar*, *er*; /oo/ spelled *oo*; /ou/ spelled *ou*, *ow*; /oi/ spelled *oi*; long e spelled *y*; syllable _*le*

HIGH-FREQUENCY WORDS

a	could	of	the	want	your
all	do	one	they	wanted	
any	eyes	school	to	what	

 Houghton Mifflin Harcourt

The Article

High-Frequency Words Taught to Date

Grade 1

a	by	find	idea	now	sing	until	book
about	call	first	into	of	small	use	care
above	car	five	is	off	soil	very	cheer
across	carry	fly	kinds	old	some	walk	children
after	caught	follow	know	once	sometimes	want	dark
again	city	food	large	one	soon	warms	ever
all	cold	for	laugh	only	sorry	was	everything
almost	come	four	learning	open	starts	wash	front
along	could	friend	light	or	stories	watch	girl
always	country	friendship	like	our	story	water	hair
and	covers	full	listen	out	studied	we	hard
animal	cried	funny	little	over	sure	were	hello
are	different	give	live	own	surprised	what	hundred
around	do	go	long	paper	take	where	kept
away	does	goes	look	party	talk	who	might
baby	done	good	loudly	people	teacher	why	mind
ball	don't	great	loved	pictures	the	window	morning
be	door	green	make	play	their	with	next
bear	down	ground	many	please	there	work	other
beautiful	draw	grow	maybe	pull	these	world	part
because	earth	happy	me	pushed	they	would	pretty
been	eat	have	minute	put	think	write	really
before	eight	he	more	read	those	years	says
began	enough	head	most	ready	thought	yellow	sky
begins	even	hear	mother	right	three	you	sleep
bird	every	heard	my	said	to	young	slowly
blue	everyone	help	myself	school	today	your	someone
both	eyes	her	near	second	together		store
boy	fall	here	never	see	too	**Grade 2**	table
bring	family	high	new	seven	took	afraid	this
brothers	far	hold	night	shall	toward	against	told
brown	father	house	no	she	try	air	
buy	few	how	noise	should	two	another	
	field	I	nothing	show	under	better	

Decoding skills taught to date: short *a*; short *i*; closed syllables (CVC); short *o*; short *u*; short *e*; long *a* (CVC*e*); long *i* (CVC*e*); /k/ spelled *c*; /s/ spelled *c*; long *o* (CVC*e*); long *u* /yoo/ (CVC*e*); long *u* /oo/ (CVC*e*); long *e* (CVC*e*); /g/ spelled *g*; /j/ spelled *g*, *dge*; blends with *r*; blends with *l*; blends with *s*; final blend *nd*; final blend *ng*; final blend *nk*; final blend *nt*; double final consonants *ll*; double final consonants *ss*; double final consonants *zz*; double final consonants *ff*; consonants -*ck*; double consonants (closed syllables); consonant digraph *th*; consonant digraph *sh*; consonant digraph *wh*; consonant digraphs *ch*, *tch*; consonant digraph *ph*; ending -*s*; ending -*ed* /ed/; ending -*ed* /d/; ending -*ed*: drop *e*; ending -*ing*: drop *e*; open syllables (CV); contractions '*ll*, '*d*; contractions '*ve*, '*re*; endings -*s*, -*es*; vowel digraphs *ai*, *ay*; vowel digraphs *ee*, *ea*; vowel digraphs *oa*, *ow*; compound words; schwa spelled *e*, *a*; schwa spelled *o*, *u*; schwa spelled *a*, *e*, *i*, *o*, *u*

Maybe she needed to relax a little bit. So she laid down on the sofa, and fell asleep.

When April woke up, she knew what she'd write about. She got out her pencil and began to write. "When you can't make up your mind…"

The Article

April had to write an article for school. She asked her family to suggest subjects she might like to write about.

April's mother suggested she write about her music lessons. No, she didn't like that at all.

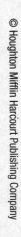

April's dad suggested she write about the time she got poison ivy. No, April did not want to write about that.

Could she choose an animal to write about? No. April didn't like any of those subjects.

April knew they wanted to be supportive, but she wanted to think of a subject that appealed to her.

She made a list of a dozen choices. But not one of them made her happy.

The Missing Bike

DECODABLE WORDS

Target Skill: schwa spelled *a, e, i, o, u*

another	Calvin	children	noticed	supposed
around	Calvin's	garage	open	

Previously Taught Skills

and	got	my	tell	wet
are	he	new	thanks	when
arms	her	no	that	yelled
as	his	not	them	you
asked	home	outside	then	
best	hope	playing	threw	
bike	inside	ran	time	
block	it	red	took	
didn't	looked	saw	up	
door	lunch	see	want	
down	mailman	seen	we	
finished	missing	so	went	
get	mom	storm	we're	

SKILLS APPLIED IN WORDS IN STORY: closed syllables (CVC); long *i* (CVCe); /k/ spelled *c*; /s/ spelled *c*; long *o* (CVCe); /g/ spelled *g*; /j/ spelled *g*; blends with *r, l, s*; final blends *nd, ng, nk, nt*; double final consonants *ll, ss*; consonants *-ck*; consonant digraphs *th, sh, wh, ch*; endings *-s, -ed* /d/, *-ed* /t/, *-ing*; open syllables (CV); contractions *'s, n't, 're*; vowel digraphs *ai, ay, ee*; compound words; schwa spelled *a, e, i, o, u* **From Grade 1:** consonants; short vowels; *r*-controlled *ar, or, er*; /o͞o/ spelled *oo*; /o͞o/ spelled *ou, ew*; /o͞o/ spelled *oo*; /ou/ spelled *ou, ow*; vowel combination *au*; long *i* spelled *y*

HIGH-FREQUENCY WORDS

a	have	said	the	to	your
find	I	some	there	was	

The Missing Bike

High-Frequency Words Taught to Date

Grade 1

a	by	find	idea	now	sing	until	book
about	call	first	into	of	small	use	care
above	car	five	is	off	soil	very	cheer
across	carry	fly	kinds	old	some	walk	children
after	caught	follow	know	once	sometimes	want	dark
again	city	food	large	one	soon	warms	ever
all	cold	for	laugh	only	sorry	was	everything
almost	come	four	learning	open	starts	wash	front
along	could	friend	light	or	stories	watch	girl
always	country	friendship	like	our	story	water	hair
and	covers	full	listen	out	studied	we	hard
animal	cried	funny	little	over	sure	were	hello
are	different	give	live	own	surprised	what	hundred
around	do	go	long	paper	take	where	kept
away	does	goes	look	party	talk	who	might
baby	done	good	loudly	people	teacher	why	mind
ball	don't	great	loved	pictures	the	window	morning
be	door	green	make	play	their	with	next
bear	down	ground	many	please	there	work	other
beautiful	draw	grow	maybe	pull	these	world	part
because	earth	happy	me	pushed	they	would	pretty
been	eat	have	minute	put	think	write	really
before	eight	he	more	read	those	years	says
began	enough	head	most	ready	thought	yellow	sky
begins	even	hear	mother	right	three	you	sleep
bird	every	heard	my	said	to	young	slowly
blue	everyone	help	myself	school	today	your	someone
both	eyes	her	near	second	together		store
boy	fall	here	never	see	too	*Grade 2*	table
bring	family	high	new	seven	took	afraid	this
brothers	far	hold	night	shall	toward	against	told
brown	father	house	no	she	try	air	
buy	few	how	noise	should	two	another	
	field	I	nothing	show	under	better	

Decoding skills taught to date: short *a*; short *i*; closed syllables (CVC); short *o*; short *u*; short *e*; long *a* (CVC*e*); long *i* (CVC*e*); /k/ spelled *c*; /s/ spelled *c*; long *o* (CVC*e*); long *u* /yoo/ (CVC*e*); long *u* /oo/ (CVC*e*); long *e* (CVC*e*); /g/ spelled *g*; /j/ spelled *g*, *dge*; blends with *r*; blends with *l*; blends with *s*; final blend *nd*; final blend *ng*; final blend *nk*; final blend *nt*; double final consonants *ll*; double final consonants *ss*; double final consonants *zz*; double final consonants *ff*; consonants -*ck*; double consonants (closed syllables); consonant digraph *th*; consonant digraph *sh*; consonant digraph *wh*; consonant digraphs *ch*, *tch*; consonant digraph *ph*; ending -*s*; ending -*ed* /ed/; ending -*ed* /d/; ending -*ed*: drop *e*; ending -*ing*: drop *e*; open syllables (CV); contractions *'ll*, *'d*; contractions *'ve*, *'re*; endings -*s*, -*es*; vowel digraphs *ai*, *ay*; vowel digraphs *ee*, *ea*; vowel digraphs *oa*, *ow*; compound words; schwa spelled *e*, *a*; schwa spelled *o*, *u*; schwa spelled *a*, *e*, *i*, *o*, *u*

"Calvin, I took your bike inside," his mom said. "We're supposed to get another storm. I didn't want it to get wet."

"Thanks, Mom!" yelled Calvin as he threw his arms around her. "You are the best!"

The Missing Bike

Calvin went outside when he finished lunch. His new bike was not there.

Calvin saw the mailman. "My red bike is missing. Have you seen it?" Calvin asked.

"No, Calvin, I have not," said the mailman. "I hope you find it."

Then Calvin saw some children playing. "My red bike is missing. Have you seen it?" Calvin asked them.

"No, Calvin, we have not," said the children. "We hope you find it."

Calvin ran up and down his block. He didn't see his bike. It was time to tell his mom that his bike was missing.

When Calvin got home, he noticed that the garage door was open. He looked inside. His mom was there. And so was his bike!

Making Things

MAKING THINGS

Target Skill: **ending *-ed*: double consonant**

dabbed	hugged	mopped	stopped

Previously Taught Skills

added	did	it	on	think
am	didn't	it's	paint	this
and	fine	just	red	up
asked	finish	like	Sam	use
beads	fun	liked	shape	way
best	gave	likes	she	when
big	Gran	make	smiled	white
black	green	making	spilled	will
bumped	had	man	string	yes
but	happen	me	thank	
can	hope	mess	that	
cleaned	I	needed	then	
cut	is	nice	things	

SKILLS APPLIED IN WORDS IN STORY: short *a*; short *i*; CVC syllable pattern; short *o*; short *u*; short *e*; long *a* (CVC*e*); long *i* (CVC*e*); /k/ spelled *c*; /s/ spelled *c*; long *o* (CVC*e*); long *u* /yōō/ (CVC*e*); /g/ spelled *g*; blends with *r*; blends with *l*; blends with *s*; final blend *nd*; final blend *ng*; final blend *nk*; double final consonants *ll*, *ss*, *dd*; double consonants (closed syllables); consonants *ck*; consonant digraphs *th*, *sh*, *ch*, *wh*; base words and ending *-s*; vowel digraphs *ai*, *ay*; base words and ending *-ed* /ed/; base words and ending *-ed* /t/; base words and ending *-ed* /d/; ending *-ed*: drop *e*; ending *-ing*: drop *e*; contractions with *'s*, *n't*; vowel digraphs *ee*, *ea*; ending *-ed*: double consonant   **From Grade 1:** consonants; short vowels; long *i* (*i*); long *e* (*e*)

HIGH-FREQUENCY WORDS

a	out	so	would
for	paper	the	you
my	said	to	

Houghton Mifflin Harcourt

Making Things

High-Frequency Words Taught to Date

Grade 1

a	call	five	kinds	once	soon	was	everything
about	car	fly	know	one	sorry	wash	front
above	carry	follow	large	only	starts	watch	girl
across	caught	food	laugh	open	stories	water	gone
after	city	for	learning	or	story	we	hair
again	cold	four	light	our	studied	were	hard
all	come	friend	like	out	sure	what	hello
almost	could	friendship	listen	over	surprised	where	horse
along	country	full	little	own	take	who	hundred
always	covers	funny	live	paper	talk	why	kept
and	cried	give	long	party	teacher	window	might
animal	different	go	look	people	the	with	mind
are	do	goes	loudly	pictures	their	work	morning
around	does	good	loved	play	there	world	next
away	done	great	make	please	these	would	other
baby	don't	green	many	pull	they	write	part
ball	door	ground	maybe	pushed	think	years	pretty
be	down	grow	me	put	those	yellow	really
bear	draw	happy	minute	read	thought	you	river
beautiful	earth	have	more	ready	three	young	saw
because	eat	he	most	right	to	your	says
been	eight	head	mother	said	today		sky
before	enough	hear	my	school	together	**Grade 2**	sleep
began	even	heard	myself	second	too	afraid	slowly
begins	every	help	near	see	took	against	someone
bird	everyone	her	never	seven	toward	air	something
blue	eyes	here	new	shall	try	also	store
both	fall	high	night	she	two	another	table
boy	family	hold	no	should	under	better	this
bring	far	house	noise	show	until	book	told
brothers	father	how	nothing	sing	use	care	
brown	few	I	now	small	very	cheer	
buy	field	idea	of	soil	walk	children	
by	find	into	off	some	want	dark	
	first	is	old	sometimes	warms	ever	

Decoding skills taught to date: short *a*; short *i*; CVC syllable pattern; short *o*; short *u*; short *e*; long *a* (CVC*e*); long *i* (CVC*e*); /k/ spelled *c*; /s/ spelled *c*; long *o* (CVC*e*); long *u* /yoo/ (CVC*e*); long *u* /oo/ (CVC*e*); long *e* (CVC*e*); /g/ spelled *g*; /j/ spelled *g, dge*; blends with *r*; blends with *l*; blends with *s*; final blend *nd*; final blend *ng*; final blend *nk*; final blend *nt*; double final consonants *ll*; double final consonants *ss*; double final consonants *ff*; double final consonants *zz*; consonants *ck*; double consonants (closed syllables); consonant digraph *th*; consonant digraph *sh*; consonant digraph *wh*; consonant digraphs *ch, tch*; consonant digraph *ph*; base words and ending -*s*; base words and ending -*ed* /ed/; base words and ending -*ed* /t/; base words and ending -*ed* /d/; base words and ending -*ing*; ending -*ed*: drop *e*; ending -*ing*: drop *e*; CV syllable pattern (open syllables); contractions with *'s, n't*; contractions with *'ll, 'd*; contractions with *'ve, 're*; base words and endings -*s, -es*; vowel digraphs *ai, ay*; vowel digraphs *ee, ea*; vowel digraphs *oa, ow*; compound words; schwa sound; ending -*ed*: double consonant

From Grade 1: consonants; short vowels; long (*i*); long *e* (*e*)

When I gave it to Gran, she asked,
"Did you make this, Sam?"

"Yes," I said. "It's for you, Gran."

"That is so nice!" she said. "Thank
you, Sam!" Then she smiled and hugged
me. She liked it!

4

Making Things

I am Sam, the make-it man. I like
making things. I am making this for my
Gran. I hope she likes it!

I cut out a big red shape. I will use
black, white, green, and red paint. Gran
and I like red the best.

1

I dabbed paint on the paper, but I bumped the paint can and the red paint spilled. I didn't think that would happen! I mopped and cleaned up my mess. I needed to finish.

2

I added beads and string. Then I stopped. It is fine just the way it is. I had fun making it. I hope Gran will like it!

3

We Baked a Cake

DECODABLE WORDS

Target Skill: ending *-ed*: double consonant

begged	clapped	rubbed	shopped	whipped

Previously Taught Skills

and	gave	last	pan	Tom
at	got	left	plate	us
baked	had	made	protect	waited
batter	hands	make	slice	we
butter	her	Meg	smiled	when
cake	him	mitts	stick	will
cut	his	mix	stove	with
each	home	Mom	than	yum
face	hot	not	that	
frosted	it	on	time	

SKILLS APPLIED IN WORDS IN STORY: short *a*; short *i*; short *o*; short *u*; short *e*; long *a* (CVC*e*); long *i* (CVC*e*); /s/ spelled *c*; long *o* (CVC*e*); /g/ spelled *g*; blends with *r*; blends with *l*; blends with *s*; final blend *nd*; double final consonants *ll*; consonants *ck*; double consonants (closed syllables); consonant digraph *th*; consonant digraph *sh*; consonant digraph *wh*; base words and ending *-s*; base words and ending *-ed* /t/; base words and ending *-ed* /d/; CV syllable pattern (open syllables); vowel digraphs *ai*, *ay*; base words and ending *-ing*; ending *-ed*: drop *e*; schwa sound; ending *-ed*: double consonant   **From Grade 1:** consonants; short vowels; long *e* (*e*); *r*-controlled vowel (*er*)

HIGH-FREQUENCY WORDS

a	from	so	would
another	good	the	
cool(ed)	more	to	
for	put	was	

Houghton Mifflin Harcourt

We Baked a Cake

High-Frequency Words Taught to Date

Grade 1

a	call	five	kinds	once	soon	was	everything
about	car	fly	know	one	sorry	wash	front
above	carry	follow	large	only	starts	watch	girl
across	caught	food	laugh	open	stories	water	gone
after	city	for	learning	or	story	we	hair
again	cold	four	light	our	studied	were	hard
all	come	friend	like	out	sure	what	hello
almost	could	friendship	listen	over	surprised	where	horse
along	country	full	little	own	take	who	hundred
always	covers	funny	live	paper	talk	why	kept
and	cried	give	long	party	teacher	window	might
animal	different	go	look	people	the	with	mind
are	do	goes	loudly	pictures	their	work	morning
around	does	good	loved	play	there	world	next
away	done	great	make	please	these	would	other
baby	don't	green	many	pull	they	write	part
ball	door	ground	maybe	pushed	think	years	pretty
be	down	grow	me	put	those	yellow	really
bear	draw	happy	minute	read	thought	you	river
beautiful	earth	have	more	ready	three	young	saw
because	eat	he	most	right	to	your	says
been	eight	head	mother	said	today		sky
before	enough	hear	my	school	together	**Grade 2**	sleep
began	even	heard	myself	second	too	afraid	slowly
begins	every	help	near	see	took	against	someone
bird	everyone	her	never	seven	toward	air	something
blue	eyes	here	new	shall	try	also	store
both	fall	high	night	she	two	another	table
boy	family	hold	no	should	under	better	this
bring	far	house	noise	show	until	book	told
brothers	father	how	nothing	sing	use	care	
brown	few	I	now	small	very	cheer	
buy	field	idea	of	soil	walk	children	
by	find	into	off	some	want	dark	
	first	is	old	sometimes	warms	ever	

Decoding skills taught to date: short *a*; short *i*; CVC syllable pattern; short *o*; short *u*; short *e*; long *a* (CVC*e*); long *i* (CVC*e*); /k/ spelled *c*; /s/ spelled *c*; long *o* (CVC*e*), long *u* /yoo/ (CVC*e*); long *u* /oo/ (CVC*e*); long *e* (CVC*e*); /g/ spelled *g*; /j/ spelled *g*, *dge*; blends with *r*, blends with *l*, blends with *s*; final blend *nd*; final blend *ng*; final blend *nk*; final blend *nt*; double final consonants *ll*; double final consonants *ss*; double final consonants *ff*; double final consonants *zz*; consonants *ck*; double consonants (closed syllables); consonant digraph *th*; consonant digraph *sh*; consonant digraph *wh*; consonant digraphs *ch*, *tch*; consonant digraph *ph*; base words and ending *-s*; base words and ending *-ed* /ed/; base words and ending *-ed* /t/; base words and ending *-ed* /d/; base words and ending *-ing*; ending *-ed*: drop *e*; ending *-ing*: drop *e*; CV syllable pattern (open syllables); contractions with *'s, n't*; contractions with *'ll, 'd*; contractions with *'ve, 're*; base words and endings *-s, -es*; vowel digraphs *ai, ay*; vowel digraphs *ee, ea*; vowel digraphs *oa, ow*; compound words; schwa sound; ending *-ed*: double consonant
From Grade 1: consonants; short vowels; long *e* (*e*); *r*-controlled vowel (*er*)

We Baked a Cake

Yum! That cake was good.

Tom begged and begged for more. Tom had more cake on his face than he had left on his plate. Mom and Meg smiled at him. Mom gave him another slice.

The last time we shopped, we got a cake mix. When we got home, we made the cake. We whipped eggs with the cake mix to make the cake batter.

4

1

We rubbed the pan with butter so the cake would not stick to the pan. We waited while the stove got hot.

Meg put on mitts and clapped her hands. The mitts will protect her hands from the hot stove.

When the cake had cooled, we frosted it. We waited for Mom to cut it. Mom cut the cake and gave us each a slice.

Alone and Together

DECODABLE WORDS

Target Skill: ending -*ing*: double consonant

clapping	hopping	skipping
getting	sipping	tapping

Previously Taught Skills

alone	eating	in	munching	spin
and	eats	is	Nate	steps
as	feet	joking	not	sticks
at	fun	jump	on	tap
away	glad	jumping	play	Tess
carrot	go	jumps	playing	will
clap	hands	keeping	rope	with
class	he	Kim	sandwich	
crunching	his	Kim's	she	
dog	home	lunch	show	
drink	hops	mom	skips	

SKILLS APPLIED IN WORDS IN STORY: short *a*; short *i*; CVC syllable pattern; short *o*; short *u*; short *e*; long *a* (CVCe); /k/ spelled *c*; long *o* (CVCe), /g/ spelled *g*; blends with *r*; blends with *l*; blends with *s*; final blend *nd*; final blend *nk*; double final consonants *ll, ss;* consonants *ck;* consonant digraph *th*; consonant digraph *sh*; consonant digraph *ch*; base words and ending -*s*; ending -*ing*: drop *e*; CV syllable pattern (open syllables); vowel digraphs *ay, ea, ee*; vowel digraph *ow*; schwa sound; ending -*ing*: double consonant
From Grade 1: consonants; short vowels; possessives with '*s*

HIGH-FREQUENCY WORDS

a	from	now	the	together
are	have	out	they	told
for	her	ready	to	too

Houghton Mifflin Harcourt

ending -*ing*: double consonant

BOOK 111

Alone and Together

High-Frequency Words Taught to Date

Grade 1

a	call	five	kinds	once	soon	was	everything
about	car	fly	know	one	sorry	wash	front
above	carry	follow	large	only	starts	watch	girl
across	caught	food	laugh	open	stories	water	gone
after	city	for	learning	or	story	we	hair
again	cold	four	light	our	studied	were	hard
all	come	friend	like	out	sure	what	hello
almost	could	friendship	listen	over	surprised	where	horse
along	country	full	little	own	take	who	hundred
always	covers	funny	live	paper	talk	why	kept
and	cried	give	long	party	teacher	window	might
animal	different	go	look	people	the	with	mind
are	do	goes	loudly	pictures	their	work	morning
around	does	good	loved	play	there	world	next
away	done	great	make	please	these	would	other
baby	don't	green	many	pull	they	write	part
ball	door	ground	maybe	pushed	think	years	pretty
be	down	grow	me	put	those	yellow	really
bear	draw	happy	minute	read	thought	you	river
beautiful	earth	have	more	ready	three	young	saw
because	eat	he	most	right	to	your	says
been	eight	head	mother	said	today		sky
before	enough	hear	my	school	together	**Grade 2**	sleep
began	even	heard	myself	second	too	afraid	slowly
begins	every	help	near	see	took	against	someone
bird	everyone	her	never	seven	toward	air	something
blue	eyes	here	new	shall	try	also	store
both	fall	high	night	she	two	another	table
boy	family	hold	no	should	under	better	this
bring	far	house	noise	show	until	book	told
brothers	father	how	nothing	sing	use	care	
brown	few	I	now	small	very	cheer	
buy	field	idea	of	soil	walk	children	
by	find	into	off	some	want	dark	
	first	is	old	sometimes	warms	ever	

Decoding skills taught to date: short *a*; short *i*; CVC syllable pattern; short *o*; short *u*; short *e*; long *a* (CVC*e*); long *i* (CVC*e*); /k/ spelled *c*; /s/ spelled *c*; long *o* (CVC*e*); long *u* /yōō/ (CVC*e*); long *u* /ōō/ (CVC*e*); long *e* (CVC*e*); /g/ spelled *g*; /j/ spelled *g*, *dge*; blends with *r*; blends with *l*; blends with *s*; final blend *nd*; final blend *ng*; final blend *nk*; final blend *nt*; double final consonants *ll, ss, zz, ff*; consonants *ck*; double consonants (closed syllables); consonant digraph *th*; consonant digraph *sh*; consonant digraph *wh*; consonant digraphs *ch, tch*; consonant digraph *ph*; base words and ending -*s*; base words and ending -*ed* /ed/; base words and ending -*ed* /t/; base words and ending -*ed* /d/; base words and ending *ing*; ending -*ed*: drop *e*; ending -*ing*: drop *e*; CV syllable pattern (open syllables); contractions with *'s, n't*; contractions with *'ll, 'd*; contractions with *'ve, 're*; base words and endings -*s, -es*; vowel digraphs *ai, ay*; vowel digraphs *ee, ea*; vowel digraphs *oa, ow*; compound words; schwa sound; ending -*ed*: double consonant; ending -*ing*: double consonant **From Grade 1:** consonants; short vowels

Now Tess, Nate, and Kim are not alone. They are joking and playing together on the steps. Tess, Nate, and Kim have fun together and alone.

BOOK 111

Alone and Together

Tess is at home. She is getting ready for a show. Tess is clapping her hands and tapping her feet. Tess will spin, clap, and tap in a class show.

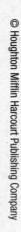

Nate is eating his lunch. He is
munching on a sandwich and crunching
as he eats carrot sticks. He is sipping his
drink and keeping his sandwich away
from his dog.

Kim is at home, too. She is skipping,
hopping, and jumping. Kim is glad as
she skips and hops with her jump rope.
Kim's mom told her to go out and play.

Day and Night

DECODABLE WORDS

Target Skill: ending -*ing*: double consonant

flapping	hopping	humming	setting	tapping

Previously Taught Skills

afraid	day	in	rising	time
am	daytime	is	seems	tired
and	eat	it	shining	toads
bees	fun	its	sleep	trees
begin	gliding	like	sleeping	up
big	go	maybe	so	waiting
bugs	hole	not	sun	waking
can	home	playing	then	will
chasing	hunt	rabbit	think	
cub	I	rest	this	

SKILLS APPLIED IN WORDS IN STORY: short *a*; short *i*; CVC syllable pattern; short *o*; short *u*; short *e;* long *a* (CVCe); long *i* (CVCe); /k/ spelled *c*; long *e* (CVCe); /g/ spelled *g*; blends with *l*; blends with *s*; final blend *nd;* final blend *nt;* consonant digraph *th;* consonant digraph *sh;* consonant digraph *ch;* base words and ending -*s;* base words and ending -*ing;* ending -*ing*: drop *e;* CV syllable pattern (open syllables); vowel digraphs *ai, ay;* vowel digraphs *ea, ee;* vowel digraphs *o, oa;* compound words; schwa sound; ending -*ing*: double consonant   **From Grade 1:** consonants; short vowels *o, oa;* compound words

HIGH-FREQUENCY WORDS

a	birds	for	one	to
animals	dark	hear	some	world
are	down	morning	the	
bear	family	night	they	

Day and Night

Houghton Mifflin Harcourt

High-Frequency Words Taught to Date

Grade 1

a	call	five	kinds	once	soon	was	everything
about	car	fly	know	one	sorry	wash	front
above	carry	follow	large	only	starts	watch	girl
across	caught	food	laugh	open	stories	water	gone
after	city	for	learning	or	story	we	hair
again	cold	four	light	our	studied	were	hard
all	come	friend	like	out	sure	what	hello
almost	could	friendship	listen	over	surprised	where	horse
along	country	full	little	own	take	who	hundred
always	covers	funny	live	paper	talk	why	kept
and	cried	give	long	party	teacher	window	might
animal	different	go	look	people	the	with	mind
are	do	goes	loudly	pictures	their	work	morning
around	does	good	loved	play	there	world	next
away	done	great	make	please	these	would	other
baby	don't	green	many	pull	they	write	part
ball	door	ground	maybe	pushed	think	years	pretty
be	down	grow	me	put	those	yellow	really
bear	draw	happy	minute	read	thought	you	river
beautiful	earth	have	more	ready	three	young	saw
because	eat	he	most	right	to	your	says
been	eight	head	mother	said	today		sky
before	enough	hear	my	school	together	**Grade 2**	sleep
began	even	heard	myself	second	too	afraid	slowly
begins	every	help	near	see	took	against	someone
bird	everyone	her	never	seven	toward	air	something
blue	eyes	here	new	shall	try	also	store
both	fall	high	night	she	two	another	table
boy	family	hold	no	should	under	better	this
bring	far	house	noise	show	until	book	told
brothers	father	how	nothing	sing	use	care	
brown	few	I	now	small	very	cheer	
buy	field	idea	of	soil	walk	children	
by	find	into	off	some	want	dark	
	first	is	old	sometimes	warms	ever	

Decoding skills taught to date: short *a*; short *i*; CVC syllable pattern; short *o*; short *u*; short *e*; long *a* (CVC*e*); long *i* (CVC*e*); /k/ spelled *c*; /s/ spelled *c*; long *o* (CVC*e*); long *u* /yōō/ (CVC*e*); long *u* /ōō/ (CVC*e*); long *e* (CVC*e*); /g/ spelled *g*; /j/ spelled *g*, *dge*; blends with *r*; blends with *l*; blends with *s*; final blend *nd*; final blend *ng*; final blend *nk*; final blend *nt*; double final consonants *ll*; double final consonants *ss*; double final consonants *zz*; double final consonants *ff*; consonants *ck*; double consonants (closed syllables); consonant digraph *th*; consonant digraph *sh*; consonant digraph *wh*; consonant digraphs *ch*, *tch*; consonant digraph *ph*; base words and ending *-s*; base words and ending *-ed* /ed/; base words and ending *-ed* /t/; base word and ending *-ed* /d/; base words and ending *-ing*; ending *-ed*: drop *e*; ending *-ing*: drop *e*; CV syllable pattern (open syllables); contractions with *'s*, *n't*; contractions with *'ll*, *'d*; contractions with *'ve*, *'re*; base words and endings *-s*, *-es*; vowel digraphs *ai*, *ay*; vowel digraphs *ee*, *ea*; vowel digraphs *oa*, *ow*; compound words; schwa sound; ending *-ed*: double consonant; ending *-ing*: double consonant   **From Grade 1:** consonants; short vowels

The sun is down. It is dark. Some animals sleep and rest. Not this one! It is waking up. It will go and hunt so it can eat.

4

Day and Night

It is time to begin the day. I am sleeping. The sun is rising. Bees are humming. I hear birds tapping in trees. The world is waking up.

1

It is daytime. The sun is shining.
Bugs are flapping and gliding.

A big bear is chasing a cub. I think
they are playing. It seems like fun!

Then the sun is setting. Toads are
hopping home. A rabbit is in its hole.
Maybe it is afraid. Maybe it is tired.
Maybe it is waiting for its family.

Dwight's Kite

DECODABLE WORDS

Target Skill: long *i* spelled *igh*, *ie*

bright	flight	might	tied
Dwight	fright	sight	tight
Dwight's	high	tie	

Previously Taught Skills

and	get	kite	sent	way
away	go	let	stand	went
back	grass	made	string	wind
be	green	not	that	with
blow	had	on	then	yellow
but	he	painted	this	
did	his	ran	time	
fell	in	reach	tree	
felt	it	sailed	up	

SKILLS APPLIED IN WORDS IN STORY: short *a*; short *i*; CVC syllable pattern; short *o*; short *u*; short *e*; long *i* (CVCe); /g/ spelled *g*; blends with *r*; blends with *l*; blends with *s*; final blend *nd*; final blend *nt*; double final consonants *ss*; consonants *ck*; double consonants (closed syllables); consonant digraph *th*; consonant digraph *ch*; ending *-ed;* CV pattern (open syllables); vowel digraphs *ai, ay, ea, ee, ow*; schwa sound; long *i* spelled *igh, ie*   **From Grade 1:** consonants; short vowels; possessives with *'s*

HIGH-FREQUENCY WORDS

a	into	out	the
could	now	saw	thought
fall	of	sky	to
good	off	sure	was

Dwight's Kite

High-Frequency Words Taught to Date

Grade 1

a	call	five	kinds	once	soon	was	doing
about	car	fly	know	one	sorry	wash	else
above	carry	follow	large	only	starts	watch	ever
across	caught	food	laugh	open	stories	water	everything
after	city	for	learning	or	story	we	front
again	cold	four	light	our	studied	were	girl
all	come	friend	like	out	sure	what	gone
almost	could	friendship	listen	over	surprised	where	hair
along	country	full	little	own	take	who	hard
always	covers	funny	live	paper	talk	why	hello
and	cried	give	long	party	teacher	window	horse
animal	different	go	look	people	the	with	hundred
are	do	goes	loudly	pictures	their	work	kept
around	does	good	loved	play	there	world	might
away	done	great	make	please	these	would	mind
baby	don't	green	many	pull	they	write	morning
ball	door	ground	maybe	pushed	think	years	next
be	down	grow	me	put	those	yellow	other
bear	draw	happy	minute	read	thought	you	part
beautiful	earth	have	more	ready	three	young	pretty
because	eat	he	most	right	to	your	really
been	eight	head	mother	said	today		river
before	enough	hear	my	school	together	**Grade 2**	room
began	even	heard	myself	second	too	afraid	saw
begins	every	help	near	see	took	against	says
bird	everyone	her	never	seven	toward	air	sky
blue	eyes	here	new	shall	try	also	sleep
both	fall	high	night	she	two	another	slowly
boy	family	hold	no	should	under	any	someone
bring	far	house	noise	show	until	better	something
brothers	father	how	nothing	sing	use	book	store
brown	few	I	now	small	very	care	table
buy	field	idea	of	soil	walk	cheer	this
by	find	into	off	some	want	children	told
	first	is	old	sometimes	warms	dark	turned

Decoding skills taught to date: short *a*; short *i*; CVC syllable pattern; short *o*; short *u*; short *e*; long *a* (CVC*e*); long *i* (CVC*e*); /k/ spelled *c*; /s/ spelled *c*; long *o* (CVC*e*), long *u* /yo͞o/ (CVC*e*); long *u* /o͞o/ (CVC*e*); long *e* (CVC*e*); /g/ spelled *g*; /j/ spelled *g, dge*; blends with *r*; blends with *l*; blends with *s*; final blend *nd*; final blend *ng*; final blend *nk*; final blend *nt*; double final consonants *ll, ss, zz, ff*; consonants *ck*; double consonants (closed syllables); consonant digraph *th*; consonant digraph *sh*; consonant digraph *wh*; consonant digraphs *ch, tch*; consonant digraph *ph*; base words and ending -*s*; base words and ending -*ed* /ed/; base words and ending -*ed* /t/; base words and ending -*ed* /d/; base words and ending -*ing*; ending -*ed*: drop *e*; ending -*ing*: drop *e*; CV syllable pattern (open syllables); contractions with '*s, n't*; contractions with '*ll*, '*d*; contractions with '*ve*, '*re*; base words and endings -*s*, -*es*; vowel digraphs *ai, ay*; vowel digraphs *ee, ea*; vowel digraphs *oa, ow*; compound words; schwa sound; ending -*ed*: double consonant; ending -*ing*: double consonant; long *i* spelled *igh, ie*

Dwight's Kite

Dwight made a kite. Dwight painted it bright yellow and green. Then Dwight tied it to a string. He made sure to tie the string tight.

Dwight's kite was in a tree. It was high, but Dwight could reach it. Dwight tied the string back on his kite. He made sure to tie it tight this time.

Then Dwight sent his kite back up into the sky. Dwight's kite string did not fall off the kite this time.

4

1

Dwight went to stand in the grass. He felt the wind blow. "Now might be the right time to let this kite go," he thought.

Dwight's kite was in flight! It went way up high. Then Dwight had a fright. The kite string fell off his kite!

Dwight's kite sailed away out of sight. "That string was <u>not</u> on tight," thought Dwight.

Then, Dwight saw his bright kite and ran to get it.

Gran's Peach Pie

DECODABLE WORDS

Target Skill: long _i_ spelled _igh_, _ie_

dried	high	pie	pies	right	tried

Previously Taught Skills

add	can	Gran's	Jean's	open	soaked	when
added	contest	had	judges	oven	thanks	which
an	crust	held	kitchen	pan	that	with
and	decide	help	laid	peach	them	
asked	drained	helped	made	peaches	then	
ate	each	in	make	plump	this	
bake	faced	is	making	prize	time	
begins	filling	it	me	secret	top	
bottom	glad	jammed	means	she	up	
bring	Gran	Jean	on	so	waited	

SKILLS APPLIED IN WORDS IN STORY: short _a_; short _i_; CVC syllable pattern; short _o_; short _u_; short _e_; long _a_ (CVC_e_); long _i_ (CVC_e_); /k/ spelled _c_; /s/ spelled _c_; /g/ spelled _g_; /j/ spelled _dge_; blends with _r_; blends with _l_; blends with _s_; final blends _nd, ng, nk_; double final consonants; double consonants (closed syllables); consonant digraph _th_; consonant digraph _sh_; consonant digraph _wh_; consonant digraphs _ch, tch_; ending _-ed_; endings _-ed, -ing_; endings _-ed, -ing_: drop e; CV syllable pattern (open syllables); endings _-s, -es_; vowel digraphs _ai, ay, ea, oa_; schwa sound; long _i_ spelled _igh_, _ie_   **From Grade 1:** consonants; short vowels; possessives with _'s_

HIGH-FREQUENCY WORDS

a	my	the	was
first	of	they	were
for	put	to	what
her	said	told	you

Houghton Mifflin Harcourt.

Gran's Peach Pie

High-Frequency Words Taught to Date

Grade 1

a	call	five	kinds	once	soon	was	doing
about	car	fly	know	one	sorry	wash	else
above	carry	follow	large	only	starts	watch	ever
across	caught	food	laugh	open	stories	water	everything
after	city	for	learning	or	story	we	front
again	cold	four	light	our	studied	were	girl
all	come	friend	like	out	sure	what	gone
almost	could	friendship	listen	over	surprised	where	hair
along	country	full	little	own	take	who	hard
always	covers	funny	live	paper	talk	why	hello
and	cried	give	long	party	teacher	window	horse
animal	different	go	look	people	the	with	hundred
are	do	goes	loudly	pictures	their	work	kept
around	does	good	loved	play	there	world	might
away	done	great	make	please	these	would	mind
baby	don't	green	many	pull	they	write	morning
ball	door	ground	maybe	pushed	think	years	next
be	down	grow	me	put	those	yellow	other
bear	draw	happy	minute	read	thought	you	part
beautiful	earth	have	more	ready	three	young	pretty
because	eat	he	most	right	to	your	really
been	eight	head	mother	said	today		river
before	enough	hear	my	school	together	**Grade 2**	room
began	even	heard	myself	second	too	afraid	saw
begins	every	help	near	see	took	against	says
bird	everyone	her	never	seven	toward	air	sky
blue	eyes	here	new	shall	try	also	sleep
both	fall	high	night	she	two	another	slowly
boy	family	hold	no	should	under	any	someone
bring	far	house	noise	show	until	better	something
brothers	father	how	nothing	sing	use	book	store
brown	few	I	now	small	very	care	table
buy	field	idea	of	soil	walk	cheer	this
by	find	into	off	some	want	children	told
	first	is	old	sometimes	warms	dark	turned

Decoding skills taught to date: short *a*; short *i*; CVC syllable pattern; short *o*; short *u*; short *e*; long *a* (CVC*e*); long *i* (CVC*e*); /k/ spelled *c*; /s/ spelled *c*; long *o* (CVC*e*), long *u* /yōō/ (CVC*e*); long *u* /ōō/ (CVC*e*); long *e* (CVC*e*); /g/ spelled *g*; /j/ spelled *g, dge*; blends with *r*; blends with *l*; blends with *s*; final blend *nd*; final blend *ng*; final blend *nk*; final blend *nt*; double final consonants *ll, ss, ff, zz*; consonants *ck*; double consonants (closed syllables); consonant digraph *th*; consonant digraph *sh*; consonant digraph *wh*; consonant digraphs *ch, tch*; consonant digraph *ph*; base words and ending -*s*; base words and ending -*ed* /ed/; base words and ending -*ed* /t/; base words and ending -*ed* /d/; base words and ending -*ing*; ending -*ed*: drop *e*; ending -*ing*: drop *e*; CV syllable pattern (open syllables); contractions with *'s, n't*; contractions with *'ll, 'd*; contractions with *'ve, 're*; base words and endings -*s*, -*es*; vowel digraphs *ai, ay*; vowel digraphs *ee, ea*; vowel digraphs *oa, ow*; compound words; schwa sound; ending -*ed*: double consonant; ending -*ing*: double consonant; long *i* spelled *igh, ie*   **From Grade 1:** consonants; short vowels; possessives with *'s*

Gran's Peach Pie

Jean and Gran were in Gran's kitchen. "You make the best peach pie, Gran," said Jean. "Can you help me make a peach pie for the pie contest?" she asked.

Jean was glad to bring her pie to the contest. The pie tent was jammed with pies. The judges ate a slice of each pie. They had to decide which pie was best.

Jean's peach pie got first prize! Jean held her pie up high and said, "This is thanks to my Gran."

Gran told Jean the secret to her peach pie. She begins with dried peaches. So Jean and Gran soaked dried peaches to make them plump.

Then Jean tried making the pie crust. Jean got it right! She made a fine bottom crust and laid it in the pie pan.

Jean drained the peaches, which had gotten plump. Gran told Jean what to add to make the pie filling. Jean added the pie filling on top of the crust. Gran's peach pie is an open-faced pie, which means that it has no top crust.

Gran helped Jean put the pie in the oven. Jean waited for the pie to bake.

Vy and the Fly

DECODABLE WORDS

Target Skill: **long *i* spelled *i*, *y***

child	I	my	try
fly	kind	shy	Vy
fry	mind	sky	

Previously Taught Skills

and	fright	named	sighs	this
away	get	needs	since	up
back	high	nice	sits	way
but	in	not	stop	will
can't	is	on	such	wish
cries	it	quite	take	with
didn't	it's	sails	that	
eat	mad	sees	then	
French	might	shame	thinks	

SKILLS APPLIED IN WORDS IN STORY: short *a*; short *i*; short *o*; short *u*; short *e*; CVC syllable pattern; long *a* (CVCe); /k/ spelled *c*; long *o* (CVCe); blends with *r*; final blend *nd*; consonants *ck*; double final consonants *ll*; blends with *s*; long *i* (CVCe); /s/ spelled *c*; consonant digraph *th*; consonant digraph *sh*; consonant digraph *ch*; base words and endings *-s*, *ed* /d/; contractions with *'s*, *n't*; vowel digraphs *ai*, *ay*; vowel digraph *ea*; schwa sound; long *i* spelled *igh*, *ie*; long *i* spelled *i*, *y*   **From Grade 1:** consonants; short vowels; /kw/ spelled *qu*

HIGH-FREQUENCY WORDS

a	pushes	wants
have	she	you
her	the	
no	to	

Houghton Mifflin Harcourt.

Vy and the Fly

High-Frequency Words Taught to Date

Grade 1

a	call	five	kinds	once	soon	was	doing
about	car	fly	know	one	sorry	wash	else
above	carry	follow	large	only	starts	watch	ever
across	caught	food	laugh	open	stories	water	everything
after	city	for	learning	or	story	we	front
again	cold	four	light	our	studied	were	girl
all	come	friend	like	out	sure	what	gone
almost	could	friendship	listen	over	surprised	where	hair
along	country	full	little	own	take	who	hard
always	covers	funny	live	paper	talk	why	hello
and	cried	give	long	party	teacher	window	horse
animal	different	go	look	people	the	with	hundred
are	do	goes	loudly	pictures	their	work	kept
around	does	good	loved	play	there	world	might
away	done	great	make	please	these	would	mind
baby	don't	green	many	pull	they	write	morning
ball	door	ground	maybe	pushed	think	years	next
be	down	grow	me	put	those	yellow	other
bear	draw	happy	minute	read	thought	you	part
beautiful	earth	have	more	ready	three	young	pretty
because	eat	he	most	right	to	your	really
been	eight	head	mother	said	today		river
before	enough	hear	my	school	together	**Grade 2**	room
began	even	heard	myself	second	too	afraid	saw
begins	every	help	near	see	took	against	says
bird	everyone	her	never	seven	toward	air	sky
blue	eyes	here	new	shall	try	also	sleep
both	fall	high	night	she	two	another	slowly
boy	family	hold	no	should	under	any	someone
bring	far	house	noise	show	until	better	something
brothers	father	how	nothing	sing	use	book	store
brown	few	I	now	small	very	care	table
buy	field	idea	of	soil	walk	cheer	this
by	find	into	off	some	want	children	told
	first	is	old	sometimes	warms	dark	turned

Decoding skills taught to date: short *a*; short *i*; CVC syllable pattern; short *o*; short *u*; short *e*; long *a* (CVC*e*); long *i* (CVC*e*); /k/ spelled *c*; /s/ spelled *c*; long *o* (CVC*e*); long *u* /yo͞o/ (CVC*e*); long *u* /o͞o/ (CVC*e*); long *e* (CVC*e*); /g/ spelled *g*; /j/ spelled *g*, *dge*; blends with *r*; blends with *l*; blends with *s*; final blend *nd*; final blend *ng*; final blend *nk*; final blend *nt*; double final consonants *ll, ss, ff, zz*; consonants *ck*; double consonants (closed syllables); consonant digraph *th*; consonant digraph *sh*; consonant digraph *wh*; consonant digraphs *ch, tch*; consonant digraph *ph*; base words and ending -*s*; base words and ending -*ed* /ed/; base words and ending -*ed* /t/; base words and ending -*ed* /d/; base words and ending -*ing*; ending -*ed*: drop *e*; ending -*ing*: drop *e*; CV syllable pattern (open syllables); contractions with *'s, n't*; contractions with *'ll* and *'d*; contractions with *'ve, 're*; base words and endings -*s, -es*; vowel digraphs *ai, ay*; vowel digraphs *ee, ea*; vowel digraphs *oa, ow*; compound words; schwa sound; ending -*ed*: double consonant; ending -*ing*: double consonant; long *i* spelled *igh, ie*; long *i* spelled *i, y* **From Grade 1:** consonants; short vowels; /kw/ spelled *qu*

Vy thinks she might get her French fry back, but then the fly is high in the sky. Since Vy is kind, she didn't mind. Will Vy get her fry back? No, that fly is way up high in the sky with the fry.

4

Vy and the Fly

A nice child named Vy sees a fly up in the sky. This fly is not shy. It sits on her French fry. This is a fright! Vy can't eat her fry. Vy needs to try to stop this fly!

1

Vy is quite a kind child, but she wants her French fry. Vy is mad.

"You can't have my fry, fly!" Vy cries. Vy pushes the fly away.

© Houghton Mifflin Harcourt Publishing Company

Vy sees the fly take the fry. It sails up in the sky. It's such a shame!

"I wish that fly didn't get my fry," Vy sighs.

The Spy

DECODABLE WORDS

Target Skill: **long *i* spelled *i, y***

dry	I	my	why
find	I'll	spy	

Previously Taught Skills

act	drank	in	Mom	tell
am	drip	is	must	used
ask	glass	it	next	went
at	hand	last	nice	will
begin	has	like	see	with
bit	hmmm	Lin	shall	
can	I	might	sighed	
Dad	I'll	milk	son	

SKILLS APPLIED IN WORDS IN STORY: short *a*; short *i*; short *o*; short *u*; short *e*; long *i* (CVC*e*); /k/ spelled *c*; /s/ spelled *c*; long *u* /yo͞o/ (CVC*e*); blends with *r*; blends with *s*; blends with *l*; CV syllable pattern (open syllables); vowel digraph *ee*; contractions with *'ll*; final blends *nd, ng, nk, nt*; double final consonants *ll, ss*; consonant digraph *th*; consonant digraph *sh*; consonant digraph *wh*; base words and ending -*ed* /d/; schwa sound; long *i* spelled *igh*; long *i* spelled *i, y*   **From Grade 1:** consonants; short vowels; final blends

HIGH-FREQUENCY WORDS

a	have	no	she	where
don't	her	of	something	you
go	know	out	the	your
good	look	said	to	

© Houghton Mifflin Harcourt Publishing Company

High-Frequency Words Taught to Date

Grade 1

a	call	five	kinds	once	soon	was	doing
about	car	fly	know	one	sorry	wash	else
above	carry	follow	large	only	starts	watch	ever
across	caught	food	laugh	open	stories	water	everything
after	city	for	learning	or	story	we	front
again	cold	four	light	our	studied	were	girl
all	come	friend	like	out	sure	what	gone
almost	could	friendship	listen	over	surprised	where	hair
along	country	full	little	own	take	who	hard
always	covers	funny	live	paper	talk	why	hello
and	cried	give	long	party	teacher	window	horse
animal	different	go	look	people	the	with	hundred
are	do	goes	loudly	pictures	their	work	kept
around	does	good	loved	play	there	world	might
away	done	great	make	please	these	would	mind
baby	don't	green	many	pull	they	write	morning
ball	door	ground	maybe	pushed	think	years	next
be	down	grow	me	put	those	yellow	other
bear	draw	happy	minute	read	thought	you	part
beautiful	earth	have	more	ready	three	young	pretty
because	eat	he	most	right	to	your	really
been	eight	head	mother	said	today		river
before	enough	hear	my	school	together	**Grade 2**	room
began	even	heard	myself	second	too	afraid	saw
begins	every	help	near	see	took	against	says
begins	everyone	her	never	seven	toward	air	sky
bird	eyes	here	new	shall	try	also	sleep
blue	fall	high	night	she	two	another	slowly
both	family	hold	no	should	under	any	someone
boy	far	house	noise	show	until	better	something
bring	father	how	nothing	sing	use	book	store
brothers	few	I	now	small	very	care	table
brown	field	idea	of	soil	walk	cheer	this
buy	find	into	off	some	want	children	told
by	first	is	old	sometimes	warms	dark	turned

Decoding skills taught to date: short *a*; short *i*; CVC syllable pattern; short *o*; short *u*; short *e*; long *a* (CVC*e*); long *i* (CVC*e*); /k/ spelled *c*; /s/ spelled *c*; long *o* (CVC*e*); long *u* /yo͞o/ (CVC*e*); long *u* /o͞o/ (CVC*e*); long *e* (CVC*e*); /g/ spelled *g*; /j/ spelled *g, dge*; blends with *r*; blends with *l*; blends with *s*; final blend *nd*; final blend *ng*; final blend *nk*; final blend *nt*; double final consonants *ll, ss, ff, zz*; consonants *ck*; double consonants (closed syllables); consonant digraph *th*; consonant digraph *sh*; consonant digraph *wh*; consonant digraphs *ch, tch*; consonant digraph *ph*; base words and ending *-s*; base words and ending *-ed* /ed/; base words and ending *-ed* /t/; base words and ending *-ed* /d/; base words and ending *-ing*; ending *-ed*: drop *e*; ending *-ing*: drop *e*; CV syllable pattern (open syllables); contractions with *'s, n't*; contractions with *'ll* and *'d*; contractions with *'ve, 're*; base words and endings *-s, -es*; vowel digraphs *ai, ay*; vowel digraphs *ee, ea*; vowel digraphs *oa, ow*; compound words; schwa sound; ending *-ed*: double consonant; ending *-ing*: double consonant; long *i* spelled *igh, ie*; long *i* spelled *i, y* **From Grade 1:** consonants; short vowels; final blends

The Spy

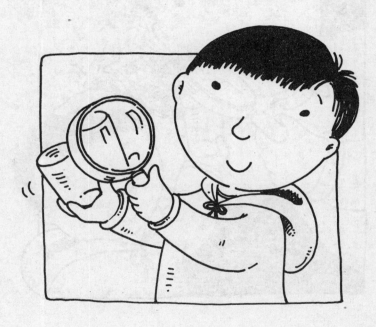

I look at my glass. It used to have
a nice bit of milk in it. "I must find out
why my glass is dry," I sighed. "I will
act like a spy. Hmmm. Where shall I
begin?"

Last, I went to ask Lin. I see
something in her hand go drip, drip, drip.

"Lin, why is my glass dry?"

"I can tell you," said Lin. "I drank
your milk!"

I am a good spy!

4

1

I'll begin with my Dad. "Dad, my glass has no milk. Why is my glass dry?"

"I don't know why, son. Ask Mom. She might know," Dad said.

Next, I went to ask Mom. "Mom, why is my glass dry?"

"I don't know why, son. Ask Lin. She might know," Mom said.

Ride and Jump

DECODABLE WORDS

Target Skill: long *e* spelled *y*

bumpy	dusty	Kenny	tiny
bunny	happy	lucky	tricky
candy	hilly	sunny	

Previously Taught Skills

am	even	hopped	lots	shop
and	fast	I	Mom	such
as	feel	if	my	take
asked	flying	is	pal	thanks
bike	fun	it	place	trail
bikes	got	it's	race	try
by	grinned	jump	ramps	up
can	had	jumped	ride	went
close	helmet	jumping	right	when
day	hills	just	rode	with

SKILLS APPLIED IN WORDS IN STORY: short *a*; short *i*; short *o*; short *u*; short *e*; CVC syllable pattern (closed syllables); long *a* (CVCe); long *i* (CVCe); /k/ spelled *c*; /s/ spelled *c*; long *o* (CVCe), /g/ spelled *g*; blends with *r*; bends with *l*; blends with *s*; final blend *nd*; double final consonants *ll*, *ss*; consonant digraph *th*; consonant digraph *sh*; base words and ending -*s*; base words and ending -*ed* /t/; base words and ending -*ed* /d/; base words and ending -*ing*; ending -*ed*: double consonant; consonant digraphs *ch*, *wh*; contractions with '*s*; final blends *mp*, *nk*, *nt*; CV syllable pattern (open syllables); vowel digraphs *ai*, *ay*; vowel digraph *ee*; vowel digraph *oa*; schwa sound; long *i* spelled *i, y, igh*; long *e* spelled *y*
From Grade 1: consonants; short vowels

HIGH-FREQUENCY WORDS

a	new	said	too	were
could	of	the	wanted	you
down	one	there	was	
for	our	to	we	

Houghton Mifflin Harcourt.

Ride and Jump

High-Frequency Words Taught to Date

Grade 1	car	follow	laugh	or	studied	what	gone
a	carry	food	learning	our	sure	where	hair
about	caught	for	light	out	surprised	who	hard
above	city	four	like	over	take	why	hello
across	cold	friend	listen	own	talk	window	horse
after	come	friendship	little	paper	teacher	with	hundred
again	could	full	live	party	the	work	kept
all	country	funny	long	people	their	world	might
almost	covers	give	look	pictures	there	would	mind
along	cried	go	loudly	play	these	write	morning
always	different	goes	loved	please	they	years	next
and	do	good	make	pull	think	yellow	other
animal	does	great	many	pushed	those	you	part
are	done	green	maybe	put	thought	young	pretty
around	don't	ground	me	read	three	your	really
away	door	grow	minute	ready	to		river
baby	down	happy	more	right	today	*Grade 2*	room
ball	draw	have	most	said	together	afraid	saw
be	earth	he	mother	school	too	against	says
bear	eat	head	my	second	took	air	sky
beautiful	eight	hear	myself	see	toward	also	sleep
because	enough	heard	near	seven	try	another	slowly
been	even	help	never	shall	two	any	someone
before	every	her	new	she	under	anything	something
began	everyone	here	night	should	until	better	store
begins	eyes	high	no	show	use	book	table
bird	fall	hold	noise	sing	very	care	this
blue	family	house	nothing	small	walk	cheer	told
both	far	how	now	soil	want	children	turned
boy	father	I	of	some	warms	dark	words
bring	few	idea	off	sometimes	was	doing	
brothers	field	into	old	soon	wash	else	
brown	find	is	once	sorry	watch	ever	
buy	first	kinds	one	starts	water	everything	
by	five	know	only	stories	we	front	
call	fly	large	open	story	were	girl	

Decoding skills taught to date: short *a*; short *i*; CVC syllable pattern; short *o*; short *u*; short *e*; long *a* (CVC*e*); long *i* (CVC*e*); /k/ spelled *c*; /s/ spelled *c*; long *o* (CVC*e*), long *u* /yōō/ (CVC*e*); long *u* /ōō/ (CVC*e*); long *e* (CVC*e*); /g/ spelled *g*; /j/ spelled *g, dge*; blends with *r*; blends with *l*; blends with *s*; final blend *nd*; final blend *ng*; final blend *nk*; final blend *nt*; double final consonants *ll*; double final consonants *ss*; double final consonants *zz*; double final consonants *ff*; consonants *ck*; double consonants (closed syllables); consonant digraph *th*; consonant digraph *sh*; consonant digraph *wh*; consonant digraphs *ch, tch*; consonant digraph *ph*; base words and ending *-s*; base words and ending *-ed* /ed/; base words and ending *-ed* /t/; base words and ending *-ed* /d/; base words and ending *-ing*; ending *-ed*: drop *e*; ending *-ing*: drop *e*; CV syllable pattern (open syllables); contractions with *'s, n't*; contractions with *'ll* and *'d*; contractions with *'ve, 're*; base words and endings *-s, -es*; vowel digraphs *ai, ay*; vowel digraphs *ee, ea*; vowel digraphs *oa, ow*; compound words; schwa sound; ending *-ed*: double consonant; ending *-ing*: double consonant; long *i* spelled *igh, ie*; long *i* spelled *i, y*; long *e* spelled *y*   **From Grade 1:** consonants; short vowels

Ride and Jump

When we got there, we rode up lots of ramps. The ramps were bumpy and tricky. Kenny and I jumped with our bikes! It was such a happy day!

I am lucky! I just got a new bike and helmet. I can ride fast. I feel as if I am flying when I ride my bike. My pal Kenny got a new bike, too. We can race.

4

1

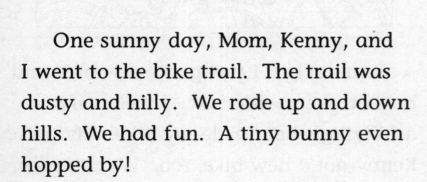

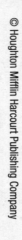

One sunny day, Mom, Kenny, and I went to the bike trail. The trail was dusty and hilly. We rode up and down hills. We had fun. A tiny bunny even hopped by!

I asked Mom if I could try jumping with my bike. Kenny wanted to try jumping, too.

Mom said, "A place by the candy shop is just right for jumping. It's close by. I can take you."

I grinned. "Thanks, Mom!"

My Kite

DECODABLE WORDS

Target Skill: *long e spelled* y

Benny	funny	sunny
Daddy	happy	windy

Previously Taught Skills

and	fly	just	prizes	way
best	flying	kite	right	which
big	games	kites	see	will
but	get	like	shop	win
cat	high	lots	stand	with
contest	him	name	sun	
dad	his	next	Sunday	
decide	I	on	that	
find	is	plays	this	
flag	it	prize	up	

SKILLS APPLIED IN WORDS IN STORY: short *a*; short *i*; CVC syllable pattern (closed syllables); short *o*; short *u*; short *e*; long *a* (CVC*e*); long *i* (CVC*e*); /k/ spelled *c*; /s/ spelled *c*; long *o* (CVC*e*); /g/ spelled *g*; blends with *r*; blends with *l*; blends with *s*; final blend *nd*; double final consonants *ll*; consonant digraphs *ch, sh, th, wh*; CV syllable pattern (open syllables); base words and endings -*s, -es*; vowel digraphs *ai, ay*; vowel digraph *ee*; schwa sound; long *i* spelled *i, y, igh*; long *e* spelled *y*   **From Grade 1:** consonants; short vowels; final blends

HIGH-FREQUENCY WORDS

a	for	new	to
are	go	of	today
be	he	the	was
call	me	there	we

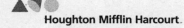

Houghton Mifflin Harcourt.

© Houghton Mifflin Harcourt Publishing Company

My Kite

High-Frequency Words Taught to Date

Grade 1

a	car	follow	laugh	or	studied	what	gone
about	carry	food	learning	our	sure	where	hair
above	caught	for	light	out	surprised	who	hard
across	city	four	like	over	take	why	hello
after	cold	friend	listen	own	talk	window	horse
again	come	friendship	little	paper	teacher	with	hundred
all	could	full	live	party	the	work	kept
almost	country	funny	long	people	their	world	might
along	covers	give	look	pictures	there	would	mind
always	cried	go	loudly	play	these	write	morning
and	different	goes	loved	please	they	years	next
animal	do	good	make	pull	think	yellow	other
are	does	great	many	pushed	those	you	part
around	done	green	maybe	put	thought	young	pretty
away	don't	ground	me	read	three	your	really
baby	door	grow	minute	ready	to		river
ball	down	happy	more	right	today	**Grade 2**	room
be	draw	have	most	said	together	afraid	saw
bear	earth	he	mother	school	too	against	says
beautiful	eat	head	my	second	took	air	sky
because	eight	hear	myself	see	toward	also	sleep
been	enough	heard	near	seven	try	another	slowly
before	even	help	never	shall	two	any	someone
began	every	her	new	she	under	anything	something
begins	everyone	here	night	should	until	better	store
bird	eyes	high	no	show	use	book	table
blue	fall	hold	noise	sing	very	care	this
both	family	house	nothing	small	walk	cheer	told
boy	far	how	now	soil	want	children	turned
bring	father	I	of	some	warms	dark	words
brothers	few	idea	off	sometimes	was	doing	
brown	field	into	old	soon	wash	else	
buy	find	is	once	sorry	watch	ever	
by	first	kinds	one	starts	water	everything	
call	five	know	only	stories	we	front	
	fly	large	open	story	were	girl	

Decoding skills taught to date: short *a*; short *i*; CVC syllable pattern (closed syllables); short *o*; short *u*; short *e*; long *a* (CVC*e*); long *i* (CVC*e*); /k/ spelled *c*; /s/ spelled *c*; long *o* (CVC*e*); long *u* /yōō/ (CVC*e*); long *u* /ōō/ (CVC*e*); long *e* (CVC*e*); /g/ spelled *g*; /j/ spelled *g*, *dge*; blends with *r*; blends with *l*; blends with *s*; final blend *nd*; final blend *ng*; final blend *nk*; final blend *nt*; double final consonants *ll*, *ss*, *ff*, *zz*; consonants *ck*; double consonants (closed syllables); consonant digraph *th*; consonant digraph *sh*; consonant digraph *wh*; consonant digraphs *ch*, *tch*; consonant digraph *ph*; base words and ending -*s*; base words and ending -*ed* /ed/; base words and ending -*ed* /t/; base words and ending -*ed* /d/; base words and ending -*ing*; ending -*ed*: drop *e*; ending -*ing*: drop *e*; CV syllable pattern (open syllables); contractions with '*s*, *n't*; contractions with '*ll* and '*d*; contractions with '*ve*, '*re*; base words and endings -*s*, -*es*; vowel digraphs *ai*, *ay*; vowel digraphs *ee*, *ea*; vowel digraphs *oa*, *ow*; compound words; schwa sound; ending -*ed*: double consonant; ending -*ing*: double consonant; long *i* spelled *igh*, *ie*; long *i* spelled *i*, *y*; long *e* spelled *y* **From Grade 1:** consonants; short vowels; final blends

My Kite

This is my dad. His name is Benny, but I call him Daddy. He is funny, and he plays games with me. We like to fly kites. Today we will get a new kite. I will find a kite I like.

1

On Sunday, it was sunny and windy. That is just right for kite flying! I fly my kite way up high. Daddy and I are happy flying my kite! Will I win a prize?

4

Daddy and I go to the kite shop.
I see lots of kites. There are funny kites,
cat kites, flag kites, and sun kites.
I decide which kite to get.

I like the flag kite best. Daddy and
I will fly this kite next Sunday. There
will be a big kite flying contest with
prizes.

Jenny Studies

DECODABLE WORDS

Target Skill: ending *-es*: change *y* to *i*

buddies	copies	pennies	tries
cities	hobbies	studies	

Previously Taught Skills

and	Friday	list	rushes	test
as	happy	Mom	sees	this
at	has	much	smiles	time
best	home	needs	snack	way
big	I	night	spell	week
can	it	on	spelled	well
class	Jenny	reads	spelling	Wendy
did	job	rest	take	when
feel	Kim	right	tell	with

SKILLS APPLIED IN WORDS IN STORY: short *a*; short *i*; short *o*; short *u*; short *e*; CVC syllable pattern (closed syllables); long *a* (CVC*e*); long *i* (CVC*e*); /k/ spelled *c*; /s/ spelled *c*; long *o* (CVC*e*); long *e* (CVC*e*); blends with *r*; blends with *l*; blends with *s*; final blend *nd*; double consonants; digraphs *th, sh, wh, ch*; base words and endings -*ed*, -*s, ing*; CV syllable pattern (open syllables); consonants *ck*; vowel digraphs *ay, ee, ea*; long *i* spelled *igh*, *ie, i*; long *e* spelled *y*; ending -*es*: change *y* to *i*   **From Grade 1:** consonants; short vowels

HIGH-FREQUENCY WORDS

a	good	says	too
always	her	she	you
do	how	the	
does	of	to	

© Houghton Mifflin Harcourt Publishing Company

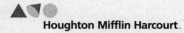

Jenny Studies

High-Frequency Words Taught to Date

Grade 1

a	car	follow	laugh	or	studied	what	gone
about	carry	food	learning	our	sure	where	hair
above	caught	for	light	out	surprised	who	hard
across	city	four	like	over	take	why	hello
after	cold	friend	listen	own	talk	window	horse
again	come	friendship	little	paper	teacher	with	hundred
all	could	full	live	party	the	work	kept
almost	country	funny	long	people	their	world	might
along	covers	give	look	pictures	there	would	mind
always	cried	go	loudly	play	these	write	morning
and	different	goes	loved	please	they	years	next
animal	do	good	make	pull	think	yellow	other
are	does	great	many	pushed	those	you	part
around	done	green	maybe	put	thought	young	pretty
away	don't	ground	me	read	three	your	really
baby	door	grow	minute	ready	to		river
ball	down	happy	more	right	today	**Grade 2**	room
be	draw	have	most	said	together	afraid	saw
bear	earth	he	mother	school	too	against	says
beautiful	eat	head	my	second	took	air	sky
because	eight	hear	myself	see	toward	also	sleep
been	enough	heard	near	seven	try	another	slowly
before	even	help	never	shall	two	any	someone
began	every	her	new	she	under	anything	something
begins	everyone	here	night	should	until	better	store
bird	eyes	high	no	show	use	book	table
blue	fall	hold	noise	sing	very	care	this
both	family	house	nothing	small	walk	cheer	told
boy	far	how	now	soil	want	children	turned
bring	father	I	of	some	warms	dark	words
brothers	few	idea	off	sometimes	was	doing	
brown	field	into	old	soon	wash	else	
buy	find	is	once	sorry	watch	ever	
by	first	kinds	one	starts	water	everything	
call	five	know	only	stories	we	front	
	fly	large	open	story	were	girl	

Decoding skills taught to date: short *a*; short *i*; short *o*; short *u*; short *e*; CVC syllable pattern (closed syllables); long *a* (CVC*e*); long *i* (CVC*e*); /k/ spelled *c*; /s/ spelled *c*; long *o* (CVC*e*); long *u* /yōo/ (CVC*e*); long *u* /ōo/ (CVC*e*); long *e* (CVC*e*); /g/ spelled *g*; /j/ spelled *g*, *dge*; blends with *r*; blends with *l*; blends with *s*; final blend *nd*; final blend *ng*; final blend *nk*; final blend *nt*; double final consonants *ll, ss, ff, zz*; consonants *ck*; double consonants (closed syllables); consonant digraph *th*; consonant digraph *sh*; consonant digraph *wh*; consonant digraphs *ch, tch*; consonant digraph *ph*; base words and ending -*s*; base words and ending -*ed* /ed/; base words and ending -*ed* /t/; base words and ending -*ing*; ending -*ed*: drop *e*; ending -*ing*: drop *e*; CV syllable pattern (open syllables); contractions with '*s* and *n't*; contractions with '*ll* and '*d*; contractions with '*ve* and '*re*; base words and endings -*s*, -*es*; vowel digraphs *ai, ay*; vowel digraphs *ee, ea*; vowel digraphs *oa, ow*; compound words; schwa sound; ending -*ed*: double consonant; ending -*ing*: double consonant; long *i* spelled *igh, ie*; long *i* spelled *i, y*; long *e* spelled *y*; ending -*es*: change *y* to *i*   **From Grade 1:** consonants; short vowels

When Jenny studies, she does well. Jenny rushes home to tell Mom. Mom sees the spelling test.

Mom says, "Good job, Jenny! How do you feel?"

Jenny smiles. "I feel h-a-p-p-y! I feel happy!"

4

Jenny Studies

Jenny always tries her best. This week she has a big spelling test. She needs to spell <u>cities</u>, <u>pennies</u>, <u>studies</u>, and <u>hobbies</u> on it. Jenny studies and studies and studies her spelling.

1

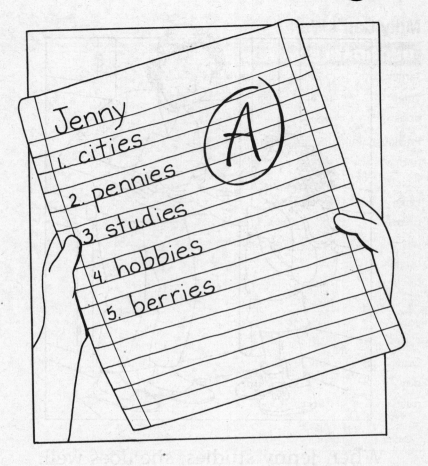

Jenny copies the spelling list. She reads her spelling list on the way home. She studies spelling at snack time. She studies with Mom at night. Jenny studies as much as she can.

On Friday, Jenny and her class take the test. Jenny does well! She spelled <u>cities</u>, <u>pennies</u>, <u>studies</u>, and the rest of the list right. Her buddies, Wendy and Kim, did well on this test, too!

Milly Can't Wait

DECODABLE WORDS

Target Skill: **ending -es: change y to i**

cities	dries	spies
cries	skies	tries

Previously Taught Skills

and	eat	it	see	those
asks	face	Let's	smell	trip
bake	feel	long	smiled	up
best	fills	make	snack	use
big	grab	Milly	snacks	wait
bucket	hands	my	still	Well
buckets	happy	needs	such	Why
by	hike	nice	sunny	wipes
can	his	not	take	yummy
Can't	home	on	that	
Dad	hot	path	them	
day	I	picks	These	
dusty	is	place	thinks	

SKILLS APPLIED IN WORDS IN STORY: short *a*; short *i*; short *o*; short *u*; short *e*; closed syllables (CVC); long *i* (CVC*e*); /k/ spelled *c*; long *e* (CVC*e*); /g/ spelled *g*; blends with *r*; blends with *l*; blends with *s*; double final consonants *ll*; consonants *ck*; schwa sound; long *e* spelled *y*; final blends *nd, ng, nk*; /s/ spelled *c*; long *a* (CVC*e*); long *o* (CVC*e*); long *u* /yo͞o/ (CVC*e*); consonant digraphs *ch, th, wh*; vowel digraphs *ai, ay, ee, ea*; contractions with *'s*, *n't*; base words and endings *-s, -ed*; long *i* spelled *i, y, ie*; ending *-es*: change *y* to *i*
From Grade 1: consonants; short vowels

HIGH-FREQUENCY WORDS

a	go	one	their	we
any	good	she	they	were
could (couldn't)	have	something	to	your
full	her	the	under	

Houghton Mifflin Harcourt

Milly Can't Wait

High-Frequency Words Taught to Date

Grade 1							
a	car	follow	laugh	or	studied	what	gone
about	carry	food	learning	our	sure	where	hair
above	caught	for	light	out	surprised	who	hard
across	city	four	like	over	take	why	hello
after	cold	friend	listen	own	talk	window	horse
again	come	friendship	little	paper	teacher	with	hundred
all	could	full	live	party	the	work	kept
almost	country	funny	long	people	their	world	might
along	covers	give	look	pictures	there	would	mind
always	cried	go	loudly	play	these	write	morning
and	different	goes	loved	please	they	years	next
animal	do	good	make	pull	think	yellow	other
are	does	great	many	pushed	those	you	part
around	done	green	maybe	put	thought	young	pretty
away	don't	ground	me	read	three	your	really
baby	door	grow	minute	ready	to		river
ball	down	happy	more	right	today	Grade 2	room
be	draw	have	most	said	together	afraid	saw
bear	earth	he	mother	school	too	against	says
beautiful	eat	head	my	second	took	air	sky
because	eight	hear	myself	see	toward	also	sleep
been	enough	heard	near	seven	try	another	slowly
before	even	help	never	shall	two	any	someone
began	every	her	new	she	under	anything	something
begins	everyone	here	night	should	until	better	store
bird	eyes	high	no	show	use	book	table
blue	fall	hold	noise	sing	very	care	this
both	family	house	nothing	small	walk	cheer	told
boy	far	how	now	soil	want	children	turned
bring	father	I	of	some	warms	dark	words
brothers	few	idea	off	sometimes	was	doing	
brown	field	into	old	soon	wash	else	
buy	find	is	once	sorry	watch	ever	
by	first	kinds	one	starts	water	everything	
call	five	know	only	stories	we	front	
	fly	large	open	story	were	girl	

Decoding skills taught to date: short *a*; short *i*; short *o*; short *u*; short *e*; CVC syllable pattern (closed syllables); long *a* (CVC*e*); long *i* (CVC*e*); /k/ spelled *c*; /s/ spelled *c*; long *o* (CVC*e*); long *u* /yōō/ (CVC*e*); long *u* /ōō/ (CVC*e*); long *e* (CVC*e*); /g/ spelled *g*; /j/ spelled *g*, *dge*; blends with *r*, blends with *l*, blends with *s*; final blend *nd*; final blend *ng*; final blend *nk*; final blend *nt*; double final consonants *ll, ss, ff, zz*; consonants *ck*; double consonants (closed syllables); consonant digraph *th*; consonant digraph *sh*; consonant digraph *wh*; consonant digraphs *ch, tch*; consonant digraph *ph*; base words and ending *-s*; base words and ending *-ed* /ed/; base words and ending *-ed* /t/; base words and ending *-ing*; ending *-ed*: drop *e*; ending *-ing*: drop *e*; CV syllable pattern (open syllables); contractions with *'s* and *n't*; contractions with *'ll* and *'d*; contractions with *'ve* and *'re*; base words and endings *-s, -es*; vowel digraphs *ai, ay*; vowel digraphs *ee, ea*; vowel digraphs *oa, ow*; compound words; schwa sound; ending *-ed*: double consonant; ending *-ing*: double consonant; long *i* spelled *igh, ie*; long *i* spelled *i, y*; long *e* spelled *y*; ending *-es*: change *y* to *i*   **From Grade 1:** consonants; short vowels

"Milly, I see your bucket! Why is it not full?" asks Dad.

"I couldn't wait," Milly cries. "These were the best snack!" Milly wipes her face and dries her hands.

"Well," Dad smiled, "we still have my bucket. We can use those. Let's go home and bake something yummy!"

4

Milly Can't Wait

One day, Milly and Dad take a trip. They go to a nice place that is not by any big cities. Milly spies something yummy. She picks, picks, picks and fills up her bucket. Dad picks, picks, picks and fills his bucket.

1

Milly and Dad grab their buckets and hike on a path. They feel happy. They hike on the long, dusty path under hot, sunny skies.

Milly needs a snack. "These smell good," she thinks. Milly tries one, and it is yummy. "These make such yummy snacks! Why not eat them?" Milly thinks.

2

3

At the Food Mart

DECODABLE WORDS

Target Skill: *r-controlled ar*

arms	cart	far	mart	parks	tart
Barb	charge	jars	park	smart	
car	Clark	large	parking	starts	

Previously Taught Skills

and	food	home	lot	rice	too
at	get	in	meat	shop	trunk
back	gets	inside	nice	soon	up
bag	go	is	not	spot	when
big	got	it	opens	tells	white
box	has	jam	plums	that	wide
bring	he	lane	pushes	then	will
checkout	helps	likes	pushing	things	with
drive	his	line	puts	three	you

SKILLS APPLIED IN WORDS IN STORY: short *a*; short *i*; CVC syllable pattern (closed syllables); short *o*; short *u*; short *e*; long *a* (CVCe); long *i* (CVCe); /k/ spelled *c*; /s/ spelled *c*; long *o* (CVCe); /g/ spelled *g*; /j/ spelled *g*, *dge*; blends with *r*; blends with *l*; blends with *s*; final blend *nd*; final blend *ng*; final blend *nk*; double final consonants *ll*, *ss*, *ff*, *zz*; consonants *ck*; consonant digraph *th*; consonant digraph *sh*; consonant digraph *wh*; consonant digraphs *ch*, *tch*; base words and ending -*s* (no spelling changes); base words and ending -*ing* (no spelling changes); CV syllable pattern (open syllables); vowel digraphs *ee*, *ea*; compound words; schwa sound spelled *a*, *e*, *i*, *o u*; r-controlled *ar*   **From Grade 1:** short vowels; consonants; long *e* spelled *e*; long *o* spelled *o*; /o͞o/ spelled *ou*, *oo*; /ou/ spelled *ou*

HIGH-FREQUENCY WORDS

a	are	hold(s)	their
after	from	of	they
again	her	the	to

At the Food Mart

 Houghton Mifflin Harcourt.

High-Frequency Words Taught to Date

Grade 1

a	car	follow	laugh	or	studied	what	girl
about	carry	food	learning	our	sure	where	gone
above	caught	for	light	out	surprised	who	hair
across	city	four	like	over	take	why	hard
after	cold	friend	listen	own	talk	window	hello
again	come	friendship	little	paper	teacher	with	horse
all	could	full	live	party	the	work	hundred
almost	country	funny	long	people	their	world	I'll
along	covers	give	look	pictures	there	would	kept
always	cried	go	loudly	play	these	write	might
and	different	goes	loved	please	they	years	mind
animal	do	good	make	pull	think	yellow	morning
are	does	great	many	pushed	those	you	next
around	done	green	maybe	put	thought	young	other
away	don't	ground	me	read	three	your	part
baby	door	grow	minute	ready	to		pretty
ball	down	happy	more	right	today	**Grade 2**	really
be	draw	have	most	said	together	afraid	river
bear	earth	he	mother	school	too	against	room
beautiful	eat	head	my	second	took	air	saw
because	eight	hear	myself	see	toward	also	says
been	enough	heard	near	seven	try	another	sky
before	even	help	never	shall	two	any	sleep
began	every	her	new	she	under	anything	slowly
begins	everyone	here	night	should	until	better	someone
bird	eyes	high	no	show	use	book	something
blue	fall	hold	noise	sing	very	care	sound
both	family	house	nothing	small	walk	cheer	store
boy	far	how	now	soil	want	children	table
bring	father	I	of	some	warms	dark	this
brothers	few	idea	off	sometimes	was	didn't	told
brown	field	into	old	soon	wash	doing	turned
buy	find	is	once	sorry	watch	else	words
by	first	kinds	one	starts	water	ever	
call	five	know	only	stories	we	everything	
	fly	large	open	story	were	front	

Decoding skills taught to date: short *a*; short *i*; CVC syllable pattern (closed syllables); short *o*; short *u*; short *e*; long *a* (CVC*e*); long *i* (CVC*e*); /k/ spelled *c*; /s/ spelled *c*; long *o* (CVC*e*); long *u* /yōo/ (CVC*e*); long *u* /ōo/ (CVC*e*); long *e* (CVC*e*); /g/ spelled *g*; /j/ spelled *g*, *dge*; blends with *r*; blends with *l*; blends with *s*; final blend *nd*; final blend *ng*; final blend *nk*; final blend *nt*; double final consonants *ll*, *ss*, *ff*, *zz*; consonants *ck*; double consonants (closed syllables); consonant digraph *th*; consonant digraph *sh*; consonant digraph *wh*; consonant digraphs *ch*, *tch*; consonant digraph *ph*; base words and ending -*s*; base words and ending -*ed* /ed/; base words and ending -*ed* /d/; base words and ending -*ed* /t/; base words and ending -*ing*; CV syllable pattern (open syllables); contractions with *'s* and *n't*; contractions with *'ll* and *'d*; contractions with *'ve* and *'re*; base words and endings -*s*, -*es*; vowel digraphs *ai*, *ay*; vowel digraphs *ee*, *ea*; vowel digraphs *oa*, *ow*; compound words; schwa sound spelled *a*, *e*, *i̇*, *o*, *u*; ending -*ed*: double consonant; ending -*ing*: double consonant; long *i* spelled *igh*, *ie*; long *i* spelled *i*, *y*; long *e* spelled *y*; ending -*es*: change *y* to *i*; r-controlled *ar* **From Grade 1:** short vowels; consonants; long *e* spelled *e*; long *o* spelled *o*; /ōo/ spelled *ou*, *oo*; /ou/ spelled *ou*

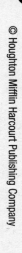

When Barb and Clark get back to the car, Barb opens the trunk. Then Clark puts inside the trunk the bag that has the things they got. Barb starts the car and they drive back home.

Barb and Clark will shop at the mart again soon.

4

At the Food Mart

Barb and Clark drive to the food mart. It is not too far from their home. Barb likes to bring Clark with her. Clark is smart and he helps Barb shop. Barb will park the car in the parking lot.

1

After Barb parks the car in a nice
spot, Barb and Clark go inside the mart.
They get a big cart.

"You are in charge of pushing the
cart," Barb tells Clark.

Clark pushes the cart up the wide
lane at the mart. He puts a big box of
white rice, meat, and a nice tart in the
cart. Then he holds a large bag of plums
in his arms. Barb gets three jars of
jam. Then Clark pushes their cart to the
checkout line.

Sharks

DECODABLE WORDS

Target Skill: *r*-controlled *ar*

dark	hard	large	scared	shark	shark's
far	harm	parts	scary	sharks	sharp

Previously Taught Skills

and	deep	in	mouth	side	until
away	down	is	need	so	up
baby	fins	it	not	stay	use
be	fish	its	pups	swim	whale
big	grow	land	right	teeth	will
but	help	lot	sea	that	with
can	huge	may	see	them	without
close	hungry	moms	seem	this	you

SKILLS APPLIED IN WORDS IN STORY: short *a*; short *i*; CVC syllable pattern (closed syllables); short *o*; short *u*; short *e*; long *a* (CVCe); long *i* (CVCe); /k/ spelled *c*; long *o* (CVCe); long *u* /yōo/ (CVCe); /g/ spelled g; /j/ spelled *g*, *dge*; blends with *r*; blends with *l*; blends with *s*; final blend *nd*; double final consonants *ll*, *ss*, *ff*, *zz*; consonant digraph *th*; consonant digraph *sh*; consonant digraph *wh*; base words and ending -*s*; base words and ending -*ed*; CV syllable pattern (open syllables); vowel digraphs *ai*, *ay*; vowel digraphs *ee*, *ea*; vowel digraphs *oa*, *ow*; compound words; schwa sound spelled *a*, *e*, *i*, *o* *u*; long *i* spelled *igh*, *ie*; long *e* spelled *y*; *r*-controlled *ar* **From Grade 1:** short vowels; consonants; long *o* spelled *o*; long *e* spelled *e*; /ōo/ spelled *ou*; singular possessives; /ou/ spelled *ou*

HIGH-FREQUENCY WORDS

a	else	live	really	they
are	eye	of	some	to
called	from	other	the	what
do	have	people	their	

© Houghton Mifflin Harcourt Publishing Company

Houghton Mifflin Harcourt

Sharks

High-Frequency Words Taught to Date

Grade 1							
a	car	follow	laugh	or	studied	what	girl
about	carry	food	learning	our	sure	where	gone
above	caught	for	light	out	surprised	who	hair
across	city	four	like	over	take	why	hard
after	cold	friend	listen	own	talk	window	hello
again	come	friendship	little	paper	teacher	with	horse
all	could	full	live	party	the	work	hundred
almost	country	funny	long	people	their	world	I'll
along	covers	give	look	pictures	there	would	kept
always	cried	go	loudly	play	these	write	might
and	different	goes	loved	please	they	years	mind
animal	do	good	make	pull	think	yellow	morning
are	does	great	many	pushed	those	you	next
around	done	green	maybe	put	thought	young	other
away	don't	ground	me	read	three	your	part
baby	door	grow	minute	ready	to		pretty
ball	down	happy	more	right	today	*Grade 2*	really
be	draw	have	most	said	together	afraid	river
bear	earth	he	mother	school	too	against	room
beautiful	eat	head	my	second	took	air	saw
because	eight	hear	myself	see	toward	also	says
been	enough	heard	near	seven	try	another	sky
before	even	help	never	shall	two	any	sleep
began	every	her	new	she	under	anything	slowly
begins	everyone	here	night	should	until	better	someone
bird	eyes	high	no	show	use	book	something
blue	fall	hold	noise	sing	very	care	sound
both	family	house	nothing	small	walk	cheer	store
boy	far	how	now	soil	want	children	table
bring	father	I	of	some	warms	dark	this
brothers	few	idea	off	sometimes	was	didn't	told
brown	field	into	old	soon	wash	doing	turned
buy	find	is	once	sorry	watch	else	words
by	first	kinds	one	starts	water	ever	
call	five	know	only	stories	we	everything	
	fly	large	open	story	were	front	

Decoding skills taught to date: short *a*; short *i*; CVC syllable pattern (closed syllables); short *o*; short *u*; short *e*; long *a* (CVC*e*); long *i* (CVC*e*); /k/ spelled *c*; /s/ spelled *c*; long *o* (CVC*e*); long *u* /yo͞o/ (CVC*e*); long *u* /o͞o/ (CVC*e*); long *e* (CVC*e*); /g/ spelled *g*; /j/ spelled *g*, *dge*; blends with *r*; blends with *l*; blends with *s*; final blend *nd*; final blend *ng*; final blend *nk*; final blend *nt*; double final consonants *ll, ss, ff, zz*; consonants *ck*; double consonants (closed syllables); consonant digraph *th*; consonant digraph *sh*; consonant digraph *wh*; consonant digraphs *ch, tch*; consonant digraph *ph*; base words and ending -*s* (no spelling changes); base words and ending -*ed* /ed/ (no spelling changes); base words and ending -*ed* /d/ (no spelling changes); base words and ending -*ed* /t/ (no spelling changes); base words and ending -*ing* (no spelling changes); ending -*ed*: drop *e*; ending -*ing*: drop *e*; CV syllable pattern (open syllables); contractions with '*s* and *n't*; contractions with '*ll* and '*d*; contractions with '*ve* and '*re*; base words and endings -*s*, -*es*; vowel digraphs *ai, ay*; vowel digraphs *ee, ea*; vowel digraphs *oa, ow*; compound words; schwa sound spelled *a, e, i, o, u*; ending -*ed*: double consonant; ending -*ing*: double consonant; long *i* spelled *igh, ie*; long *i* spelled *i, y*; long *e* spelled *y*; ending -*es*: change *y* to *i*; r-controlled *ar* **From Grade 1:** short vowels; consonants; long *o* spelled *o*; long *e* spelled *e*; /o͞o/ spelled *ou*; singular possessives; /ou/ spelled *ou*

Sharks

Some sharks can harm people but a lot of them do not. The whale shark is a large shark. It may seem huge and scary, but do not be scared! The whale shark will not harm you.

Sharks are fish. Some sharks live close to land. Other sharks live far away. They swim in deep, dark parts of the sea. Sharks use their fins to swim up and down and from side to side.

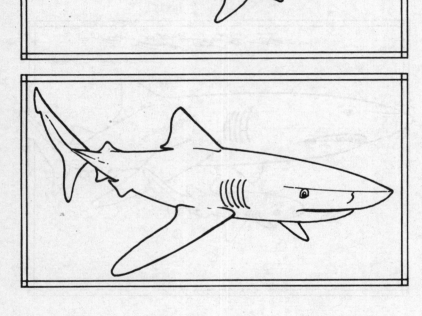

Baby sharks are called pups. Pups have hard, sharp teeth. Pups can swim without help, so their moms do not need to stay with them until they grow up.

This shark is hungry. You can see the shark's really sharp teeth in its big mouth. What else can you see? That is right! You can see its fins and you can see its eye.

Mort's Porch

DECODABLE WORDS

Target Skill: r-controlled *or, ore*

before	morning	organ	short
glories	Mort	porch	snore
more	Mort's	porridge	

Previously Taught Skills

an	cat	in	not	sit
and	close	kept	on	sits
asleep	didn't	like	open	songs
at	had	liked	played	starts
ate	happy	long	pole	than
be	he	made	sang	that
big	he's	make	sat	tried
bowl	his	music	shhh	when
but	hot	night	singing	with

SKILLS APPLIED IN WORDS IN STORY: short *a*; short *i*; short *o*; short *u*; short *e*; long *a* (CVC*e*); long *i* (CVC*e*); /k/ spelled *c*; long *o* (CVC*e*); /g/ spelled *g*; /j/ spelled *g*, *dge*; blends with *r*; blends with *l*; blends with *s*; final blend *nd*; final blend *ng*; double consonants (closed syllables); consonant digraph *th*; consonant digraph *sh*; consonant digraph *wh*; consonant digraphs *ch*, *tch*; base words and ending -*s*; base words and ending -*ed*; base words and ending -*ing*; ending -*ed*: drop *e*; CV syllable pattern (open syllables); contractions with *'s*; base words and endings -*s*, -*es*; vowel digraphs *ai*, *ay*; vowel digraphs *oa*, *ow*; schwa sound spelled *a, e, i, o u*; long *i* spelled *igh*, *ie*; long *i* spelled *i, y*; long *e* spelled *y*; ending -*es*: change *y* to *i*; r-controlled *ar*; r-controlled *or*, *ore*   **From Grade 1:** short vowels; consonants; single possessives; long *e* spelled *e*; /z/ spelled *s*

HIGH-FREQUENCY WORDS

all	good	of	the	watch(ed)
anything	hear(s)	sometimes	to	watch(es)
bird(s)	near	sound	too	

© Houghton Mifflin Harcourt Publishing Company

Mort's Porch

High-Frequency Words Taught to Date

© Houghton Mifflin Harcourt Publishing Company

Grade 1						Grade 2	
a	carry	for	like	own	teacher	work	horse
about	caught	four	listen	paper	the	world	hundred
above	city	friend	little	party	their	would	I'll
across	cold	friendship	live	people	there	write	I've
after	come	full	long	pictures	these	years	kept
again	could	funny	look	play	they	yellow	might
all	country	give	loudly	please	think	you	mind
almost	covers	go	loved	pull	those	young	morning
along	cried	goes	make	pushed	thought	your	next
always	different	good	many	put	three		other
and	do	great	maybe	read	to	**Grade 2**	part
animal	does	green	me	ready	today	afraid	pretty
are	done	ground	minute	right	together	against	really
around	don't	grow	more	said	too	air	river
away	door	happy	most	school	took	also	room
baby	down	have	mother	second	toward	another	saw
ball	draw	he	my	see	try	any	says
be	earth	head	myself	seven	two	anything	sky
bear	eat	hear	near	shall	under	being	sleep
beautiful	eight	heard	never	she	until	better	slowly
because	enough	help	new	should	use	book	someone
been	even	her	night	show	very	care	something
before	every	here	no	sing	walk	cheer	sound
began	everyone	high	noise	small	want	children	stood
begins	eyes	hold	nothing	soil	warms	dark	store
bird	fall	house	now	some	was	didn't	table
blue	family	how	of	sometimes	wash	doing	tall
both	far	I	off	soon	watch	else	this
boy	father	idea	old	sorry	water	ever	told
bring	few	into	once	starts	we	everything	turned
brothers	field	is	one	stories	were	flower	words
brown	find	kinds	only	story	what	front	
buy	first	know	open	studied	where	girl	
by	five	large	or	sure	who	gone	
call	fly	laugh	our	surprised	why	hair	
car	follow	learning	out	take	window	hard	
	food	light	over	talk	with	hello	

Decoding skills taught to date: short *a*; short *i*; CVC syllable pattern (closed syllables); short *o*; short *u*; short *e*; long *a* (CVC*e*); long *i* (CVC*e*); /k/ spelled *c*; /s/ spelled *c*; long *o* (CVC*e*); long *u* /yoo/ (CVC*e*); long *u* /oo/ (CVC*e*); long *e* (CVC*e*); /g/ spelled *g*; /j/ spelled *g*, *dge*; blends with *r*; blends with *l*; blends with *s*; final blends *nd, ng, nk, nt*; double final consonants *ll, ss, ff, zz*; consonants *ck*; double consonants (closed syllables); consonant digraphs *th, sh, wh, ch, tch, ph*; base words and endings *-s, -ed* /ed/, *-ed* /d/, *-ed* /t/, *-ing*; CV syllable pattern (open syllables); contractions with *'s, n't, 'll, 'd, 've, 're*; base words and endings *-s, -es*; vowel digraphs *ai, ay, ee, ea*; vowel digraphs *oa, ow*; compound words; schwa sound spelled *a, e, i, o, u*; ending *-ed*: double consonant; ending *-ing*: double consonant; long *i* spelled *igh, ie*; long *i* spelled *i, y*; long *e* spelled *y*; ending *-es*: change *y* to *i*; *r*-controlled *ar, or, ore*   **From Grade 1:** short vowels; consonants; single possessives; long *e* spelled *e*; /z/ spelled *s*

Mort's Porch

Mort sat on his porch in the morning. He watched the morning glories on the porch pole open. He ate his big bowl of hot porridge. Mort liked to sit on his porch more than anything!

Mort sits on his porch at night, too. He watches the morning glories on the porch pole close. He hears the birds near his porch singing good night.

Before long, Mort starts to snore! Shhh! He's asleep!

4

1

Mort had an organ on his porch. Sometimes he played songs on his organ. Mort tried to make the organ sound like the birds that sang near his porch. But Mort didn't sound like the birds. He didn't sound good at all!

Mort played more and more songs on his organ. Mort's cat liked to be on the porch with Mort, but not when he played his organ music. Mort kept his songs short and that made his cat happy.

Chores Before the Seashore

DECODABLE WORDS

Target Skill: *r-controlled or, ore*

before	chores	forgot	shore	store	torn
bored	corn	more	shoreline	thorn	
chore	Flora	seashore	shorts	tore	

Previously Taught Skills

about	crabs	it's	not	saw	wait
and	crawl	last	now	she	way
asked	fix	make	on	so	we
at	fixed	mess	patch	stitched	went
back	get	Mom	pick	that	wet
bed	go	must	rock	that's	when
big	got	my	room	then	with
by	home	need	rose	this	you
can	I	next	sand	time	
close	in	nice	sat	up	

SKILLS APPLIED IN WORDS IN STORY: short *a*; short *i*; short *o*; short *u*; short *e*; long *a* (CVC*e*); long *i* (CVC*e*); /k/ spelled *c*; /s/ spelled *c*; long *o* (CVC*e*); /g/ spelled *g*; blends with *r*; blends with *l*; blends with *s*; final blend *nd*; final blend *nt*; double final consonants *ll*, *ss*, *ff*, *zz*; consonants *ck*; consonant digraph *th*; consonant digraph *sh*; consonant digraph *wh*; consonant digraphs *ch*, *tch*; base words and ending *-ed*; CV syllable pattern; contractions with '*s*; base words and endings *-s*, *-es*; vowel digraphs *ai*, *ay*; vowel digraphs *ee*, *ea*; compound words; schwa sound spelled *a*, *e*, *i*, *o*, *u*; long *i* spelled *i*, *y*; r-controlled *or*, *ore*   **From Grade 1:** short vowels; consonants; long *e* spelled *e*; long *o* spelled *o*; /o͞o/ spelled *ou*, *oo*; /ou/ spelled *ou*, *ow*; /ô/ spelled *aw*

HIGH-FREQUENCY WORDS

a	done	one	they	walked
birds	door	said	to	was
do	her	the	told	your

Houghton Mifflin Harcourt

High-Frequency Words Taught to Date

Grade 1							
a	carry	for	like	own	teacher	work	horse
about	caught	four	listen	paper	the	world	hundred
above	city	friend	little	party	their	would	I'll
across	cold	friendship	live	people	there	write	I've
after	come	full	long	pictures	these	years	kept
again	could	funny	look	play	they	yellow	might
all	country	give	loudly	please	think	you	mind
almost	covers	go	loved	pull	those	young	morning
along	cried	goes	make	pushed	thought	your	next
always	different	good	many	put	three		other
and	do	great	maybe	read	to	**Grade 2**	part
animal	does	green	me	ready	today	afraid	pretty
are	don't	ground	minute	right	together	against	really
around	door	grow	more	said	too	air	river
away	down	happy	most	school	took	also	room
baby	draw	have	mother	second	toward	another	saw
ball	earth	he	my	see	try	any	says
be	eat	head	myself	seven	two	anything	sky
bear	eight	hear	near	shall	under	being	sleep
beautiful	enough	heard	never	she	until	better	slowly
because	even	help	new	should	use	book	someone
been	every	her	night	show	very	care	something
before	everyone	here	no	sing	walk	cheer	sound
began	eyes	high	noise	small	want	children	stood
begins	fall	hold	nothing	soil	warms	dark	store
bird	family	house	now	some	was	didn't	table
blue	far	how	of	sometimes	wash	doing	tall
both	father	I	off	soon	watch	else	this
boy	few	idea	old	sorry	water	ever	told
bring	field	into	once	starts	we	everything	turned
brothers	find	is	one	stories	were	flower	words
brown	first	kinds	only	story	what	front	
buy	five	know	open	studied	where	girl	
by	fly	large	or	sure	who	gone	
call	follow	laugh	our	surprised	why	hair	
car	food	learning	out	take	window	hard	
		light	over	talk	with	hello	

Decoding skills taught to date: short *a*; short *i*; CVC closed syllables; short *o*; short *u*; short *e*; long *a* (CVC*e*); long *i* (CVC*e*); /k/ spelled *c*; /s/ spelled *c*; long *o* (CVC*e*); long *u* /yoo/ (CVC*e*); long *u* /oo/ (CVC*e*); long *e* (CVC*e*); /g/ spelled *g*; /j/ spelled *g, dge*; blends with *r*; blends with *l*; blends with *s*; final blend *nd*; final blend *ng*; final blend *nk*; final blend *nt*; double final consonants *ll, ss, ff, zz*; consonants *ck*; double consonants (closed syllables); consonant digraphs *th, sh, wh, ch, tch, ph*; base words and ending -*s*; base words and ending -*ed* /ed/; base words and ending -*ed* /d/; base words and ending -*ed* /t/; base words and ending -*ing*; CV open syllables; contractions with *'s, n't, 'll, 'd, 've, 're*; base words and endings -*s, -es*; vowel digraphs *ai, ay, ee, ea, oa, ow*; compound words; schwa sound; ending -*ed*: double consonant; ending -*ing*: double consonant; long *i* spelled *igh, ie, i, y*; long *e* spelled *y*; ending -*es*: change *y* to *i*; r-controlled *ar*; r-controlled *or, ore*   **From Grade 1:** short vowels; consonants; long *e* spelled *e*; long *o* spelled *o*; /oo/ spelled *ou, oo*; /ou/ spelled *ou, ow*; /ô/ spelled *aw*

At last, Flora was done with her chores! So Flora and her mom went to the seashore. They walked by the shoreline and saw nice shore birds. Then Flora sat on a rock and saw crabs crawl by on the wet sand. Flora was not bored now!

4

Chores Before the Seashore

Flora was bored. "Can we go to the seashore?" she asked.

"Flora, you forgot about your chores," said Mom. "You must get more corn before we can go to the shore. Go to the store next door."

1

© Houghton Mifflin Harcourt Publishing Company

Flora went to the store and got more corn. On her way back home, she walked so close to roses that she tore her shorts on a thorn.

"Now I need to fix my shorts," said Flora. "That's one more chore I need to do before I can go to the seashore!"

Flora stitched a big patch on her shorts when she got home.

"I got more corn," she told Mom. "And I fixed my torn shorts. Now it's time to go!"

"Wait!" said Mom. "You must make your bed and pick up the mess in this room."

2

3

Mister Fern's Big Day

DECODABLE WORDS

Target Skill: *r-controlled er*

border	cooler	Fern's	matters	poster
cheaper	disaster	flowers	Mister	toaster
cider	Fern	grocer's	perhaps	

Previously Taught Skills

am	day	home	made	sorry	too
and	dropped	I	Miss	started	we
at	for	in	no	stuff	went
be	get	is	on	such	will
big	got	isn't	party	sudden	with
Bunny	had	it	planned	then	
cake	he	its	put	think	
cried	Hen	jug	sandwiches	this	
crispy	his	like	so	time	

SKILLS APPLIED IN WORDS IN STORY: short *a*; short *i*; CVC syllable pattern (closed syllables); short *o*; short *u*; short *e*; long *a* (CVC*e*); long *i* (CVC*e*); /k/ spelled *c*; /s/ spelled *c*; long *o* (CVC*e*); /g/ spelled *g*; blends with *r*; blends with *l*; blends with *s*; final blend *nd*; final blend *nk*; final blend *nt*; double final consonants *ll, ss, ff, zz*; double consonants (closed syllables); consonant digraph *th*; consonant digraphs *ch, tch*; base words and ending -*s*; base words and ending -*ed*; base words and ending -*ing*; CV syllable pattern (open syllables); contractions with *n't*; base words and endings -*s*, -*es*; vowel digraphs *ai, ay*; vowel digraphs *ee, ea*; vowel digraphs *oa, ow*; schwa sound spelled *a, e, i, o, u*; ending -*ed*: double consonant; long *i* spelled *igh, ie*; long *i* spelled *i, y*; long *e* spelled *y*; ending -*es*: change *y* to *i*; r-controlled *ar*, r-controlled *or*, *ore*; r-controlled *er* **From Grade 1:** short vowels; consonants; single possessives; long *e* spelled *e*; long *o* spelled *o*; /o͞o/ spelled *oo*; /z/ spelled *s*

HIGH-FREQUENCY WORDS

a	friend(s)	of	smaller	to	your
all	from	said	surprised	walked	
anyway	great	saw	the	want(ed)	
around	hav(ing)	should	they	what	

Houghton Mifflin Harcourt.

Mister Fern's Big Day

Happy Birthday

High-Frequency Words Taught to Date

Grade 1

a	carry	for	like	own	teacher	work	hello
about	caught	four	listen	paper	the	world	horse
above	city	friend	little	party	their	would	hundred
across	cold	friendship	live	people	there	write	I'll
after	come	full	long	pictures	these	years	I've
again	could	funny	look	play	they	yellow	kept
all	country	give	loudly	please	think	you	might
almost	covers	go	loved	pull	those	young	mind
along	cried	goes	make	pushed	thought	your	morning
always	different	good	many	put	three		move
and	do	great	maybe	read	to	**Grade 2**	next
animal	does	green	me	ready	today	afraid	other
are	done	ground	minute	right	together	against	part
around	don't	grow	more	said	too	air	pretty
away	door	happy	most	school	took	also	really
baby	down	have	mother	second	toward	another	river
ball	draw	he	my	see	try	any	room
be	earth	head	myself	seven	two	anything	saw
bear	eat	hear	near	shall	under	behind	says
beautiful	eight	heard	never	she	until	being	sky
because	enough	help	new	should	use	better	sleep
been	even	her	night	show	very	book	slowly
before	every	here	no	sing	walk	care	someone
began	everyone	high	noise	small	want	cheer	something
begins	eyes	hold	nothing	soil	warms	children	sound
bird	fall	house	now	some	was	dark	stood
blue	family	how	of	sometimes	wash	didn't	store
both	far	I	off	soon	watch	doing	table
boy	father	idea	old	sorry	water	else	tall
bring	few	into	once	starts	we	ever	this
brothers	field	is	one	stories	were	everything	told
brown	find	kinds	only	story	what	flower	turned
buy	first	know	open	studied	where	front	voice
by	five	large	or	sure	who	girl	words
call	fly	laugh	our	surprised	why	gone	
car	follow	learning	out	take	window	hair	
	food	light	over	talk	with	hard	

Decoding skills taught to date: short *a*; short *i*; CVC closed syllables; short *o*; short *u*; short *e*; long *a* (CVC*e*); long *i* (CVC*e*); /k/ spelled *c*; /s/ spelled *c*; long *o* (CVC*e*); long *u* /yōō/ (CVC*e*); long *u* /ōō/ (CVC*e*); long *e* (CVC*e*); /g/ spelled *g*; /j/ spelled *g*, *dge*; blends with *r*; blends with *l*; blends with *s*; final blend *nd*; final blend *ng*; final blend *nk*; final blend *nt*; double final consonants *ll*, *ss*, *ff*, *zz*; consonants *ck*; double consonants (closed syllables); consonant digraphs *th*, *sh*, *wh*, *ch*, *tch*, *ph*; base words and ending *-s*; base words and ending *-ed* /ed/; base words and ending *-ed* /d/; base words and ending *-ed* /t/; base words and ending *-ing*; CV open syllables; contractions with *'s*, *n't*, *'ll*, *'d*, *'ve*, *'re*; base words and endings *-s*, *-es*; vowel digraphs *ai*, *ay*, *ee*, *ea*, *oa*, *ow*; compound words; schwa sound; ending *-ed*: double consonant; ending *-ing*: double consonant; long *i* spelled *igh*, *ie*, *i*, *y*; long *e* spelled *y*; ending *-es*: change *y* to *i*; r-controlled *ar*; r-controlled *or*, *ore*; r-controlled *er*
From Grade 1: short vowels; consonants; single possessives; long *e* spelled *e*; long *o* spelled *o*; /ōō/ spelled *oo*; /z/ spelled *s*

Mister Fern's Big Day

All of a sudden, Mister Fern walked in. He saw the big poster with the border of flowers.

"I am sorry your party is such a disaster," said Miss Hen.

"No, it isn't," said Mister Fern. "Having friends is what matters!" So Mister Fern and his friends had a great time anyway!

Mister Bunny and Miss Hen planned a party for Mister Fern. They wanted Mister Fern to be surprised on his big day!

Mister Bunny and Miss Hen made a big poster with flowers around its border.

"I think Mister Fern will like this," said Miss Hen.

Mister Bunny and Miss Hen went to the grocer's to get stuff for the party. They got sandwiches and cake. Then they got cider from the cooler.

"I like cider," said Mister Bunny. "Perhaps we should get this big jug."

"No," said Miss Hen. "The smaller jug of cider is cheaper."

At home, Miss Hen put the sandwiches in the toaster. The sandwiches started to get too crispy!

Then Mister Bunny dropped Mister Fern's cake!

"This is a disaster!" cried Miss Hen.

Amber and Her Corn

DECODABLE WORDS

Target Skill: *r-controlled er*

Amber	farmer	herself	perhaps
Amber's	ferns	higher	shorter
eaters	her	louder	stronger

Previously Taught Skills

and	corn	had	left	plan	will
asked	dogs	happy	like	she	with
asks	filled	has	lot	soon	
ate	free	helps	lots	still	
barn	garden	huge	loud	them	
big	get	I	maybe	then	
but	getting	is	munched	this	
can	good	it	now	too	
cats	got	just	on	top	
chicks	grow	keeps	pile	way	

SKILLS APPLIED IN WORDS IN STORY: short *a*; short *i*; CVC syllable pattern (closed syllables); short *o*; short *u*; short *e*; long *a* (CVC*e*); long *i* (CVC*e*); /k/ spelled *c*; long *u* /yōō/ (CVC*e*); /g/ spelled *g*; /j/ spelled *g, dge*; blends with *r*; blends with *l*; blends with *s*; final blend *nd*; final blend *ng*; double final consonants *ll, ss, ff, zz*; consonants *ck*; consonant digraph *th*; consonant digraph *sh*; consonant digraphs *ch, tch*; base words and ending -*s*; base words and ending -*ed*; base words and ending -*ing*; CV syllable pattern (open syllables); vowel digraphs *ai, ay*; vowel digraphs *ee, ea*; vowel digraphs *oa, ow*; compound words; schwa sound spelled *a, e, i, o, u*; ending -*ing*: double consonant; long *i* spelled *igh, ie, i, y*; long *e* spelled *y*; r-controlled *ar*; r-controlled *or, ore*; r-controlled *er*   **From Grade 1:** short vowels; consonants; /z/ spelled *s*; long *e* spelled *e*; /ōō/ spelled *oo*; /ōō/ spelled *oo*; single possessives; /ou/ spelled *ou, ow*

HIGH-FREQUENCY WORDS

a	do	many	the	to
all	friends	of	there	were
call(ed)	know	said	they	what

Houghton Mifflin Harcourt

© Houghton Mifflin Harcourt Publishing Company

Amber and Her Corn

© Houghton Mifflin Harcourt Publishing Company

High-Frequency Words Taught to Date

Grade 1

a, about, above, across, after, again, all, almost, along, always, and, animal, are, around, away, baby, ball, be, bear, beautiful, because, been, before, began, begins, bird, blue, both, boy, bring, brothers, brown, buy, by, call, car, carry, caught, city, cold, come, could, country, covers, cried, different, do, does, done, don't, door, down, draw, earth, eat, eight, enough, even, every, everyone, eyes, fall, family, far, father, few, field, find, first, five, fly, follow, food, for, four, friend, friendship, full, funny, give, go, goes, good, great, green, ground, grow, happy, have, he, head, hear, heard, help, her, here, high, hold, house, how, I, idea, into, is, kinds, know, large, laugh, learning, light, like, listen, little, live, long, look, loudly, loved, make, many, maybe, me, minute, more, most, mother, my, myself, near, never, new, night, no, noise, nothing, now, of, off, old, once, one, only, open, or, our, out, over, own, paper, party, people, pictures, play, please, pull, pushed, put, read, ready, right, said, school, second, see, seven, shall, she, should, show, sing, small, soil, some, sometimes, soon, sorry, starts, stories, story, studied, sure, surprised, take, talk, teacher, the, their, there, these, they, think, those, thought, three, to, today, together, too, took, toward, try, two, under, until, use, very, walk, want, warms, was, wash, watch, water, we, were, what, where, who, why, window, with, work, world, would, write, years, yellow, you, young, your

Grade 2

afraid, against, air, also, another, any, anything, behind, being, better, book, care, cheer, children, dark, didn't, doing, else, ever, everything, flower, front, girl, gone, hair, hard, hello, horse, hundred, I'll, I've, kept, might, mind, morning, move, next, other, part, pretty, really, river, room, saw, says, sky, sleep, slowly, someone, something, sound, stood, store, table, tall, this, told, turned, voice, words

---

Decoding skills taught to date: short *a*; short *i*; CVC syllable pattern (closed syllables); short *o*; short *u*; short *e*; long *a* (CVC*e*); long *i* (CVC*e*); /k/ spelled *c*; /s/ spelled *c*; long *o* (CVC*e*); long *u* /yōō/ (CVC*e*); long *u* /ōō/ (CVC*e*); long *e* (CVC*e*); /g/ spelled *g*; /j/ spelled *g*, *dge*; blends with *r*; blends with *l*; blends with *s*; final blend *nd*; final blend *ng*; final blend *nk*; final blend *nt*; double final consonants *ll*, *ss*, *ff*, *zz*; consonants *ck*; double consonants (closed syllables); consonant digraphs *th*, *sh*, *wh*, *ch*, *tch*, *ph*; base words and endings *-s*, *-ed* /ed/, *-ed* /d/, *-ed* /t/, *-ing*; open syllables; contractions with *'s*, *n't*, *'ll*, *'d*, *'ve*, *'re*; base words and endings *-s*, *-es*; vowel digraphs *ai*, *ay*, *ee*, *ea*, *oa*, *ow*; compound words; schwa sound; ending *-ed*: double consonant; ending *-ing*: double consonant; long *i* spelled *igh*, *ie*, *i*, *y*; long *e* spelled *y*; ending *-es*: change *y* to *i*; r-controlled *ar*; r-controlled *or*, *ore*; r-controlled *er*
From Grade 1: short vowels; consonants; /z/ spelled *s*; long *e* spelled *e*; /ōō/ spelled *oo*; /ōō/ spelled *oo*; single possessives; /ou/ spelled *ou*, *ow*

Amber and Her Corn

Amber is a farmer. She has a big barn filled to the top with corn. "This huge pile keeps getting higher and higher!" she said. "What can I do with all this corn?" Soon, she had a good plan!

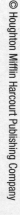

"I know what I will do!" said Amber. She called her farmer friends. They were happy to get free chicks!

Now Amber's pile of corn is shorter, but there is still a lot left. "Maybe cats and dogs like corn, too?" Amber asks herself.

4

1

"Corn helps chicks grow stronger!"
she said. "Perhaps I will get lots of
chicks!"

Amber's chicks were good eaters.
The chicks ate lots and lots of corn, but
then they ate Amber's garden. The
chicks munched on Amber's ferns!

The chicks were loud. "It is too loud!"
Amber called to them, but the chicks just
got louder and louder!

Now there were way too many chicks.
"What can I do?" Amber asked herself.

A Bird Nest

DECODABLE WORDS

Target Skill: *r-controlled ir, ur*

bird	birds	dirt	disturb	stir	turns

Previously Taught Skills

after	get	long	rope	waiting
and	grass	make	saw	warm
at	had	making	see	webs
began	hatch	male	sitting	weeks
careful	her	mom	stems	with
close	him	mud	taking	wove
cute	home	my	them	
dad	I	nest	then	
did	in	nests	times	
eggs	is	next	too	
ever	it	not	tree	
for	keeping	on	twigs	
fun	leaves	protect	used	

SKILLS APPLIED IN WORDS IN STORY: short *a;* short *i;* short *o;* short *u;* short *e;* long *a* (CVC*e*); /k/ spelled *c;* long *o* (CVC*e*); long *u* /yōō/ (CVC*e*); /g/ spelled *g;* blends with *r;* blends with *l;* blends with *s;* final blend *nd;* final blend *ng;* double final consonants *ss;* consonant digraph *th;* consonant digraph *tch;* base words and ending *-s;* base words and ending *-ed* /d/; base words and ending *-ing;* ending *-ing:* drop *e;* vowel digraph *ai;* vowel digraphs *ee, ea;* long *i* spelled *i, y;* r-controlled *or;* r-controlled *er;* r-controlled *ir, ur*   **From Grade 1:** consonants; short vowels; final blend *st;* vowel combination *aw;* vowel digraph *oo* /oo/

HIGH-FREQUENCY WORDS

a	have	they	you
another	he	to	
because	said	wanted	
could	small	was	
few	the	were	

Houghton Mifflin Harcourt

A Bird Nest

High-Frequency Words Taught to Date

Grade 1

a	carry	for	like	own	teacher	work	hello
about	caught	four	listen	paper	the	world	horse
above	city	friend	little	party	their	would	hundred
across	cold	friendship	live	people	there	write	I'll
after	come	full	long	pictures	these	years	I've
again	could	funny	look	play	they	yellow	kept
all	country	give	loudly	please	think	you	might
almost	covers	go	loved	pull	those	young	mind
along	cried	goes	make	pushed	thought	your	morning
always	different	good	many	put	three		move
and	do	great	maybe	read	to	**Grade 2**	next
animal	does	green	me	ready	today	afraid	other
are	done	ground	minute	right	together	against	part
around	don't	grow	more	said	too	air	pretty
away	door	happy	most	school	took	also	really
baby	down	have	mother	second	toward	another	river
ball	draw	he	my	see	try	any	room
be	earth	head	myself	seven	two	anything	saw
bear	eat	hear	near	shall	under	behind	says
beautiful	eight	heard	never	she	until	being	sky
because	enough	help	new	should	use	better	sleep
been	even	her	night	show	very	book	slowly
before	every	here	no	sing	walk	care	someone
began	everyone	high	noise	small	want	cheer	something
begins	eyes	hold	nothing	soil	warms	children	sound
bird	fall	house	now	some	was	dark	stood
blue	family	how	of	sometimes	wash	didn't	store
both	far	I	off	soon	watch	doing	table
boy	father	idea	old	sorry	water	else	tall
bring	few	into	once	starts	we	ever	this
brothers	field	is	one	stories	were	everything	told
brown	find	kinds	only	story	what	flower	turned
buy	first	know	open	studied	where	front	voice
by	five	large	or	sure	who	girl	words
call	fly	laugh	our	surprised	why	gone	
car	follow	learning	out	take	window	hair	
	food	light	over	talk	with	hard	

Decoding skills taught to date: short *a*; short *i*; CVC syllable pattern; short *o*; short *u*; short *e*; long *a* (CVC*e*); long *i* (CVC*e*); /k/ spelled *c*; /s/ spelled *c*; long *o* (CVC*e*), long *u* /yōō/ (CVC*e*); long *u* /ōō/ (CVC*e*); long *e* (CVC*e*); /g/ spelled *g*; /j/ spelled *g, dge*; blends with *r*; blends with *l*; blends with *s*; final blend *nd*; final blend *ng*; final blend *nk*; final blend *nt*; double final consonants *ll*; double final consonants *ss*; double final consonants *zz*; double final consonants *ff*; consonants *ck*; double consonants (closed syllables); consonant digraph *th*; consonant digraph *sh*; consonant digraph *wh*; consonant digraphs *ch, tch*; consonant digraph *ph*; base words and ending -*s*; base words and ending -*ed* /ed/; base words and ending -*ed* /t/; base words and ending -*ed* /d/; base words and ending -*ing*; ending -*ed*: drop *e*; ending -*ing*: drop *e*; CV syllable pattern (open syllables); contractions with '*s, n't*; contractions with '*ve, 're*; base words and endings -*s, -es*; vowel digraphs *ai, ay*; vowel digraphs *ee, ea*; vowel digraphs *oa, ow*; compound words; schwa sound; ending -*ed*: double consonant; ending -*ing*: double consonant; long *i* spelled *igh, ie*; long *i* spelled *i, y*; long *e* spelled *y*; ending -*es*: change *y* to *i*; r-controlled *ar*; r-controlled *or, ore*; r-controlled *er*; r-controlled *ir, ur* **From Grade 1:** consonants; short vowels; final blend *st*; vowel combination *aw*; vowel digraph *oo* /oo/

A Bird Nest

Did you ever see birds make nests? I have, and it is fun to see. I saw a bird make a nest in a tree next to my home. It began with long grass stems. Then it wove them.

At times, I could see the male sitting on the eggs keeping them warm. Mom bird and dad bird were taking turns in the nest. After a few weeks, cute birds began to stir!

Dad said the male bird was making a nest for eggs. He used rope he had. Mud, dirt, twigs, leaves, and webs were used. I was careful not to disturb him.

2

Next, another bird was sitting on eggs. Dad said it was mom bird. I was waiting for the eggs to hatch. I did not get too close because mom bird wanted to protect her eggs.

3

Beach Trip

DECODABLE WORDS

Target Skill: *r-controlled ir, ur*

bird	burned	hurts	sunburn

Previously Taught Skills

am	for	itch	packs	trip
and	get	joy	plan	trunks
arms	glass	jump	play	unpack
at	Gramps	last	screams	up
bag	Granny	long	seat	us
beach	has	makes	seatbelt	use
block	help	Mom	so	uses
buggy	her	my	stay	up
can	I	next	stuffed	van
click	ice	off	summer	waves
Dad	in	on	sun	will
flip	is	Pam	tea	with
flops	it	pack	time	

SKILLS APPLIED IN WORDS IN STORY: short *a, i, o, u, e*; long *a, i*; u /yōō/ (CVC*e*); /k/ spelled *c*; /g/ spelled *g*; blends with *r, l, s*; final blend *nd*; double final consonants *ll*; double consonants (closed syllables); consonants *ck;* consonant digraph *tch*; base words and endings *-s, -ed /t/, -ed /d/*; vowel digraphs *ay, ea*; compound words; long *i* spelled *i, y*; long *e* spelled *y*; r-controlled *ar, er, ir, ur*   **From Grade 1:** consonants; short vowels; final blend *mp*

HIGH-FREQUENCY WORDS

a	family	me	she	they
all	happy	of	sure	to
are	have	puts	the	we
don't	live	really	there	

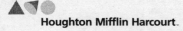
© Houghton Mifflin Harcourt Publishing Company

Beach Trip

High-Frequency Words Taught to Date

Grade 1	carry	for	like	own	teacher	work	hello
a	caught	four	listen	paper	the	world	horse
about	city	friend	little	party	their	would	hundred
above	cold	friendship	live	people	there	write	I'll
across	come	full	long	pictures	these	years	I've
after	could	funny	look	play	they	yellow	kept
again	country	give	loudly	please	think	you	might
all	covers	go	loved	pull	those	young	mind
almost	cried	goes	make	pushed	thought	your	morning
along	different	good	many	put	three		move
always	do	great	maybe	read	to	*Grade 2*	next
and	does	green	me	ready	today	afraid	other
animal	done	ground	minute	right	together	against	part
are	don't	grow	more	said	too	air	pretty
around	door	happy	most	school	took	also	really
away	down	have	mother	second	toward	another	river
baby	draw	he	my	see	try	any	room
ball	earth	head	myself	seven	two	anything	saw
be	eat	hear	near	shall	under	behind	says
bear	eight	heard	never	she	until	being	sky
beautiful	enough	help	new	should	use	better	sleep
because	even	her	night	show	very	book	slowly
been	every	here	no	sing	walk	care	someone
before	everyone	high	noise	small	want	cheer	something
began	eyes	hold	nothing	soil	warms	children	sound
begins	fall	house	now	some	was	dark	stood
bird	family	how	of	sometimes	wash	didn't	store
blue	far	I	off	soon	watch	doing	table
both	father	idea	old	sorry	water	else	tall
boy	few	into	once	starts	we	ever	this
bring	field	is	one	stories	were	everything	told
brothers	find	kinds	only	story	what	flower	turned
brown	first	know	open	studied	where	front	voice
buy	five	large	or	sure	who	girl	words
by	fly	laugh	our	surprised	why	gone	
call	follow	learning	out	take	window	hair	
car	food	light	over	talk	with	hard	

Decoding skills taught to date: short *a*; short *i*; CVC syllable pattern; short *o*; short *u*; short *e*; long *a* (CVC*e*); long *i* (CVC*e*); /k/ spelled *c*; /s/ spelled *c*; long *o* (CVC*e*), long *u* /yōō/ (CVC*e*); long *u* /ōō/ (CVC*e*); long *e* (CVC*e*); /g/ spelled *g*; /j/ spelled *g*, *dge*; blends with *r*; blends with *l*; blends with *s*; final blend *nd*; final blend *ng*; final blend *nk*; final blend *nt*; double final consonants *ll*; double final consonants *ss*; double final consonants *ff*; double final consonants *zz*; consonants *ck*; double consonants (closed syllables); consonant digraph *th*; consonant digraph *sh*; consonant digraph *wh*; consonant digraphs *ch*, *tch*; consonant digraph *ph*; base words and ending -*s*; base words and ending -*ed* /ed/; base words and ending -*ed* /t/; base words and ending -*ed* /d/; base words and ending -*ing*; ending -*ed*: drop *e*; ending -*ing*: drop *e*; CV syllable pattern (open syllables); contractions with '*s*, *n't*; contractions with '*ve*, '*re*; base words and endings -*s*, -*es*; vowel digraphs *ai*, *ay*; vowel digraphs *ee*, *ea*; vowel digraphs *oa*, *ow*; compound words; schwa sound; ending -*ed*: double consonant; ending -*ing*: double consonant; long *i* spelled *igh*, *ie*; long *i* spelled *i*, *y*; long *e* spelled *y*; ending -*es*: change *y* to *i*; r-controlled *ar*; r-controlled *or*, *ore*; r-controlled *er*; r-controlled *ir*, *ur*   **From Grade 1:** consonants; short vowels; final blend *mp*

Beach Trip

Mom packs the beach buggy, and I get my trunks and flip flops. Mom puts sun block on Pam and me. I play in the waves. Pam puts her arms up and screams with joy!

My family packs for a trip to the beach. We plan to stay there all summer. Mom has sun block in her beach bag for us to use so we don't get burned. A sunburn really hurts and can itch.

© Houghton Mifflin Harcourt Publishing Company

Mom and Dad pack up the van. Pam is in her seat. She has her stuffed bird and is happy. I jump in next to her, click my seatbelt, and we are off.

At long last, we are at the beach. Granny and Gramps live there. They help us unpack the van. We have a glass of ice tea. Gramps makes the best ice tea.

2

3

A Role in the Play

DECODABLE WORDS

Target Skill: **homophone pairs (with high-frequency words in parentheses)**

for/(four)   (hear)/(here)   sea/see

Previously Taught Skills

and	for	leaves	picks	tried
asks	fun	like	play	turn
at	got	lines	rock	up
bit	happy	Miss	role	wait
boat	has	mom	smiles	waits
bus	her	needs	so	when
can	I	next	stage	wide
cannot	in	nine	stand	will
cast	is	on	step	
class	it	out	tells	
dance	kids	part	them	
excited	Kitty	parts	this	
first	lead	Peach	time	

SKILLS APPLIED IN WORDS IN STORY: short *a, i, o, u, e*; long *a, i,* (CVC*e*); /k/ spelled *c*; /s/ spelled *c*; /g/ spelled *g*; /j/ spelled *g*; blends with *r, l, s*; final blend *nd*; double final consonants *ll, ss*; consonant digraph *th*; CV syllable pattern (open syllables); base words and ending *-s*; vowel digraphs *ai, ay, ee, ea*; long *i* spelled *ie, i*; long *e* spelled *y*; r-controlled *ar, er, ur*; homophones   **From Grade 1:** consonants; short vowels; final blend *mp*

HIGH-FREQUENCY WORDS

a	here	the	you
be	many	to	
four	of	today	
have	says	what	
hear	she	who	

Houghton Mifflin Harcourt.

A Role in the Play

High-Frequency Words Taught to Date

Grade 1

a	carry	for	like	own	teacher	work	hair
about	caught	four	listen	paper	the	world	hard
above	city	friend	little	party	their	would	hello
across	cold	friendship	live	people	there	write	horse
after	come	full	long	pictures	these	years	hundred
again	could	funny	look	play	they	yellow	I'll
all	country	give	loudly	please	think	you	I've
almost	covers	go	loved	pull	those	young	kept
along	cried	goes	make	pushed	thought	your	might
always	different	good	many	put	three		mind
and	do	great	maybe	read	to	**Grade 2**	morning
animal	does	green	me	ready	today	afraid	move
are	done	ground	minute	right	together	against	next
around	don't	grow	more	said	too	air	other
away	door	happy	most	school	took	also	part
baby	down	have	mother	second	toward	another	pretty
ball	draw	he	my	see	try	any	really
be	earth	head	myself	seven	two	anything	river
bear	eat	hear	near	shall	under	behind	room
beautiful	eight	heard	never	she	until	being	saw
because	enough	help	new	should	use	better	says
been	even	her	night	show	very	book	sky
before	every	here	no	sing	walk	care	sleep
began	everyone	high	noise	small	want	cheer	slowly
begins	eyes	hold	nothing	soil	warms	children	someone
bird	fall	house	now	some	was	dark	something
blue	family	how	of	sometimes	wash	didn't	sound
both	far	I	off	soon	watch	doing	stood
boy	father	idea	old	sorry	water	else	store
bring	few	into	once	starts	we	ever	table
brothers	field	is	one	stories	were	everything	tall
brown	find	kinds	only	story	what	floor	this
buy	first	know	open	studied	where	flower	told
by	five	large	or	sure	who	found	turned
call	fly	laugh	our	surprised	why	front	voice
car	follow	learning	out	take	window	girl	what's
	food	light	over	talk	with	gone	words

Decoding skills taught to date: short *a*; short *i*; CVC syllable pattern; short *o*; short *u*; short *e*; long *a* (CVC*e*); long *i* (CVC*e*); /k/ spelled *c*; /s/ spelled *c*; long *o* (CVC*e*), long *u* /yōō/ (CVC*e*); long *u* /ōō/ (CVC*e*); long *e* (CVC*e*); /g/ spelled *g*; /j/ spelled *g*, *dge*; blends with *r*; blends with *l*; blends with *s*; final blend *nd*; final blend *ng*; final blend *nk*; final blend *nt*; double final consonants *ll*; double final consonants *ss*; double final consonants *ff*; double final consonants *zz*; consonants *ck*; double consonants (closed syllables); consonant digraph *th*; consonant digraph *sh*; consonant digraph *wh*; consonant digraphs *ch*, *tch*; consonant digraph *ph*; base words and ending -*s*; base words and ending -*ed* /ed/; base words and ending -*ed* /t/; base words and ending -*ed* /d/; base words and ending -*ing*; ending -*ed*: drop *e*; ending -*ing*: drop *e*; CV syllable pattern (open syllables); contractions with '*s*, *n't*; contractions with '*ve*, '*re*; base words and endings -*s*, -*es*; vowel digraphs *ai*, *ay*; vowel digraphs *ee*, *ea*; vowel digraphs *oa*, *ow*; compound words; schwa sound; ending -*ed*: double consonant; ending -*ing*: double consonant; long *i* spelled *igh*, *ie*; long *i* spelled *i*, *y*; long *e* spelled *y*; ending -*es*: change *y* to *i*; r-controlled *ar*; r-controlled *or*, *ore*; r-controlled *er*; r-controlled *ir*, *ur*; homophones **From Grade 1:** consonants; short vowels; final blend *mp*

At last, the play is today. Kitty is a bit excited! When Kitty leaves for the bus, her mom tells her, "Have fun! See you at the play!" Kitty smiles wide.

4

A Role in the Play

Our Play

Lead Role - Kitty

Kitty is so happy. She tried out for the class play, and she got the lead role. It is the first time Kitty will be on stage. Kitty cannot wait.

1

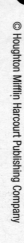

First, the cast has to repeat the parts.
Kitty needs to hear the many parts.
Miss Peach tells her, "Stand here for this
part. You will be on a boat at sea."

Kitty waits for her turn to read her
lines.

Next, Miss Peach asks, "Can I have
four kids who like to dance?"

Nine kids step up. Miss Peach picks
four of them and says, "Time to rock!"

A Boat Ride

DECODABLE WORDS

Target Skill: homophone pairs

road/rode   sea/see   weak/week

Previously Taught Skills

am	fish	his	mile	safe	time
and	fishing	I	need	smooth	too
at	float	in	nice	so	took
best	for	is	off	stay	until
block	fun	it	on	sun	us
boat	go	keep	or	take	vests
can	good	life	out	taking	waves
cannot	Gramps	like	pole	tasted	while
day	great	long	rest	that	wish
docked	grilled	look	rested	then	
far	has	lunch	ride	three	

SKILLS APPLIED IN WORDS IN STORY: short *a*; short *i*; short *o*; short *u*; short *e*; long *a* (CVCe); long *i* (CVCe); /k/ spelled *c*; long *o* (CVCe); /g/ spelled *g*; blends with *r*; blends with *l*; blends with *s*; final blend *nd*; final blend *ng*; double final consonants *ll*; double final consonants *ff*; consonants *ck*; consonant digraph *th*; consonant digraph *sh*; base words and ending *-s*; base words and ending *-ed* /t/; base words and ending *-ing*; vowel digraph *ay*; vowel digraphs *ee, ea*; vowel digraph *oa*; *r*-controlled *or, ore*; homophones
From Grade 1: consonants; short vowels; vowel combination *ou*; vowel digraph *oo* /oo/

HIGH-FREQUENCY WORDS

a	away	put	the	water
also	could	said	to	we
are	(in)to	says	today	you

 Houghton Mifflin Harcourt.

A Boat Ride

High-Frequency Words Taught to Date

Grade 1

a	carry	for	like	own	teacher	work	hair
about	caught	four	listen	paper	the	world	hard
above	city	friend	little	party	their	would	hello
across	cold	friendship	live	people	there	write	horse
after	come	full	long	pictures	these	years	hundred
again	could	funny	look	play	they	yellow	I'll
all	country	give	loudly	please	think	you	I've
almost	covers	go	loved	pull	those	young	kept
along	cried	goes	make	pushed	thought	your	might
always	different	good	many	put	three		mind
and	do	great	maybe	read	to	*Grade 2*	morning
animal	does	green	me	ready	today	afraid	move
are	done	ground	minute	right	together	against	next
around	don't	grow	more	said	too	air	other
away	door	happy	most	school	took	also	part
baby	down	have	mother	second	toward	another	pretty
ball	draw	he	my	see	try	any	really
be	earth	head	myself	seven	two	anything	river
bear	eat	hear	near	shall	under	behind	room
beautiful	eight	heard	never	she	until	being	saw
because	enough	help	new	should	use	better	says
been	even	her	night	show	very	book	sky
before	every	here	no	sing	walk	care	sleep
began	everyone	high	noise	small	want	cheer	slowly
begins	eyes	hold	nothing	soil	warms	children	someone
bird	fall	house	now	some	was	dark	something
blue	family	how	of	sometimes	wash	didn't	sound
both	far	I	off	soon	watch	doing	stood
boy	father	idea	old	sorry	water	else	store
bring	few	into	once	starts	we	ever	table
brothers	field	is	one	stories	were	everything	tall
brown	find	kinds	only	story	what	floor	this
buy	first	know	open	studied	where	flower	told
by	five	large	or	sure	who	found	turned
call	fly	laugh	our	surprised	why	front	voice
car	follow	learning	out	take	window	girl	what's
	food	light	over	talk	with	gone	words

Decoding skills taught to date: short *a*; short *i*; CVC syllable pattern; short *o*; short *u*; short *e*; long *a* (CVC*e*); long *i* (CVC*e*); /k/ spelled *c*; /s/ spelled *c*; long *o* (CVC*e*); long *u* /yōō/ (CVC*e*); long *u* /ōō/ (CVC*e*); long *e* (CVC*e*); /g/ spelled *g*; /j/ spelled *g*, *dge*; blends with *r*; blends with *l*; blends with *s*; final blend *nd*; final blend *ng*; final blend *nk*; final blend *nt*; double final consonants *ll*; double final consonants *ss*; double final consonants *zz*; double final consonants *ff*; consonants *ck*; double consonants (closed syllables); consonant digraph *th*; consonant digraph *sh*; consonant digraph *wh*; consonant digraphs *ch*, *tch*; consonant digraph *ph*; base words and ending -*s*; base words and ending -*ed* /ed/; base words and ending -*ed* /t/; base words and ending -*ed* /d/; base words and ending -*ing*; ending -*ed*: drop *e*; ending -*ing*: drop *e*; CV syllable pattern (open syllables); contractions with *'s, n't*; contractions with *'ve, 're*; base words and endings -*s*, -*es*; vowel digraphs *ai*, *ay*; vowel digraphs *ee*, *ea*; vowel digraphs *oa*, *ow*; compound words; schwa sound; ending -*ed*: double consonant; ending -*ing*: double consonant; long *i* spelled *igh*, *ie*; long *i* spelled *i*, *y*; long *e* spelled *y*; ending -*es*: change *y* to *i*; r-controlled *ar*; r-controlled *or*, *ore*; r-controlled *er*; r-controlled *ir*, *ur*; homophones **From Grade 1:** consonants; short vowels; vowel combination *ou*; vowel digraph *oo* /oo/

"Good! Good! I like fish!" I said.

We rode in the boat for a long while until lunch. Then we docked and grilled the fish. It tasted great. I wish we could stay on that boat for a week.

4

A Boat Ride

Can you see the boat? It is time for a nice ride on the sea. We need to put life vests on. We need sun block to keep us safe, too.

1

We cannot take a boat on the road. It has to float on the sea. The waves are weak, so Gramps says it is the best day for a smooth boat ride.

Off we go. We rode a mile out, and then rested. It is fun to rest and look out at the far away sea. Gramps took out his fishing pole and said, "I am fishing for lunch."

Faster or Not?

DECODABLE WORDS

Target Skill: ending -er: double consonant

bigger	faster	smarter	stronger

Previously Taught Skills

a	did	join	slow	uphill
am	each	just	snack	us
an	fast	let's	soon	wagon
apple	first	look	spotted	waved
ate	Frog	looked	started	well
by	get	may	stop	when
beat	go	not	than	will
big	Goat	on	then	wise
but	her	or	this	
came	hill	over	too	
can	how	Owl	top	
chuckled	I	race	Tory	
claimed	is	ran	Turtle	
cried	it	set	up	

SKILLS APPLIED IN WORDS IN STORY: short *a, i, o, u, e*; long *a* (CVCe); /k/ and /s/ spelled *c*; /g/ spelled *g*; blends with *l*, blends with *s*; double final consonants *ll*; consonants *ck*; consonant digraphs *th, ch*; contraction *'s*; vowel digraphs *ay, ea*; vowel digraph *ow*; long *i* spelled *y*; r-controlled *ar, or, er*; ending -er: double consonant   **From Grade 1:** consonants; vowel digraph *oo* /o͞o/; /oo/ spelled *oo, ou*; vowel combination *ow*

HIGH-FREQUENCY WORDS

a	do	other	the	who
animals	everyone	pull	there	you
are	horse	said	they	
be	laughed	she	to	

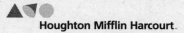

Houghton Mifflin Harcourt

Faster or Not?

High-Frequency Words Taught to Date

Grade 1

a	carry	for	like	own	teacher	work	hair
about	caught	four	listen	paper	the	world	hard
above	city	friend	little	party	their	would	hello
across	cold	friendship	live	people	there	write	horse
after	come	full	long	pictures	these	years	hundred
again	could	funny	look	play	they	yellow	I'll
all	country	give	loudly	please	think	you	I've
almost	covers	go	loved	pull	those	young	kept
along	cried	goes	make	pushed	thought	your	might
always	different	good	many	put	three		mind
and	do	great	maybe	read	to	**Grade 2**	morning
animal	does	green	me	ready	today	afraid	move
are	done	ground	minute	right	together	against	next
around	don't	grow	more	said	too	air	other
away	door	happy	most	school	took	also	part
baby	down	have	mother	second	toward	another	pretty
ball	draw	he	my	see	try	any	really
be	earth	head	myself	seven	two	anything	river
bear	eat	hear	near	shall	under	behind	room
beautiful	eight	heard	never	she	until	being	saw
because	enough	help	new	should	use	better	says
been	even	her	night	show	very	book	sky
before	every	here	no	sing	walk	care	sleep
began	everyone	high	noise	small	want	cheer	slowly
begins	eyes	hold	nothing	soil	warms	children	someone
bird	fall	house	now	some	was	dark	something
blue	family	how	of	sometimes	wash	didn't	sound
both	far	I	off	soon	watch	doing	stood
boy	father	idea	old	sorry	water	else	store
bring	few	into	once	starts	we	ever	table
brothers	field	is	one	stories	were	everything	tall
brown	find	kinds	only	story	what	floor	this
buy	first	know	open	studied	where	flower	told
by	five	large	or	sure	who	found	turned
call	fly	laugh	our	surprised	why	front	voice
car	follow	learning	out	take	window	girl	what's
	food	light	over	talk	with	gone	words

Decoding skills taught to date: short *a*; short *i*; short *o*; short *u*; short *e*; CVC closed syllables; long *a* (CVC*e*); long *i* (CVC*e*); /k/ spelled *c*; /s/ spelled *c*; long *o* (CVC*e*); long *u* /yōō/ (CVC*e*); long *u* /ōō/ (CVC*e*); long *e* (CVC*e*); /g/ spelled *g*; /j/ spelled *g*, *dge*; blends with *r*; blends with *l*; blends with *s*; final blend *nd*; final blend *ng*; final blend *nk*; final blend *nt*; double final consonants *ll*, *ss*, *ff*, *zz*; consonants *ck*; double consonants (closed syllables); consonant digraphs *th*, *sh*, *wh*, *ch*, *tch*, *ph*; base words and endings *-s*, *-ed* /ed/, *-ed* /t/, *-ed* /d/, *ing*, *es*; CV open syllables; contractions with *'s*, *n't*, *'ll*, *'d*, *'ve*, *'re*; vowel digraphs *ai* and *ay*, *ee* and *ea*, *oa* and *ow*; compound words; schwa sound; long *i* spelled *igh*, *ie*, *i*, *y*; long *e* spelled *y*; ending *-es*: change *y* to *i*; r-controlled *ar*, *or*, *ore*, *er*, *ir*, *ur*; homophones; ending *-er*: double consonant

"You beat us!" the animals cried. "How did you do it?"

"Well," chuckled Tory. "I may not be faster, but I am smarter. When the race started, I did not stop. I just ran!"

Everyone laughed. Then each ate an apple snack.

Faster or Not?

"Let's race up the big hill," said Tory Turtle. "Who will get there first? Get set! GO!"

"I will," laughed Frog. "You are too slow."

"Tory may be slow," cried Goat, "but I am fast!"

© Houghton Mifflin Harcourt Publishing Company

Soon, other animals came by. Each claimed to be faster.

"I am not just faster," Goat said, "I am stronger! I can pull a wagon!"

"I can pull a bigger wagon!" said Horse!

"Stop!" cried wise Owl, "The race is over! Look!"

The animals looked uphill. They spotted Tory on top. Tory waved.

They ran up the big hill to join her.

Little Bird's Flight

DECODABLE WORDS

Target Skill: ending -*er*: double consonant

bigger	colder	harder	longer	warmer
brighter	cooler	lighter	older	wiser

Previously Taught Skills

an	days	her	little	pals	tiny
and	eat	here	long	place	trip
as	flight	hides	look	seeds	warm
back	fly	home	lots	shook	we
bird	food	in	much	sky	went
birds	for	is	must	snow	when
brrr	freeze	it	need	soon	will
but	gets	it's	not	spring	wings
can	got	just	now	stopped	winter
chirped	ground	lakes	nuts	strength	with
cried	happy	let's	on	sunny	yes

SKILLS APPLIED IN WORDS IN STORY: short *a, i, o, u, e*; long *a* (CVC*e*); long *i* (CVC*e*); /k/ and /s/ spelled *c*; long *o* (CVC*e*); /g/ spelled *g*; blends with *r*; blends with *l*; blends with *s*; final blends *nd, ng*; consonants *ck*; consonant digraphs *sh, wh, ch*; base words and endings -*s,* -*ed* /t/, -*ed* /d/; vowel digraphs *ay, ee*; vowel digraph *ow*; long *i* spelled *igh, y*; long *e,* spelled *y*; r-controlled *ar, er, ir*   **From Grade 1:** consonants; possessives with *'s*; vowel digraphs *oo* /o͞o/, /oo/; syllable _*le*; vowel combinations *ou, ow*

HIGH-FREQUENCY WORDS

a	flew	she	there	today	were
away	of	sometimes	they	was	you
find	said	the		to	we

Houghton Mifflin Harcourt

Little Bird's Flight

High-Frequency Words Taught to Date

Grade 1							
a	carry	for	like	own	teacher	work	hair
about	caught	four	listen	paper	the	world	hard
above	city	friend	little	party	their	would	hello
across	cold	friendship	live	people	there	write	horse
after	come	full	long	pictures	these	years	hundred
again	could	funny	look	play	they	yellow	I'll
all	country	give	loudly	please	think	you	I've
almost	covers	go	loved	pull	those	young	kept
along	cried	goes	make	pushed	thought	your	might
always	different	good	many	put	three		mind
and	do	great	maybe	read	to	**Grade 2**	morning
animal	does	green	me	ready	today	afraid	move
are	done	ground	minute	right	together	against	next
around	don't	grow	more	said	too	air	other
away	door	happy	most	school	took	also	part
baby	down	have	mother	second	toward	another	pretty
ball	draw	he	my	see	try	any	really
be	earth	head	myself	seven	two	anything	river
bear	eat	hear	near	shall	under	behind	room
beautiful	eight	heard	never	she	until	being	saw
because	enough	help	new	should	use	better	says
been	even	her	night	show	very	book	sky
before	every	here	no	sing	walk	care	sleep
began	everyone	high	noise	small	want	cheer	slowly
begins	eyes	hold	nothing	soil	warms	children	someone
bird	fall	house	now	some	was	dark	something
blue	family	how	of	sometimes	wash	didn't	sound
both	far	I	off	soon	watch	doing	stood
boy	father	idea	old	sorry	water	else	store
bring	few	into	once	starts	we	ever	table
brothers	field	is	one	stories	were	everything	tall
brown	find	kinds	only	story	what	floor	this
buy	first	know	open	studied	where	flower	told
by	five	large	or	sure	who	found	turned
call	fly	laugh	our	surprised	why	front	voice
car	follow	learning	out	take	window	girl	what's
	food	light	over	talk	with	gone	words

Decoding skills taught to date: short *a*; short *i*; short *o*; short *u*; short *e*; closed syllables; long *a* (CVC*e*); long *i* (CVC*e*); /k/ spelled *c*; /s/ spelled *c*; long *o* (CVC*e*); long *u* /yoo/ (CVC*e*); long *u* /oo/ (CVC*e*); long *e* (CVC*e*); /g/ spelled *g*; /j/ spelled *g*, *dge*; blends with *r*; blends with *l*; blends with *s*; final blend *nd*; final blend *ng*; final blend *nk*; final blend *nt*; double final consonants *ll, ss, ff, zz*; consonants *ck*; double consonants (closed syllables); consonant digraphs *th, sh, wh, ch, tch, ph*; base words and endings -*s*, -*ed* /ed/, -*ed* /t/, -*ed* /d/, *ing, es*; open syllables; contractions with *'s, n't, 'll, 'd, 've, 're*; vowel digraphs *ai, ay, ee, ea*; vowel digraphs *oa, ow*; compound words; schwa sound; long *i* spelled *igh, ie, i, y*; long *e* spelled *y*; ending -*es*: change *y* to *i*; r-controlled *ar, or, ore, er, ir, ur*; homophones; ending -*er*: double consonant

Little Bird and her pals were happy in the warm, sunny place. In spring, they went back home.

"Now it is warmer here," said Little Bird. "We can find food. And when it gets colder, we will just fly to a warmer place!"

Little Bird's Flight

"Brrr!" cried Little Bird as she shook her tiny wings. "It is much cooler today!"

"Yes," said a bigger bird. "We must find a warmer place for the winter."

"Eat lots of seeds," said an older and wiser bird. "You will need strength for the long trip!"

Soon Little Bird flew away. Bigger and older birds went with her. Sometimes they stopped to eat. But there was not much food.

"It's harder to find food," said an older bird. "Snow hides the ground, and lakes freeze."

The birds flew on. Soon the sky got lighter and brighter. The days got longer and warmer.

"Let's look for a home here," chirped Little Bird. "We can find lots of nuts and seeds to eat!"

Pumpkin and Prizes

DECODABLE WORDS

Target Skill: ending -*est*: double consonant

biggest	scariest	smallest
saddest	silliest	

Previously Taught Skills

and	dripped	judges	pointed	think
as	dry	Lee	prize	this
asked	face	let's	prizes	too
at	for	like	proudly	we
be	gave	looked	pumpkin	will
best	get	made	pumpkins	win
Carlo	got	Mandy	Sam	winner
contest	had	Miss	she	with
crying	he	Mr. (Mister)	silly	yes
did	I	on	Smith	
didn't	is	paint	so	
down	it	picked	they	

SKILLS APPLIED IN WORDS IN STORY: short *a*; short *i*; short *o*; short *u*; short *e*; CVC closed syllables; long *a* (CVC*e*); long *i* (CVC*e*); /k/ spelled *c*; /j/ spelled *g*, *dge*; blends with *r*; blends with *s*; final blends *nd, nk, nt*; double final consonants *ll*; consonants *ck*; consonant digraphs *th, sh*; base words and endings -*ed*/ed/, -*ed* /t/, -*ing*, -*es*; CV open syllables; contractions with *'s*, *n't*; vowel digraphs *ai* and *ay*, *ee* and *ea*; endings -*ed*, -*er*: double consonant; long *i* spelled *i*, *y*; long *e* spelled *y*; r-controlled *ar, or, er*; ending -*est*: double consonant **From Grade 1:** consonants, /z/ spelled *s*; phonogram -*ump*; long *e* (*e, ee*); vowel digraphs *oo* /o͞o/; /oo/ spelled *oo*; vowel combinations *ou, ow*; suffix -*ly*

HIGH-FREQUENCY WORDS

a	have	said	was
eyes	laugh(ed)	the	were
from	one	there	who

Houghton Mifflin Harcourt

Pumpkin and Prizes

High-Frequency Words Taught to Date

Grade 1

a	carry	for	like	own	teacher	work	hair
about	caught	four	listen	paper	the	world	hard
above	city	friend	little	party	their	would	hello
across	cold	friendship	live	people	there	write	horse
after	come	full	long	pictures	these	years	hundred
again	could	funny	look	play	they	yellow	I'll
all	country	give	loudly	please	think	you	I've
almost	covers	go	loved	pull	those	young	kept
along	cried	goes	make	pushed	thought	your	might
always	different	good	many	put	three		mind
and	do	great	maybe	read	to	*Grade 2*	morning
animal	does	green	me	ready	today	afraid	move
are	done	ground	minute	right	together	against	next
around	don't	grow	more	said	too	air	other
away	door	happy	most	school	took	also	part
baby	down	have	mother	second	toward	another	pretty
ball	draw	he	my	see	try	any	really
be	earth	head	myself	seven	two	anything	river
bear	eat	hear	near	shall	under	behind	room
beautiful	eight	heard	never	she	until	being	saw
because	enough	help	new	should	use	better	says
been	even	her	night	show	very	book	sky
before	every	here	no	sing	walk	care	sleep
began	everyone	high	noise	small	want	cheer	slowly
begins	eyes	hold	nothing	soil	warms	children	someone
bird	fall	house	now	some	was	dark	something
blue	family	how	of	sometimes	wash	didn't	sound
both	far	I	off	soon	watch	doing	stood
boy	father	idea	old	sorry	water	else	store
bring	few	into	once	starts	we	ever	table
brothers	field	is	one	stories	were	everything	tall
brown	find	kinds	only	story	what	floor	this
buy	first	know	open	studied	where	flower	told
by	five	large	or	sure	who	found	turned
call	fly	laugh	our	surprised	why	front	voice
car	follow	learning	out	take	window	girl	what's
	food	light	over	talk	with	gone	words

Decoding skills taught to date: short *a*; short *i*; short *o*; short *u*; short *e*; CVC closed syllables; long *a* (CVC*e*); long *i* (CVC*e*); /k/ spelled *c*; /s/ spelled *c*; long *o* (CVC*e*); long *u* /yo͞o/ (CVC*e*); long *u* /o͞o/ (CVC*e*); long *e* (CVC*e*); /g/ spelled *g*; /j/ spelled *g*, *dge*; blends with *r*; blends with *l*; blends with *s*; final blend *nd*; final blend *ng*; final blend *nk*; final blend *nt*; double final consonants *ll*, *ss*, *ff*, *zz*; consonants *ck*; double consonants (closed syllables); consonant digraphs *th*, *sh*, *wh*, *ch*, *tch*, *ph*; base words and endings -*s*, -*ed* /ed/, -*ed* /t/, -*ed* /d/, *ing*, *es*; CV open syllables; contractions with *'s*, *n't*, *'ll*, *'d*, *'ve*, *'re*; vowel digraphs *ai* and *ay*, *ee* and *ea*, *oa* and *ow*; compound words; schwa sound; long *i* spelled *igh*, *ie*, *i*, *y*; long *e*, spelled *y*; ending -*es*: change *y* to *i*; r-controlled *ar*, *or*, *ore*, *er*, *ir*, *ur*; homophones; ending -*er*: double consonant; ending -*est*: double consonant   **From Grade 1:** consonants; /z/ spelled *s*; phonogram -*ump*; long *e* (*e*, *ee*); vowel digraphs *oo*; /oo/ spelled *oo*; vowel combinations *ou*, *ow*; suffix -*ly*

I looked at my pumpkin. The paint didn't dry on the eyes! It dripped down from its eyes like it was crying!

"Who made this?" asked Mr. Lee.

"I did," I said.

"It can get a prize . . . for the saddest!" laughed Miss Smith.

So I got a prize, too!

4

Pumpkin and Prizes

"Let's have a pumpkin contest," said Miss Smith. "The best pumpkins will win a prize!"

"Will there be a prize for the biggest?" I asked.

"Yes," Miss Smith said. "And there will be a prize for the smallest, the silliest, and the scariest!"

1

Miss Smith and Mr. Lee were the judges. They picked the best pumpkins.

Sam was a winner. He had the smallest pumpkin.

Mandy was a winner, too. She had the biggest pumpkin!

"Who made this one?" asked Mr. Lee. He pointed at a pumpkin with a silly face.

"I did," Carlo said proudly.

"We think it is the silliest!" said Mr. Lee as he gave Carlo a prize.

Did You Know?

DECODABLE WORDS

Target Skill: ending -est: double consonant

biggest	highest	loudest	slowest	tallest
coldest	hottest	oldest	smallest	
fastest	longest	shortest	strongest	

Previously Taught Skills

a	cat	is	ostrich	that
about	did	it	our	them
an	elephant	kind	out	they
and	falcon	know	peak	things
beak	find	land	pelican	tiny
big	from	lift	read	tree(s)
bigger	full	like	redwood	up
bird	has	look	sailfish	whale
blue	how	monkeys	sea	you
book(s)	hummingbird	more	shapes	
bugs	I	much	sizes	
but	in	on	sky	
can	Internet	or	than	

SKILLS APPLIED IN WORDS IN STORY: short a, i, o, u, e; closed syllables; long a (CVCe); long i (CVCe); /g/ spelled g; blends with r, l, s; final blends nd, ng, nt, nk; double final consonants ll; consonant digraphs th, wh, sh, ch, ph; base words and endings -s, -ing; open syllables; vowel digraphs ai, ee, ea; compound words; schwa sound; long i spelled i; long e spelled y, ey; r-controlled ore, er, ir, or; ending -er: double consonant; ending -est: double consonant **From Grade 1:** consonants; /z/ spelled s; consonant digraph kn; digraph oo /ōō/; /oo/ spelled ou, ue; vowel combinations ou, ow

HIGH-FREQUENCY WORDS

all	are	many	to	where
also	come	of	wall	world
animal(s)	earth	the	what	

Houghton Mifflin Harcourt

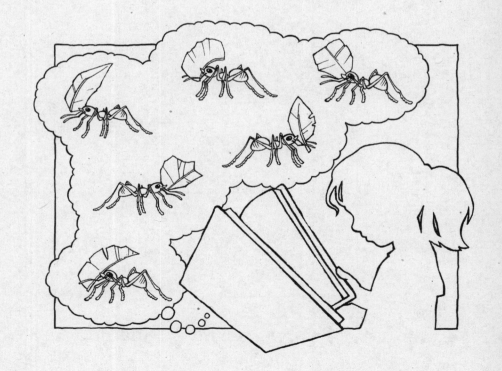

High-Frequency Words Taught to Date

Grade 1							
a	carry	for	like	own	teacher	work	hair
about	caught	four	listen	paper	the	world	hard
above	city	friend	little	party	their	would	hello
across	cold	friendship	live	people	there	write	horse
after	come	full	long	pictures	these	years	hundred
again	could	funny	look	play	they	yellow	I'll
all	country	give	loudly	please	think	you	I've
almost	covers	go	loved	pull	those	young	kept
along	cried	goes	make	pushed	thought	your	might
always	different	good	many	put	three		mind
and	do	great	maybe	read	to	**Grade 2**	morning
animal	does	green	me	ready	today	afraid	move
are	done	ground	minute	right	together	against	next
around	don't	grow	more	said	too	air	other
away	door	happy	most	school	took	also	part
baby	down	have	mother	second	toward	another	pretty
ball	draw	he	my	see	try	any	really
be	earth	head	myself	seven	two	anything	river
bear	eat	hear	near	shall	under	behind	room
beautiful	eight	heard	never	she	until	being	saw
because	enough	help	new	should	use	better	says
been	even	her	night	show	very	book	sky
before	every	here	no	sing	walk	care	sleep
began	everyone	high	noise	small	want	cheer	slowly
begins	eyes	hold	nothing	soil	warms	children	someone
bird	fall	house	now	some	was	dark	something
blue	family	how	of	sometimes	wash	didn't	sound
both	far	I	off	soon	watch	doing	stood
boy	father	idea	old	sorry	water	else	store
bring	few	into	once	starts	we	ever	table
brothers	field	is	one	stories	were	everything	tall
brown	find	kinds	only	story	what	floor	this
buy	first	know	open	studied	where	flower	told
by	five	large	or	sure	who	found	turned
call	fly	laugh	our	surprised	why	front	voice
car	follow	learning	out	take	window	girl	what's
	food	light	over	talk	with	gone	words

Decoding skills taught to date: short *a*; short *i*; short *o*; short *u*; short *e*; CVC closed syllables; long *a* (CVC*e*); long *i* (CVC*e*); /k/ spelled *c*; /s/ spelled *c*; long *o* (CVC*e*); long *u* /yōō/ (CVC*e*); long *u* /ōō/ (CVC*e*); long *e* (CVC*e*); /g/ spelled *g*; /j/ spelled *g*, *dge*; blends with *r*; blends with *l*; blends with *s*; final blend *nd*; final blend *ng*; final blend *nk*; final blend *nt*; double final consonants *ll*, *ss*, *ff*, *zz*; consonants *ck*; double consonants (closed syllables); consonant digraphs *th*, *sh*, *wh*, *ch*, *tch*, *ph*; base words and endings *-s*, *-ed* /ed/, *-ed* /t/, *-ed* /d/, *ing*, *es*; CV open syllables; contractions with *'s*, *n't*, *'ll*, *'d*, *'ve*, *'re*; vowel digraphs *ai* and *ay*, *ee* and *ea*, *oa* and *ow*; compound words; schwa sound; long *i* spelled *igh*, *ie*, *i*, *y*; long *e*, spelled *y*; ending *-es*: change *y* to *i*; r-controlled *ar*, *or*, *ore*, *er*, *ir*, *ur*; homophones; ending *-er*: double consonant; ending *-est*: double consonant   **From Grade 1:** consonants; /z/ spelled *s*; consonant digraph *kn*; digraph *oo* /ōō/; /oo/ spelled *ou*, *ue*; vowel combinations *ou*, *ow*

Did You Know?

Our world is full of many things. They come in all shapes and sizes. I like to read about them.

Did you know that a blue whale is the biggest animal in the sea? It is also the loudest. The biggest land animal is an elephant. Monkeys are the loudest animals on land.

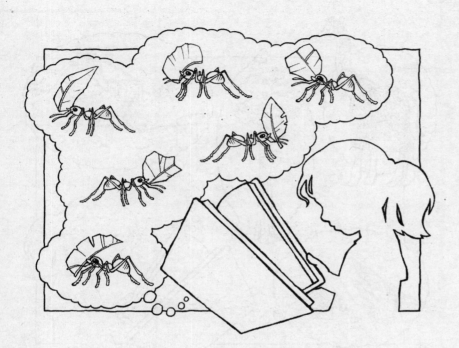

Did you know that the strongest animals are tiny bugs? They can lift things much bigger than they are!

You can find out more about the slowest, coldest, hottest, or shortest things. How? Read a book about them. You can also look them up on the Internet!

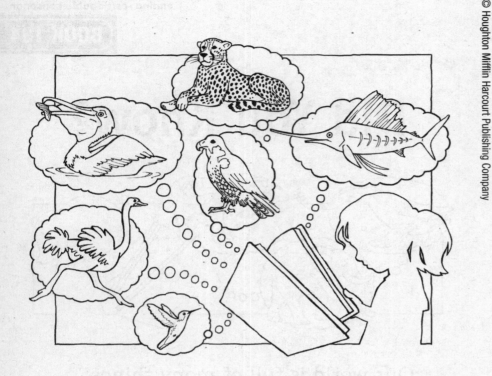

Did you know that the fastest animal on land is a kind of big cat? A sailfish is fastest in the sea. A falcon is the fastest bird in the sky. I know this from books!

The biggest bird on earth is the ostrich. The smallest is a hummingbird. A pelican has the longest beak.

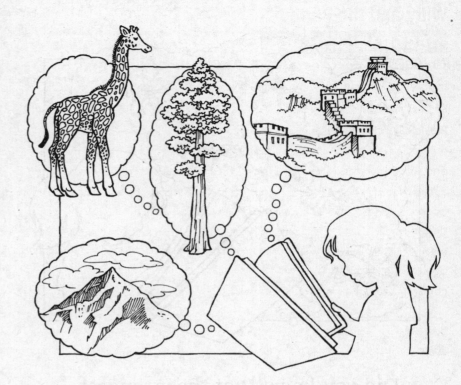

Did you know that a redwood is the tallest tree? A redwood is also one of the oldest trees in the world.

You can also read to find out what the tallest animal is, what the highest peak is, or where the longest wall is!

Willy and the Puppy

DECODABLE WORDS

Target Skill: **suffix -y**

breezy	cloudy	gloomy	stormy
chilly	fluffy	snowy	windy

Previously Taught Skills

a	face	jumped	puppy	too
and	for	long	puppy's	we
asked	get	looked	scarf	will
back	got	made	sky	Willy
began	had	maybe	snow	Willy's
blew	happy	Mom	snowflakes	wind
boy	his	not	soon	window
can	I	now	stepped	
city	in	out	then	
day	inside	outside	think	
even	it	played	time	

SKILLS APPLIED IN WORDS IN STORY: short *a*; short *i*; short *o*; short *u*; short *e*; CVC closed syllables; long *a* (CVC*e*); long *i* (CVC*e*); /k/ spelled *c*; /s/ *spelled c*; /g/ spelled *g*; blends with *r*; blends with *l*; blends with *s*; final blends *nd, ng, nk*; double final consonants *ll, ff*; consonants *ck*; double consonants (closed syllables); consonant digraphs *th, sh, ch*; base words and endings *-s, -ed* /t/, *-ed* /d/; CV open syllables; vowel digraph *ay*; vowel digraph *ow*; compound words; schwa sound; long *i* spelled *y*; long *e* spelled *y*; r-controlled *ar, or*; suffix *-y* **From Grade 1:** consonants; long *e* (*e, ee*); final blend *mp*; possessives with *'s*; vowel digraph *oo* /ōō/; /oo/ spelled *oo*; vowel combinations *ou, ow, ew, oy*

HIGH-FREQUENCY WORDS

also	go	the	very
been	into	they	was
fall	said	to	were

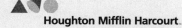
Houghton Mifflin Harcourt

© Houghton Mifflin Harcourt Publishing Company

suffix *-y*

BOOK 135

Willy and the Puppy

© Houghton Mifflin Harcourt Publishing Company

High-Frequency Words Taught to Date

Grade 1

a	carry	for	like	own	teacher	work	hair
about	caught	four	listen	paper	the	world	hard
above	city	friend	little	party	their	would	hello
across	cold	friendship	live	people	there	write	horse
after	come	full	long	pictures	these	years	hundred
again	could	funny	look	play	they	yellow	I'll
all	country	give	loudly	please	think	you	I've
almost	covers	go	loved	pull	those	young	kept
along	cried	goes	make	pushed	thought	your	might
always	different	good	many	put	three		mind
and	do	great	maybe	read	to	**Grade 2**	morning
animal	does	green	me	ready	today	afraid	move
are	done	ground	minute	right	together	against	next
around	don't	grow	more	said	too	air	other
away	door	happy	most	school	took	also	part
baby	down	have	mother	second	toward	another	pretty
ball	draw	he	my	see	try	any	really
be	earth	head	myself	seven	two	anything	river
bear	eat	hear	near	shall	under	behind	room
beautiful	eight	heard	never	she	until	being	saw
because	enough	help	new	should	use	better	says
been	even	her	night	show	very	book	sky
before	every	here	no	sing	walk	care	sleep
began	everyone	high	noise	small	want	cheer	slowly
begins	eyes	hold	nothing	soil	warms	children	someone
bird	fall	house	now	some	was	dark	something
blue	family	how	of	sometimes	wash	didn't	stand
both	far	I	off	soon	watch	doing	stood
boy	father	idea	old	sorry	water	else	store
bring	few	into	once	starts	we	ever	table
brothers	field	is	one	stories	were	everything	tall
brown	find	kinds	only	story	what	floor	this
buy	first	know	open	studied	where	flower	told
by	five	large	or	sure	who	found	turned
call	fly	laugh	our	surprised	why	front	voice
car	follow	learning	out	take	window	girl	what's
	food	light	over	talk	with	gone	words

Decoding skills taught to date: short *a*; short *i*; CVC closed syllables; short *o*; short *u*; short *e*; long *a* (CVC*e*); long *i* (CVC*e*); /k/ spelled *c*; /s/ spelled *c*; long *o* (CVC*e*); long *u* /yoo/ (CVC*e*); long *u* /oo/ (CVC*e*); long *e* (CVC*e*); /g/ spelled *g*; /j/ spelled *g*, *dge*; blends with *r*; blends with *l*; blends with *s*; final blend *nd*; final blend *ng*; final blend *nk*; final blend *nt*; double final consonants *ll*, *ss*, *ff*, *zz*; consonants *ck*; double consonants (closed syllables); consonant digraphs *th*, *sh*, *wh*, *ch*, *tch*, *ph*; base words and ending -*s*; base words and ending -*ed* /ed/; base words and ending -*ed* /d/; base words and ending -*ed* /t/; base words and ending -*ing*; base words and ending -*ed*; CV open syllables; contractions *s* with '*s*, *n't*, '*ll*, '*d*, '*ve*, '*re*; base words and endings -*s*, -*es*; vowel digraphs *ai*, *ay*, *ee*, *ea*, *oa*, *ow*; compound words; schwa sound; endings -*s*, -*ed*: double consonant; ending -*ing*: double consonant; long *i* spelled *igh*, *ie*, *i*, *y*; long *e* spelled *y*; ending -*es*: change *y* to *i*; r-controlled *ar*; r-controlled *or*, *ore*; r-controlled *er*; r-controlled *ir*, *ur*; homophones; ending -*er*: double consonant; ending -*est*: double consonant; suffix -*y* **From Grade 1:** consonants; long *e* (*e*, *ee*); final blend *mp*; possessives with '*s*; vowel digraph *oo* /oo/; /oo/ spelled *oo*; vowel combinations *ou*, *ow*, *ew*, *oy*

Now it was not too windy to go outside. A happy Willy and his puppy jumped into the fluffy snow. They played and played in the fluffy snow. They even made a snow boy and a snow puppy!

Willy and the Puppy

It was a chilly day. Willy and his puppy stepped outside.

The sky was cloudy and gloomy. A breezy wind blew Willy's scarf. It also blew in the puppy's face.

Soon it got very, very windy. Willy and his puppy had to go back inside. "I think it will get stormy," said Willy. "Maybe it will even get snowy!"

It had not been snowy in Willy's city for a long, long time.

Willy and his puppy looked out the window. Then fluffy snowflakes began to fall! Willy and his puppy were happy.

"Mom, can we play outside?" asked Willy.

Three Messy Sheep

DECODABLE WORDS

Target Skill: **suffix –y**

cloudy	fuzzy	mucky	shaggy
fluffy	messy	muddy	

Previously Taught Skills

and	far	I	on	three
at	faster	in	open	way
ate	fell	is	out	we
bad	Fen	it	played	went
be	Fin	last	rain	wet
Ben	for	latch	ran	will
closed	gate	leaned	see	
day	get	leaped	sheep	
did	got	looking	sky	
drip	grass	moaned	so	
drop	harder	mud	soft	
each	he	nice	splashed	
eat	home	not	swung	

SKILLS APPLIED IN WORDS IN STORY: short *a, i, o, u, e*; CVC syllable pattern (closed syllables); long *a, i, o* (CVC*e*); /k/ spelled *c*; /s/ spelled *c*; /g/ spelled *g*; blends with *r, l, s*; final blends *nd, ft, ng, nt*; double final consonants *ll, ss, ff, zz*; consonant digraphs *th, sh, ch, tch*; base words and endings *-ed* /d/, *-ed* /t/, *-ing*; CV syllable pattern (open syllables); vowel digraphs *ai, ay, ee, ea*; vowel digraph *oa*; long *i* spelled *y*; long *e* spelled *y*; r-controlled *ar, or*; ending *-er*: double consonant; suffix *-y* **From Grade 1:** consonants; short vowels; long *e* (*e, ee*); /oo/ spelled *oo*; vowel combination *ou*

HIGH-FREQUENCY WORDS

are	here	the	was
field	one	they	were
friends	said	to	

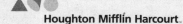

Houghton Mifflin Harcourt.

© Houghton Mifflin Harcourt Publishing Company

suffix *-y*

BOOK 136

Three Messy Sheep

High-Frequency Words Taught to Date

Grade 1

a	caught	friend	live	pictures	they	you	kept
about	city	friendship	long	play	think	young	might
above	cold	full	look	please	those	your	mind
across	come	funny	loudly	pull	thought		morning
after	could	give	loved	pushed	three	*Grade 2*	move
again	country	go	make	put	to	afraid	next
all	covers	goes	many	read	today	against	other
almost	cried	good	maybe	ready	together	air	part
along	different	great	me	right	too	also	pretty
always	do	green	minute	said	took	another	really
and	does	ground	more	school	toward	any	river
animal	done	grow	most	second	try	anything	room
are	don't	happy	mother	see	two	behind	saw
around	door	have	my	seven	under	being	says
away	down	he	myself	shall	until	better	sky
baby	draw	head	near	she	use	book	sleep
ball	earth	hear	never	should	very	care	slowly
be	eat	heard	new	show	walk	cheer	someone
bear	eight	help	night	sing	want	children	something
beautiful	enough	her	no	small	warms	dark	stand
because	even	here	noise	soil	was	didn't	stood
been	every	high	nothing	some	wash	doing	store
before	everyone	hold	now	sometimes	watch	else	table
began	eyes	house	of	soon	water	ever	tall
begins	fall	how	off	sorry	we	everything	this
bird	family	I	old	starts	were	floor	told
blue	far	idea	once	stories	what	flower	turned
both	father	into	one	story	where	found	voice
boy	few	is	only	studied	who	front	what's
bring	field	kinds	open	sure	why	girl	words
brothers	find	know	or	surprised	window	gone	
brown	first	large	our	take	with	hair	
buy	five	laugh	out	talk	work	hard	
by	fly	learning	over	teacher	world	hello	
call	follow	light	own	the	would	horse	
car	food	like	paper	their	write	hundred	
carry	four	little	party	there	years	I'll	
				these	yellow	I've	

Decoding skills taught to date: short *a*; short *i*; CVC syllable pattern (closed syllables); short *o*; short *u*; short *e*; long *a* (CVC*e*); long *i* (CVC*e*); /k/ spelled *c*; /s/ spelled *c*; long *o* (CVC*e*); long *u* /yōō/ (CVC*e*); long *u* /ōō/ (CVC*e*); long *e* (CVC*e*); /g/ spelled *g*; /j/ spelled *g*, *dge*; blends with *r*; blends with *l*; blends with *s*; final blend *nd*; final blend *ng*; final blend *nk*; final blend *nt*; double final consonants *ll*, *ss*, *ff*, *zz*; consonants *ck*; double consonants (closed syllables); consonant digraph *th*; consonant digraph *sh*; consonant digraph *wh*; consonant digraphs *ch*, *tch*; consonant digraph *ph*; base words and ending -*s*; base words and ending -*ed* /ed/; base words and ending -*ed* /d/; base words and ending -*ed* /t/; base words and ending -*ing*; CV syllable pattern (open syllables); contractions with '*s* and *n't*; contractions with '*ll* and '*d*; contractions with '*ve* and '*re*; base words and endings -*s*, -*es*; vowel digraphs *ai*, *ay*; vowel digraphs *ee*, *ea*; vowel digraphs *oa*, *ow*; compound words; schwa sound; ending -*ed*: double consonant; ending -*ing*: double consonant; long *i* spelled *igh*, *ie*; long *i* spelled *i*, *y*; long *e* spelled *y*; ending -*es*: change *y* to *i*; r-controlled *ar*; r-controlled *or*, *ore*; r-controlled *er*; r-controlled *ir*, *ur*; homophones, ending -*er*: double consonant; ending -*est*: double consonant; suffix -*y* **From Grade 1:** consonants; short vowels; long *e* (*e*, *ee*); /oo/ spelled *oo*

Three Messy Sheep

"It is so bad to be wet," moaned Ben.

So the sheep ran home. They went faster and faster. They splashed in mucky mud on the way.

At last Fen, Fin, and Ben got home.

"We are three muddy, messy sheep," Fen said.

Fin, Fen, and Ben were friends. Fin was fluffy. Fen was fuzzy. Ben was shaggy. They ate grass in the field. They leaped and played each day.

4

1

One day, the gate latch was not closed. So Fin leaned on it. The gate swung open.

"I will eat soft grass out here," he said.

Out went Fin. Out went Fen and Ben.

The three sheep went far looking for nice grass. Fen, Fin, and Ben ate and ate. They did not see the sky get cloudy.

Drip, drop, drip, drop. Rain fell harder and harder. The three sheep got so wet.

© Houghton Mifflin Harcourt Publishing Company

The Big Race

DECODABLE WORDS

Target Skill: **suffix -ly**

badly	gladly	quickly	slowly
briskly	nicely	sadly	

Previously Taught Skills

a	fine	I	rock	time
and	finish	Kit	Sam	turns
at	flag	last	same	up
Ben	for	Lee	sat	us
best	Fran	line	say	when
big	Fred	lined	so	will
both	go	not	started	win
crowd	got	on	starting	with
did	had	place	stepped	yelled
end	he	prize	stop	
ever	held	puffed	take	
faster	his	race	that's	
fell	huffed	ran	this	

SKILLS APPLIED IN WORDS IN STORY: short *a, i, o, u, e*; CVC syllable pattern (closed syllables); long *a* (CVC*e*); long *i* (CVC*e*); /s/ spelled *c*; /g/ spelled *g*; blends with *r, l, s;* final blends *nd, ft, st*; double final consonants *ll, ff*; consonants *ck*; double consonants (closed syllables); consonant digraphs *th, sh, wh*; base words and ending *-s*; base words and ending *-ed* /d/; base words and ending *-ed* /t/; base words and ending *-ing*; contractions with *'s*; vowel digraphs *ay, ee*; long *o* spelled *ow*; endings *-ed, ing*: double consonant; long *i* spelled *e, y*; long *e* spelled *y*; r-controlled *ar, ore, ur*; ending *-er*: double consonant; suffix *-ly*   **From Grade 1** consonants; long vowel *o* (CV); vowel combination *ow*

HIGH-FREQUENCY WORDS

animals	said	they	was
caught	the	to	you

© Houghton Mifflin Harcourt Publishing Company

The Big Race

High-Frequency Words Taught to Date

Grade 1							I've
a	caught	friend	live	pictures	they	you	kept
about	city	friendship	long	play	think	young	knew
above	cold	full	look	please	those	your	might
across	come	funny	loudly	pull	thought		mind
after	could	give	loved	pushed	three	**Grade 2**	morning
again	country	go	make	put	to	afraid	move
all	covers	goes	many	read	today	against	next
almost	cried	good	maybe	ready	together	air	other
along	different	great	me	right	too	also	part
always	do	green	minute	said	took	another	pretty
and	does	ground	more	school	toward	any	really
animal	done	grow	most	second	try	anything	river
are	don't	happy	mother	see	two	behind	room
around	door	have	my	seven	under	being	saw
away	down	head	myself	shall	until	better	says
baby	draw	hear	near	she	use	book	sky
ball	earth	heard	never	should	very	care	sleep
be	eat	help	new	show	walk	cheer	slowly
bear	eight	her	night	sing	want	children	someone
beautiful	enough	here	no	small	warms	coming	something
because	even	high	noise	soil	was	dark	stand
been	every	hold	nothing	some	wash	didn't	stood
before	everyone	house	now	sometimes	watch	doing	store
began	eyes	how	of	soon	water	else	table
begins	fall	I	off	sorry	we	ever	tall
bird	family	idea	old	starts	were	everything	this
blue	far	into	once	stories	what	floor	though
both	father	is	one	story	where	flower	told
boy	few	kinds	only	studied	who	found	turned
bring	field	know	open	sure	why	front	voice
brothers	find	large	or	surprised	window	girl	what's
brown	first	laugh	our	take	with	gone	words
buy	five	learning	out	talk	work	hair	
by	fly	light	over	teacher	world	hard	
call	follow	like	own	the	would	hello	
car	food	listen	paper	their	write	horse	
carry	four	little	party	there	years	hundred	
			people	these	yellow	I'll	

Decoding skills taught to date: short *a*; short *i*; CVC syllable pattern (closed syllables); short *o*; short *u*; short *e*; long *a* (CVC*e*); long *i*, (CVC*e*); /k/ spelled *c*; /s/ spelled *c*; long *o* (CVC*e*); long *u* /yōō/ (CVC*e*); long *u* /ōō/ (CVC*e*); long *e* (CVC*e*); /g/ spelled *g*; /j/ spelled *g*, *dge*; blends with *r*; blends with *l*; blends with *s*; final blend *nd*; final blend *ng*; final blend *nk*; final blend *nt*; double final consonants *ll, ss, ff, zz*; consonants *ck*; double consonants (closed syllables); consonant digraph *th*; consonant digraph *sh*; consonant digraph *wh*; consonant digraphs *ch, tch*; consonant digraph *ph*; base words and ending -*s*; base words and ending -*ed* /ed/; base words and ending -*ed* /d/; base words and ending -*ed* /t/; base words and ending -*ing*; CV syllable pattern (open syllables); contractions with '*s* and *n't*; contractions with '*ll* and '*d*; contractions with '*ve* and '*re*; base words and endings -*s*, -*es*; vowel digraphs *ai, ay*; vowel digraphs *ee, ea*; vowel digraphs *oa, ow*; compound words; schwa sound; ending -*ed*: double consonant; ending -*ing*: double consonant; long *i* spelled *igh, ie*; long *i* spelled *i, y*; long *e* spelled *y*; ending -*es*: change *y* to *i*; r-controlled *ar*; r-controlled *or, ore*; r-controlled *er*; r-controlled *ir, ur*; homophones; ending -*er*: double consonant; ending -*est*: double consonant; suffix -*y*; suffix -*ly* **From Grade 1:** consonants; long vowel *o* (CV); vowel combination *ow*

"I gladly say you both win," said Sam.
"You will take turns with the prize."

"That's fine with us," Fran and Fred
said nicely. They held up the big prize.
This was the best race ever.

4

© Houghton Mifflin Harcourt Publishing Company .

The Big Race

The animals lined up for the big race.
The crowd yelled.
Sam stepped up to the starting line.
He got his flag up. "Go!" he yelled.
The flag fell. The race started briskly.

1

Kit ran badly. Lee ran slowly. They sadly fell to last place.

Ben huffed and puffed. He had to stop. He sat on a big rock and did not finish the race.

Fran and Fred ran quickly. When Fred ran faster, Fran caught up. So Fran and Fred got to the end at the same time.

Little Fish

DECODABLE WORDS

Target Skill: **suffix -ly**

bravely	dimly	really	wisely
deeply	quickly	sharply	

Previously Taught Skills

a	fast	it	sea	them
and	fins	its	see	up
big	fish	just	shakes	way
but	flips	leads	show	why
can	go	leaps	so	will
click	he	let's	splashes	with
dad	his	likes	swim	
dark	I	long	swims	
deep	in	not	teeth	
down	is	plan	tell	

SKILLS APPLIED IN WORDS IN STORY: short *a*; short *i*; CVC syllable pattern (closed syllables); short *o*; short *u*; short *e*; long *a, i* (CVC*e*); /k/ spelled *c*; /g/ spelled *g*; blends with *r*; blends with *l*; blends with *s*; final blend *nd*; final blend *ng*; double final consonants *ll*; consonants *ck*; consonant digraph *th*; consonant digraph *sh*; consonant digraph *wh*; base words and ending *-s* (no spelling changes, drop *e* before ending); CV syllable pattern (open syllables); contractions with *'s*; base words and endings *-s, -es*; vowel digraph *ay*; vowel digraphs *ee, ea*; vowel digraph *ow*; long *i* spelled *y*; r-controlled *ar*; suffix *-ly*
From Grade 1: consonants, short vowels; vowel combination *ow*

HIGH-FREQUENCY WORDS

again	little	they	water
good	said	to	you
idea	the	wants	

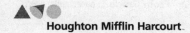

Houghton Mifflin Harcourt

Little Fish

High-Frequency Words Taught to Date

Grade 1							
a	caught	friend	live	pictures	they	you	I've
about	city	friendship	long	play	think	young	kept
above	cold	full	look	please	those	your	knew
across	come	funny	loudly	pull	thought		might
after	could	give	loved	pushed	three	**Grade 2**	mind
again	country	go	make	put	to	afraid	morning
all	covers	goes	many	read	today	against	move
almost	cried	good	maybe	ready	together	air	next
along	different	great	me	right	too	also	other
always	do	green	minute	said	took	another	part
and	does	ground	more	school	toward	any	pretty
animal	done	grow	most	second	try	anything	really
are	don't	happy	mother	see	two	behind	river
around	door	have	my	seven	under	being	room
away	down	head	myself	shall	until	better	saw
baby	draw	hear	near	she	use	book	says
ball	earth	heard	never	should	very	care	sky
be	eat	help	new	show	walk	cheer	sleep
bear	eight	her	night	sing	want	children	slowly
beautiful	enough	here	no	small	warms	coming	someone
because	even	high	noise	soil	was	dark	something
been	every	hold	nothing	some	wash	didn't	stand
before	everyone	house	now	sometimes	watch	doing	stood
began	eyes	how	of	soon	water	else	store
begins	fall	I	off	sorry	we	ever	table
bird	family	idea	old	starts	were	everything	tall
blue	far	into	once	stories	what	floor	this
both	father	is	one	story	where	flower	though
boy	few	kinds	only	studied	who	found	told
bring	field	know	open	sure	why	front	turned
brothers	find	large	or	surprised	window	girl	voice
brown	first	laugh	our	take	with	gone	what's
buy	five	learning	out	talk	work	hair	words
by	fly	light	over	teacher	world	hard	
call	follow	like	own	the	would	hello	
car	food	listen	paper	their	write	horse	
carry	four	little	party	there	years	hundred	
			people	these	yellow	I'll	

Decoding skills taught to date: short *a*; short *i*; CVC syllable pattern (closed syllables); short *o*; short *u*; short *e*; long *a* (CVC*e*); long *i* (CVC*e*); /k/ spelled *c*; /s/ spelled *c*; long *o* (CVC*e*); long *u* /yōō/ (CVC*e*); long *u* /ōō/ (CVC*e*); long *e* (CVC*e*); /g/ spelled *g*; /j/ spelled *g, dge*; blends with *r*; blends with *l*; blends with *s*; final blend *nd*; final blend *ng*; final blend *nk*; final blend *nt*; double final consonants *ll, ss, ff, zz*; consonants *ck*; double consonants (closed syllables); consonant digraph *th*; consonant digraph *sh*; consonant digraph *wh*; consonant digraphs *ch, tch*; consonant digraph *ph*; base words and ending -*s*; base words and ending -*ed* /ed/; base words and ending -*ed* /d/; base words and ending -*ed* /t/; base words and ending -*ing*; CV syllable pattern (open syllables); contractions with *'s* and *n't*; contractions with *'ll* and *'d*; contractions with *'ve* and *'re*; base words and endings -*s*, -*es*; vowel digraphs *ai, ay*; vowel digraphs *ee, ea*; vowel digraphs *oa, ow*; compound words; schwa sound; ending -*ed*: double consonant; ending -*ing*: double consonant; long *i* spelled *igh, ie*; long *i* spelled *i, y*; long *e* spelled *y*; ending -*es*: change *y* to *i*; r-controlled *ar*; r-controlled *or, ore*; r-controlled *er*; r-controlled *ir, ur*; homophones; ending -*er*: double consonant; ending -*est*: double consonant; suffix -*y*; suffix -*ly*   **From Grade 1:** consonants; short vowels; vowel combination *ow*

Little Fish

Little Fish likes to swim. He swims fast. He leaps and splashes. But he really wants to swim deep down in the sea.

A big fish swims fast to them. Its long teeth click sharply. Little Fish shakes. He flips his fins and swims quickly up, up, up.

"You will not go so deep again, will you?" said Dad wisely.

Little Fish is with his dad. He tells his plan to swim deep.

"It is not a good idea to swim deeply. But let's go and I will show you why," said Dad.

Down in the sea they swim. Dad leads the way. The water is dark. Little Fish can just see dimly. But he swims bravely.

2

3

Rob Sings a Song

DECODABLE WORDS

Target Skill: **suffix** *-ful*

helpful	hopeful	hurtful	joyful	thankful

Previously Taught Skills

am	had	nice	sings	tune
and	hard	not	smiled	weeks
bad	he	notes	song	went
but	him	Rabbit	so	when
can	his	Rob	stay	will
clapped	in	sang	still	wished
cracking	is	scream	sweet	with
day	it	see	teach	
did	Lark	she	that	
for	liked	shrill	then	
glass	made	sing	think	
good	me	singing	try	

SKILLS APPLIED IN WORDS IN STORY: short *a, i, o, u, e*; CVC syllable pattern (closed syllables); long *a, i, o* (CVC*e*); /k/ spelled *c*; /s/ spelled *c*; long *u* /yōō/ (CVC*e*); /g/ spelled *g*; blends with *r, l, s*; final blends *nd, ng, nk, nt*; double final consonants *ll, ss*; consonants *ck*; double consonants (closed syllables); consonant digraphs *th, sh, wh, ch*; base words and endings *-s, -ed* /d/, *-ed* /t/, *-ing*; CV syllable pattern (open syllables); vowel digraphs *ee, ea*; ending *-ed*: double consonant; long *i* spelled *y*; r-controlled *ar, or, ur*; suffix *-ful*
From Grade 1: consonants; short vowels; long e (*e, ee*); vowel digraph *oo*; vowel diphthong *oy*

HIGH-FREQUENCY WORDS

a	I	one	to	work(ed)
could	never	said	was	you
heard	of	sound	were	your

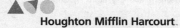

© Houghton Mifflin Harcourt Publishing Company

Rob Sings a Song

High-Frequency Words Taught to Date

Grade 1							
a	caught	friend	live	pictures	they	you	I've
about	city	friendship	long	play	think	young	kept
above	cold	full	look	please	those	your	knew
across	come	funny	loudly	pull	thought		might
after	could	give	loved	pushed	three	**Grade 2**	mind
again	country	go	make	put	to	afraid	morning
all	covers	goes	many	read	today	against	move
almost	cried	good	maybe	ready	together	air	next
along	different	great	me	right	too	also	other
always	do	green	minute	said	took	another	part
and	does	ground	more	school	toward	any	pretty
animal	done	grow	most	second	try	anything	really
are	don't	happy	mother	see	two	behind	river
around	door	have	my	seven	under	being	room
away	down	he	myself	shall	until	better	saw
baby	draw	head	near	she	use	book	says
ball	earth	hear	never	should	very	care	sky
be	eat	heard	new	show	walk	cheer	sleep
bear	eight	help	night	sing	want	children	slowly
beautiful	enough	her	no	small	warms	coming	someone
because	even	here	noise	soil	was	dark	something
been	every	high	nothing	some	wash	didn't	sound
before	everyone	hold	now	sometimes	watch	doing	stood
began	eyes	house	of	soon	water	else	store
begins	fall	how	off	sorry	we	ever	table
bird	family	I	old	starts	were	everything	tall
blue	far	idea	once	stories	what	floor	this
both	father	into	one	story	where	flower	though
boy	few	is	only	studied	who	found	told
bring	field	kinds	open	sure	why	front	turned
brothers	find	know	or	surprised	window	girl	voice
brown	first	large	our	take	with	gone	what's
buy	five	laugh	out	talk	work	hair	words
by	fly	learning	over	teacher	world	hard	
call	follow	light	own	the	would	hello	
car	food	like	paper	their	write	horse	
carry	four	listen	party	there	years	hundred	
		little	people	these	yellow	I'll	

Decoding skills taught to date: short *a*; short *i*; CVC syllable pattern (closed syllables); short *o*; short *u*; short *e*; long *a* (CVC*e*); long *i* (CVC*e*); /k/ spelled *c*; /s/ spelled *c*; long *o* (CVC*e*); long *u* /yōō/ (CVC*e*); long *u* /ōō/ (CVC*e*); long *e* (CVC*e*); /g/ spelled *g*; /j/ spelled *g*, *dge*; blends with *r*; blends with *l*; blends with *s*; final blend *nd*; final blend *ng*; final blend *nk*; final blend *nt*; double final consonants *ll*, *ss*, *ff*, *zz*; consonants *ck*; double consonants (closed syllables); consonant digraph *th*; consonant digraph *sh*; consonant digraph *wh*; consonant digraphs *ch*, *tch*; consonant digraph *ph*; base words and ending -*s*; base words and ending -*ed* /ed/; base words and ending -*ed* /d/; base words and ending -*ed* /t/; base words and ending -*ing*; CV syllable pattern (open syllables); contractions with *'s* and *n't*; contractions with *'ll* and *'d*; contractions with *'ve* and *'re*; base words and endings -*s*, -*es*; vowel digraphs *ai*, *ay*; vowel digraphs *ee*, *ea*; vowel digraphs *oa*, *ow*; compound words; schwa sound; ending -*ed*: double consonant; ending -*ing*: double consonant; long *i* spelled *igh*, *ie*; long *i* spelled *i*, *y*; long *e* spelled *y*; ending -*es*: change *y* to *i*; *r*-controlled *ar*; *r*-controlled *or*, *ore*; *r*-controlled *er*; *r*-controlled *ir*, *ur*; homophones; ending -*er*: double consonant; ending -*est*: double consonant; suffix -*y*; suffix -*ly*; suffix -*ful*

Rob Sings a Song

Then one day, Rob sang. It was a nice song. It was good.

Lark clapped and smiled. "That is a sweet tune," she said.

"I am thankful that you were so helpful," said Rob. He and Lark smiled.

Rob Rabbit wished he could sing, but his singing was bad. He could not stay in tune. He sang and sang, but his notes never made a nice sound.

Rob went to see Lark. "Your singing is joyful," said Rob. "I am hopeful you can teach me to sing."

Lark had heard that Rob could not sing, but she liked him.

"I will try," she said.

Lark worked with Rob for weeks. Rob did try hard, but when he sang, it was still bad. His notes made Lark think of cracking glass.

"That is not a song. It is a scream," said Lark. "It is hurtful and shrill."

2

3

Goat and Toad's Lunch

© Houghton Mifflin Harcourt Publishing Company

DECODABLE WORDS

Target Skill: **suffix** *-ful*

basketful	handful	mouthful	painful	restful

Previously Taught Skills

am	felt	in	nice	that
and	for	is	on	them
at	gave	it	packed	things
back	go	I've	panted	this
basket	Goat	last	picnic	three
became	had	let's	ready	Toad
before	hard	lift	rest	Toad's
better	harder	like	so	up
but	he	lunch	spot	will
croaked	hill	met	stop	
eat	his	moaned	tasted	

SKILLS APPLIED IN WORDS IN STORY: short *a, i, o, u, e*; CVC syllable pattern (closed); long *a, i* (CVCe); /k/ spelled *c*; /s/ spelled *c*; /g/ spelled *g*; blends with *r*; blends with *s*; final blends *nd, ng, nt*; double final consonants *ll*; consonants *ck*; double consonants (closed syllables); consonant digraphs *th, ch*; base words and endings *-s, -ed* /ed/, /t/ (no spelling changes, drop *e* before ending); CV syllable pattern (open); contractions with *'s, 've*; base words and ending *-s*; vowel digraphs *ai, ee, ea*; vowel digraph *oa*; long *e* spelled *y*; r-controlled *ar, or, ore, er*; ending *-er*: double consonant; suffix *-ful*   **From Grade 1:** consonants, short vowels; short *e* spelled *ea*; long *e* (*e, ee*); vowel combination *ou* (as in *out*); possessive *'s*

HIGH-FREQUENCY WORDS

a	food	of	the	you
carry	good	our	to	
come	here	put	was	
could	I	said	what	

Houghton Mifflin Harcourt

Goat and Toad's Lunch

High-Frequency Words Taught to Date

Grade 1							
a	caught	friend	live	pictures	they	you	I've
about	city	friendship	long	play	think	young	kept
above	cold	full	look	please	those	your	knew
across	come	funny	loudly	pull	thought		might
after	could	give	loved	pushed	three	**Grade 2**	mind
again	country	go	make	put	to	afraid	morning
all	covers	goes	many	read	today	against	move
almost	cried	good	maybe	ready	together	air	next
along	different	great	me	right	too	also	other
always	do	green	minute	said	took	another	part
and	does	ground	more	school	toward	any	pretty
animal	done	grow	most	second	try	anything	really
are	don't	happy	mother	see	two	behind	river
around	door	have	my	seven	under	being	room
away	down	he	myself	shall	until	better	saw
baby	draw	head	near	she	use	book	says
ball	earth	hear	never	should	very	care	sky
be	eat	heard	new	show	walk	cheer	sleep
bear	eight	help	night	sing	want	children	slowly
beautiful	enough	her	no	small	warms	coming	someone
because	even	here	noise	soil	was	dark	something
been	every	high	nothing	some	wash	didn't	sound
before	everyone	hold	now	sometimes	watch	doing	stood
began	eyes	house	of	soon	water	else	store
begins	fall	how	off	sorry	we	ever	table
bird	family	I	old	starts	were	everything	tall
blue	far	idea	once	stories	what	floor	this
both	father	into	one	story	where	flower	though
boy	few	is	only	studied	who	found	told
bring	field	kinds	open	sure	why	front	turned
brothers	find	know	or	surprised	window	girl	voice
brown	first	large	our	take	with	gone	what's
buy	five	laugh	out	talk	work	hair	words
by	fly	learning	over	teacher	world	hard	
call	follow	light	own	the	would	hello	
car	food	like	paper	their	write	horse	
carry	for	listen	party	there	years	hundred	
	four	little	people	these	yellow	I'll	

Decoding skills taught to date: short *a*; short *i*; CVC syllable pattern (closed syllables); short *o*; short *u*; short *e*; long *a* (CVC*e*); long *i* (CVC*e*); /k/ spelled *c*; /s/ spelled *c*; long *o* (CVC*e*); long *u* /yoo/ (CVC*e*); long *u* /oo/ (CVC*e*); long *e* (CVC*e*); /g/ spelled *g*; /j/ spelled *g, dge*; blends with *r*; blends with *l*; blends with *s*; final blend *nd*; final blend *ng*; final blend *nk*; final blend *nt*; double final consonants *ll, ss, ff, zz*; consonants *ck*; double consonants (closed syllables); consonant digraph *th*; consonant digraph *sh*; consonant digraph *wh*; consonant digraphs *ch, tch*; consonant digraph *ph*; base words and ending -*s*; base words and ending -*ed* /ed/; base words and ending -*ed* /d/; base words and ending -*ed* /t/; base words and ending -*ing*; CV syllable pattern (open syllables); contractions with *'s* and *n't*; contractions with *'ll* and *'d*; contractions with *'ve* and *'re*; base words and endings -*s*, -*es*; vowel digraphs *ai, ay*; vowel digraphs *ee, ea*; vowel digraphs *oa, ow*; compound words; schwa sound; ending -*ed*: double consonant; ending -*ing*: double consonant; long *i* spelled *igh, ie*; long *i* spelled *i, y*; long *e* spelled *y*; ending -*es*: change *y* to *i*; r-controlled *ar*; r-controlled *or, ore*; r-controlled *er*; r-controlled *ir, ur*; homophones; ending -*er*: double consonant; ending -*est*: double consonant; suffix -*y*; suffix -*ly*; suffix -*ful*

"Let's stop," panted Goat.

"It is restful in this spot. Let's eat," said Toad.

Goat had to rest before he could eat. At last, he had a mouthful of food. It tasted good, and Goat felt better.

4

Goat and Toad's Lunch

Goat met Toad for a picnic. "I am here for our picnic," Goat said.

"I am ready, so let's go!" said Toad. "I've packed this basketful of food for lunch." He gave the basket to Goat.

1

The basket was hard to lift. "What is in this basket?" moaned Goat. "It is a handful to carry."

"I put in three nice things," croaked Toad. "You will like them."

The basket became harder and harder to carry. Goat had it on his back, but that became painful.

"Come on," said Toad. "Carry it up the hill."

2

3

I Love Vacation!

DECODABLE WORDS

Target Skill: **syllable -*tion***

action	motion	station
lotion	protection	vacation

Previously Taught Skills

a	Gabe	mom	seashore	wait
all	get	my	sleepy	waves
at	go	nap	spot	we
back	he	on	stay	week
before	here	our	sunburn	will
can	house	out	suntan	you
don't	I	pulls	swim	
family	is	put	take	
feel	it	rocks	then	
for	just	run	this	
forth	makes	says	too	
from	me	seagulls	train	

SKILLS APPLIED IN WORDS IN STORY: short *a*; short *i*; short *o*; short *u*; short *e*; closed syllables (CVC); long *a* (CVC*e*); /k/ spelled *c*; /g/ spelled *g*; blends with *r*; blends with *l*; blends with *s*; double final consonants *ll*; consonants *ck*; consonant digraphs *th, sh*; base words and ending *-s*; open syllables (CV); contractions with *n't*; vowel digraphs *ai* and *ay*, *ee* and *ea*; compound words; schwa sound; long *i* spelled *I, y*; long *e* spelled *y*; r-controlled *or, ore, ur*; homophones; suffix *-y*; syllable *-tion*   **From Grade 1:** consonants; short vowels; /z/ spelled *s*; long *e* (*e, ee*); /ōō/ spelled *ou*; vowel combination *ou*

HIGH-FREQUENCY WORDS

all	come(s)	love	the	watch(es)
and	house	of	to	
are	little	one	want	

▲▼● Houghton Mifflin Harcourt.

I Love Vacation!

High-Frequency Words Taught to Date

Grade 1	caught	friend	live	pictures	they	you	I've
a	city	friendship	long	play	think	young	kept
about	cold	full	look	please	those	your	knew
above	come	funny	loudly	pull	thought		might
across	could	give	loved	pushed	three	*Grade 2*	mind
after	country	go	make	put	to	afraid	morning
again	covers	goes	many	read	today	against	move
all	cried	good	maybe	ready	together	air	next
almost	different	great	me	right	too	also	other
along	do	green	minute	said	took	another	part
always	does	ground	more	school	toward	any	pretty
and	done	grow	most	second	try	anything	really
animal	don't	happy	mother	see	two	behind	river
are	door	have	my	seven	under	being	room
around	down	he	myself	shall	until	better	saw
away	draw	head	near	she	use	book	says
baby	earth	hear	never	should	very	care	sky
ball	eat	heard	new	show	walk	cheer	sleep
be	eight	help	night	sing	want	children	slowly
bear	enough	her	no	small	warms	coming	someone
beautiful	even	here	noise	soil	was	dark	something
because	every	high	nothing	some	wash	didn't	sound
been	everyone	hold	now	sometimes	watch	doing	stood
before	eyes	house	of	soon	water	else	store
began	fall	how	off	sorry	we	ever	table
begins	family	I	old	starts	were	everything	tall
bird	far	idea	once	stories	what	floor	this
blue	father	into	one	story	where	flower	though
both	few	is	only	studied	who	found	told
boy	field	kinds	open	sure	why	front	turned
bring	find	know	or	surprised	window	girl	voice
brothers	first	large	our	take	with	gone	what's
brown	five	laugh	out	talk	work	hair	words
buy	fly	learning	over	teacher	world	hard	
by	follow	light	own	the	would	hello	
call	food	like	paper	their	write	horse	
car	for	listen	party	there	years	hundred	
carry	four	little	people	these	yellow	I'll	

Decoding skills taught to date: short *a*; short *i*; CVC syllable pattern (closed syllables); short *o*; short *u*; short *e*; long *a* (CVC*e*); long *i* (CVC*e*); /k/ spelled *c*; /s/ spelled *c*; long *o* (CVC*e*); long *u* /yōō/ (CVC*e*); long u /ōō/ (CVC*e*); long *e* (CVC*e*); /g/ spelled *g*; /j/ spelled *g*, *dge*; blends with *r*; blends with *l*; blends with *s*; final blend *nd*; final blend *ng*; final blend *nk*; final blend *nt*; double final consonants *ll, ss, ff, zz*; consonants *ck*; double consonants (closed syllables); consonant digraph *th*; consonant digraph *sh*; consonant digraph *wh*; consonant digraphs *ch, tch*; consonant digraph *ph*; base words and ending *-s*; base words and ending *-ed* /ed/; base words and ending *-ed* /t/; base word and ending *-ing*; CV syllable pattern (open syllables); contractions with *'s* and *n't*; contractions with *'ll* and *'d*; contractions with *'ve* and *'re*; base words and endings *-s, -es*; vowel digraphs *ai, ay*; vowel digraphs *ee, ea*; vowel digraphs *oa, ow*; compound words; schwa sound; ending *-ed*: double consonant; ending *-ing*: double consonant; long *i* spelled *igh, ie*; long *i* spelled *i, y*; long e spelled *y*; ending *-es*: change *y* to *i*; r-controlled *ar*; r-controlled *or, ore*; r-controlled *er*; r-controlled *ir, ur*; homophones; ending *-er*: double consonant; ending *-est*: double consonant; suffix *-y*; suffix *-ly*; suffix *-ful*; syllable *-tion*

"You don't want to get a sunburn,"
Mom says. "Put on this suntan lotion for
protection."

We all put on suntan lotion. Then
we go for a swim. Don't you just love a
vacation?

I Love Vacation!

←TRAIN

My family will go on vacation! We
will stay at the seashore for one week.
We get to take a train from the station to
the seashore.

We wait at the station for the train.
Here it comes!

We get on the train. Then it pulls out of the station. I can feel the motion of the train. It rocks back and forth.

The motion makes me sleepy. I take a nap before we get to our vacation spot.

We are here! I run to our vacation house.

Gabe is too little to run. He just watches the motion of the waves and the action of the seagulls.

A Space Station

DECODABLE WORDS

Target Skill: syllable *-tion*

connection	protection	station
motion	section	

Previously Taught Skills

a	fly	it	our	up
after	food	last	outfit	us
always	for	make	outside	we
an	get	makes	put	while
astronauts	go	must	show(ed)	will
be	he	need	space	with
bring	helmet	needs	spaceship	
call(ed)	home	next	things	
can	if	on	this	
day	in	orbit	trip	
fix	is	orbits	try	

SKILLS APPLIED IN WORDS IN STORY: short *a*; short *i*; short *o*; short *u*; short *e*; closed syllables (CVC); long *a* (CVCe); long *i* (CVCe); /k/ spelled *c*; long *o* (CVCe); /g/ spelled *g*; blends with *r*; blends with *l*; blends with *s*; final blend *ng*; double final consonants *ll*; consonant digraphs *th, sh, wh*; base words and ending -*s*; open syllables (CV); vowel digraphs *ai* and *ay*, *ee* and *ea*; vowel digraphs *oa, ow*; compound words; schwa sound; long *i* spelled *y*; *r*-controlled *or*; homophones; syllable -*tion* **From Grade 1:** consonants; long *e* (*e, ee*); /o͞o/ spelled *oo*; vowel combinations *ou, au*

HIGH-FREQUENCY WORDS

and	gear	one	the	want(s)
around	live	other	their	who
Earth	move(s)	said	they	work
every	of	sometimes	to	

Houghton Mifflin Harcourt.

A Space Station

High-Frequency Words Taught to Date

Grade 1							
a	caught	friend	live	pictures	they	you	I've
about	city	friendship	long	play	think	young	kept
above	cold	full	look	please	those	your	knew
across	come	funny	loudly	pull	thought		might
after	could	give	loved	pushed	three	**Grade 2**	mind
again	country	go	make	put	to	afraid	morning
all	covers	goes	many	read	today	against	move
almost	cried	good	maybe	ready	together	air	next
along	different	great	me	right	too	also	other
always	do	green	minute	said	took	another	part
and	does	ground	more	school	toward	any	pretty
animal	done	grow	most	second	try	anything	really
are	don't	happy	mother	see	two	behind	river
around	door	have	my	seven	under	being	room
away	down	he	myself	shall	until	better	saw
baby	draw	head	near	she	use	book	says
ball	earth	hear	never	should	very	care	sky
be	eat	heard	new	show	walk	cheer	sleep
bear	eight	help	night	sing	want	children	slowly
beautiful	enough	her	no	small	warms	coming	someone
because	even	here	noise	soil	was	dark	something
been	every	high	nothing	some	wash	didn't	sound
before	everyone	hold	now	sometimes	watch	doing	stood
began	eyes	house	of	soon	water	else	store
begins	fall	how	off	sorry	we	ever	table
bird	family	I	old	starts	were	everything	tall
blue	far	idea	once	stories	what	floor	this
both	father	into	one	story	where	flower	though
boy	few	is	only	studied	who	found	told
bring	field	kinds	open	sure	why	front	turned
brothers	find	know	or	surprised	window	girl	voice
brown	first	large	our	take	with	gone	what's
buy	five	laugh	out	talk	work	hair	words
by	fly	learning	over	teacher	world	hard	
call	follow	light	own	the	would	hello	
car	food	like	paper	their	write	horse	
carry	for	listen	party	there	years	hundred	
	four	little	people	these	yellow	I'll	

Decoding skills taught to date: short *a*; short *i*; CVC syllable pattern (closed syllables); short *o*; short *u*; short *e*; long *a* (CVC*e*); long *i* (CVC*e*); /k/ spelled *c*; /s/ spelled *c*; long *o* (CVC*e*); long *u* /y$\overline{oo}$/ (CVC*e*); long *u* /$\overline{oo}$/ (CVC*e*); long *e* (CVC*e*); /g/ spelled *g*; /j/ spelled *g*, *dge*; blends with *r*; blends with *l*; blends with *s*; final blend *nd*; final blend *ng*; final blend *nk*; final blend *nt*; double final consonants *ll, ss, ff, zz*; consonants *ck*; double consonants (closed syllables); consonant digraph *th*; consonant digraph *sh*; consonant digraph *wh*; consonant digraphs *ch, tch*; consonant digraph *ph*; base words and ending *-s*; base words and ending *-ed* /ed/; base words and ending *-ed* /t/; base words and ending *-ing*; CV syllable pattern (open syllables); contractions with *'s* and *n't*; contractions with *'ll* and *'d*; contractions with *'ve* and *'re*; base words and endings *-s, -es*; vowel digraphs *ai, ay*; vowel digraphs *ee, ea*; vowel digraphs *oa, ow*; compound words; schwa sound; ending *-ed*: double consonant; ending *-ing*: double consonant; long *i* spelled *igh, ie*; long *i* spelled *i, y*; long *e* spelled *y*; ending *-es*: change *y* to *i*; r-controlled *ar*; r-controlled *or, ore*; r-controlled *er*; r-controlled *ir, ur*; homophones; ending *-er*: double consonant; ending *-est*: double consonant; suffix *-y*; suffix *-ly*; suffix *-ful*; syllable *-tion*

A Space Station

The last astronaut showed us a space outfit.

"Sometimes we need to fix a section outside the space station," he said. "If we go outside of the space station, we must put on this gear for protection. Who wants to try on a space helmet?"

Astronauts can fly in a spaceship up to the space station. The space station will be their home while they work in space.

One astronaut said, "The space station is always in motion. It moves around Earth. This trip is called an orbit. The space station makes 16 orbits every day!"

The next astronaut said, "Our spaceship needs to make a connection with the space station. After we make the connection, we can get on to the space station. We will bring space food and other things we need while we live on the space station."

Painting Pictures

DECODABLE WORDS

Target Skill: syllable *-ture*

creature	features	nature	pictures
creature's	future	pasture	texture
creatures	mixture	picture	

Previously Taught Skills

a	farm	in	my	smooth
and	first	is	on	thick
as	fun	it	paint	thin
be	grass	kitchen	painting	think
big	hangs	like(s)	paper	this
bumpy	has	make	place	use
can	he	makes	she	well
Dad	I	mix	shows	with
den	I'll	Mom	silly	you

SKILLS APPLIED IN WORDS IN STORY: short *a*; short *i*; short *o*; short *u*; short *e*; closed syllables (CVC); long *a* (CVC*e*); long *i* (CVC*e*); /k/ spelled *c*; /s/ spelled *c*; /g/ spelled *g*; blends with *r*; blends with *s*; final blend *nd*; final blend *ng*; final blend *nk*; final blend *nt*; double final consonants *ll*, *ss*; consonant digraphs *th, tch*; base words and endings -*s*, -*ed* /d/, -*ing*; contraction with *'ll*; vowel digraphs *ai* and *ay*, *ee* and *ea*; schwa sound; long *i* spelled *I, y*; long *e* spelled *y*; r-controlled *ar, er, ir*; homophones; suffix -*y*; syllable -*ture*
From Grade 1: consonants; /z/ spelled *s*; long *e* (*e, ee*); long *o* spelled *ow*; /o͞o/ spelled *ou*

HIGH-FREQUENCY WORDS

animal(s)	give(s)	the	want
are	of	to	what
do	or	use(d)	

Houghton Mifflin Harcourt

Painting Pictures

High-Frequency Words Taught to Date

Grade 1							
a	caught	friend	live	pictures	they	you	I've
about	city	friendship	long	play	think	young	kept
above	cold	full	look	please	those	your	knew
across	come	funny	loudly	pull	thought		might
after	could	give	loved	pushed	three	**Grade 2**	mind
again	country	go	make	put	to	afraid	morning
all	covers	goes	many	read	today	against	move
almost	cried	good	maybe	ready	together	air	next
along	different	great	me	right	too	also	other
always	do	green	minute	said	took	another	part
and	does	ground	more	school	toward	any	pretty
animal	done	grow	most	second	try	anything	really
are	don't	happy	mother	see	two	behind	river
around	door	have	my	seven	under	being	room
away	down	he	myself	shall	until	better	saw
baby	draw	head	near	she	use	book	says
ball	earth	hear	never	should	very	care	sky
be	eat	heard	new	show	walk	cheer	sleep
bear	eight	help	night	sing	want	children	slowly
beautiful	enough	her	no	small	warms	coming	someone
because	even	here	noise	soil	was	dark	something
been	every	high	nothing	some	wash	didn't	sound
before	everyone	hold	now	sometimes	watch	doing	stood
began	eyes	house	of	soon	water	else	store
begins	fall	how	off	sorry	we	ever	table
bird	family	I	old	starts	were	everything	tall
blue	far	idea	once	stories	what	floor	this
both	father	into	one	story	where	flower	though
boy	few	is	only	studied	who	found	told
bring	field	kinds	open	sure	why	front	turned
brothers	find	know	or	surprised	window	girl	voice
brown	first	large	our	take	with	gone	what's
buy	five	laugh	out	talk	work	hair	words
by	fly	learning	over	teacher	world	hard	
call	follow	light	own	the	would	hello	
car	food	like	paper	their	write	horse	
carry	for	listen	party	there	years	hundred	
	four	little	people	these	yellow	I'll	

Decoding skills taught to date: short *a*; short *i*; CVC syllable pattern (closed syllables); short *o*; short *u*; short *e*; long *a* (CVC*e*); long *i* (CVC*e*); /k/ spelled *c*; /s/ spelled *c*; long *o* (CVC*e*); long *u* /yōō/ (CVC*e*); long *u* /ōō/ (CVC*e*); long *e* (CVC*e*); /g/ spelled *g*; /j/ spelled *g, dge*; blends with *r*; blends with *l*; blends with *s*; final blend *nd*; final blend *ng*; final blend *nk*; final blend *nt*; double final consonants *ll, ss, ff, zz*; consonants *ck*; double consonants (closed syllables); consonant digraph *th*; consonant digraph *sh*; consonant digraph *wh*; consonant digraphs *ch, tch*; consonant digraph *ph*; base words and ending -*s*; base words and ending -*ed* /ed/; base words and ending -*ed* /t/; base words and ending -*ing*; CV syllable pattern (open syllables); contractions with *'s* and *n't*; contractions with *'ll* and *'d*; contractions with *'ve* and *'re*; base words and endings -*s, -es*; vowel digraphs *ai, ay*; vowel digraphs *ee, ea*; vowel digraphs *oa, ow*; compound words; schwa sound; ending -*ed*: double consonant; ending -*ing*: double consonant; long *i* spelled *igh, ie*; long *i* spelled *i, y*; long *e* spelled *y*; ending -*es*: change *y* to *i*; r-controlled *ar*; r-controlled *or, ore*; r-controlled *er*; r-controlled *ir, ur*; homophones; ending -*er*: double consonant; ending -*est*: double consonant; suffix -*y*; suffix -*ly*; suffix -*ful*; syllable -*tion*; syllable -*ture*

Dad likes my bumpy creature picture. He hangs it in the den. Mom likes my pasture picture. She hangs it in the kitchen. What pictures do you think I'll paint in the future?

© Houghton Mifflin Harcourt Publishing Company

Painting Pictures

I like to paint pictures. First, I mix the paint. I can make the paint mixture thick or thin.

A thin mixture has a smooth texture. A thick mixture makes a bumpy texture on the paper.

I like to paint silly creatures. I want this creature's features to be bumpy. I use a thick paint mixture. It makes a bumpy texture. Bumpy creature pictures are fun to paint!

I paint pictures of nature as well. This picture shows a pasture. It is a big place with grass and farm animals. I used a thin paint mixture. It gives the pasture picture a smooth texture.

Pasture Creatures

DECODABLE WORDS

Target Skill: **syllable *-ture***

adventure	captured	creatures	pasture
capture	creature	mixture	puncture

Previously Taught Skills

a	got	is	nice	this
Al	grass	it	on	too
an	grasshopper	jar	placed	we
and	he	kept	planned	went
asked	holes	leaves	pointed	while
boys	home	let	put	will
bugs	homes	lid	Sam	yes
did	hurried	long	see	you
farm	I	look	so	
for	if	more	that	
go	in	net	then	

SKILLS APPLIED IN WORDS IN STORY: short *a*; short *i*; short *o*; short *u*; short *e*; closed syllables (CVC); long *a* (CVCe); long *i* (CVCe); /k/ spelled *c*; /s/ spelled *c*; long *o* (CVCe); /g/ spelled *g*; blends with *r*; blends with *l*; final blend *nd*; final blend *ng*; final blend *nt*; double final consonants *ll, ss*; double consonants (closed syllables); consonant digraphs *th, wh*; base words and endings *-s, -ed* /ed/, *-ed* /t/, *-ed* /d/; CV syllable pattern (open syllables); vowel digraphs *ee* and *ea*; compound words; schwa sound; long *i* spelled *I*; ending *-ed*: change *y* to *i*; r-controlled *ar, ur, or, ore*; homophones; syllable *-ture*   **From Grade 1:** *consonants*; /z/ spelled *s*; long *e* (*e, ee*); vowel digraphs *oo, /o͞o/*; /o͞o/ spelled *ou*; vowel combinations *oy, oi*

HIGH-FREQUENCY WORDS

call(ed)	live(d)	the	to
have	of	their	would
into	said	they	

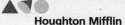

Houghton Mifflin Harcourt.

Pasture Creatures

High-Frequency Words Taught to Date

Grade 1							
a	caught	friend	live	pictures	they	you	I've
about	city	friendship	long	play	think	young	kept
above	cold	full	look	please	those	your	knew
across	come	funny	loudly	pull	thought		might
after	could	give	loved	pushed	three	**Grade 2**	mind
again	country	go	make	put	to	afraid	morning
all	covers	goes	many	read	today	against	move
almost	cried	good	maybe	ready	together	air	next
along	different	great	me	right	too	also	other
always	do	green	minute	said	took	another	part
and	does	ground	more	school	toward	any	pretty
animal	done	grow	most	second	try	anything	really
are	don't	happy	mother	see	two	behind	river
around	door	have	my	seven	under	being	room
away	down	he	myself	shall	until	better	saw
baby	draw	head	near	she	use	book	says
ball	earth	hear	never	should	very	care	sky
be	eat	heard	new	show	walk	cheer	sleep
bear	eight	help	night	sing	want	children	slowly
beautiful	enough	her	no	small	warms	coming	someone
because	even	here	noise	soil	was	dark	something
been	every	high	nothing	some	wash	didn't	sound
before	everyone	hold	now	sometimes	watch	doing	stood
began	eyes	house	of	soon	water	else	store
begins	fall	how	off	sorry	we	ever	table
bird	family	I	old	starts	were	everything	tall
blue	far	idea	once	stories	what	floor	this
both	father	into	one	story	where	flower	though
boy	few	is	only	studied	who	found	told
bring	field	kinds	open	sure	why	front	turned
brothers	find	know	or	surprised	window	girl	voice
brown	first	large	our	take	with	gone	what's
buy	five	laugh	out	talk	work	hair	words
by	fly	learning	over	teacher	world	hard	
call	follow	light	own	the	would	hello	
car	food	like	paper	their	write	horse	
carry	for	listen	party	there	years	hundred	
	four	little	people	these	yellow	I'll	

Decoding skills taught to date: short *a*; short *i*; CVC syllable pattern (closed syllables); short *o*; short *u*; short *e*; long *a* (CVC*e*); long *i* (CVC*e*); /k/ spelled *c*; /s/ spelled *c*; long *o* (CVC*e*); long *u* /yo͞o/ (CVC*e*); long *u* /o͞o/ (CVC*e*); long *e* (CVC*e*); /g/ spelled *g*; /j/ spelled *g*, *dge*; blends with *r*; blends with *l*; blends with *s*; final blend *nd*; final blend *ng*; final blend *nk*; final blend *nt*; double final consonants *ll*, *ss*, *ff*, *zz*; consonants *ck*; double consonants (closed syllables); consonant digraph *th*; consonant digraph *sh*; consonant digraph *wh*; consonant digraphs *ch*, *tch*; consonant digraph *ph*; base words and ending -*s*; base words and ending -*ed* /ed/; base words and ending -*ed* /t/; base words and ending -*ing*; CV syllable pattern (open syllables); contractions with *'s* and *n't*; contractions with *'ll* and *'d*; contractions with *'ve* and *'re*; base words and endings -*s*, -*es*; vowel digraphs *ai*, *ay*; vowel digraphs *ee*, *ea*; vowel digraphs *oa*, *ow*; compound words; schwa sound; ending -*ed*: double consonant; ending -*ing*: double consonant; long *i* spelled *igh*, *ie*; long *i* spelled *i*, *y*; long *e* spelled *y*; endings -*es*: change *y* to *i*; *r*-controlled *ar*; *r*-controlled *or*, *ore*; *r*-controlled *er*; *r*-controlled *ir*, *ur*; homophones; ending -*er*: double consonant; ending -*est*: double consonant; suffix -*y*; suffix -*ly*; suffix -*ful*; syllable -*tion*; syllable -*ture*

Sam and Al captured more creatures in the pasture. They kept the creatures in the jar for a while. Then the boys let the pasture creatures go.

"So long, creatures," called Sam and Al. The creatures hurried to their homes in the pasture.

4

Pasture Creatures

Sam and Al planned an adventure on the farm. They would capture bugs that lived in the farm pasture.

The boys got a net and a jar. Then they went into the pasture to look for creatures.

1

"Did you puncture holes in the lid of the jar?" Sam asked Al.

"Yes," said Al. "I put in a mixture of grass and leaves, too. If we capture creatures, they will have a nice home!"

Al pointed. "I see a creature. Capture it, Sam!"

Sam captured the creature in the net. Then he and Al placed the creature in the jar.

"This creature is a grasshopper," said Sam.

From Unhappy to Happy

DECODABLE WORDS

Target Skill: prefix *un-*

unhappy	unload	unpack

Previously Taught Skills

and	drive	I	she	we're
Ann	ends	is	she's	when
asks	feel	it	smile	will
at	for	leaving	smiles	
back	glad	long	still	
be	going	make	them	
boxes	Granddad	Mom	then	
but	happy	more	think	
Carl	hard	Parks	wave	
day	help	see	we	

SKILLS APPLIED IN WORDS IN STORY: short *a*; short *i*; CVC syllable pattern (closed syllables); short *u*; short *e*; long *a* (CVC*e*); long *i* (CVC*e*); /k/ spelled *c*; long *o* (CVC*e*); /g/ spelled *g*; blends with *r, l, s*; final blends *nd, ng, nk*; double final consonants *ll*; consonants *ck*; double consonants (closed syllables); consonant digraphs *th, sh, wh*; endings -*s*, -*ed*, -*ing*; endings -*ed*, -*ing*: drop e; CV syllable pattern (open syllables); contractions with '*s*, '*re*; endings -*s*, -*es*; vowel digraphs *ay, ea, ee*; compound words; long *i* spelled *i*; long *e* spelled *y*; *r*-controlled *ar, or, ore*; prefix *un-*

HIGH-FREQUENCY WORDS

all	family	here	the	too
are	friends	mov(ing)	their	watching
children	from	says	to	work

From Unhappy to Happy

 Houghton Mifflin Harcourt.

High-Frequency Words Taught to Date

Grade 1							I've
a	caught	friend	live	pictures	they	you	kept
about	city	friendship	long	play	think	young	knew
above	cold	full	look	please	those	your	might
across	come	funny	loudly	pull	thought		mind
after	could	give	loved	pushed	three	**Grade 2**	morning
again	country	go	make	put	to	afraid	move
all	covers	goes	many	read	today	against	next
almost	cried	good	maybe	ready	together	air	other
along	different	great	me	right	too	also	part
always	do	green	minute	said	took	another	pretty
and	does	ground	more	school	toward	any	really
animal	done	grow	most	second	try	anything	river
are	don't	happy	mother	see	two	behind	room
around	door	have	my	seven	under	being	saw
away	down	he	myself	shall	until	better	says
baby	draw	head	near	she	use	book	sky
ball	earth	hear	never	should	very	care	sleep
be	eat	heard	new	show	walk	cheer	slowly
bear	eight	help	night	sing	want	children	someone
beautiful	enough	her	no	small	warms	coming	something
because	even	here	noise	soil	was	dark	sound
been	every	high	nothing	some	wash	didn't	stood
before	everyone	hold	now	sometimes	watch	doing	store
began	eyes	house	of	soon	water	else	table
begins	fall	how	off	sorry	we	ever	tall
bird	family	I	old	starts	were	everything	this
blue	far	idea	once	stories	what	floor	though
both	father	into	one	story	where	flower	told
boy	few	is	only	studied	who	found	turned
bring	field	kinds	open	sure	why	front	voice
brothers	find	know	or	surprised	window	girl	what's
brown	first	large	our	take	with	gone	without
buy	five	laugh	out	talk	work	hair	words
by	fly	learning	over	teacher	world	hard	
call	follow	light	own	the	would	hello	
car	food	like	paper	their	write	horse	
carry	for	listen	party	there	years	hundred	
	four	little	people	these	yellow	I'll	

Decoding skills taught to date: short *a*, short *i*, CVC syllable pattern (closed); short *o*, short *u*, short *e*; long *a* (CVC*e*), long *i* (CVC*e*); /k/ spelled *c*; /s/ spelled *c*; long *o* (CVC*e*), long *u* /yōō/ (CVC*e*), long *u* /ōō/ (CVC*e*), long *e* (CVC*e*); /g/ spelled *g*; /j/ spelled *g*, *dge*; blends with *r*, *l*, *s*; final blends *nd*, *ng*, *nk*, *nt*; double final consonants *ll*, *ss*, *ff*, *zz*; consonants *ck*; double consonant (closed syllables); consonant digraphs *th*, *sh*, *wh*, *ch*, *tch*, *ph*; endings -*s*, -*ed*; endings -*ed*, -*ing*: drop *e*; CV syllable pattern (open syllables); contractions with '*s* and *n't*; contractions with '*ll*, '*d*, '*ve*, '*re*; endings -*s*, -*es*; vowel digraphs *ai*, *ay*, *ee*, *ea*, *oa*, *ow*; compound words; schwa sound; endings -*ed*, -*ing*: double consonant; long *i* spelled *igh*, *ie*, *i*, *y*; long *e* spelled *y*; ending -*es*: change *y* to *i*; r-controlled *ar*, *or*, *ore*, *er*, *ir*, *ur*; homophones; endings -*er*, -*est*: double consonant; suffixes -*y*, -*ly*, -*ful*; syllables -*tion*, -*ture*; prefix *un*- **From Grade 1:** consonants; short vowels

Then Carl and Ann see children watching them. The children wave at Carl and Ann. Carl and Ann wave back.

"I think we will make friends and be happy here," Ann says.

From Unhappy to Happy

It is moving day for the Parks family. Carl and Ann are unhappy to be leaving their friends. "Will we make friends?" Carl asks Mom.

"We're all going to make more friends," she says. Mom smiles, but she's unhappy, too.

Mom, Carl, Ann, and Granddad are
all glad when the long drive ends. Mom
and Granddad smile, but Carl and Ann
still feel unhappy.

Mom and Granddad unload boxes.
Carl and Ann help unpack. Moving is
hard work.

Be a Bug Spy!

DECODABLE WORDS

Target Skill: prefix *un-*

unlucky   unsafe   unwell

Previously Taught Skills

and	closely	leaf	plant	that
be	eating	like	plants	them
bee	find	lucky	rock	trees
big	finding	make	safe	under
bite	for	may	smart	up
bug	hard	might	so	will
bugs	hopping	not	spot	
but	hurt	on	spy	
by	if	or	start	
can	in	park	stem	
check	is	pick	stems	
close	it	places	sting	

SKILLS APPLIED IN WORDS IN STORY: short *a*, short *i*, CVC syllable pattern (closed), short *o*, short *u*, short *e*, long *a* (CVC*e*); long *i* (CVC*e*), /k/ spelled *c*; long *o* (CVC*e*), /g/ spelled *g*; blends with *l, s*; final blends *nd, ng, nt*; consonants *ck*; consonant digraphs *th, ch*; endings -*s*, -*ing*; CV syllable pattern (open syllables); endings -*s*, -*es*; vowel digraphs *ai, ee, ea*; schwa sound; ending -*ing*: double consonant; long *i* spelled *igh, y*; *r*-controlled *ar, or*; suffixes -*y*, -*ly*, -*ful*; prefix *un*-

HIGH-FREQUENCY WORDS

a	don't	how	most	to
are	flower	look	the	you
care(ful)	flowers	many	their	

© Houghton Mifflin Harcourt Publishing Company

Be a Bug Spy!

High-Frequency Words Taught to Date

Grade 1

a	caught	friend	live	pictures	they	you	I've
about	city	friendship	long	play	think	young	kept
above	cold	full	look	please	those	your	knew
across	come	funny	loudly	pull	thought		might
after	could	give	loved	pushed	three	*Grade 2*	mind
again	country	go	make	put	to	afraid	morning
all	covers	goes	many	read	today	against	move
almost	cried	good	maybe	ready	together	air	next
along	different	great	me	right	too	also	other
always	do	green	minute	said	took	another	part
and	does	ground	more	school	toward	any	pretty
animal	done	grow	most	second	try	anything	really
are	don't	happy	mother	see	two	behind	river
around	door	have	my	seven	under	being	room
away	down	he	myself	shall	until	better	saw
baby	draw	head	near	she	use	book	says
ball	earth	hear	never	should	very	care	sky
be	eat	heard	new	show	walk	cheer	sleep
bear	eight	help	night	sing	want	children	slowly
beautiful	enough	her	no	small	warms	coming	someone
because	even	here	noise	soil	was	dark	something
been	every	high	nothing	some	wash	didn't	sound
before	everyone	hold	now	sometimes	watch	doing	stood
began	eyes	house	of	soon	water	else	store
begins	fall	how	off	sorry	we	ever	table
bird	family	I	old	starts	were	everything	tall
blue	far	idea	once	stories	what	floor	this
both	father	into	one	story	where	flower	though
boy	few	is	only	studied	who	found	told
bring	field	kinds	open	sure	why	front	turned
brothers	find	know	or	surprised	window	girl	voice
brown	first	large	our	take	with	gone	what's
buy	five	laugh	out	talk	work	hair	without
by	fly	learning	over	teacher	world	hard	words
call	follow	light	own	the	would	hello	
car	food	like	paper	their	write	horse	
carry	for	listen	party	there	years	hundred	
	four	little	people	these	yellow	I'll	

Decoding skills taught to date: short *a*, short *i*, CVC syllable pattern (closed), short *o*, short *u*, short *e*, long *a* (CVCe), long *i* (CVCe), /k/ spelled *c*; /s/ spelled *c*; long *o* (CVCe), long *u* /yōō/ (CVCe), long *u* /ōō/ (CVCe), long *e* (CVCe), /g/ spelled *g*; /j/ spelled *g*, *dge*; blends with *r, l, s*; final blends *nd, ng, nk, nt*; double final consonants *ll, ss, ff, zz*; consonants *ck*; double consonant (closed syllables); consonant digraphs *th, sh, wh, ch, tch, ph*; endings *-s, -ed*; endings *-ed, -ing*: drop *e*; CV syllable pattern (open syllables); contractions with *'s* and *n't*; contractions with *'ll, 'd, 've, 're*; endings *-s, -es*; vowel digraphs *ai, ay, ee, ea, oa, ow*; compound words; schwa sound; endings *-ed, -ing*: double consonant; long *i* spelled *igh, ie, i, y*; long *e* spelled *y*; ending *-es*: change *y* to *i*; r-controlled *ar, or, ore, er, ir, ur*; homophones; endings *-er, -est*: double consonant; suffixes *-y, -ly, -ful*; syllables *-tion, -ture*; prefix *un-* **From Grade 1:** consonants; short vowels

Look closely for bugs, but be smart. It is unsafe to pick up bugs that might bite or sting you. Their bites can make you unwell. So be careful, and don't get close to bugs that might hurt you.

Be a Bug Spy!

If you like bugs, you can be a bug spy. Most bugs are not big, but you can find them if you look for them.

It is not hard to spy bugs in a park. Start by finding bugs on plants. Check plant stems and flowers. You may spy bugs eating plants or hopping up trees.

Look closely and you can spy a bee on a flower or a bug on a leaf. Can you spy a bug under a rock? Will you be lucky or unlucky? How many bugs can you spot under a big rock?

Writing Time

DECODABLE WORDS

Target Skill: prefix _re-_

recheck   reread   rethink

Previously Taught Skills

after	copy	happen	make	reading	that	whole
and	day	happy	Miss	right	then	will
ask	did	helped	missing	Rose	things	with
asking	draft(s)	I	my	sat	think(s)	yes
be	events	in	need	sentences	this	
begin	find	is	not	she	time	
by	finish	it	on	spelling	turns	
changes	first	just	order	stories	understand	
chat	fix	last	partner(s)	story	us	
check	for	Lee	partner's	take	we	
class	fresh	liked	perfect	tell	when	

SKILLS APPLIED IN WORDS IN STORY: short _a_, short _i_, CVC syllable pattern (closed), short _o_, short _u_, short _e_, long _a_ (CVC_e_), long _i_ (CVC_e_), long _o_ (CVC_e_), /g/ spelled _g_; /j/ spelled _g_; blends with _r, l, s_; final blends _nd, ng, nk_; double final consonants _ll, ss_; consonants _ck_; consonant digraphs _th, wh, ch_; base words and ending -_ed_ /t/; ending -_ing_: drop _e_; CV syllable pattern (open syllables); contractions with _'ll_; base words and ending -_s_; vowel digraphs _ay, ee, ea_; long _o_ spelled _o_; compound words; long _e_ spelled _y_; ending -_es_: change _y_ to _i_; r-controlled _or, ir_; prefix _re-_

HIGH-FREQUENCY WORDS

about	next	there	was	writ(ing)
anything	our	to	were	you
are	said	took	what	your
does	the	want	work	

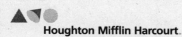
Houghton Mifflin Harcourt.

Writing Time

High-Frequency Words Taught to Date

Grade 1							I've
a	caught	friend	live	pictures	they	you	kept
about	city	friendship	long	play	think	young	knew
above	cold	full	look	please	those	your	might
across	come	funny	loudly	pull	thought		mind
after	could	give	loved	pushed	three	*Grade 2*	morning
again	country	go	make	put	to	afraid	move
all	covers	goes	many	read	today	against	next
almost	cried	good	maybe	ready	together	air	other
along	different	great	me	right	too	also	part
always	do	green	minute	said	took	another	pretty
and	does	ground	more	school	toward	any	really
animal	done	grow	most	second	try	anything	river
are	don't	happy	mother	see	two	behind	room
around	door	have	my	seven	under	being	saw
away	down	he	myself	shall	until	better	says
baby	draw	head	near	she	use	book	sky
ball	earth	hear	never	should	very	care	sleep
be	eat	heard	new	show	walk	cheer	slowly
bear	eight	help	night	sing	want	children	someone
beautiful	enough	her	no	small	warms	coming	something
because	even	here	noise	soil	was	dark	sound
been	every	high	nothing	some	wash	didn't	stood
before	everyone	hold	now	sometimes	watch	doing	store
began	eyes	house	of	soon	water	else	table
begins	fall	how	off	sorry	we	ever	tall
bird	family	I	old	starts	were	everything	this
blue	far	idea	once	stories	what	floor	though
both	father	into	one	story	where	flower	told
boy	few	is	only	studied	who	found	turned
bring	field	kinds	open	sure	why	front	voice
brothers	find	know	or	surprised	window	girl	what's
brown	first	large	our	take	with	gone	without
buy	five	laugh	out	talk	work	hair	words
by	fly	learning	over	teacher	world	hard	
call	follow	light	own	the	would	hello	
car	food	like	paper	their	write	horse	
carry	for	listen	party	there	years	hundred	
	four	little	people	these	yellow	I'll	

Decoding skills taught to date: short *a*; short *i*; CVC syllable pattern (closed); short *o*; short *u*; short *e*; long *a* (CVC*e*); long *i* (CVC*e*); /k/ spelled *c*; /s/ spelled *c*; long *o* (CVC*e*); long *u* /yo͞o/ (CVC*e*); long *u* /o͞o/ (CVC*e*); long *e* (CVC*e*); /g/ spelled *g*; /j/ spelled *g, dge*; blends with *r, l, s*; final blends *nd, ng, nk, nt*; double final consonants *ll, ss, ff, zz*; consonants *ck*; double consonant (closed syllables); consonant digraphs *th, sh, wh, ch, tch, ph*; base words and endings *-s, -ed*; endings *-ed, -ing*: drop *e*; CV syllable pattern (open syllables); contractions with *'s* and *n't*; contractions with *'ll, 'd, 've, 're*; endings *-s, -es*; vowel digraphs *ai, ay, ee, ea, oa, ow*; compound words; schwa sound; endings *-ed, -ing*: double consonant; long *i* spelled *igh, ie, i, y*; long *e* spelled *y*; ending *-es*: change *y* to *i*; *r*-controlled *ar, or, ore, er, ir, ur*; homophones; endings *-er, -est*: double consonant; suffixes *-y, -ly, -ful*; syllables *-tion, -ture*; prefixes *un-, re-* **Grade 1** consonants; short vowels

Writing Time

Miss Lee said, "Class, it is time to work on your stories. Begin your first drafts. What will happen first, next, and last? This draft does not need to be perfect. After you finish, there will be time to reread the drafts with partners and make changes."

When we were happy with our stories, it was time to recheck spelling and fix our sentences. When the stories were just right, we made a fresh copy.

We took turns reading our stories. I think the class liked my story. I liked it.

4

1

The next day, we sat with partners. Miss Lee said, "Take turns reading your stories. Ask what your partner thinks. Chat about your partner's story."

"Miss Lee?" Rose said. "After we reread with our partners, we find things we need to fix and things we want to change. Is that right?"

"Yes!" said the whole class.

Miss Lee helped us by asking, "Did you tell the whole story? Are events in order? Is anything missing?" Then she said, "Rethink parts that your partners didn't understand."

Recycle and Reuse

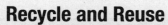

DECODABLE WORDS

Target Skill: **prefix** *re-*

recycle   refilling   reuse

Previously Taught Skills

and	drink	landfills	or	toss
as	dump	less	paper	trash
away	get	longer	rid	trashcans
bags	girl	lot	she	until
be	glass	lunch	so	use
bin	go	made	that	waste
box	her	make	then	way
burn	homes	may	these	we
burned	in	much	things	
but	is	need	this	
can	it	no	throw	
cans	it's	not	throwing	

SKILLS APPLIED IN WORDS IN STORY: short *a*; short *i*; CVC syllable pattern (closed); short *o*; short *u*; short *e*; long *a* (CVC*e*); /k/ spelled *c*; long *o* (CVC*e*); long *u* /yoo/ (CVC*e*); long *e* (CV, CVC*e*); /g/ spelled *g*; blends with *r, l, s*; final blends *nd, ng, nk*; double final consonants *ll, ss*; consonant digraphs *th, sh, ch*; endings *-s, -ed, -ing*; CV syllable pattern (open syllables); contractions with *'s*; vowel digraphs *ay, ee, ow*; compound words; schwa sound; *r*-controlled *or, er, ir, ur*; ending *-er*: double consonant; prefix *re-*

HIGH-FREQUENCY WORDS

a	don't	other	what
all	how	our	where
do	into	put	work
do(ing)	of	the	you
does	one	to	

Houghton Mifflin Harcourt

Recycle and Reuse

High-Frequency Words Taught to Date

Grade 1

a	caught	friend	live	pictures	they	you	I've
about	city	friendship	long	play	think	young	kept
above	cold	full	look	please	those	your	knew
across	come	funny	loudly	pull	thought		might
after	could	give	loved	pushed	three	**Grade 2**	mind
again	country	go	make	put	to	afraid	morning
all	covers	goes	many	read	today	against	move
almost	cried	good	maybe	ready	together	air	next
along	different	great	me	right	too	also	other
always	do	green	minute	said	took	another	part
and	does	ground	more	school	toward	any	pretty
animal	done	grow	most	second	try	anything	really
are	don't	happy	mother	see	two	behind	river
around	door	have	my	seven	under	being	room
away	down	he	myself	shall	until	better	saw
baby	draw	head	near	she	use	book	says
ball	earth	hear	never	should	very	care	sky
be	eat	heard	new	show	walk	cheer	sleep
bear	eight	help	night	sing	want	children	slowly
beautiful	enough	her	no	small	warms	coming	someone
because	even	here	noise	soil	was	dark	something
been	every	high	nothing	some	wash	didn't	sound
before	everyone	hold	now	sometimes	watch	doing	stood
began	eyes	house	of	soon	water	else	store
begins	fall	how	off	sorry	we	ever	table
bird	family	I	old	starts	were	everything	tall
blue	far	idea	once	stories	what	floor	this
both	father	into	one	story	where	flower	though
boy	few	is	only	studied	who	found	told
bring	field	kinds	open	sure	why	front	turned
brothers	find	know	or	surprised	window	girl	voice
brown	first	large	our	take	with	gone	what's
buy	five	laugh	out	talk	work	hair	without
by	fly	learning	over	teacher	world	hard	words
call	follow	light	own	the	would	hello	
car	food	like	paper	their	write	horse	
carry	for	listen	party	there	years	hundred	
	four	little	people	these	yellow	I'll	

Decoding skills taught to date: short *a*; short *i*; CVC syllable pattern (closed); short *o*; short *u*; short *e*; long *a* (CVC*e*); long *i* (CVC*e*); /k/ spelled *c*; /s/ spelled *c*; long *o* (CVC*e*); long *u* /yōō/ (CVC*e*); long *u* /ōō/ (CVC*e*); long *e* (CVC*e*); /g/ spelled *g*; /j/ spelled *g*, *dge*; blends with *r, l, s*; final blends *nd, ng, nk, nt*; double final consonants *ll, ss, ff, zz*; consonants *ck*; double consonant (closed syllables); consonant digraphs *th, sh, wh, ch, tch, ph*; endings -*s*, -*ed*; endings -*ed*, -*ing*: drop *e*; CV syllable pattern (open syllables); contractions with '*s* and *n't*; contractions with '*ll*, '*d*, '*ve*, '*re*; endings -*s*, -*es*; vowel digraphs *ai, ay, ee, ea, oa, ow*; compound words; schwa sound; endings -*ed*, -*ing*: double consonant; long *i* spelled *igh, ie, i, y*; long *e* spelled *y*; ending -*es*: change *y* to *i*; r-controlled *ar, or, ore, er, ir, ur*; homophones; endings -*er*, -*est*: double consonant; suffixes -*y*, -*ly*, -*ful*; syllables -*tion*, -*ture*; prefixes *un-, re-* **From Grade 1:** consonants; short vowels

Recycle and reuse. It's not waste until you waste it!

4

Recycle and Reuse

We make a lot of trash in our homes and where we work. Then we throw it away. We put it in trashcans to get rid of it.

Where does all that trash go? It may get burned. It may go into landfills, or to the dump.

1

How can we make less trash so we don't burn as much or dump so much in landfills?

One way is to waste less. We can recycle what we no longer need. We can put glass, paper, and cans in a recycle bin. Then these things can be made into other things.

We make less waste when we reuse things. Use a lunch box, not bags that you toss in the trash. Do what this girl is doing. She is refilling her drink can, not throwing it away.

Growing Plants

DECODABLE WORDS

Target Skill: **prefix *over-***

overeager	overgrown	overreact	overtake

Previously Taught Skills

advice	can	growing	make	sunlight
and	dirt	hard	may	that
as	drain	harder	much	this
at	dry	if	need	time
be	easy	in	no	wait
beds	follow	is	not	weeds
begin	for	it	or	when
big	garden	just	plant	will
bit	get	letting	plants	with
but	grow	like	strong	

SKILLS APPLIED IN WORDS IN STORY: short *a*; short *i*; CVC syllable pattern (closed); short *o*; short *u*; short *e*; long *a* (CVCe); long *i* (CVCe); /k/ spelled *c*; /s/ spelled *c*; /g/ spelled *g*; blends with *r, l, s*; final blends *nd, ng, nt*; double final consonants *ll*; double consonants (closed syllables); consonant digraphs *th, wh, ch*; ending *–s*; ending *-ing*; CV syllable pattern (open); vowel digraphs *ai, ay, ee, ea, ow*; compound words; schwa sound; ending *-ing*: double consonant; long *i* spelled *igh, y*; long *e* spelled *y*; r-controlled *ar, or, er, ir*; ending *-er*: double consonant; suffix *-y*; prefixes *re-, over-*   **From Grade 1:** consonants; short vowels

HIGH-FREQUENCY WORDS

a	don't	to	your
air	out	too	
are	the	water	
do	they	you	

Houghton Mifflin Harcourt

Growing Plants

High-Frequency Words Taught to Date

Grade 1							
a	caught	friend	live	pictures	they	you	I've
about	city	friendship	long	play	think	young	kept
above	cold	full	look	please	those	your	knew
across	come	funny	loudly	pull	thought		might
after	could	give	loved	pushed	three	**Grade 2**	mind
again	country	go	make	put	to	afraid	morning
all	covers	goes	many	read	today	against	move
almost	cried	good	maybe	ready	together	air	next
along	different	great	me	right	too	also	other
always	do	green	minute	said	took	another	part
and	does	ground	more	school	toward	any	pretty
animal	done	grow	most	second	try	anything	really
are	don't	happy	mother	see	two	behind	river
around	door	have	my	seven	under	being	room
away	down	he	myself	shall	until	better	saw
baby	draw	head	near	she	use	book	says
ball	earth	hear	never	should	very	care	sky
be	eat	heard	new	show	walk	cheer	sleep
bear	eight	help	night	sing	want	children	slowly
beautiful	enough	her	no	small	warms	coming	someone
because	even	here	noise	soil	was	dark	something
been	every	high	nothing	some	wash	didn't	sound
before	everyone	hold	now	sometimes	watch	doing	stood
began	eyes	house	of	soon	water	else	store
begins	fall	how	off	sorry	we	ever	table
bird	family	I	old	starts	were	everything	tall
blue	far	idea	once	stories	what	floor	this
both	father	into	one	story	where	flower	though
boy	few	is	only	studied	who	found	told
bring	field	kinds	open	sure	why	front	turned
brothers	find	know	or	surprised	window	girl	voice
brown	first	large	our	take	with	gone	what's
buy	five	laugh	out	talk	work	hair	without
by	fly	learning	over	teacher	world	hard	words
call	follow	light	own	the	would	hello	
car	food	like	paper	their	write	horse	
carry	for	listen	party	there	years	hundred	
	four	little	people	these	yellow	I'll	

Decoding skills taught to date: short *a*; short *i*; closed syllables (CVC); short *o*; short *u*; short *e*; long *a* (CVC*e*); long *i* (CVC*e*); /k/ spelled *c*; /s/ spelled *c*; long *o* (CVC*e*); long *u* /yōō/ (CVC*e*); long *u* /ōō/ (CVC*e*); long *e* (CVC*e*); /g/ spelled *g*; /j/ spelled *g, dge*; blends with *r*; blends with *l*; blends with *s*; final blend *nd*; final blend *ng*; final blend *nk*; final blend *nt*; double final consonants *ll, ss, ff, zz*; consonants *ck*; double consonants (closed syllables); consonant digraphs *th, sh, wh, ch, tch, ph*; ending -*s*; ending -*ed* /ed/; ending -*ed* /t/; ending -*ing*; CV syllable pattern (open syllables); contractions *'s, n't*; contractions *'ll, 'd*; contractions *'ve, 're*; endings -*s, -es*; vowel digraphs *ai, ay, ea, ee, oa, ow*; endings -*ed, -ing*: drop *e*; compound words; schwa sound; endings -*ed, -ing*: double consonant; long *i* spelled *igh, ie*; long *i* spelled *i, y*; long *e* spelled *y*; ending -*es*: change *y* to *i*; *r*-controlled *ar, or, ore, er, ir, ur*; homophones; endings -*er, -est*: double consonant; suffixes -*y, -ly, -ful*; syllables -*tion, -ture*; prefixes *un-, re-, over-*

If you follow this advice, the plants in your garden will grow big and strong in no time!

Growing Plants

If you like plants, you can plant a garden.

Plants may be easy or hard to grow in a garden. Plants need air, sunlight, water, dirt, and time to grow. Don't be overeager as you begin. Just do a bit at a time.

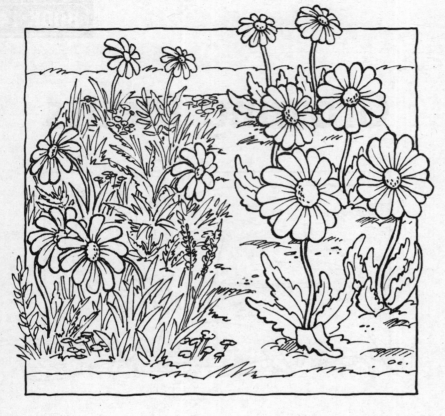

Plants need air and sunlight. Letting weeds overtake your garden plants will make it hard for your plants to grow. When garden beds get overgrown with weeds, it is harder for plants to get the air and sunlight that they need.

Plants need water, but not too much. If your plants get too much water, don't overreact. Just drain the garden as much as you can, and wait for the sun to dry it out.

Is Liz Late?

DECODABLE WORDS

Target Skill: **prefix _over-_**

overcast   overdid   oversleep

Previously Taught Skills

afraid	Dan	it	not	then
after	day	Jess	on	think
am	did	just	park	tried
and	didn't	late	quickly	up
as	dressed	least	raining	wait
ate	find	Liz	ran	we
be	for	long	really	went
bed	glad	make	rubbed	with
bench	had	meet	see	woke
but	happy	missed	set	
came	I	morning	she	
can't	in	night	stairs	
cried	is	no	start	

SKILLS APPLIED IN WORDS IN STORY: short _a_; short _i_; CVC syllable pattern (closed); short _o_; short _u_; short _e_; long _a_ (CVCe); /k/ spelled _c_; /g/ spelled _g_; blends with _r_, _l_, _s_; final blends _nd_, _ng_, _nk_, _nt_; double final consonants _ss_; consonants _ck_; double consonants (closed syllables); consonant digraphs _th_, _sh_, _wh_, _ch_; endings _-s_, _-ed_, _-ing_; contractions with _n't_; vowel digraphs _ai_, _ay_, _ee_, _ea_; schwa sound; ending _-ed_: double consonant; long _i_ spelled _igh_, _i_, _ie_; long _e_ spelled _y_; r-controlled _ar_, _er_; suffix _-ly_; prefix _over-_

HIGH-FREQUENCY WORDS

a	eyes	said	to
are	next	the	too
call(ed)	off	they	want
don't	one	thought	was

Houghton Mifflin Harcourt.

© Houghton Mifflin Harcourt Publishing Company

Is Liz Late?

High-Frequency Words Taught to Date

Grade 1

a	caught	friend	live	pictures	they	you
about	city	friendship	long	play	think	young
above	cold	full	look	please	those	your
across	come	funny	loudly	pull	thought	
after	could	give	loved	pushed	three	**Grade 2**
again	country	go	make	put	to	afraid
all	covers	goes	many	read	today	against
almost	cried	good	maybe	ready	together	air
along	different	great	me	right	too	also
always	do	green	minute	said	took	another
and	does	ground	more	school	toward	any
animal	done	grow	most	second	try	anything
are	don't	happy	mother	see	two	behind
around	door	have	my	seven	under	being
away	down	he	myself	shall	until	better
baby	draw	head	near	she	use	book
ball	earth	hear	never	should	very	care
be	eat	heard	new	show	walk	cheer
bear	eight	help	night	sing	want	children
beautiful	enough	her	no	small	warms	coming
because	even	here	noise	soil	was	dark
been	every	high	nothing	some	wash	didn't
before	everyone	hold	now	sometimes	watch	doing
began	eyes	house	of	soon	water	else
begins	fall	how	off	sorry	we	ever
bird	family	I	old	starts	were	everything
blue	far	idea	once	stories	what	floor
both	father	into	one	story	where	flower
boy	few	is	only	studied	who	found
bring	field	kinds	open	sure	why	front
brothers	find	know	or	surprised	window	girl
brown	first	large	our	take	with	gone
buy	five	laugh	out	talk	work	hair
by	fly	learning	over	teacher	world	hard
call	follow	light	own	the	would	hello
car	food	like	paper	their	write	horse
carry	for	listen	party	there	years	hundred
	four	little	people	these	yellow	I'll

I've
kept
knew
might
mind
morning
move
next
other
part
pretty
really
river
room
saw
says
sky
sleep
slowly
someone
something
sound
stood
store
table
tall
this
though
told
turned
voice
what's
without
words

Decoding skills taught to date: short *a*; short *i*; CVC syllable pattern (closed syllables); short *o*; short *u*; short *e*; long *a* (CVC*e*); long *i* (CVC*e*); /k/ spelled *c*; /s/ spelled *c*; long *o* (CVC*e*); long *u* /yōō/ (CVC*e*); long *u* /ōō/ (CVC*e*); long *e* (CVC*e*); /g/ spelled *g*; /j/ spelled *g*, *dge*; blends with *r*; blends with *l*; blends with *s*; final blend *nd*; final blend *ng*; final blend *nk*; final blend *nt*; double final consonants *ll, ss, ff, zz*; consonants *ck*; double consonants (closed syllables); consonant digraph *th*; consonant digraph *sh*; consonant digraph *wh*; consonant digraphs *ch, tch*; consonant digraph *ph*; ending *-s*; ending *-ed*; ending *-ing*; open syllables (CV); contractions *'s, n't*; contractions *'ll, 'd*; contractions *'ve, 're*; endings *-s, -es*; vowel digraphs *ai, ay, ea, ee, oa, ow*; endings *-ed, -ing*: drop *e*; compound words; schwa sound; endings *-ed, -ing*: double consonant; long *i* spelled *igh, ie, i, y*; long *e* spelled *y*; ending *-es*: change *y* to *i*; r-controlled *ar, or, ore, er, ir, ur*; homophones; endings *-er, -est*: double consonant; suffixes *-y, -ly, -ful*; syllables *-tion, -ture*; prefixes *un-, re-, over-*

Just then, Jess and Dan came up to her. Liz was happy to see them. "Liz!" they called. "Are we late?"

"I thought I was late," said Liz. "Am I glad to see you!"

Is Liz Late?

One night, Liz stayed up late after a long day. She really overdid it, and she had to meet Dan and Jess in the park the next morning. She rubbed her eyes as she went up the stairs to bed.

The next morning, Liz woke up with a start. "No, no!" she cried. "Did I oversleep? I can't be late! I don't want to make Jess and Dan wait!"

She quickly dressed and ate and set off for the park.

The day was overcast, but at least it was not raining. Liz ran to the park and tried to find Jess and Dan. She didn't see them.

She was afraid she was too late and had missed them. She sat on a bench to think.

Baking a Cake

DECODABLE WORDS

Target Skill: prefix *pre-*

preheat   premade   prepare

Previously Taught Skills

and	everything	is	pans	that
back	fill	it	press	then
bake	first	lightly	rack	time
baking	follow	longer	read	until
batter	frost	make	scratch	use
be	frosted	mix	set	wait
big	frosting	must	so	way
bowl	get	need	springs	when
cake	grease	not	steps	will
can	hot	on	stick	with
center	if	or	stove	
eat	in	own	tell	

SKILLS APPLIED IN WORDS IN STORY: short *a*; short *i*; CVC syllable pattern (closed syllables); short *o*; short *u*; short *e*; long *a* (CVCe); long *i* (CVCe); /k/ spelled *c*; /s/ spelled *c*; long *o* (CVCe); long *u* /yo͞o/ (CVCe); /g/ spelled *g*; blends with *r, s*; final blend *ng*; double final consonants *ll, ss*; consonants *ck*; double consonants (closed syllables); consonant digraphs *th, wh, tch*; endings *-s, -ed*; CV syllable pattern (open syllables); vowel digraphs *ai, ay, ee, ea, ow*; endings *-ed, -ing*: drop e; compound words; schwa sound; long *i* spelled *igh*; long *e* spelled *e, y*; r-controlled *or, er, ir*; ending *-er*: double consonant; suffix *-ly*; prefix *pre-*

HIGH-FREQUENCY WORDS

a	one	you
done	the	your
from	to	

Houghton Mifflin Harcourt.

Baking a Cake

High-Frequency Words Taught to Date

Grade 1

a	caught	friend	live	pictures	they	you	I've
about	city	friendship	long	play	think	young	kept
above	cold	full	look	please	those	your	knew
across	come	funny	loudly	pull	thought		might
after	could	give	loved	pushed	three	**Grade 2**	mind
again	country	go	make	put	to	afraid	morning
all	covers	goes	many	read	today	against	move
almost	cried	good	maybe	ready	together	air	next
along	different	great	me	right	too	also	other
always	do	green	minute	said	took	another	part
and	does	ground	more	school	toward	any	pretty
animal	done	grow	most	second	try	anything	really
are	don't	happy	mother	see	two	behind	river
around	door	have	my	seven	under	being	room
away	down	he	myself	shall	until	better	saw
baby	draw	head	near	she	use	book	says
ball	earth	hear	never	should	very	care	sky
be	eat	heard	new	show	walk	cheer	sleep
bear	eight	help	night	sing	want	children	slowly
beautiful	enough	her	no	small	warms	coming	someone
because	even	here	noise	soil	was	dark	something
been	every	high	nothing	some	wash	didn't	sound
before	everyone	hold	now	sometimes	watch	doing	stood
began	eyes	house	of	soon	water	else	store
begins	fall	how	off	sorry	we	ever	table
bird	family	I	old	starts	were	everything	tall
blue	far	idea	once	stories	what	floor	this
both	father	into	one	story	where	flower	though
boy	few	is	only	studied	who	found	told
bring	field	kinds	open	sure	why	front	turned
brothers	find	know	or	surprised	window	girl	voice
brown	first	large	our	take	with	gone	what's
buy	five	laugh	out	talk	work	hair	without
by	fly	learning	over	teacher	world	hard	words
call	follow	light	own	the	would	hello	
car	food	like	paper	their	write	horse	
carry	for	listen	party	there	years	hundred	
	four	little	people	these	yellow	I'll	

Decoding skills taught to date: short *a*; short *i*; closed syllables (CVC); short *o*; short *u*; short *e*; long *a* (CVC*e*); long *i* (CVC*e*); /k/ spelled *c*; /s/ spelled *c*; long *o* (CVC*e*); long *u* /yōō/ (CVC*e*); long *u* /ōō/ (CVC*e*); long *e* (CVC*e*); /g/ spelled *g*; /j/ spelled *g, dge*; blends with *r*; blends with *l*; blends with *s*; final blend *nd*; final blend *ng*; final blend *nk*; final blend *nt*; double final consonants *ll, ss, ff, zz*; consonants *ck*; double consonants (closed syllables); consonant digraphs *th, sh, wh, ch, tch, ph*; endings -*s*, -*ed*, -*ing*; open syllables (CV); contractions '*s, n't*; contractions '*ll, 'd*; contractions '*ve, 're*; endings -*s*, -*es*; vowel digraphs *ai, ay, ea, ee, oa, ow*; endings -*ed*, -*ing*: drop *e*; compound words; schwa sound; endings -*ed*, -*ing*: double consonant; long *i* spelled *igh, ie, i, y*; long *e* spelled *y*; ending -*es*: change *y* to *i*; r-controlled *ar*; r-controlled *or, ore*; r-controlled *er*; r-controlled *ir, ur*; homophones; endings -*er*, -*est*: double consonant; suffixes -*y*, -*ly*, -*ful*; syllables -*tion*, -*ture*; prefixes *un-, re-, over-, pre-*

Set the cake on a rack and wait until it is no longer hot. Then it will be time to frost the cake. Make your own frosting or use premade.

When the cake is frosted, it is time to eat cake!

Baking a Cake

To bake a cake, you must follow the steps. You can use a cake mix or bake from scratch.

First, read the steps and prepare everything you will need.

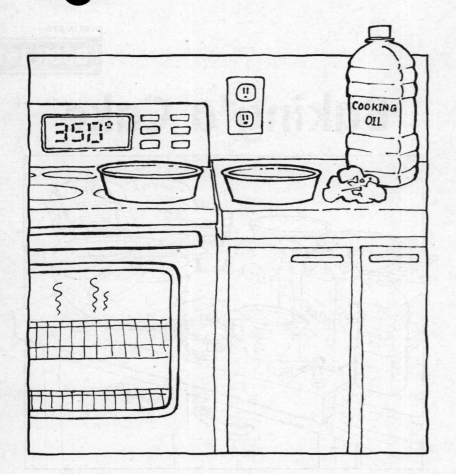

Preheat the stove. Grease the cake pans so that the cake will not stick.

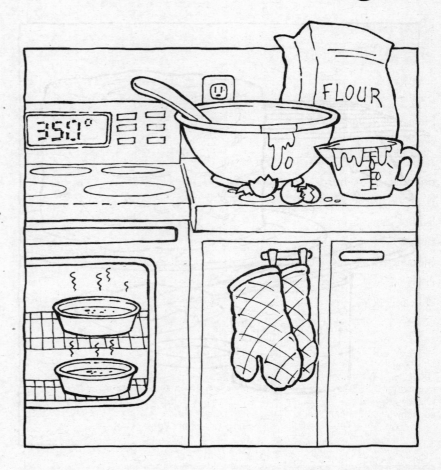

Follow the steps to make the cake batter in a big bowl. Then fill the cake pans with batter.

Bake the cake until it is done. One way to tell if a cake is done is to press it lightly in the center. If it springs back, it is done.

Meg Studies

DECODABLE WORDS

Target Skill: prefix *pre-*

predictions   prehistoric   prehistory

Previously Taught Skills

ago	did	likes	reads	time
and	easy	long	recorded	turns
animals	hard	make	right	under
based	her	Meg	see	up
before	histories	more	seems	wait
bit	if	on	seems	whole
blanket	is	opens	studies	will
can't	it	or	study	
check	just	pictures	things	
curls	light	read	this	

SKILLS APPLIED IN WORDS IN STORY: short *a*; short *i*; CVC syllable pattern (closed); short *o*; short *u*; short *e*; long *a* (CVCe); long *i* (CVCe); /k/ spelled *c*; /g/ spelled *g*; blends with *l*; blends with *s*; final blends *nd*, *ng*; double final consonants *ll*; consonants *ck*; consonant digraph *th*; consonant digraph *sh*; consonant digraph *wh*; consonant digraphs *ch, tch*; ending *-s*; ending *-ed*: drop *e*; CV syllable pattern (open); vowel digraphs *ai, ay, ee, ea*; schwa sound; long *i* spelled *igh*; long *e* spelled *y*; ending *-es*: change *y* to *i*; r-controlled *ar, or, ore, ur*; suffix *-y*; syllables *-tion, -ture*; prefix *pre-*   **From Grade 1:** consonants; short vowels; possessives with *'s*

HIGH-FREQUENCY WORDS

a	book('s)	people	they
about	one	the	to
book	out	their	too

Houghton Mifflin Harcourt

Meg Studies

High-Frequency Words Taught to Date

Grade 1							
a	caught	friend	live	pictures	they	you	I've
about	city	friendship	long	play	think	young	kept
above	cold	full	look	please	those	your	knew
across	come	funny	loudly	pull	thought		might
after	could	give	loved	pushed	three	**Grade 2**	mind
again	country	go	make	put	to	afraid	morning
all	covers	goes	many	read	today	against	move
almost	cried	good	maybe	ready	together	air	next
along	different	great	me	right	too	also	other
always	do	green	minute	said	took	another	part
and	does	ground	more	school	toward	any	pretty
animal	done	grow	most	second	try	anything	really
are	don't	happy	mother	see	two	behind	river
around	door	have	my	seven	under	being	room
away	down	he	myself	shall	until	better	saw
baby	draw	head	near	she	use	book	says
ball	earth	hear	never	should	very	care	sky
be	eat	heard	new	show	walk	cheer	sleep
bear	eight	help	night	sing	want	children	slowly
beautiful	enough	her	no	small	warms	coming	someone
because	even	here	noise	soil	was	dark	something
been	every	high	nothing	some	wash	didn't	sound
before	everyone	hold	now	sometimes	watch	doing	stood
began	eyes	house	of	soon	water	else	store
begins	fall	how	off	sorry	we	ever	table
bird	family	I	old	starts	were	everything	tall
blue	far	idea	once	stories	what	floor	this
both	father	into	one	story	where	flower	though
boy	few	is	only	studied	who	found	told
bring	field	kinds	open	sure	why	front	turned
brothers	find	know	or	surprised	window	girl	voice
brown	first	large	our	take	with	gone	what's
buy	five	laugh	out	talk	work	hair	without
by	fly	learning	over	teacher	world	hard	words
call	follow	light	own	the	would	hello	
car	food	like	paper	their	write	horse	
carry	for	listen	party	there	years	hundred	
	four	little	people	these	yellow	I'll	

Decoding skills taught to date: short *a*; short *i*; closed syllables (CVC); short *o*; short *u*; short *e*; long *a* (CVC*e*); long *i* (CVC*e*); /k/ spelled *c*; /s/ spelled *c*; long *o* (CVC*e*); long *u* /yoō/ (CVC*e*); long *u* /oō/ (CVC*e*); long *e* (CVC*e*); /g/ spelled *g*; /j/ spelled *g, dge*; blends with *r*; blends with *l*; blends with *s*; final blends *nd, ng, nk, nt*; double final consonants *ll, ss, ff, zz*; consonants *ck*; double consonants (closed syllables); consonant digraphs *th, sh, wh, ch, tch, ph*; endings *-s, -ed, -ing*; open syllables (CV); contractions *'s, n't*; contractions *'ll, 'd*; contractions *'ve, 're*; endings *-s, -es*; vowel digraphs *ai, ay, ea, ee, oa, ow*; endings *-ed, -ing*: drop *e*; compound words; schwa sound; endings *-ed, -ing*: double consonant; long *i* spelled *igh, ie, i, y*; long *e* spelled *y*; ending *-es*: change *y* to *i*; r-controlled *ar*; r-controlled *or, ore*; r-controlled *er*; r-controlled *ir, ur*; homophones; endings *-er, -est*: double consonant; suffixes *-y, -ly, -ful*; syllables *-tion, -ture*; prefixes *un-, re-, over-, pre-*

Meg will read the whole book. She curls up under a blanket and turns on her light. She can't wait to read it!

4

Meg Studies

Meg likes to study prehistory, or the time before people recorded their histories. She likes to read about prehistoric animals and the things they did so long ago.

1

Meg makes predictions based on a book's pictures. This one is about prehistoric animals. Meg opens it up to check it out.

Meg reads a bit to see if the book is too easy or too hard. It seems just right, so Meg reads more.

Jeff Makes a Mistake

DECODABLE WORDS

Target Skill: **prefix** *mis-*

misbehave   mistake   misunderstanding

Previously Taught Skills

and	get	it	off	take
at	had	Jan	on	that
back	happened	Jeff	pal	then
big	helped	know	park	Wag
by	hide	leash	play	Wag's
chat	himself	Lee	right	went
did	his	made	rule	while
didn't	I	makes	see	whole
dog	I'll	mean	sign	will
dogs	in	must	sister	with
followed	is	my	smiled	yelled
fun	isn't	not	stay	

SKILLS APPLIED IN WORDS IN STORY: short *a*; short *i*; short *o*; short *e*; short *u*; CVC syllable pattern (closed syllables); long *a* (CVC*e*); long *i* (CVC*e*); long *o* (CVC*e*); long *u* /o͞o/ (CVC*e*); /g/ spelled *g*; blends with *l*; blends with *s*; final blend *nd*; final blend *nt*; double final consonants *ll, ff*; consonants *ck*; consonant digraph *th*; consonant digraph *sh*; consonant digraph *wh*; consonant digraphs *ch, tch*; ending -*ed* /d/; ending -*ed* /t/; ending -*ing*; open syllables (CV); contraction *n't*; contraction *'ll*; endings -*s*, -*es*; vowel digraphs *ee, ea*; vowel digraphs *oa, ow*; compound words; schwa sound; long *i* spelled *igh, ie*; long *i* spelled *i, y*; r-controlled *ar*; r-controlled *er*; prefix *mis-*   **From Grade 1:** consonants; short vowels; final blends; possessives with *'s*

HIGH-FREQUENCY WORDS

a	he	she	thought	what
all	look (looked)	the	to	you
don't	said	they	was	

Houghton Mifflin Harcourt

© Houghton Mifflin Harcourt Publishing Company

prefix mis-

BOOK 153

Jeff Makes a Mistake

High-Frequency Words Taught to Date

Grade 1	caught	friend	live	pictures	they	you	I've
a	city	friendship	long	play	think	young	kept
about	cold	full	look	please	those	your	knew
above	come	funny	loudly	pull	thought		might
across	could	give	loved	pushed	three	**Grade 2**	mind
after	country	go	make	put	to	afraid	morning
again	covers	goes	many	read	today	against	move
all	cried	good	maybe	ready	together	air	next
almost	different	great	me	right	too	also	other
along	do	green	minute	said	took	another	part
always	does	ground	more	school	toward	any	pretty
and	done	grow	most	second	try	anything	really
animal	don't	happy	mother	see	two	behind	river
are	door	have	my	seven	under	being	room
around	down	he	myself	shall	until	better	saw
away	draw	head	near	she	use	book	says
baby	earth	hear	never	should	very	care	sky
ball	eat	heard	new	show	walk	cheer	sleep
be	eight	help	night	sing	want	children	slowly
bear	enough	her	no	small	warms	coming	someone
beautiful	even	here	noise	soil	was	dark	something
because	every	high	nothing	some	wash	didn't	sound
been	everyone	hold	now	sometimes	watch	doing	stood
before	eyes	house	of	soon	water	else	store
began	fall	how	off	sorry	we	ever	table
begins	family	I	old	starts	were	everything	tall
bird	far	idea	once	stories	what	floor	this
blue	father	into	one	story	where	flower	though
both	few	is	only	studied	who	found	told
boy	field	kinds	open	sure	why	front	turned
bring	find	know	or	surprised	window	girl	voice
brothers	first	large	our	take	with	gone	what's
brown	five	laugh	out	talk	work	hair	without
buy	fly	learning	over	teacher	world	hard	words
by	follow	light	own	the	would	hello	
call	food	like	paper	their	write	horse	
car	for	listen	party	there	years	hundred	
carry	four	little	people	these	yellow	I'll	

Decoding skills taught to date: short *a*; short *i*; CVC syllable pattern (closed syllables); short *o*; short *u*; short *e*; long *a* (CVC*e*); long *i* (CVC*e*); /k/ spelled *c*; /s/ spelled *c*; long *o* (CVC*e*); long *u* /yōō/ (CVC*e*); long *u* /ōō/ (CVC*e*); long *e* (CVC*e*); /g/ spelled *g*; /j/ spelled *g, dge*; blends with *r*; blends with *l*; blends with *s*; final blend *nd*; final blend *ng*; final blend *nk*; final blend *nt*; double final consonants *ll, ss, ff, zz*; consonants *ck*; double consonants (closed syllables); consonant digraph *th*; consonant digraph *sh*; consonant digraph *wh*; consonant digraphs *ch, tch*; consonant digraph *ph*; ending *-s*; ending *-ed* /ed/; ending *-ed* /d/; ending *-ed* /t/; ending *-ing*; ending *-ed*: drop *e*; ending *-ing*: drop *e*; CV syllable pattern (open syllables); contractions *'s, n't*; contractions *'ll, 'd*; contractions *'ve, 're*; endings *-s, -es*; vowel digraphs *ai, ay*; vowel digraphs *ee, ea*; vowel digraphs *oa, ow*; compound words; schwa sound; ending *-ed*: double consonant; ending *-ing*: double consonant; long *i* spelled *igh, ie*; long *i* spelled *i, y*; long *e* spelled *y*; ending *-es*: change *y* to *i*; r-controlled *ar*; r-controlled *or, ore*; r-controlled *er*; r-controlled *ir, ur*; homophones; ending *-er*: double consonant; ending *-est*: double consonant; suffix *-y*; suffix *-ly*; suffix *-ful*; syllable *-tion*; syllable *-ture*; prefix *un-*; prefix *re-*; prefix *over-*; prefix *pre-*; prefix *mis-*

Jeff Makes a Mistake

Jan smiled and said, "I see what happened. Jeff did not see the whole sign. It is a misunderstanding!"

Jan helped Jeff get Wag back on his leash. She said, "Lee, I know you didn't mean to hide the rule!" Then they all went and had fun at the park.

Jeff went to the park with his big sister Jan and his dog Wag.

Jan said, "I'll chat with my pal Lee while you play with Wag. Don't misbehave!"

4

1

Jeff looked at the sign by Lee. He thought the rule was <u>Dogs off leash in park</u>. Jeff made a mistake! Jeff said to himself, "I will not misbehave. I'll take off Wag's leash."

Jeff said, "I followed the rule, Jan!"
Jan yelled, "Jeff, that isn't right! Wag must stay on his leash at the park!"

Max Gets Dressed

DECODABLE WORDS

Target Skill: **prefix *mis-***

misbuttoned   mismatched   mistake

Previously Taught Skills

and	for	made	rebuttoned	spoke
before	get	Max	replaced	surprise
but	gets	Max's	right	then
by	had	Mike	see	up
came	I	Mom	shirt	wake
Dad	in	myself	shorts	while
did	it	nice	show	will
dressed	job	not	smiled	woke
fine	let's	on	socks	wore

SKILLS APPLIED IN WORDS IN STORY: short *a*; short *i*; short *o*; short *u*; short *e*; CVC syllable pattern (closed syllables); /g/ spelled *g*; long *a* (CVC*e*); long *i* (CVC*e*); /k/ spelled *c*; /s/ spelled *c*; long *o* (CVC*e*); blends with *r*; blends with *l*; blends with *s*; final blend *nd*; double final consonants *ll, ss*; consonants *ck*; double consonants (closed syllables); consonant digraph *th*; consonant digraph *sh*; consonant digraph *wh*; ending *-s*; ending *-ed* /t/; CV syllable pattern (open syllables); contraction *'s*; vowel digraph *ow*; schwa sound; long *i* spelled *igh*; long *i* spelled *i, y*; r-controlled *or, ore*; r-controlled *er*; r-controlled *ir, ur*; prefix *re-*; compound words; prefix *mis-*   **From Grade 1:** consonants; short vowels; final blends; possessives with *'s*

HIGH-FREQUENCY WORDS

a	else	knew	soon	what
be	everyone	said	to	work
brother	he	something	was	you

Houghton Mifflin Harcourt.

Max Gets Dressed

© Houghton Mifflin Harcourt Publishing Company

High-Frequency Words Taught to Date

Grade 1

a	caught	friend	live	pictures	they	you	I've
about	city	friendship	long	play	think	young	kept
above	cold	full	look	please	those	your	knew
across	come	funny	loudly	pull	thought		might
after	could	give	loved	pushed	three	**Grade 2**	mind
again	country	go	make	put	to	afraid	morning
all	covers	goes	many	read	today	against	move
almost	cried	good	maybe	ready	together	air	next
along	different	great	me	right	too	also	other
always	do	green	minute	said	took	another	part
and	does	ground	more	school	toward	any	pretty
animal	done	grow	most	second	try	anything	really
are	don't	happy	mother	see	two	behind	river
around	door	have	my	seven	under	being	room
away	down	he	myself	shall	until	better	saw
baby	draw	head	near	she	use	book	says
ball	earth	hear	never	should	very	care	sky
be	eat	heard	new	show	walk	cheer	sleep
bear	eight	help	night	sing	want	children	slowly
beautiful	enough	her	no	small	warms	coming	someone
because	even	here	noise	soil	was	dark	something
been	every	high	nothing	some	wash	didn't	sound
before	everyone	hold	now	sometimes	watch	doing	stood
began	eyes	house	of	soon	water	else	store
begins	fall	how	off	sorry	we	ever	table
bird	family	I	old	starts	were	everything	tall
blue	far	idea	once	stories	what	floor	this
both	father	into	one	story	where	flower	though
boy	few	is	only	studied	who	found	told
bring	field	kinds	open	sure	why	front	turned
brothers	find	know	or	surprised	window	girl	voice
brown	first	large	our	take	with	gone	what's
buy	five	laugh	out	talk	work	hair	without
by	fly	learning	over	teacher	world	hard	words
call	follow	light	own	the	would	hello	
car	food	like	paper	their	write	horse	
carry	four	listen	party	there	years	hundred	
		little	people	these	yellow	I'll	

Decoding skills taught to date: short *a*; short *i*; short *o*; short *u*; short *e*; CVC syllable pattern (closed syllables); long *a* (CVC*e*); long *i* (CVC*e*); /k/ spelled *c*; /s/ spelled *c*; long *o* (CVC*e*); long *u* /yōō/ (CVC*e*); long *u* /ōō/ (CVC*e*); long *e* (CVC*e*); /g/ spelled *g*; /j/ spelled *g*, *dge*; blends with *r*; blends with *l*; blends with *s*; final blend *nd*; final blend *ng*; final blend *nk*; final blend *nt*; double final consonants *ll, ss, ff, zz*; consonants *ck*; double consonants (closed syllables); consonant digraph *th*; consonant digraph *sh*; consonant digraph *wh*; consonant digraphs *ch, tch*; consonant digraph *ph*; ending *-s*; ending *-ed* /ed/; ending *-ed* /d/; ending *-ed* /t/; ending *-ing*; ending *-ed*: drop *e*; ending *-ing*: drop *e*; CV syllable pattern (open syllables); contractions *'s, n't*; contractions *'ll, 'd*; contractions *'ve, 're*; endings *-s, -es*; vowel digraphs *ai, ay*; vowel digraphs *ee, ea*; vowel digraphs *oa, ow*; compound words; schwa sound; ending *-ed*: double consonant; ending *-ing*: double consonant; long *i* spelled *igh, ie*; long *i* spelled *i, y*; long *e* spelled *y*; ending *-es*: change *y* to *i*; r-controlled *ar*; r-controlled *or, ore*; r-controlled *er*; r-controlled *ir, ur*; homophones; ending *-er*: double consonant; ending *-est*: double consonant; suffix *-y*; suffix *-ly*; suffix *-ful*; syllable *-tion*; syllable *-ture*; prefix *un-*; prefix *re-*; prefix *over-*; prefix *pre-*; prefix *mis-*

Mike said, "Nice work, Max!"

While he spoke, Mike rebuttoned Max's shirt. He replaced Max's mismatched socks.

Then Mike said, "Let's show Mom and Dad what a fine job you did!"

4

Max Gets Dressed

Max woke up before everyone else. Max said, "I will get dressed by myself. It will be a nice surprise for Mom and Dad."

1

Soon Max had on shorts, a shirt, and socks. But something was not right. Max knew he had made a mistake.

Max's brother Mike came in to wake Max up. Max said, "See, Mike? I dressed myself."

Mike smiled. Max wore a misbuttoned shirt. He wore mismatched socks.

The Knitting Knight

DECODABLE WORDS

Target Skill: silent consonants *kn*, *gn*

gnats	kneel	knight	knitted	knocked	know
knapsack	knelt	knit	knitting	knots	

Previously Taught Skills

and	designed	his	not	showed	untie
asked	did	home	on	signs	well
at	dress	I	packed	Sir	went
away	find	in	pants	sitting	when
before	followed	it	Peach	snacks	will
big	for	kind	person's	teach	yarn
Bill	gave	last	polite	teacher	
but	gift	liked	Princess	then	
can	gifts	met	quest	this	
chase	him	next	return	tie	
day	himself	nice	rock	tiny	

SKILLS APPLIED IN WORDS IN STORY: short *a*; short *i*; short *o*; short *u*; short *e*; long *a* (CVC*e*); long *i* (CVC*e*); /k/ spelled *c*; /s/ spelled *c*; CVC syllable pattern (closed syllables); CV syllable pattern (open syllables); /g/ spelled *g*; long *o* (CVC*e*); blends with *r*; blends with *s*; final blend *nd*; final blend *nt*; double final consonants *ll, ss*; consonants *ck*; double consonants (closed syllables); consonant digraph *th*; consonant digraph *sh*; consonant digraph *wh*; consonant digraph *ch*; ending -*s*; ending -*ed*; ending -*ing*; vowel digraph *ay*; vowel digraphs *ee, ea*; vowel digraph *ow*; compound words; schwa sound; ending -*ing*: double consonant; long *i* spelled *igh, ie, i*; long *e* spelled *y*; r-controlled *ar, er, or, ore, ur*; prefix *re*-; prefix *un*-; silent consonants *kn, gn* **From Grade 1:** consonants; short vowels; /kw/ spelled *qu*; final blends; possessives with '*s*

HIGH-FREQUENCY WORDS

a	great	me	to	you
could	he	out	was	
give	how	the	would	

© Houghton Mifflin Harcourt Publishing Company

The Knitting Knight

High-Frequency Words Taught to Date

Grade 1							I've
a	caught	friend	live	pictures	they	you	kept
about	city	friendship	long	play	think	young	knew
above	cold	full	look	please	those	your	might
across	come	funny	loudly	pull	thought		mind
after	could	give	loved	pushed	three	**Grade 2**	morning
again	country	go	make	put	to	afraid	move
all	covers	goes	many	read	today	against	next
almost	cried	good	maybe	ready	together	air	other
along	different	great	me	right	too	also	part
always	do	green	minute	said	took	another	pretty
and	does	ground	more	school	toward	any	really
animal	done	grow	most	second	try	anything	river
are	don't	happy	mother	see	two	behind	room
around	door	have	my	seven	under	being	saw
away	down	he	myself	shall	until	better	says
baby	draw	head	near	she	use	book	sky
ball	earth	hear	never	should	very	care	sleep
be	eat	heard	new	show	walk	cheer	slowly
bear	eight	help	night	sing	want	children	someone
beautiful	enough	her	no	small	warms	coming	something
because	even	here	noise	soil	was	dark	sound
been	every	high	nothing	some	wash	didn't	stood
before	everyone	hold	now	sometimes	watch	doing	store
began	eyes	house	of	soon	water	else	table
begins	fall	how	off	sorry	we	ever	tall
bird	family	I	old	starts	were	everything	this
blue	far	idea	once	stories	what	floor	though
both	father	into	one	story	where	flower	told
boy	few	is	only	studied	who	found	turned
bring	field	kinds	open	sure	why	front	voice
brothers	find	know	or	surprised	window	girl	what's
brown	first	large	our	take	with	gone	without
buy	five	laugh	out	talk	work	hair	words
by	fly	learning	over	teacher	world	hard	
call	follow	light	own	the	would	hello	
car	food	like	paper	their	write	horse	
carry	for	listen	party	there	years	hundred	
	four	little	people	these	yellow	I'll	

Decoding skills taught to date: short *a*; short *i*; CVC syllable pattern (closed syllables); short *o*; short *u*; short *e*; long *a* (CVC*e*); long *i* (CVC*e*); /k/ spelled *c*; /s/ spelled *c*; long *o* (CVC*e*); long *u* /yōō/ (CVC*e*); long *u* /ōō/ (CVC*e*); long *e* (CVC*e*); /g/ spelled *g*; /j/ spelled *g*, *dge*; blends with *r*; blends with *l*; blends with *s*; final blend *nd*; final blend *ng*; final blend *nk*; final blend *nt*; double final consonants *ll*, *ss*, *ff*, *zz*; consonants *ck*; double consonants (closed syllables); consonant digraph *th*; consonant digraph *sh*; consonant digraph *wh*; consonant digraphs *ch*, *tch*; consonant digraph *ph*; ending -*s*; ending -*ed* /ed/; ending -*ed* /d/; ending -*ed* /t/; ending -*ing*; ending -*ed*: drop *e*; ending -*ing*: drop *e*; CV syllable pattern (open syllables); contractions *'s*, *n't*; contractions *'ll*, *'d*; contractions *'ve*, *'re*; endings -*s*, -*es*; vowel digraphs *ai*, *ay*; vowel digraphs *ee*, *ea*; vowel digraphs *oa*, *ow*; compound words; schwa sound; ending -*ed*: double consonant; ending -*ing*: double consonant; long *i* spelled *igh*, *ie*; long *i* spelled *i*, *y*; long *e* spelled *y*; ending -*es*: change *y* to *i*; r-controlled *ar*; r-controlled *or*, *ore*; r-controlled *er*; r-controlled *ir*, *ur*; homophones; ending -*er*: double consonant; ending -*est*: double consonant; suffix -*y*; suffix -*ly*; suffix -*ful*; syllable -*tion*; syllable -*ture*; prefix *un*-; prefix *re*-; prefix *over*-; prefix *pre*-; prefix *mis*-; silent consonants *kn*, *gn*

The knitting knight showed Sir Bill how to knit. At last, Sir Bill knitted well! Then he went home. He designed and knitted a dress for Princess Peach. Princess Peach liked it and gave Sir Bill a nice gift in return.

4

The Knitting Knight

Sir Bill was a great knight. He would kneel and give nice gifts to Princess Peach. Sir Bill was polite and knocked when he went to a person's home. He could tie and untie big knots and chase away tiny gnats.

But he did not know how to knit.

1

"Can I find out how to knit?" Sir Bill asked himself. He packed his yarn and snacks in his knapsack. Then the knight followed signs on his quest to find a knitting teacher.

The next day, Sir Bill met a knight sitting on a rock. This knight was knitting pants! Sir Bill knelt before him and asked, "Kind knight, will you teach me to knit?"

Ben Knocks

DECODABLE WORDS

Target Skill: silent consonants *kn, gn*

Gnome	knit	knock
knack	knits	knocking
knapsack	knitting	knocks
Knight	knob	knows

Previously Taught Skills

and	grab	inside	sees	when
barks	Gran	is	sits	which
Ben	grandson	just	sitting	will
best	Gran's	likes	smiles	with
brings	help	make	teaching	yarn
cat	helps	my	that	yells
designs	her	nice	time	yes
dog	him	on	try	
each	his	runs	turns	
for	in	see	weekend	

SKILLS APPLIED IN WORDS IN STORY: short *a*; short *i*; short *o*; short *e*; short *u*; CVC syllable pattern (closed syllables); final blend *ng*; long *a* (CVC*e*); /s/ spelled *c*; /g/ spelled *g*; consonant digraph *wh*; long *i* (CVC*e*); /k/ spelled *c*; long *o* (CVC*e*); blends with *r*; blends with *s*; final blend *nd*; double final consonants *ll*; consonants *ck*; double consonants (closed syllables); consonant digraph *th*; consonant digraph *ch*; ending -*s*; ending -*ing*; CV syllable pattern (open syllables); schwa sound; vowel digraphs *ee, ea*; vowel digraph *ow*; compound words; ending -*ing*: double consonant; long *i* spelled *igh, ie, y*; r-controlled *ar, er, or, ur*; silent consonants *kn, gn* **From Grade 1:** consonants; short vowels; final blends; possessives with *'s*

HIGH-FREQUENCY WORDS

a	door	he	says	to
calls	goes	house	she	today
come	have	out	the	too

Houghton Mifflin Harcourt.

Ben Knocks

© Houghton Mifflin Harcourt Publishing Company

High-Frequency Words Taught to Date

Grade 1

a	caught	friend	live	pictures	they	you
about	city	friendship	long	play	think	young
above	cold	full	look	please	those	your
across	come	funny	loudly	pull	thought	
after	could	give	loved	pushed	three	**Grade 2**
again	country	go	make	put	to	afraid
all	covers	goes	many	read	today	against
almost	cried	good	maybe	ready	together	air
along	different	great	me	right	too	also
always	do	green	minute	said	took	another
and	does	ground	more	school	toward	any
animal	done	grow	most	second	try	anything
are	don't	happy	mother	see	two	behind
around	door	have	my	seven	under	being
away	down	he	myself	shall	until	better
baby	draw	head	near	she	use	book
ball	earth	hear	never	should	very	care
be	eat	heard	new	show	walk	cheer
bear	eight	help	night	sing	want	children
beautiful	enough	her	no	small	warms	coming
because	even	here	noise	soil	was	dark
been	every	high	nothing	some	wash	didn't
before	everyone	hold	now	sometimes	watch	doing
began	eyes	house	of	soon	water	else
begins	fall	how	off	sorry	we	ever
bird	family	I	old	starts	were	everything
blue	far	idea	once	stories	what	floor
both	father	into	one	story	where	flower
boy	few	is	only	studied	who	found
bring	field	kinds	open	sure	why	front
brothers	find	know	or	surprised	window	girl
brown	first	large	our	take	with	gone
buy	five	laugh	out	talk	work	hair
by	fly	learning	over	teacher	world	hard
call	follow	light	own	the	would	hello
car	food	like	paper	their	write	horse
carry	for	listen	party	there	years	hundred
	four	little	people	these	yellow	I'll

I've
kept
knew
might
mind
morning
move
next
other
part
pretty
really
river
room
saw
says
sky
sleep
slowly
someone
something
sound
stood
store
table
tall
this
though
told
turned
voice
what's
without
words

Decoding skills taught to date: short *a*; short *i*; CVC syllable pattern (closed syllables); short *o*; short *u*; short *e*; long *a* (CVC*e*); long *i* (CVC*e*); /k/ spelled *c*; /s/ spelled *c*; long *o* (CVC*e*); long *u* /yoo/ (CVC*e*); long *u* /oo/ (CVC*e*); long *e* (CVC*e*); /g/ spelled *g*; /j/ spelled *g*, *dge*; blends with *r*; blends with *l*; blends with *s*; final blend *nd*; final blend *ng*; final blend *nk*; final blend *nt*; double final consonants: *ll*, *ss*, *ff*, *zz*; consonants *ck*; double consonants (closed syllables); consonant digraph *th*; consonant digraph *sh*; consonant digraph *wh*; consonant digraphs *ch*, *tch*; consonant digraph *ph*; ending *-s*; ending *-ed* /ed/; ending *-ed* /d/; ending *-ed* /t/; ending *-ing*; ending *-ed*: drop *e*; ending *-ing*: drop *e*; CV syllable pattern (open syllables); contractions *'s*, *n't*; contractions *'ll*, *'d*; contractions *'ve*, *'re*; endings *-s*, *-es*; vowel digraphs *ai*, *ay*; vowel digraphs *ee*, *ea*; vowel digraphs *oa*, *ow*; compound words; schwa sound; ending *-ed*: double consonant; ending *-ing*: double consonant; long *i* spelled *igh*, *ie*; long *i* spelled *i*, *y*; long *e* spelled *y*; ending *-es*: change *y* to *i*; r-controlled *ar*; r-controlled *or*, *ore*; r-controlled *er*; r-controlled *ir*, *ur*; homophones; ending *-er*: double consonant; ending *-est*: double consonant; suffix *-y*; suffix *-ly*; suffix *-ful*; syllable *-tion*; syllable *-ture*; prefix *un-*; prefix *re-*; prefix *over-*; prefix *pre-*; prefix *mis-*; silent consonants *kn*, *gn*

Gran is teaching Ben to knit. Ben knows which yarn will make nice designs. He sits and helps Gran when she knits. Gnome and Knight try to help, too! Ben and Gran have a knack for knitting.

4

Ben Knocks

Each weekend, Ben runs to Gran's house to see her. He brings his knapsack with him. Ben knocks on her door. Knock, knock, knock!

Each time, Gran's dog, Gnome, sees Ben and barks.

1

Today, Gran is sitting inside with her cat, Knight. Gran is knitting with yarn. She likes to knit.

Gran knows Ben is knocking. "Is that my best grandson, Ben?" she calls out.

"Just grab the knob and come in!" Gran yells.

"Yes, Gran," says Ben. He turns the knob and goes in to see Gran. Gran smiles when she sees Ben.

Climbing with Lamb

© Houghton Mifflin Harcourt Publishing Company

BOOK 157

DECODABLE WORDS

Target Skill: **silent consonants *mb***

climb	climbing	lamb	thumb
climbers	crumbs	limb	

Previously Taught Skills

and	gets	Mom	stuffed	will
better	help	more	take	with
cake	hills	my	takes	
can	hurt	on	tell	
cannot	I	show	that	
eat	is	sit	then	
feed	kit	slice	trees	
feels	low	stay	until	
first-aid	means	steps	when	

SKILLS APPLIED IN WORDS IN STORY: short *a*; short *i*; short *o*; short *u*; short *e*; CVC syllable pattern (closed syllables); /g/ spelled *g*; compound words; long *a* (CVCe); long *i* (CVCe); /k/ spelled *c*; /s/ spelled *c*; blends with *r*; blends with *l*; blends with *s*; final blend *nd*; double final consonants *ll*, *ff*; consonant digraph *th*; consonant digraph *sh*; consonant digraph *wh*; ending -*ing*; ending -*s*; ending -*ed* /t/; vowel digraphs *ai, ay*; vowel digraphs *ee, ea*; vowel digraph *ow*; long *i* spelled *i, y*; r-controlled *ar*; r-controlled *ore*; r-controlled *er*; r-controlled *ir, ur*; suffix -*ful*; silent consonants *mb*   **From Grade 1:** consonants; short vowels; final blends

HIGH-FREQUENCY WORDS

a	care	head	of	too
again	careful	look	out	want
are	don't	love	she	
be	down	me	the	
calls	good	near	to	

Climbing with Lamb

High-Frequency Words Taught to Date

Grade 1

a	caught	friend	live	pictures	they	you	I've
about	city	friendship	long	play	think	young	kept
above	cold	full	look	please	those	your	knew
across	come	funny	loudly	pull	thought		might
after	could	give	loved	pushed	three	*Grade 2*	mind
again	country	go	make	put	to	afraid	morning
all	covers	goes	many	read	today	against	move
almost	cried	good	maybe	ready	together	air	next
along	different	great	me	right	too	also	other
always	do	green	minute	said	took	another	part
and	does	ground	more	school	toward	any	pretty
animal	done	grow	most	second	try	anything	really
are	don't	happy	mother	see	two	behind	river
around	door	have	my	seven	under	being	room
away	down	head	myself	shall	until	better	saw
baby	draw	hear	near	she	use	book	says
ball	earth	heard	never	should	very	care	sky
be	eat	help	new	show	walk	cheer	sleep
bear	eight	her	night	sing	want	children	slowly
beautiful	enough	here	no	small	warms	coming	someone
because	even	high	noise	soil	was	dark	something
been	every	hold	nothing	some	wash	didn't	sound
before	everyone	house	now	sometimes	watch	doing	stood
began	eyes	how	of	soon	water	else	store
begins	fall	I	off	sorry	we	ever	table
bird	family	idea	old	starts	were	everything	tall
blue	far	into	once	stories	what	floor	this
both	father	is	one	story	where	flower	though
boy	few	kinds	only	studied	who	found	told
bring	field	know	open	sure	why	front	turned
brothers	find	large	or	surprised	window	girl	voice
brown	first	laugh	our	take	with	gone	what's
buy	five	learning	out	talk	work	hair	without
by	follow	light	over	teacher	world	hard	words
call	food	like	own	the	would	hello	
car	for	listen	paper	their	write	horse	
carry	four	little	party	there	years	hundred	
			people	these	yellow	I'll	

Decoding skills taught to date: short *a*; short *i*; short *o*; short *u*; short *e*; CVC syllable pattern (closed syllables); long *a* (CVC*e*); long *i* (CVC*e*); /k/ spelled *c*; /s/ spelled *c*; long *o* (CVC*e*); long *u* /y$\overline{oo}$/ (CVC*e*); long *u* /$\overline{oo}$/ (CVC*e*); long *e* (CVC*e*); /g/ spelled *g*, /j/ spelled *g*, *dge*; blends with *r*; blends with *l*; blends with *s*; final blend *nd*; final blend *ng*; final blend *nk*; final blend *nt*; double final consonants *ll, ss, ff, zz*; consonants *ck*; double consonants (closed syllables); consonant digraph *th*; consonant digraph *sh*; consonant digraph *wh*; consonant digraphs *ch, tch*; consonant digraph *ph*; ending *-s*; ending *-ed* /ed/; ending *-ed* /d/; ending *-ed* /t/; ending *-ing*; ending *-ed*: drop *e*; ending *-ing*: drop *e*; CV syllable pattern (open syllables); contractions *'s, n't*; contractions *'ll, 'd*; contractions *'ve, 're*; endings *-s, -es*; vowel digraphs *ai, ay*; vowel digraphs *ee, ea*; vowel digraphs *oa, ow*; compound words; schwa sound; ending *-ed*: double consonant; ending *-ing*: double consonant; long *i* spelled *igh, ie*; long *i* spelled *i, y*; long *e* spelled *y*; ending *-es*: change *y* to *i*; r-controlled *ar*; r-controlled *or, ore*; r-controlled *er*; r-controlled *ir, ur*; homophones; ending *-er*: double consonant; ending *-est*: double consonant; suffix *-y*; suffix *-ly*; suffix *-ful*; syllable *-tion*; syllable *-ture*; prefix *un-*; prefix *re-*; prefix *over-*; prefix *pre-*; prefix *mis-*; silent consonants *kn, gn*; silent consonants *mb*

Climbing with Lamb

Look! My thumb feels better. That means I can climb again!

Lamb and I head out to climb the limb. I tell Lamb that I will be more careful.

I don't want to hurt my thumb again!

I love to climb. I climb steps. I climb hills. I climb trees.

When I climb, I take my stuffed lamb with me. I help Lamb climb, too.

Lamb and I are good climbers.

4

1

I sit on a low limb with Lamb. I eat a slice of cake. I feed the crumbs to Lamb.

Then Mom calls. Lamb and I climb down. On the climb down, I hurt my thumb on the limb.

I show my thumb to Mom. Mom gets out the first-aid kit and takes care of my thumb. I cannot climb until my thumb is better.

Lamb will stay with me. My thumb feels better when Lamb is near. She is a good lamb.

Crumb Cake

DECODABLE WORDS

Target Skill: silent consonants *mb*

climbs	crumb	crumbs	thumbs

Previously Taught Skills

and	eggs	last	on	until
at	fingers	like	pan	up
baked	finished	long	reach	use
bakes	first	lots	slice	wait
best	for	make	smells	yum
bowl	gets	makes	start	yummy
butter	hardly	milk	stir	
cake	help	mix	sweet	
can	her	mixed	then	
crunchy	I	mixing	things	
dump	in	Mom	this	
each	is	more	time	
eat	it	next	top	

SKILLS APPLIED IN WORDS IN STORY: short *a*; short *i*; short *o*; short *u*; short *e*; CVC syllable pattern (closed syllables); /s/ spelled *c*; /g/ spelled *g*; long *a* (CVCe); long *i* (CVCe); /k/ spelled *c*; long *u* /yo͞o/ (CVCe); blends with *r*; blends with *l*; blends with *s*; final blend *nd*; final blend *ng*; double final consonants *ll*; double consonants (closed syllables); consonant digraph *th*; consonant digraph *sh*; consonant digraph *ch*; ending -*s*; ending -*ed* /t/; ending -*ing*; vowel digraph *ai*; vowel digraphs *ee, ea*; vowel digraph *ow*; long *e* spelled *y*; long *i* spelled *i*; suffix -*y*; r-controlled *ar*; r-controlled *or, ore*; r-controlled *er*; r-controlled *ir*; suffix -*ly*; silent consonants *mb* **From Grade 1:** consonants; short vowels; final blends

HIGH-FREQUENCY WORDS

a	into	puts	to
all	of	she	we
go	our	the	

Houghton Mifflin Harcourt.

Crumb Cake

High-Frequency Words Taught to Date

Grade 1							
a	caught	friend	live	pictures	they	you	I've
about	city	friendship	long	play	think	young	kept
above	cold	full	look	please	those	your	knew
across	come	funny	loudly	pull	thought		might
after	could	give	loved	pushed	three	**Grade 2**	mind
again	country	go	make	put	to	afraid	morning
all	covers	goes	many	read	today	against	move
almost	cried	good	maybe	ready	together	air	next
along	different	great	me	right	too	also	other
always	do	green	minute	said	took	another	part
and	does	ground	more	school	toward	any	pretty
animal	done	grow	most	second	try	anything	really
are	don't	happy	mother	see	two	behind	river
around	door	have	my	seven	under	being	room
away	down	he	myself	shall	until	better	saw
baby	draw	head	near	she	use	book	says
ball	earth	hear	never	should	very	care	sky
be	eat	heard	new	show	walk	cheer	sleep
bear	eight	help	night	sing	want	children	slowly
beautiful	enough	her	no	small	warms	coming	someone
because	even	here	noise	soil	was	dark	something
been	every	high	nothing	some	wash	didn't	sound
before	everyone	hold	now	sometimes	watch	doing	stood
began	eyes	house	of	soon	water	else	store
begins	fall	how	off	sorry	we	ever	table
bird	family	I	old	starts	were	everything	tall
blue	far	idea	once	stories	what	floor	this
both	father	into	one	story	where	flower	though
boy	few	is	only	studied	who	found	told
bring	field	kinds	open	sure	why	front	turned
brothers	find	know	or	surprised	window	girl	voice
brown	first	large	our	take	with	gone	what's
buy	five	laugh	out	talk	work	hair	without
by	fly	learning	over	teacher	world	hard	words
call	follow	light	own	the	would	hello	
car	food	like	paper	their	write	horse	
carry	for	listen	party	there	years	hundred	
	four	little	people	these	yellow	I'll	

Decoding skills taught to date: short *a*; short *i*; short *o*; short *u*; short *e*; CVC syllable pattern (closed syllables); long *a* (CVC*e*); long *i* (CVC*e*); /k/ spelled *c*; /s/ spelled *c*; long *o* (CVC*e*); long *u* /yo͞o/ (CVC*e*); long *u* /o͞o/ (CVC*e*); long *e* (CVC*e*); /g/ spelled *g*; /j/ spelled *g, dge*; blends with *r*; blends with *l*; blends with *s*; final blend *nd*; final blend *ng*; final blend *nk*; final blend *nt*; double final consonants *ll, ss, ff, zz*; consonants *ck*; double consonants (closed syllables); consonant digraph *th*; consonant digraph *sh*; consonant digraph *wh*; consonant digraphs *ch, tch*; consonant digraph *ph*; ending *-s*; ending *-ed* /ed/; ending *-ed* /d/; ending *-ed* /t/; ending *-ing*; ending *-ed*: drop *e*; ending *-ing*: drop *e*; CV syllable pattern (open syllables); contractions *'s, n't*; contractions *'ll, 'd*; contractions *'ve, 're*; endings *-s, -es*; vowel digraphs *ai, ay*; vowel digraphs *ee, ea*; vowel digraphs *oa, ow*; compound words; schwa sound; ending *-ed*: double consonant; ending *-ing*: double consonant; long *i* spelled *igh, ie*; long *i* spelled *i, y*; long *e* spelled *y*; ending *-es*: change *y* to *i*; r-controlled *ar*; r-controlled *or, ore*; r-controlled *er*; r-controlled *ir, ur*; homophones; ending *-er*: double consonant; ending *-est*: double consonant; suffix *-y*; suffix *-ly*; suffix *-ful*; syllable *-tion*; syllable *-ture*; prefix *un-*; prefix *re-*; prefix *over-*; prefix *pre-*; prefix *mis-*; silent consonants *kn, gn*; silent consonants *mb*

Crumb Cake

Mom makes the best crumb cake.
I like to help her make the crumb cake.

First, Mom climbs up to reach the mixing bowl. She gets it, and then I start mixing.

The crumb cake bakes for a long time. I can hardly wait!

At last, it is finished, and it smells yummy! Mom and I each eat a slice. I like the crunchy crumbs on this sweet crumb cake. Yum, yum!

4

1

Lots of things go in the bowl to make crumb cake. Mom puts in eggs. I add milk, butter, and more things. Next, we stir the crumb cake until it is all mixed.

I dump the crumb cake mix into the pan. Then Mom makes the crumbs for the crumb cake. We use our fingers and thumbs to add the crumbs on top. Then the crumb cake is baked.

Ren Wren Wraps

DECODABLE WORDS

Target Skill: **silent consonants *wr***

unwraps	wraps	Wren's
wrapping	Wren	writes

Previously Taught Skills

and	hands	it's	playing	tape
big	hard	likes	quickly	thank
box	has	lines	Ren	thinks
cuts	her	lot	rest	this
day	his	name	rips	time
dots	in	nice	Ron	will
for	inside	on	such	with
fun	is	paper	surprise	
gift	it	plane	tag	

SKILLS APPLIED IN WORDS IN STORY: short *a*; short *i*; short *o*; short *e*; short *u*; CVC syllable pattern (closed syllables); long *a* (CVC*e*); long *i* (CVC*e*); /k/ spelled *c*; /s/ spelled *c*; /g/ spelled *g*; final blend *nd*; final blend *nk*; consonant digraph *th*; endings -*s*, -*ing*; ending -*ing*: double consonant; schwa sound; prefix *un*-; double final consonants *ll*; consonants *ck*; blends with *r*; blends with *l*; blends with *s*; r-controlled *ar*, *er*, *or*, *ur*; compound words; contraction *'s*; CV syllable pattern (open syllables); vowel digraph *ay*; suffix -*ly*; consonant digraph *ch*; silent consonants *wr* **From Grade 1:** consonants; short vowels; /kw/ spelled *qu*; final blends; possessives with *'s*

HIGH-FREQUENCY WORDS

a	gives	says	to
be	have	she	what
do	he	the	work
give	of	there	you

© Houghton Mifflin Harcourt Publishing Company

Houghton Mifflin Harcourt

Ren Wren Wraps

High-Frequency Words Taught to Date

Grade 1	caught	friend	live	pictures	they	you	I've
a	city	friendship	long	play	think	young	kept
about	cold	full	look	please	those	your	knew
above	come	funny	loudly	pull	thought		might
across	could	give	loved	pushed	three	*Grade 2*	mind
after	country	go	make	put	to	afraid	morning
again	covers	goes	many	read	today	against	move
all	cried	good	maybe	ready	together	air	next
almost	different	great	me	right	too	also	other
along	do	green	minute	said	took	another	part
always	does	ground	more	school	toward	any	pretty
and	done	grow	most	second	try	anything	really
animal	don't	happy	mother	see	two	behind	river
are	door	have	my	seven	under	being	room
around	down	he	myself	shall	until	better	saw
away	draw	head	near	she	use	book	says
baby	earth	hear	never	should	very	care	sky
ball	eat	heard	new	show	walk	cheer	sleep
be	eight	help	night	sing	want	children	slowly
bear	enough	her	no	small	warms	coming	someone
beautiful	even	here	noise	soil	was	dark	something
because	every	high	nothing	some	wash	didn't	sound
been	everyone	hold	now	sometimes	watch	doing	stood
before	eyes	house	of	soon	water	else	store
began	fall	how	off	sorry	we	ever	table
begins	family	I	old	starts	were	everything	tall
bird	far	idea	once	stories	what	floor	this
blue	father	into	one	story	where	flower	though
both	few	is	only	studied	who	found	told
boy	field	kinds	open	sure	why	front	turned
bring	find	know	or	surprised	window	girl	voice
brothers	first	large	our	take	with	gone	what's
brown	five	laugh	out	talk	work	hair	without
buy	fly	learning	over	teacher	world	hard	words
by	follow	light	own	the	would	hello	
call	food	like	paper	their	write	horse	
car	for	listen	party	there	years	hundred	
carry	four	little	people	these	yellow	I'll	

Decoding skills taught to date: short *a, i, o, u, e*; CVC syllable pattern (closed syllables); long *a* (CVC*e*); long *i* (CVC*e*); /k/ spelled *c*; /s/ spelled *c*; long *o* (CVC*e*); long *u* /yo͞o/ (CVC*e*); long *u* /o͞o/ (CVC*e*); long *e* (CVC*e*); /g/ spelled *g*; /j/ spelled *g, dge*; blends with *r*; blends with *l*; blends with *s*; final blend *nd*; final blend *ng*; final blend *nk*; final blend *nt*; double final consonants *ll, ss, ff, zz*; consonants *ck*; double consonants (closed syllables); consonant digraph *th*; consonant digraph *sh*; consonant digraph *wh*; consonant digraphs *ch, tch*; consonant digraph *ph*; ending *-s*; ending *-ed* /ed/; ending *-ed* /d/; ending *-ed* /t/; ending *-ing*; ending *-ed*: drop *e*; ending *-ing*: drop *e*; CV syllable pattern (open syllables); contractions *'s, n't*; contractions *'ll, 'd*; contractions *'ve, 're*; endings *-s, -es*; vowel digraphs *ai, ay*; vowel digraphs *ee, ea*; vowel digraphs *oa, ow*; compound words; schwa sound; ending *-ed*: double consonant; ending *-ing*: double consonant; long *i* spelled *igh, ie*; long *i* spelled *i, y*; long *e* spelled *y*; ending *-es*: change *y* to *i*; r-controlled *ar*; r-controlled *or, ore*; r-controlled *er*; r-controlled *ir, ur*; homophones; ending *-er*: double consonant; ending *-est*: double consonant; suffix *-y*; suffix *-ly*; suffix *-ful*; syllable *-tion*; syllable *-ture*; prefix *un-*; prefix *re-*; prefix *over-*; prefix *pre-*; prefix *mis-*; silent consonants *kn, gn*; silent consonants *mb*; silent consonants *wr*

Ren Wren gives the gift to Ron Wren.
Ron rips the paper and quickly unwraps
the box.

Ron Wren likes his plane a lot. He
says, "This is a big surprise! Thank you,
Ren. It is such a nice gift."

Ren Wren and Ron Wren have fun playing
with the plane for the rest of the day.

4

Ren Wren Wraps

Ren Wren has a big box in her hands.
There is a plane inside the box. What
will Ren Wren do with this box?

1

Ren Wren has tape and nice wrapping paper with dots and lines on it. She cuts the paper and wraps the box. It is hard work!

Ren Wren writes Ron Wren's name on a tag. It's time to give this gift to Ron Wren. Ren thinks this gift will be a big surprise to Ron!

© Houghton Mifflin Harcourt Publishing Company

Ren Wren Writes

DECODABLE WORDS

Target Skill: **silent consonants *wr***

shipwrecks	wrecked	Wren	write	writing
wrapping	wrecks	Wren's	writes	wrong

Previously Taught Skills

and	gets	Mom	paper	then
asks	has	name	pen	things
Ben	her	next	Ren	thinks
can	his	not	sheet	tries
car	if	on	show	with
fills	is	own	shows	
for	kinds	page	stop	
funny	lines	pages	tells	
get	makes	pals	that	

SKILLS APPLIED IN WORDS IN STORY: short *a*; short *i*; short *o*; short *e*; short *u*; CVC syllable pattern (closed syllables); long *a* (CVCe); long *i* (CVCe); /j/ spelled *g*; final blend *nd*; consonant digraph *th*; consonant digraph *sh*; ending *-s*; ending *-ed* /t/; ending *-ing*: drop *e*; vowel digraph *ow*; schwa sound; long *i* spelled *i, y, ie*; r-controlled *ar, er*; /k/ spelled *c*; /g/ spelled *g*; blends with *s*; double final consonants *ll*; final blend *ng*; final blend *nk*; compound words; double consonants (closed syllables); CV syllable pattern (open syllables); contraction *'s*; ending *-ing*: double consonant; ending *-es*: change *y* to *i*; long *e* spelled *y*; silent consonants *wr*   **From Grade 1:** consonants; short vowels; possessives with *'s*; final blends

HIGH-FREQUENCY WORDS

a	does	she	too
about	he	the	wants
all	of	to	what

Ren Wren Writes

High-Frequency Words Taught to Date

Grade 1	caught	friend	live	pictures	they	you	I've
a	city	friendship	long	play	think	young	kept
about	cold	full	look	please	those	your	knew
above	come	funny	loudly	pull	thought		might
across	could	give	loved	pushed	three	*Grade 2*	mind
after	country	go	make	put	to	afraid	morning
again	covers	goes	many	read	today	against	move
all	cried	good	maybe	ready	together	air	next
almost	different	great	me	right	too	also	other
along	do	green	minute	said	took	another	part
always	does	ground	more	school	toward	any	pretty
and	done	grow	most	second	try	anything	really
animal	don't	happy	mother	see	two	behind	river
are	door	have	my	seven	under	being	room
around	down	he	myself	shall	until	better	saw
away	draw	head	near	she	use	book	says
baby	earth	hear	never	should	very	care	sky
ball	eat	heard	new	show	walk	cheer	sleep
be	eight	help	night	sing	want	children	slowly
bear	enough	her	no	small	warms	coming	someone
beautiful	even	here	noise	soil	was	dark	something
because	every	high	nothing	some	wash	didn't	sound
been	everyone	hold	now	sometimes	watch	doing	stood
before	eyes	house	of	soon	water	else	store
began	fall	how	off	sorry	we	ever	table
begins	family	I	old	starts	were	everything	tall
bird	far	idea	once	stories	what	floor	this
blue	father	into	one	story	where	flower	though
both	few	is	only	studied	who	found	told
boy	field	kinds	open	sure	why	front	turned
bring	find	know	or	surprised	window	girl	voice
brothers	first	large	our	take	with	gone	what's
brown	five	laugh	out	talk	work	hair	without
buy	fly	learning	over	teacher	world	hard	words
by	follow	light	own	the	would	hello	
call	food	like	paper	their	write	horse	
car	for	listen	party	there	years	hundred	
carry	four	little	people	these	yellow	I'll	

Decoding skills taught to date: short *a, i, o, u, e*; CVC syllable pattern (closed syllables); long *a* (CVC*e*); long *i* (CVC*e*); /k/ spelled *c*; /s/ spelled *c*; long *o* (CVC*e*); long *u* /yōō/ (CVC*e*); long *u* /ōō/ (CVC*e*); long *e* (CVC*e*); /g/ spelled *g*; /j/ spelled *g, dge*; blends with *r*; blends with *l*; blends with *s*; final blend *nd*; final blend *ng*; final blend *nk*; final blend *nt*; double final consonants *ll, ss, ff, zz*; consonants *ck*; double consonants (closed syllables); consonant digraph *th*; consonant digraph *sh*; consonant digraph *wh*; consonant digraphs *ch, tch*; consonant digraph *ph*; ending *-s*; ending *-ed* /ed/; ending *-ed* /d/; ending *-ed* /t/; ending *-ing*; ending *-ed*: drop *e*; ending *-ing*: drop *e*; CV syllable pattern (open syllables); contractions '*s, n't*; contractions '*ll, 'd*; contractions '*ve, 're*; endings *-s, -es*; vowel digraphs *ai, ay*; vowel digraphs *ee, ea*; vowel digraphs *oa, ow*; compound words; schwa sound; ending *-ed*: double consonant; ending *-ing*: double consonant; long *i* spelled *igh, ie*; long *i* spelled *i, y*; long *e* spelled *y*; ending *-es*: change *y* to *i*; r-controlled *ar*; r-controlled *or, ore*; r-controlled *er*; r-controlled *ir, ur*; homophones; ending *-er*: double consonant; ending *-est*: double consonant; suffix *-y*; suffix *-ly*; suffix *-ful*; syllable *-tion*; syllable *-ture*; prefix *un-*; prefix *re-*; prefix *over-*; prefix *pre-*; prefix *mis-*; silent consonants *kn, gn*; silent consonants *mb*; silent consonants *wr*

Ren Wren shows Mom her writing.
She does not show Mom the page that
Ben wrecked.

Ren Wren tells Mom that Ben wants
to write, too. She asks Mom if Ben can
get his own paper for writing.

4

Ren Wren Writes

Ren Wren has a pen. Ren Wren writes
her name on a sheet of paper. Then she
thinks about what to write next.

1

© Houghton Mifflin Harcourt Publishing Company

Ren Wren writes about all kinds of things. She writes about wrapping gifts. She writes about her pals. She writes about car wrecks and shipwrecks.

Ren Wren fills pages and pages with her writing.

Ben Wren gets a pen. He tries to write and makes funny lines on Ren Wren's pages. Ren thinks that is wrong and asks Ben to stop.

Paul Caused It!

DECODABLE WORDS

Target Skill: /ô/ spelled *au, aw*

because	caused	launch	Paul	straw
cause	fault	launched	saw	

Previously Taught Skills

am	fine	it	right	this
and	finish	just	sat	tip
at	get	lunch	she	try
bench	hand	lunchtime	so	under
but	happen	Meg	sorry	up
can	he	mess	spilled	we
catch	help	milk	split	wet
clean	her	my	standing	when
drinking	his	on	sticky	with
eat	I	park	still	yelled
fell	is	reached	then	yes

SKILLS APPLIED IN WORDS IN STORY: short *a*; short *i*; CVC syllable pattern; short *o*; short *u*; short *e*; long *i* (CVC*e*); /k/ spelled *c*; /g/ spelled *g*; blends with *r*; blends with *l*; blends with *s*; final blend *nd*; final blend *nk*; double final consonants *ll*, *ss*, *ff*, *zz*; consonants *ck*; double consonants (closed syllables); consonant digraphs *th*, *sh*, *wh*, *ch*, *tch*; base words and ending -*ed*; base words and ending -*ing*; CV syllable pattern (open syllables); vowel digraphs *ee*, *ea*; compound words; schwa spelled *a, e, i, o, u*; long *i* spelled *igh, ie*; long *i* spelled *i, y*; long *e* spelled *y*; r-controlled *ar, or, er*; suffix -*y*; /ô/ spelled *au, aw* **From Grade 1:** short vowels; consonants; long *e* spelled *e*; long *o* spelled *o*

HIGH-FREQUENCY WORDS

a	down	said	was	you
all	food	the	were	
around	out	to	what	

© Houghton Mifflin Harcourt Publishing Company

Paul Caused It!

High-Frequency Words Taught to Date

Grade 1

a	caught	friend	live	pictures	they	you	I've
about	city	friendship	long	play	think	young	kept
above	cold	full	look	please	those	your	knew
across	come	funny	loudly	pull	thought		leaves
after	could	give	loved	pushed	three	*Grade 2*	might
again	country	go	make	put	to	afraid	mind
all	covers	goes	many	read	today	against	morning
almost	cried	good	maybe	ready	together	air	move
along	different	great	me	right	too	also	next
always	do	green	minute	said	took	another	other
and	does	ground	more	school	toward	any	part
animal	done	grow	most	second	try	anything	pretty
are	don't	happy	mother	see	two	behind	really
around	door	have	my	seven	under	being	river
away	down	he	myself	shall	until	better	room
baby	draw	head	near	she	use	book	saw
ball	earth	hear	never	should	very	care	says
be	eat	heard	new	show	walk	cheer	sky
bear	eight	help	night	sing	want	children	sleep
beautiful	enough	her	no	small	warms	coming	slowly
because	even	here	noise	soil	was	dark	someone
been	every	high	nothing	some	wash	didn't	something
before	everyone	hold	now	sometimes	watch	doing	sound
began	eyes	house	of	soon	water	else	stood
begins	fall	how	off	sorry	we	ever	store
bird	family	I	old	starts	were	everything	table
blue	far	idea	once	stories	what	floor	tall
both	father	into	one	story	where	flower	this
boy	few	is	only	studied	who	found	though
bring	field	kinds	open	sure	why	front	through
brothers	find	know	or	surprised	window	girl	told
brown	first	large	our	take	with	gone	turned
buy	five	laugh	out	talk	work	hair	voice
by	fly	learning	over	teacher	world	hard	what's
call	follow	light	own	the	would	hello	without
car	food	like	paper	their	write	horse	words
carry	for	listen	party	there	years	hundred	
	four	little	people	these	yellow	I'll	

Decoding skills taught to date: short *a*; short *i*; CVC syllable pattern; short *o*; short *u*; short *e*; long *a* (CVC*e*); long *i* (CVC*e*); /k/ spelled *c*; /s/ spelled *c*; long *o* (CVC*e*); long *u* /yōō/ (CVC*e*); long *u* /ōō/ (CVC*e*); long *e* (CVC*e*); /g/ spelled *g*; /j/ spelled *g*, *dge*; blends with *r*; blends with *l*; blends with *s*; final blend *nd*; final blend *ng*; final blend *nk*; final blend *nt*; double final consonants *ll*, *ss*, *ff*, *zz*; consonants *ck*; double consonants (closed syllables); consonant digraphs *th*, *sh*, *wh*, *ch*, *tch*, *ph*; base words and ending *-s*; base words and ending *-ed*; base words and ending *-ing*; CV syllable pattern (open syllables); contractions with *'s* and *n't*; contractions with *'ll* and *'d*; contractions with *'ve* and *'re*; base words and endings *-s*, *-es*; vowel digraphs *ai*, *ay*; vowel digraphs *ee*, *ea*; vowel digraphs *oa*, *ow*; compound words; schwa spelled *a*, *e*, *i*, *o*, *u*; ending *-ed*: double consonant; ending *-ing*: double consonant; long *i* spelled *igh*, *ie*; long *i* spelled *i*, *y*; long *e* spelled *y*; ending *-es*: change *y* to *i*; r-controlled *ar*, *or*, *ore*, *er*, *ir*, *ur*; homophones; ending *-er*: double consonant; ending *-est*: double consonant; suffixes *-y*, *-ly*, *-ful*; syllables *-tion*, *-ture*; prefixes *un-*, *re-*, *over-*, *pre-*, *mis-*; silent consonants *kn*, *gn*, *mb*, *wr*; /ô/ spelled *au*, *aw*
From Grade 1: short vowels; consonants; long *e* spelled *e*; long *o* spelled *o*

"I am so, so sorry," said Paul. "It was my fault! I was the cause!"

"My food is all around," said Meg, "but it is fine because we can clean up the mess."

"Yes, we can," said Paul. "Then we can split what we can still eat!"

4

Paul Caused It!

At lunchtime, Paul was at the park. He was drinking his milk with a straw. He saw a bench so he sat down to finish drinking. When Paul sat on the bench, he caused it to tip! The food launched up, up, up!

1

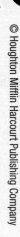

Meg saw it all happen. "My lunch," she yelled. "You caused my food to launch up!"

Paul reached up with his hand to try to help Meg catch her lunch.

Just then, the straw fell out and the milk spilled. Paul and Meg were standing right under the milk when it spilled! This caused Paul and Meg to get wet and sticky!

Paul Takes a Jaunt

DECODABLE WORDS

Target Skill: /ô/ spelled *au*, *aw*

cause	draws	jaunt	Paul's	saw
dawn	fault	launch	pause	taut
draw	hauls	Paul	raw	yawns

Previously Taught Skills

and	for	last	seagulls	trips
as	fun	lot	seeks	unties
at	gets	make	set	watch
away	has	not	sets	when
boat	he	on	short	while
but	his	plans	still	
can't	inside	rope	take	
cold	is	sail	takes	
dock	it	sailboat	trip	

SKILLS APPLIED IN WORDS IN STORY: short *a*; short *i*; CVC syllable pattern; short *o*; short *u*; short *e*; long *a* (CVC*e*); long *i* (CVC*e*); /k/ spelled *c*; long *o* (CVC*e*); /g/ spelled *g*; blends with *r*; blends with *l*; blends with *s*; final blend *nd*; final blend *nt*; double final consonants *ll*, *ss*, *ff*, *zz*; consonants *ck*; consonant digraphs *sh*, *wh*, *ch*, *tch*; base words and ending -*s*; CV syllable pattern (open syllables); contractions with *n't*; base words and endings -*s*, -*es*; vowel digraphs *ai*, *ay*; vowel digraphs *ee*, *ea*; vowel digraphs *oa*, *ow*; compound words; schwa spelled *a*, *e*, *i*, *o*, *u*; long *i* spelled *i*, *y*; ending -*es*: change *y* to *i*; *r*-controlled *or*; prefix *un*-; /ô/ spelled *au*, *aw* **From Grade 1:** short vowels; consonants; long *e* spelled *e*; long *o* spelled *o*; single possessives

HIGH-FREQUENCY WORDS

a	does	off	to
air	from	the	was
all	of	there	what

Houghton Mifflin Harcourt.

/ô/ spelled au, aw

BOOK 162

Paul Takes a Jaunt

High-Frequency Words Taught to Date

Grade 1

a	caught	friend	live	pictures	they	you
about	city	friendship	long	play	think	young
above	cold	full	look	please	those	your
across	come	funny	loudly	pull	thought	
after	could	give	loved	pushed	three	**Grade 2**
again	country	go	make	put	to	afraid
all	covers	goes	many	read	today	against
almost	cried	good	maybe	ready	together	air
along	different	great	me	right	too	also
always	do	green	minute	said	took	another
and	does	ground	more	school	toward	any
animal	done	grow	most	second	try	anything
are	don't	happy	mother	see	two	behind
around	door	have	my	seven	under	being
away	down	he	myself	shall	until	better
baby	draw	head	near	she	use	book
ball	earth	hear	never	should	very	care
be	eat	heard	new	show	walk	cheer
bear	eight	help	night	sing	want	children
beautiful	enough	her	no	small	warms	coming
because	even	here	noise	soil	was	dark
been	every	high	nothing	some	wash	didn't
before	everyone	hold	now	sometimes	watch	doing
began	eyes	house	of	soon	water	else
begins	fall	how	off	sorry	we	ever
bird	family	I	old	starts	were	everything
blue	far	idea	once	stories	what	floor
both	father	into	one	story	where	flower
boy	few	is	only	studied	who	found
bring	field	kinds	open	sure	why	front
brothers	find	know	or	surprised	window	girl
brown	first	large	our	take	with	gone
buy	five	laugh	out	talk	work	hair
by	fly	learning	over	teacher	world	hard
call	follow	light	own	the	would	hello
car	food	like	paper	their	write	horse
carry	for	listen	party	there	years	hundred
	four	little	people	these	yellow	I'll

I've
kept
knew
leaves
might
mind
morning
move
next
other
part
pretty
really
river
room
saw
says
sky
sleep
slowly
someone
something
sound
stood
store
table
tall
this
though
through
told
turned
voice
what's
without
words

Decoding skills taught to date: short *a*; short *i*; CVC syllable pattern; short *o*; short *u*; short *e*; long *a* (CVC*e*); long *i* (CVC*e*); /k/ spelled *c*; /s/ spelled *c*; long *o* (CVC*e*); long *u* /yōō/ (CVC*e*); long *u* /ōō/ (CVC*e*); long *e* (CVC*e*); /g/ spelled *g*; /j/ spelled *g*, *dge*; blends with *r*; blends with *l*; blends with *s*; final blend *nd*; final blend *ng*; final blend *nk*; final blend *nt*; double final consonants *ll*, *ss*, *ff*, *zz*; consonants *ck*; double consonants (closed syllables); consonant digraphs *th*, *sh*, *wh*, *ch*, *tch*, *ph*; base words and ending *-s*; base words and ending *-ed*; base words and ending *-ing*; CV syllable pattern (open syllables); contractions with *'s* and *n't*; contractions with *'ll* and *'d*; contractions with *'ve* and *'re*; base words and endings *-s*, *-es*; vowel digraphs *ai*, *ay*; vowel digraphs *ee*, *ea*; vowel digraphs *oa*, *ow*; compound words; schwa spelled *a*, *e*, *i*, *o*, *u*; ending *-ed*: double consonant; ending *-ing*: double consonant; long *i* spelled *igh*, *ie*; long *i* spelled *i*, *y*; long *e* spelled *y*; ending *-es*: change *y* to *i*; r-controlled *ar*, *or*, *ore*, *er*, *ir*, *ur*; homophones; ending *-er*: double consonant; ending *-est*: double consonant; suffixes *-y*, *-ly*, *-ful*; syllables *-tion*, *-ture*; prefixes *un-*, *re-*, *over-*, *pre-*, *mis-*; silent consonants *kn*, *gn*, *mb*, *wr*; /ô/ spelled *au*, *aw*
From Grade 1: short vowels; consonants; long *e* spelled *e*; long *o* spelled *o*; single possessives

It is still dawn as Paul's boat draws
away from the dock. Seagulls watch as
he sets off on his jaunt! Paul has a lot of
fun when he gets to take short trips on
his sailboat!

4

Paul Takes a Jaunt

Paul yawns. It is dawn. The air is
raw, but not cold.

Paul plans to take a short trip on his
boat. He hauls on a rope to make the sail
taut. Paul's boat is all set for the jaunt.

1

The boat does not draw away from the dock. Paul can't launch his boat. There is a pause while Paul seeks the cause.

At last, Paul saw what was at fault. The rope from the boat to the dock was still taut! Paul unties the rope and hauls it inside the boat.

A Walk in the Fall

DECODABLE WORDS

Target Skill: /ô/ spelled *al*, *a*

àll	always	fall	walk
almost	ball	sidewalk	water
also	call	talk	

Previously Taught Skills

after	fun	kids	play	tells
and	go	let's	put	that
as	has	likes	right	that's
away	he	me	run	throw
can	I	Mom	she	throws
close	in	nice	slip	today
day	is	no	so	us
far	it	on	such	we
for	it's	Paul	takes	with

SKILLS APPLIED IN WORDS IN STORY: short *a*; short *i*; CVC syllable pattern; short *o*; short *u*; short *e*; long *a* (CVC*e*); long *i* (CVC*e*); /k/ spelled *c*; /s/ spelled *c*; long *o* (CVC*e*); /g/ spelled *g*; blends with *r*; blends with *l*; blends with *s*; final blend *nd*; double final consonants *ll*, *ss*, *ff*, *zz*; consonant digraphs *th*, *sh*, *ch*; base words and ending *-s*; CV syllable pattern (open syllables); contractions with *'s*; vowel digraphs *ai*, *ay*; vowel digraphs *oa*, *ow*; compound words; schwa spelled *a*, *e*, *i*, *o*, *u*; long *i* spelled *igh*, *ie*; long *i* spelled *i*, *y*; r-controlled *ar*, *or*, *er*; /ô/ spelled *au*, *aw*, *al*, *a* **From Grade 1:** short vowels; consonants; long *o* spelled *o*; long *e* spelled *e*

HIGH-FREQUENCY WORDS

a	else	here	to	wants
anyone	great	the	too	was
comes	have	there('s)	want	

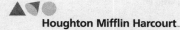
Houghton Mifflin Harcourt.

A Walk in the Fall

High-Frequency Words Taught to Date

Grade 1	caught	friend	live	pictures	they	you	I've
a	city	friendship	long	play	think	young	kept
about	cold	full	look	please	those	your	knew
above	come	funny	loudly	pull	thought		leaves
across	could	give	loved	pushed	three	*Grade 2*	might
after	country	go	make	put	to	afraid	mind
again	covers	goes	many	read	today	against	morning
all	cried	good	maybe	ready	together	air	move
almost	different	great	me	right	too	also	next
along	do	green	minute	said	took	another	other
always	does	ground	more	school	toward	any	part
and	done	grow	most	second	try	anything	pretty
animal	don't	happy	mother	see	two	behind	really
are	door	have	my	seven	under	being	river
around	down	he	myself	shall	until	better	room
away	draw	head	near	she	use	book	saw
baby	earth	hear	never	should	very	care	says
ball	eat	heard	new	show	walk	cheer	sky
be	eight	help	night	sing	want	children	sleep
bear	enough	her	no	small	warms	coming	slowly
beautiful	even	here	noise	soil	was	dark	someone
because	every	high	nothing	some	wash	didn't	something
been	everyone	hold	now	sometimes	watch	doing	sound
before	eyes	house	of	soon	water	else	stood
began	fall	how	off	sorry	we	ever	store
begins	family	I	old	starts	were	everything	table
bird	far	idea	once	stories	what	floor	tall
blue	father	into	one	story	where	flower	this
both	few	is	only	studied	who	found	though
boy	field	kinds	open	sure	why	front	through
bring	find	know	or	surprised	window	girl	told
brothers	first	large	our	take	with	gone	turned
brown	five	laugh	out	talk	work	hair	voice
buy	fly	learning	over	teacher	world	hard	what's
by	follow	light	own	the	would	hello	without
call	food	like	paper	their	write	horse	words
car	for	listen	party	there	years	hundred	
carry	four	little	people	these	yellow	I'll	

Decoding skills taught to date: short *a*; short *i*; CVC syllable pattern; short *o*; short *u*; short *e*; long *a* (CVC*e*); long *i* (CVC*e*); /k/ spelled *c*; /s/ spelled *c*; long *o* (CVC*e*); long *u* /yoo/ (CVC*e*); long *u* /oo/ (CVC*e*); long *e* (CVC*e*); /g/ spelled *g*; /j/ spelled *g*, *dge*; blends with *r*; blends with *l*; blends with *s*; final blend *nd*; final blend *ng*; final blend *nk*; final blend *nt*; double final consonants *ll*, *ss*, *ff*, *zz*; consonants *ck*; double consonants (closed syllables); consonant digraphs *th*, *sh*, *wh*, *ch*, *tch*, *ph*; base words and ending *-s*; base words and ending *-ed*; base words and ending *-ing*; CV syllable pattern (open syllables); contractions with *'s* and *n't*; contractions with *'ll* and *'d*; contractions with *'ve* and *'re*; base words and endings *-s*, *-es*; vowel digraphs *ai*, *ay*; vowel digraphs *ee*, *ea*; vowel digraphs *oa*, *ow*; compound words; schwa spelled *a*, *e*, *i*, *o*, *u*; ending *-ed*: double consonant; ending *-ing*: double consonant; long *i* spelled *igh*, *ie*; long *i* spelled *i*, *y*; long *e* spelled *y*; ending *-es*: change *y* to *i*; r-controlled *ar*, *or*, *ore*, *er*, *ir*, *ur*; homophones; ending *-er*: double consonant; ending *-est*: double consonant; suffixes *-y*, *-ly*, *-ful*; syllables *-tion*, *-ture*; prefixes *un-*, *re-*, *over-*, *pre-*, *mis-*; silent consonants *kn*, *gn*, *mb*, *wr*; /ô/ spelled *au*, *aw*, *al*, *a*
From Grade 1: short vowels; consonants; long *o* spelled *o*; long *e* spelled *e*

A Walk in the Fall

"Kids, put the ball away," Mom tells us. "It's such a nice day. Let's walk. Let's talk. Let's have fun in the fall."

As always, Mom is right. We all have a great day.

Today is a nice fall day, so Paul and I want to go for a walk.

"Anyone else want to go?" we call. Mom tells us she also wants to go. That's nice! We can all go for a walk!

Paul takes a ball. He always has a ball and likes to play with it.

"Paul!" I call. "Throw me the ball!"

"All right! Here it comes!"

Paul throws the ball. He throws it too far!

I run after the ball. No! There's water on the sidewalk.

I slip and almost fall! That was close.

Water in the Hall!

DECODABLE WORDS

Target Skill: /ô/ spelled *al*, *a*

all	call	fall	small	wall
almost	called	hall	walk	water
always	chalk	hallway	walked	

Previously Taught Skills

about	day	he	looking	right	turned
and	desk	his	math	run	up
around	didn't	huge	mess	see	us
at	down	hurt	my	slide	very
away	face	I	not	slip	wait
back	finish	in	on	stopped	we
bell	for	is	or	teacher	went
big	gather	just	out	tell	when
bit	get	keep	over	that	will
came	go	left	problem	things	
can	going	let's	put	this	
cleaned	happy	lined	rang	told	

SKILLS APPLIED IN WORDS IN STORY: short *a*; short *i*; short *o*; short *u*; short *e*; long *a* (CVC*e*); long *i* (CVC*e*); /k/ spelled *c*; /s/ spelled *c*; long *u* /yōō/ (CVC*e*); /g/ spelled *g*; /j/ spelled *g*, *dge*; blends with *l*; blends with *s*; final blend *nd*; final blend *ng*; final blend *nt*; double final consonants *ll*, *ss*, *ff*, *zz*; consonants *ck*; double consonants (closed syllables); consonant digraphs *th*, *sh*, *wh*, *ch*; base words and ending -*s*; base words and ending -*ed*; base words and ending -*ing*; CV syllable pattern (open syllables); contractions with '*s* and *n't*; vowel digraphs *ai*, *ay*; vowel digraphs *ee*, *ea*; compound words; schwa spelled *a*, *e*, *i*, *o*, *u*; ending -*ed*: double consonant; long *i* spelled *igh*, *ie*; long *i* spelled *i*, *y*; long *e* spelled *y*; r-controlled *or*, *er*, *ur*; suffix -*ful*; /ô/ spelled *au*, *aw*, *al*, *a* **From Grade 1:** short vowels; consonants; /ou/ spelled *ou*, *ow*; long *e* spelled *e*; long *o* spelled *o*; /ōō/ spelled *oo*

HIGH-FREQUENCY WORDS

a	don't	have	school	to	were
care(ful)	floor	here	someone	want	what
could	from	our	the	was	

Houghton Mifflin Harcourt

Water in the Hall!

High-Frequency Words Taught to Date

Grade 1	caught	friend	live	pictures	they	you	I've
a	city	friendship	long	play	think	young	kept
about	cold	full	look	please	those	your	knew
above	come	funny	loudly	pull	thought		leaves
across	could	give	loved	pushed	three	**Grade 2**	might
after	country	go	make	put	to	afraid	mind
again	covers	goes	many	read	today	against	morning
all	cried	good	maybe	ready	together	air	move
almost	different	great	me	right	too	also	next
along	do	green	minute	said	took	another	other
always	does	ground	more	school	toward	any	part
and	done	grow	most	second	try	anything	pretty
animal	don't	happy	mother	see	two	behind	really
are	door	have	my	seven	under	being	river
around	down	he	myself	shall	until	better	room
away	draw	head	near	she	use	book	saw
baby	earth	hear	never	should	very	care	says
ball	eat	heard	new	show	walk	cheer	sky
be	eight	help	night	sing	want	children	sleep
bear	enough	her	no	small	warms	coming	slowly
beautiful	even	here	noise	soil	was	dark	someone
because	every	high	nothing	some	wash	didn't	something
been	everyone	hold	now	sometimes	watch	doing	sound
before	eyes	house	of	soon	water	else	stood
began	fall	how	off	sorry	we	ever	store
begins	family	I	old	starts	were	everything	table
bird	far	idea	once	stories	what	floor	tall
blue	father	into	one	story	where	flower	this
both	few	is	only	studied	who	found	though
boy	field	kinds	open	sure	why	front	through
bring	find	know	or	surprised	window	girl	told
brothers	first	large	our	take	with	gone	turned
brown	five	laugh	out	talk	work	hair	voice
buy	fly	learning	over	teacher	world	hard	what's
by	follow	light	own	the	would	hello	without
call	food	like	paper	their	write	horse	words
car	for	listen	party	there	years	hundred	
carry	four	little	people	these	yellow	I'll	

Decoding skills taught to date: short *a*; short *i*; CVC syllable pattern; short *o*; short *u*; short *e*; long *a* (CVC*e*); long *i* (CVC*e*); /k/ spelled *c*; /s/ spelled *c*; long *o* (CVC*e*); long *u* /yōo/ (CVC*e*); long *u* /ōo/ (CVC*e*); long *e* (CVC*e*); /g/ spelled *g*; /j/ spelled *g*, *dge*; blends with *r*; blends with *l*; blends with *s*; final blend *nd*; final blend *ng*; final blend *nk*; final blend *nt*; double final consonants *ll*, *ss*, *ff*, *zz*; consonants *ck*; double consonants (closed syllables); consonant digraphs *th*, *sh*, *wh*, *ch*, *tch*, *ph*; base words and ending -*s*; base words and ending -*ed*; base words and ending -*ing*; CV syllable pattern (open syllables); contractions with *'s* and *n't*; contractions with *'ll* and *'d*; contractions with *'ve* and *'re*; base words and endings -*s*, -*es*; vowel digraphs *ai*, *ay*; vowel digraphs *ee*, *ea*; vowel digraphs *oa*, *ow*; compound words; schwa spelled *a*, *e*, *i*, *o*, *u*; ending -*ed*: double consonant; ending -*ing*: double consonant; long *i* spelled *igh*, *ie*; long *i* spelled *i*, *y*; long *e* spelled *y*; ending -*es*: change *y* to *i*; r-controlled *ar*, *or*, *ore*, *er*, *ir*, *ur*; homophones; ending -*er*: double consonant; ending -*est*: double consonant; suffixes -*y*, -*ly*, -*ful*; syllables -*tion*, -*ture*; prefixes *un*-, *re*-, *over*-, *pre*-, *mis*-; silent consonants *kn*, *gn*, *mb*, *wr*; /ô/ spelled *au*, *aw*, *al*, *a*
From Grade 1: short vowels; consonants; /ou/ spelled *ou*, *ow*; long *e* spelled *e*; long *o* spelled *o*; /ōo/ spelled *oo*

Water in the Hall!

Our teacher is always very careful.
He told us to walk, not run, in the hall.
He didn't want us to slip or slide on the
water and get hurt.

"Let's keep the small problem small!" he
called. "Don't fall or get water all over!"

I was about to finish a math problem
when the bell on the wall rang. The
school day was over!

I put the chalk away and went back
to my desk to gather all my things.

4

1

We all lined up and were about to go out to the hallway when our teacher stopped us.

"Wait right here for a bit," he told us. "We have a small problem in the hall. I can see water on the floor."

He turned around and walked down the hall to see what was going on.

When he came back, we could tell that he was not happy from just looking at his face.

"That small problem was almost a huge problem. Someone left the water on! I will call to get this big mess cleaned up right away."

An Author Thinks and Thinks

DECODABLE WORDS

Target Skill: /ô/ spelled *o*

broth	cloth	moss	soft	strong	tossing

Previously Taught Skills

about	bright	flies	more	sitting	thinking
an	can	hawk	much	sleepy	thinks
and	dawn	he	next	snacks	this
around	day	him	nice	so	trees
at	desk	his	on	starts	will
August	draped	in	out	story	window
author	draws	is	over	summer	write
bald	drink	it	picnic	sun	yawns
behind	eagle	job	scrap	tall	
big	eat	launches	sees	then	
bird	finish	makes	sits	think	

SKILLS APPLIED IN WORDS IN STORY: short *a*; short *i*; CVC syllable pattern; short *o*; short *u*; short *e*; long *a* (CVC*e*); long *i* (CVC*e*); /k/ spelled *c*; /s/ spelled *c*; /g/ spelled *g*; blends with *r*; blends with *l*; blends with *s*; final blend *nd*; final blend *ng*; final blend *nk*; double final consonants *ll*, *ss*, *ff*, *zz*; consonants *ck*; double consonants (closed syllables); consonant digraphs *th*, *sh*, *ch*; base words and ending -*s*; base words and ending -*ed*; base words and ending -*ing*; CV syllable pattern (open syllables); base words and endings -*s*, -*es*; vowel digraphs *ai*, *ay*; vowel digraphs *ee*, *ea*; vowel digraphs *oa*, *ow*; schwa spelled *a*, *e*, *i*, *o*, *u*; ending -*ing*: double consonant; long *i* spelled *igh*, *ie*; long *i* spelled *i*, *y*; long *e* spelled *y*; ending -*es*: change *y* to *i*; r-controlled *ar*, *or*, *ore*, *er*, *ir*; suffix -*y*; silent consonants *wr*; /ô/ spelled *au*, *aw*, *al*, *a*, *o* **From Grade 1:** short vowels; consonants; long *e* spelled *e*; long *o* spelled *o*; syllable _*le*; /ou/ spelled *ou*

HIGH-FREQUENCY WORDS

a	for	into	people	to
air	head	look(ing)	some	what
another	idea(s)	of	the	

© Houghton Mifflin Harcourt Publishing Company

Houghton Mifflin Harcourt.

An Author Thinks and Thinks

High-Frequency Words Taught to Date

Grade 1

a	caught	friend	live	pictures	they	you	I've
about	city	friendship	long	play	think	young	leaves
above	cold	full	look	please	those	your	kept
across	come	funny	loudly	pull	thought		might
after	could	give	loved	pushed	three	*Grade 2*	mind
again	country	go	make	put	to	afraid	morning
all	covers	goes	many	read	today	against	move
almost	cried	good	maybe	ready	together	air	next
along	different	great	me	right	too	also	other
always	do	green	minute	said	took	another	part
and	does	ground	more	school	toward	any	pretty
animal	done	grow	most	second	try	anything	really
are	don't	happy	mother	see	two	behind	river
around	door	have	my	seven	under	being	room
away	down	he	myself	shall	until	better	saw
baby	draw	head	near	she	use	book	says
ball	earth	hear	never	should	very	care	sky
be	eat	heard	new	show	walk	cheer	sleep
bear	eight	help	night	sing	want	children	slowly
beautiful	enough	her	no	small	warms	coming	someone
because	even	here	noise	soil	was	dark	something
been	every	high	nothing	some	wash	didn't	sound
before	everyone	hold	now	sometimes	watch	doing	stood
began	eyes	house	of	soon	water	else	store
begins	fall	how	off	sorry	we	ever	table
bird	family	I	old	starts	were	everything	tall
blue	far	idea	once	stories	what	floor	this
both	father	into	one	story	where	flower	through
boy	few	is	only	studied	who	front	told
bring	field	kinds	open	sure	why	found	turned
brothers	find	know	or	surprised	window	girl	voice
brown	first	large	our	take	with	gone	what's
buy	five	laugh	out	talk	work	hair	without
by	fly	learning	over	teacher	world	hard	words
call	follow	light	own	the	would	hello	
car	food	like	paper	their	write	horse	
carry	for	listen	party	there	years	hundred	
	four	little	people	these	yellow	I'll	

Decoding skills taught to date: short *a*; short *i*; CVC syllable pattern; short *o*; short *u*; short *e*; long *a* (CVC*e*); long *i* (CVC*e*); /k/ spelled *c*; /s/ spelled *c*; long *o* (CVC*e*); long *u* /yōō/ (CVC*e*); long *u* /ōō/ (CVC*e*); long *e* (CVC*e*); /g/ spelled *g*; /j/ spelled *g*, *dge*; blends with *r*; blends with *l*; blends with *s*; final blend *nd*; final blend *ng*; final blend *nk*; final blend *nt*; double final consonants *ll*, *ss*, *ff*, *zz*; consonants *ck*; double consonants (closed syllables); consonant digraphs *th*, *sh*, *wh*, *ch*, *tch*, *ph*; base words and ending -*s*; base words and ending -*ed*; base words and ending -*ing*; CV syllable pattern (open syllables); contractions with *'s* and *n't*; contractions with *'ll* and *'d*; contractions with *'ve* and *'re*; base words and endings -*s*, -*es*; vowel digraphs *ai*, *ay*; vowel digraphs *ee*, *ea*; vowel digraphs *oa*, *ow*; compound words; schwa spelled *a*, *e*, *i*, *o*, *u*; ending -*ed*: double consonant; ending -*ing*: double consonant; long *i* spelled *igh*, *ie*; long *i* spelled *i*, *y*; long *e* spelled *y*; ending -*es*: change *y* to *i*; r-controlled *ar*, *or*, *ore*, *er*, *ir*, *ur*; homophones; ending -*er*: double consonant; ending -*est*: double consonant; suffixes -*y*, -*ly*, -*ful*; syllables -*tion*, -*ture*; prefixes *un*-, *re*-, *over*-, *pre*-, *mis*-; silent consonants *kn*, *gn*, *mb*, *wr*; /ô/ spelled *au*, *aw*, *al*, *a*, *o*   **From Grade 1:** short vowels; consonants; long *e* spelled *e*; long *o* spelled *o*; syllable _*le*; /ou/ spelled *ou*

The author yawns. He is sleepy.
He will finish his story another day.

He draws on what he sees around
him for ideas, and what he sees makes
him think about so much more.

What a nice job!

4

An Author Thinks and Thinks

This author sits at his desk, thinking
and thinking. He is looking out the
window and tossing ideas around in
his head.

It is a nice day. The sun is bright.
What can he write about?

1

He sees a big hawk. The strong bird makes him think of a bald eagle.

He starts to write a story about a bald eagle at dawn. The eagle launches into the air and flies over the tall trees.

2

Then he sees a scrap of soft cloth draped behind him. This makes him think of a summer picnic.

He starts to write about a picnic in August. Sitting next to some moss, the people drink broth and eat snacks.

3

A Launch at Dawn

DECODABLE WORDS

Target Skill: /ô/ spelled *o*

blastoff	boss	long	off	strong	toss

Previously Taught Skills

afraid	can't	Hawk	it	person	think
also	dawn	Hawk's	just	pumps	thinks
an	fall	he	launch	put	this
and	float	helmet	lot	rocket	time
applaud	for	he's	lots	see	Tom
astronaut	Friday	him	luck	shape	train
at	fun	his	make	stay	up
awful	go	home	my	take	when
be	goes	I	name	tests	while
but	going	in	need	that	will
calls	had	is	no	them	with
can	happen	isn't	on	things	yell

SKILLS APPLIED IN WORDS IN STORY: short *a*; short *i*; CVC syllable pattern; short *o*; short *u*; short *e*; long *a* (CVC*e*); long *i* (CVC*e*); /k/ spelled *c*; /s/ spelled *c*; long *o* (CVC*e*); /g/ spelled *g*; blends with *r*; blends with *l*; blends with *s*; final blend *nd*; final blend *ng*; final blend *nk*; double final consonants *ll*, *ss*, *ff*, *zz*; consonants *ck*; double consonants (closed syllables); consonant digraphs *th*, *sh*, *wh*, *ch*; base words and ending -*s*; CV syllable pattern (open syllables); contractions with *'s* and *n't*; base words and endings -*s*, -*es*; vowel digraphs *ai*, *ay*; vowel digraphs *ee*, *ea*; vowel digraphs *oa*, *ow*; compound words; schwa spelled *a*, *e*, *i*, *o*, *u*; long *i* spelled *i*, *y*; r-controlled *or*, *er*; suffix -*ful*; /ô/ spelled *au*, *aw*, *al*, *a*, *o* **From Grade 1**: short vowels; consonants; long *e* spelled *e*; long *o* spelled *o*; single possessives

HIGH-FREQUENCY WORDS

a	care(ful)	everyone	people	they
air	come	good	sure	to
because	don't	have	the	was
before	down	of	there	would

Houghton Mifflin Harcourt.

A Launch at Dawn

High-Frequency Words Taught to Date

Grade 1

a	caught	friend	live	pictures	they	you	I've
about	city	friendship	long	play	think	young	kept
above	cold	full	look	please	those	your	knew
across	come	funny	loudly	pull	thought		leaves
after	could	give	loved	pushed	three	**Grade 2**	might
again	country	go	make	put	to	afraid	mind
all	covers	goes	many	read	today	against	morning
almost	cried	good	maybe	ready	together	air	move
along	different	great	me	right	too	also	next
always	do	green	minute	said	took	another	other
and	does	ground	more	school	toward	any	part
animal	done	grow	most	second	try	anything	pretty
are	don't	happy	mother	see	two	behind	really
around	door	have	my	seven	under	being	river
away	down	he	myself	shall	until	better	room
baby	draw	head	near	she	use	book	saw
ball	earth	hear	never	should	very	care	says
be	eat	heard	new	show	walk	cheer	sky
bear	eight	help	night	sing	want	children	sleep
beautiful	enough	her	no	small	warms	coming	slowly
because	even	here	noise	soil	was	dark	someone
been	every	high	nothing	some	wash	didn't	something
before	everyone	hold	now	sometimes	watch	doing	sound
began	eyes	house	of	soon	water	else	stood
begins	fall	how	off	sorry	we	ever	store
bird	family	I	old	starts	were	everything	table
blue	far	idea	once	stories	what	floor	tall
both	father	into	one	story	where	flower	this
boy	few	is	only	studied	who	found	though
bring	field	kinds	open	sure	why	front	through
brothers	find	know	or	surprised	window	girl	told
brown	first	large	our	take	with	gone	turned
buy	five	laugh	out	talk	work	hair	voice
by	fly	learning	over	teacher	world	hard	what's
call	follow	light	own	the	would	hello	without
car	food	like	paper	their	write	horse	words
carry	for	listen	party	there	years	hundred	
	four	little	people	these	yellow	I'll	

Decoding skills taught to date: short *a*; short *i*; CVC syllable pattern; short *o*; short *u*; short *e*; long *a* (CVC*e*); long *i* (CVC*e*); /k/ spelled *c*; /s/ spelled *c*; long *o* (CVC*e*); long *u* /yoo/ (CVC*e*); long *u* /oo/ (CVC*e*); long *e* (CVC*e*); /g/ spelled *g*; /j/ spelled *g*, *dge*; blends with *r*; blends with *l*; blends with *s*; final blend *nd*; final blend *ng*; final blend *nk*; final blend *nt*; double final consonants *ll*, *ss*, *ff*, *zz*; consonants *ck*; double consonants (closed syllables); consonant digraphs *th*, *sh*, *wh*, *ch*, *tch*, *ph*; base words and ending -*s*; base words and ending -*ed*; base words and ending -*ing*; CV syllable pattern (open syllables); contractions with *'s* and *n't*; contractions with *'ll* and *'d*; contractions with *'ve* and *'re*; base words and endings -*s*, -*es*; vowel digraphs *ai*, *ay*; vowel digraphs *ee*, *ea*; vowel digraphs *oa*, *ow*; compound words; schwa spelled *a*, *e*, *i*, *o*, *u*; ending -*ed*: double consonant; ending -*ing*: double consonant; long *i* spelled *igh*, *ie*; long *i* spelled *i*, *y*; long *e* spelled *y*; ending -*es*: change *y* to *i*; r-controlled *ar*, *or*, *ore*, *er*, *ir*, *ur*; homophones; ending -*er*: double consonant; ending -*est*: double consonant; suffixes -*y*, -*ly*, -*ful*; syllables -*tion*, -*ture*; prefixes *un*-, *re*-, *over*-, *pre*-, *mis*-; silent consonants *kn*, *gn*, *mb*, *wr*; /ô/ spelled *au*, *aw*, *al*, *a*, *o* **From Grade 1:** short vowels; consonants; long *e* spelled *e*; long *o* spelled *o*; single possessives

On Friday, a lot of people will come see the launch. They will yell and applaud.

Blastoff! There goes Hawk! Good luck!

4

A Launch at Dawn

This is my boss. His name is Tom, but everyone calls him Hawk. He is an astronaut!

Hawk had to train for a long time before going to space. He had to take lots of tests and stay in shape. He had to make sure he was strong!

1

On Friday, Hawk will go to space! His rocket will launch at dawn. The rocket will be Hawk's home while he's in space.

A lot can happen when a person goes to space. I would be afraid to go, but my boss isn't. Hawk thinks it will be fun. I think it would be awful!

Hawk will have to put on a helmet that pumps air. Hawk can't take the helmet off because there is no air in space!

Also, Hawk will need to be careful with his things. He can't just toss them up in the air! Things float in space. They don't fall down!

2

3

Under the Moon

BOOK 167

DECODABLE WORDS

Target Skill: /o͞o/ spelled *oo, ou*

brood	food	hoot	raccoon	smooth	through
cool	group	Moon	room	soon	

Previously Taught Skills

and	bright	gets	its	reads	tries
animals	bugs	glow	keep	right	try
asleep	by	go	lake	rising	under
at	can	goes	large	see	underwater
away	closer	he	light	she	up
babies	den	her	mom	sky	use
baby	eat	high	nest	sleep	wade
back	falls	him	night	small	wakes
bed	feed	his	now	story	water
big	find	in	or	tall	will
birds	for	inside	over	then	window
boy	gathers	is	plants	trees	wings

SKILLS APPLIED IN WORDS IN STORY: short *a*; short *i*; CVC syllable pattern; short *o*; short *u*; short *e*; long *a* (CVCe); long *i* (CVCe); /k/ spelled *c*; long *o* (CVCe); long *u* /yo͞o/ (CVCe); /g/ spelled *g*; /j/ spelled *g*; blends with *r*; blends with *l*; blends with *s*; final blend *nd*; final blend *ng*; final blend *nt*; double final consonants *ll, ss, ff, zz*; consonants *ck*; double consonants (closed syllables); consonant digraphs *th, sh*; base words and ending -*s*; base words and ending -*ing*; CV syllable pattern (open syllables); base words and endings -*s*, -*es*; vowel digraph *ay*; vowel digraphs *ee, ea*; vowel digraph *ow*; compound words; schwa spelled *a, e, i, o, u*; long *i* spelled *igh*; long *i* spelled *i, y*; long *e* spelled *y*; ending -*es*: change *y* to *i*; r-controlled *ar, or, er, ir*; /ô/ spelled *al, a*; /o͞o/ spelled *oo, ou* **From Grade 1:** short vowels; consonants; long *o* spelled *o*; long *e* spelled *e*; /ou/ spelled *ow*; vowel diphthong *oy*

HIGH-FREQUENCY WORDS

a	air	hear(s)	look(s)	out	to
about	from	leaves	of	the	

© Houghton Mifflin Harcourt Publishing Company

Under the Moon

High-Frequency Words Taught to Date

Grade 1	city	full	loudly	pushed	to	against	mind
a	cold	funny	loved	put	today	ago	morning
about	come	give	make	read	together	air	move
above	could	go	many	ready	too	alone	next
across	country	goes	maybe	right	took	also	other
after	covers	good	me	said	toward	another	part
again	cried	great	minute	school	try	any	pretty
all	different	green	more	second	two	anything	really
almost	do	ground	most	see	under	behind	river
along	does	grow	mother	seven	until	being	room
always	done	happy	my	shall	use	better	saw
and	don't	have	myself	she	very	book	says
animal	door	he	near	should	walk	care	sky
are	down	head	never	show	want	cheer	sleep
around	draw	hear	new	sing	warms	children	slowly
away	earth	heard	night	small	was	coming	someone
baby	eat	help	no	soil	wash	dark	something
ball	eight	her	noise	some	watch	didn't	sound
be	enough	here	nothing	sometimes	water	doing	stood
bear	even	high	now	soon	we	else	store
beautiful	every	hold	of	sorry	were	ever	table
because	everyone	house	off	starts	what	everything	tall
been	eyes	how	old	stories	where	floor	this
before	fall	I	once	story	who	flower	though
began	family	idea	one	studied	why	found	through
begins	far	into	only	sure	window	front	told
bird	father	is	open	surprised	with	girl	turned
blue	few	kinds	or	take	work	gone	voice
both	field	know	our	talk	world	hair	what's
boy	find	large	out	teacher	would	hard	without
bring	first	laugh	over	the	write	hello	won't
brothers	five	learning	own	their	years	horse	words
brown	fly	light	paper	there	yellow	hundred	
buy	follow	like	party	these	you	I'll	
by	food	listen	people	they	young	I've	
call	for	little	pictures	think	your	kept	
car	four	live	play	those		knew	
carry	friend	long	please	thought	*Grade 2*	leaves	
caught	friendship	look	pull	three	afraid	might	

Decoding skills taught to date: short *a*; short *i*; CVC syllable pattern; short *o*; short *u*; short *e*; long *a* (CVC*e*); long *i* (CVC*e*); /k/ spelled *c*; /s/ spelled *c*; long *o* (CVC*e*); long *u* /yōō/ (CVC*e*); long *u* /ōō/ (CVC*e*); long *e* (CVC*e*); /g/ spelled *g*; /j/ spelled *g*, *dge*; blends with *r*, blends with *l*, blends with *s*; final blend *-nd*; final blend *ng*; final blend *nk*; final blend *nt*; double final consonants *ll*, *ss*, *ff*, *zz*; consonants *ck*; double consonants (closed syllables); consonant digraphs *th*, *sh*, *wh*, *ch*, *tch*, *ph*; base words and ending *-s*; base words and ending *-ed*; base words and ending *-ing*; CV syllable pattern (open syllables); contractions with *'s* and *n't*; contractions with *'ll* and *'d*; contractions with *'ve* and *'re*; base words and endings *-s*, *-es*; vowel digraphs *ai*, *ay*; vowel digraphs *ee*, *ea*; vowel digraphs *oa*, *ow*; compound words; schwa spelled *a*, *e*, *i*, *o*, *u*; ending *-ed*: double consonant; ending *-ing*: double consonant; long *i* spelled *igh*, *ie*; long *i* spelled *i*, *y*; long *e* spelled *y*; ending *-es*: change *y* to *i*; r-controlled *ar*, *or*, *ore*, *er*, *ir*, *ur*; homophones; ending *-er*: double consonant; ending *-est*: double consonant; suffixes *-y*, *-ly*, *-ful*; syllables *-tion*, *-ture*; prefixes *un-*, *re-*, *over-*, *pre-*, *mis-*; silent consonants *kn*, *gn*, *mb*, *wr*; /ô/ spelled *au*, *aw*, *al*, *a*, *o*; /ōō/ spelled *oo*, *ou* **From Grade 1:** short vowels; consonants; long *o* spelled *o*; long *e* spelled *e*; /ou/ spelled *ow*; vowel diphthong *oy*

A boy is in his room. He gets in his
bed. He can see the bright glow of the
Moon through his big window. His mom
reads him a story about the Moon in the
night sky. Soon, he falls asleep by the
light of the Moon.

Under the Moon

Right now, the Moon is rising over
the tall trees. A mom and her baby
wade through the cool water. The large
animals try to find food underwater.

Soon, the animals will wade out of the
cool water and go to sleep.

4

1

The Moon is rising over the small lake. A mom gathers its brood closer. A brood is a group of baby birds. The mom will use its smooth wings to keep the cool night air away from her nest.

2

The Moon is high in the night sky. A raccoon wakes up and leaves her den. The raccoon looks for her food at night. She tries to find bugs or small plants to eat.

Then the raccoon hears a hoot. She goes back inside her den to feed her babies.

3

Soup Group

BOOK 168

DECODABLE WORDS

Target Skill: /o͞o/ spelled *oo*, *ou*

cool	group	noodles	soup
food	Lou	shoo	you

Previously Taught Skills

a	ginger	make	peas	three
and	got	members	pot	tried
ate	green	met	showed	week
best	how	mom	smelled	weeks
cat	it	next	sneak	will
chicken	Kim	or	slurp	with
cried	last	Pam	then	yummy
dad	liked	Pam's	thick	
garlic	made	pea	this	

SKILLS APPLIED IN WORDS IN STORY: short *a*; short *i*; closed syllables (CVC); short *o*; short *e*; long *a* (CVC*e*); long *i* (CVC*e*); /k/ spelled *c*; consonant *g* (hard *g*); /j/ spelled *g*, *dge*; blends with *r*; blends with *s*; final blend *nd*; double final consonants *ll*; consonants *ck*; consonant digraph *th*; consonant digraph *sh*; ending *-s*; ending *-ed* /t/; vowel digraphs *ee*, *ea*; vowel digraph *ow*; r-controlled *ar*; r-controlled *or*; r-controlled *er*; /o͞o/ spelled *oo*, *ou*
From Grade 1: consonants; short vowels; vowel combination *ow*

HIGH-FREQUENCY WORDS

a	every	some	think	what
ago	loved	the	to	were
do	of	they	was	

© Houghton Mifflin Harcourt Publishing Company

High-Frequency Words Taught to Date

Grade 1	city	full	loudly	pushed	to	against	mind
a	cold	funny	loved	put	today	ago	morning
about	come	give	make	read	together	air	move
above	could	go	many	ready	too	alone	next
across	country	goes	maybe	right	took	also	other
after	covers	good	me	said	toward	another	part
again	cried	great	minute	school	try	any	pretty
all	different	green	more	second	two	anything	really
almost	do	ground	most	see	under	behind	river
along	does	grow	mother	seven	until	being	room
always	done	happy	my	shall	use	better	saw
and	don't	have	myself	she	very	book	says
animal	door	he	near	should	walk	care	sky
are	down	head	never	show	want	cheer	sleep
around	draw	hear	new	sing	warms	children	slowly
away	earth	heard	night	small	was	coming	someone
baby	eat	help	no	soil	wash	dark	something
ball	eight	her	noise	some	watch	didn't	sound
be	enough	here	nothing	sometimes	water	doing	stood
bear	even	high	now	soon	we	else	store
beautiful	every	hold	of	sorry	were	ever	table
because	everyone	house	off	starts	what	everything	tall
been	eyes	how	old	stories	where	floor	this
before	fall	I	once	story	who	flower	though
began	family	idea	one	studied	why	found	through
begins	far	into	only	sure	window	front	told
bird	father	is	open	surprised	with	girl	turned
blue	few	kinds	or	take	work	gone	voice
both	field	know	our	talk	world	hair	what's
boy	find	large	out	teacher	would	hard	without
bring	first	laugh	over	the	write	hello	won't
brothers	five	learning	own	their	years	horse	words
brown	fly	light	paper	there	yellow	hundred	
buy	follow	like	party	these	you	I'll	
by	food	listen	people	they	young	I've	
call	for	little	pictures	think	your	kept	
car	four	live	play	those		knew	
carry	friend	long	please	thought	*Grade 2*	leaves	
caught	friendship	look	pull	three	afraid	might	

Decoding skills taught to date: short *a*; short *i*; closed syllables (CVC: short *a*, *i*); short *o*; short *u*; short *e*; closed syllables (CVC: short *o*, *u*, *e*); long *a* (CVC*e*); long *i* (CVC*e*); /k/ spelled *c*; /s/ spelled *c*; long *o* (CVC*e*); long *u* /yo͞o/ (CVC*e*); long *u* /o͞o/ (CVC*e*); long *e* (CVC*e*); consonant *g* (hard *g*); /j/ spelled *g*, *dge*; blends with *r*; blends with *l*; blends with *s*; final blend *nd*; final blend *ng*; final blend *nk*; final blend *nt*; double final consonants *ll*, *ss*, *ff*, *zz*; consonants *ck*; double consonants (closed syllables); consonant digraph *th*; consonant digraph *sh*; consonant digraph *wh*; consonant digraphs *ch*, *tch*; consonant digraph *ph*; ending *-s*; ending *-ed* /ed/; ending *-ed* /d/; ending *-ed* /t/; ending *-ing*; ending *-ed*: drop *e*; ending *-ing*: drop *e*; open syllables (CV); contractions *'s*, *n't*; contractions *'ll*, *'d*; contractions *'ve*, *'re*; endings *-s*, *-es*; vowel digraphs *ai*, *ay*; vowel digraphs *ee*, *ea*; vowel digraphs *oa*, *ow*; compound words; schwa spelled *a*, *e*, *i*, *o*, *u*; ending *-ed*: double consonant; ending *-ing*: double consonant; long *i* spelled *igh*, *ie*; long *i* spelled *i*, *y*; long *e* spelled *y*; ending *-es*: change *y* to *i*; *r*-controlled *ar*; *r*-controlled *or*, *ore*; *r*-controlled *er*; *r*-controlled *ir*, *ur*; homophones; ending *-er*: double consonant; ending *-est*: double consonant; suffix *-y*; suffix *-ly*; suffix *-ful*; syllable *-tion*; syllable *-ture*; prefix *un-*; prefix *re-*; prefix *over-*; prefix *pre-*; prefix *mis-*; silent consonants *kn*, *gn*; silent consonants *mb*; silent consonants *wr*; /ô/ spelled *au*, *aw*; /ô/ spelled *al*, *a*; /ô/ spelled *o*; /o͞o/ spelled *oo*, *ou* **From Grade 1:** consonants; short vowels; vowel combination *ow*

Soup Group

Lou, Pam, and Kim were members of a soup group. Every week, the soup group met to make the best food: soup!

The soup group made the soup with a mom or dad. Then the soup group ate the soup!

This week, Kim showed the group how to make ginger and garlic soup. They loved it!

What soup do you think the soup group will make next?

Three weeks ago, Lou got a pot and some peas. The soup group made pea soup.

Cool! It was green and thick! The soup group liked the pea soup.

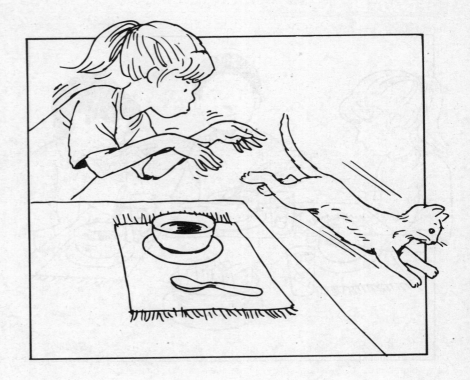

Last week, the soup group made chicken soup with noodles.

The chicken soup smelled yummy! Pam's cat tried to sneak a slurp.

"Shoo, shoo!" Pam cried.

Stew Crew

DECODABLE WORDS

Target Skill: /oo/ spelled *ew, ue*

blew	crew	few	stew	Tuesday
blue	dew	grew	threw	
chew	Drew	knew	true	

Previously Taught Skills

and	decided	is	picked	up
asked	dinner	it's	pot	went
ate	fine	kitchen	rules	wet
can	first	liked	so	what
chives	food	make	started	with
cried	garden	meat	that	yes
cut	his	mom	then	
dad	I	needed	this	
dad's	in	on	turnips	

SKILLS APPLIED IN WORDS IN STORY: short *a*; short *i*; closed syllables; short *o*; short *u*; short *e*; long *a* (CVC*e*); /k/ spelled *c*; long *u* /oo/ (CVC*e*); consonant *g* (hard *g*); blends with *r*; blends with *s*; final blend *nd*; consonant digraph *th*; consonant digraph *wh*; consonant digraph *ch*; ending *-s*; ending *-ed* /ed/; ending *-ed* /t/; open syllables (CV); contractions '*s*; vowel digraphs *ee, ea*; *r*-controlled *ar*; *r*-controlled *ir, ur*; /ô/ spelled *al, a*; /oo/ spelled *oo, ou*; /oo/ spelled *ew, ue*   **From Grade 1:** consonants; short vowels

HIGH-FREQUENCY WORDS

a	he	some	to	were
are	(in)to	the	was	where
be	said	they	we	would

Houghton Mifflin Harcourt.

/oo/ spelled *ew, ue*

BOOK 169

Stew Crew

High-Frequency Words Taught to Date

Grade 1	city	full	loudly	pushed	to	against	mind
a	cold	funny	loved	put	today	ago	morning
about	come	give	make	read	together	air	move
above	could	go	many	ready	too	alone	next
across	country	goes	maybe	right	took	also	other
after	covers	good	me	said	toward	another	part
again	cried	great	minute	school	try	any	pretty
all	different	green	more	second	two	anything	really
almost	do	ground	most	see	under	behind	river
along	does	grow	mother	seven	until	being	room
always	done	happy	my	shall	use	better	saw
and	don't	have	myself	she	very	book	says
animal	door	he	near	should	walk	care	sky
are	down	head	never	show	want	cheer	sleep
around	draw	hear	new	sing	warms	children	slowly
away	earth	heard	night	small	was	coming	someone
baby	eat	help	no	soil	wash	dark	something
ball	eight	her	noise	some	watch	didn't	sound
be	enough	here	nothing	sometimes	water	doing	stood
bear	even	high	now	soon	we	else	store
beautiful	every	hold	of	sorry	were	ever	table
because	everyone	house	off	starts	what	everything	tall
been	eyes	how	old	stories	where	floor	this
before	fall	I	once	story	who	flower	though
began	family	idea	one	studied	why	found	through
begins	far	into	only	sure	window	front	told
bird	father	is	open	surprised	with	girl	turned
blue	few	kinds	or	take	work	gone	voice
both	field	know	our	talk	world	hair	what's
boy	find	large	out	teacher	would	hard	without
bring	first	laugh	over	the	write	hello	won't
brothers	five	learning	own	their	years	horse	words
brown	fly	light	paper	there	yellow	hundred	
buy	follow	like	party	these	you	I'll	
by	food	listen	people	they	young	I've	
call	for	little	pictures	think	your	kept	
car	four	live	play	those		knew	
carry	friend	long	please	thought	*Grade 2*	leaves	
caught	friendship	look	pull	three	afraid	might	

Decoding skills taught to date: short *a*; short *i*; closed syllables (CVC: short *a, i*); short *o*; short *u*; short *e*; closed syllables (CVC: short *o, u, e*); long *a* (CVC*e*); long *i* (CVC*e*); /k/ spelled *c*; /s/ spelled *c*; long *o* (CVC*e*); long *u* /yo͞o/ (CVC*e*); long *u* /o͞o/ (CVC*e*); long *e* (CVC*e*); consonant *g* (hard *g*); /j/ spelled *g, dge*; blends with *r*; blends with *l*; blends with *s*; final blend *nd*; final blend *ng*; final blend *nk*; final blend *nt*; double final consonants *ll, ss, ff, zz*; consonants *ck*; double consonants (closed syllables); consonant digraph *th*; consonant digraph *sh*; consonant digraph *wh*; consonant digraphs *ch, tch*; consonant digraph *ph*; ending *-s*; ending *-ed* /ed/; ending *-ed* /d/; ending *-ed* /t/; ending *-ing*; ending *-ed*: drop *e*; ending *-ing*: drop *e*; open syllables (CV); contractions *'s, n't*; contractions *'ll, 'd*; contractions *'ve, 're*; endings *-s, -es*; vowel digraphs *ai, ay*; vowel digraphs *ee, ea*; vowel digraphs *oa, ow*; compound words; schwa spelled *a, e, i, o, u*; ending *-ed*: double consonant; ending *-ing*: double consonant; long *i* spelled *igh, ie*; long *i* spelled *i, y*; long *e* spelled *y*; ending *-es*: change *y* to *i*; r-controlled *ar*; r-controlled *or, ore*; r-controlled *er*; r-controlled *ir, ur*; homophones; ending *-er*: double consonant; ending *-est*: double consonant; suffix *-y*; suffix *-ly*; suffix *-ful*; syllable *-tion*; syllable *-ture*; prefix *un-*; prefix *re-*; prefix *over-*; prefix *pre-*; prefix *mis-*; silent consonants *kn, gn*; silent consonants *mb*; silent consonants *wr*; /ô/ spelled *au, aw*; /ô/ spelled *al, a*; /ô/ spelled *o*; /o͞o/ spelled *oo, ou*; /o͞o/ spelled *ew, ue*   **From Grade 1:** consonants; short vowels

Stew Crew

Drew asked his dad to dinner. His dad blew on the stew. Then he ate some and started to chew.

He said, "I knew it. This is fine stew!"

"So true! Mom and I are the stew crew!" cried Drew.

Drew decided to make dinner on Tuesday. He knew his mom and dad liked stew.

He asked, "Mom, can I make some stew?"

"Yes," said his mom. "We can be the stew crew!"

First, Drew went to his dad's garden
where his dad grew chives and turnips.
The garden was wet with dew.

Drew picked what he needed. Drew
knew the chives would make fine stew!

In the kitchen, Drew knew the rules.
They cut up meat and a few chives.

They threw the food into a blue pot.
Drew knew that he and his mom were
a fine stew crew!

2

3

Blue Sue

DECODABLE WORDS

Target Skill: /o͞o/ spelled *ew, ue*

Andrew	clues	knew	Sue
blue	drew	new	true

Previously Taught Skills

and	draw	it	picked	these
art	family	it's	shells	things
at	fun	laces	shirts	too
beach	had	look	showed	took
blooms	her	make	skirts	water
bunch	him	named	sky	went
class	I	next	so	will
color	I'll	nice	socks	wore
day	is	on	that	

SKILLS APPLIED IN WORDS IN STORY: short *a*; short *i*; short *o*; short *u*; short *e*; long *a* (CVC*e*); long *i* (CVC*e*); /k/ spelled *c*; /s/ spelled *c*; long *e* (CVC*e*); blends with *r*; blends with *l*; blends with *s*; final blend *nd*; final blend *ng*; final blend *nt*; double final consonants *ll*; consonants *ck*; consonant digraph *th*; consonant digraph *sh*; consonant digraph *ch*; ending *-s*; ending *-ed* /d/; open syllables (CV); contraction *'s*; vowel digraph *ay*; vowel digraph *ea*; vowel digraph *ow*; long *i* spelled *i, y*; r-controlled *ar*; r-controlled *or, ore*; r-controlled *er*; r-controlled *ir*; /ô/ spelled *aw*; /ô/ spelled *a*; /o͞o/ spelled *oo*; /o͞o/ spelled *ew, ue*
From Grade 1: consonants; short vowels; digraph *kn*; vowel digraph *oo* /oo/

HIGH-FREQUENCY WORDS

a	brother	loved	said	they	would
are	every(thing)	of	she	to	

© Houghton Mifflin Harcourt Publishing Company

Houghton Mifflin Harcourt

High-Frequency Words Taught to Date

Grade 1							
a	city	full	loudly	pushed	to	against	mind
about	cold	funny	loved	put	today	ago	morning
above	come	give	make	read	together	air	move
across	could	go	many	ready	too	alone	next
after	country	goes	maybe	right	took	also	other
again	covers	good	me	said	toward	another	part
all	cried	great	minute	school	try	any	pretty
almost	different	green	more	second	two	anything	really
along	do	ground	most	see	under	behind	river
always	does	grow	mother	seven	until	being	room
and	done	happy	my	shall	use	better	saw
animal	don't	have	myself	she	very	book	says
are	door	he	near	should	walk	care	sky
around	down	head	never	show	want	cheer	sleep
away	draw	hear	new	sing	warms	children	slowly
baby	earth	heard	night	small	was	coming	someone
ball	eat	help	no	soil	wash	dark	something
be	eight	her	noise	some	watch	didn't	sound
bear	enough	here	nothing	sometimes	water	doing	stood
beautiful	even	high	now	soon	we	else	store
because	every	hold	of	sorry	were	ever	table
been	everyone	house	off	starts	what	everything	tall
before	eyes	how	old	stories	where	floor	this
began	fall	I	once	story	who	flower	though
begins	family	idea	one	studied	why	found	through
bird	far	into	only	sure	window	front	told
blue	father	is	open	surprised	with	girl	turned
both	few	kinds	or	take	work	gone	voice
boy	field	know	our	talk	world	hair	what's
bring	find	large	out	teacher	would	hard	without
brothers	first	laugh	over	the	write	hello	won't
brown	five	learning	own	their	years	horse	words
buy	fly	light	paper	there	yellow	hundred	
by	follow	like	party	these	you	I'll	
call	food	listen	people	they	young	I've	
car	for	little	pictures	think	your	kept	
carry	four	live	play	those		knew	
carry	friend	long	please	thought	**Grade 2**	leaves	
caught	friendship	look	pull	three	afraid	might	

Decoding skills taught to date: short *a*; short *i*; closed syllables (CVC: short *a, i*); short *o*; short *u*; short *e*; closed syllables (CVC: short *o, u, e*); long *a* (CVC*e*); long *i* (CVC*e*); /k/ spelled *c*; /s/ spelled *c*; long *o* (CVC*e*); long *u* /yōō/ (CVC*e*); long *u* /ōō/ (CVC*e*); long *e* (CVC*e*); consonant *g* (hard *g*); /j/ spelled *g, dge*; blends with *r*; blends with *l*; blends with *s*; final blend *nd*; final blend *ng*; final blend *nk*; final blend *nt*; double final consonants *ll, ss, ff, zz*; consonants *ck*; double consonants (closed syllables); consonant digraph *th*; consonant digraph *sh*; consonant digraph *wh*; consonant digraphs *ch, tch*; consonant digraph *ph*; ending *-s*; ending *-ed* /ed/; ending *-ed* /d/; ending *-ed* /t/; ending *-ing*; ending *-ed*: drop *e*; ending *-ing*: drop *e*; open syllables (CV); contractions *'s, n't*; contractions *'ll, 'd*; contractions *'ve, 're*; endings *-s, -es*; vowel digraphs *ai, ay*; vowel digraphs *ee, ea*; vowel digraphs *oa, ow*; compound words; schwa spelled *a, e, i, o, u*; ending *-ed*: double consonant; ending *-ing*: double consonant; long *i* spelled *igh, ie*; long *i* spelled *i, y*; long *e* spelled *y*; ending *-es*: change *y* to *i*; r-controlled *ar*; r-controlled *or, ore*; r-controlled *er*; r-controlled *ir, ur*; homophones; ending *-er*: double consonant; ending *-est*: double consonant; suffix *-y*; suffix *-ly*; suffix *-ful*; syllable *-tion*; syllable *-ture*; prefix *un-*; prefix *re-*; prefix *over-*; prefix *pre-*; prefix *mis-*; silent consonants *kn, gn*; silent consonants *mb*; silent consonants *wr*; /ô/ spelled *au, aw*; /ô/ spelled *al, a*; /ô/ spelled *o*; /ōō/ spelled *oo, ou*; /ōō/ spelled *ew, ue* **From Grade 1:** consonants; short vowels; digraph *kn*; vowel digraph *oo* /oo/

Sue took her new picture to art class. She named it "Blue Blooms."

"I knew flowers would make a nice picture," said Sue. "So I drew blue blooms!"

4

Blue Sue

Sue loved the color blue. Her shirts and her skirts were blue. Her socks and her laces were blue.

Everything Sue wore had blue in it. It's true!

1

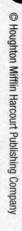

Sue and her family went to the beach. Sue showed blue things to her brother, Andrew.

"Look at these clues, Andrew," said Sue. "The water is blue. The sky is blue. These shells are blue, too!"

The next day, Sue took Andrew to look at flowers. Sue showed him the new blue blooms. They picked a bunch.

"I'll draw a new picture of these blue flowers," said Sue. "That will be fun."

Looking for Bigfoot

DECODABLE WORDS

Target Skill: /o͝o/ spelled *oo*

Bigfoot	cookbook	looking	woof
book	Cookie	stood	
brook	good	took	
cook	looked	woods	

Previously Taught Skills

about	dinner	in	out	think
and	find	is	real	time
at	for	it	see	too
birds	frogs	listened	Shh	trees
but	had	Mmm	smelled	well
came	hi	my	speaking	with
Dad	his	night	started	
didn't	I	no	still	

SKILLS APPLIED IN WORDS IN STORY: short *a*; short *i*; closed syllables; short *u*; long *i* (CVC*e*); /k/ spelled *c*; consonant *g* (hard *g*); blends with *r*; blends with *s*; final blend *nd*; final blend *nk*; double final consonants *ll*; consonant digraph *th*; consonant digraph *wh*; ending -*s*; ending -*ed* /d/; ending -*ed* /t/; ending -*ing*; open syllables (CV); contraction *n't*; vowel digraph *ay*; vowel digraphs *ee, ea*; compound words; long *i* spelled *igh*; long *i* spelled *i*; r-controlled *ar*; r-controlled *er*; /o͞o/ spelled *oo*; /o͝o/ spelled *oo* **From Grade 1:** consonants; short vowels; vowel combination *ou*

HIGH-FREQUENCY WORDS

a	he	read	there	were
could	hear	said	to	you
do	heard	saw	today	
does	into	the	we	

Houghton Mifflin Harcourt.

Looking for Bigfoot

High-Frequency Words Taught to Date

Grade 1							
a	city	full	loudly	pushed	to	against	mind
about	cold	funny	loved	put	today	ago	morning
above	come	give	make	read	together	air	move
across	could	go	many	ready	too	alone	next
after	country	goes	maybe	right	took	also	other
again	covers	good	me	said	toward	another	outside
all	cried	great	minute	school	try	any	part
almost	different	green	more	second	two	anything	pretty
along	do	ground	most	see	under	behind	really
always	does	grow	mother	seven	until	being	river
and	done	happy	my	shall	use	better	room
animal	don't	have	myself	she	very	book	saw
are	door	he	near	should	walk	care	says
around	down	head	never	show	want	cheer	sky
away	draw	hear	new	sing	warms	children	sleep
baby	earth	heard	night	small	was	coming	slowly
ball	eat	help	no	soil	wash	dark	someone
be	eight	her	noise	some	watch	didn't	something
bear	enough	here	nothing	sometimes	water	doing	sound
beautiful	even	high	now	soon	we	else	stood
because	every	hold	of	sorry	were	ever	store
been	everyone	house	off	starts	what	everything	table
before	eyes	how	old	stories	where	floor	tall
began	fall	I	once	story	who	flower	this
begins	family	idea	one	studied	why	found	though
bird	far	into	only	sure	window	front	through
blue	father	is	open	surprised	with	girl	told
both	few	kinds	or	take	work	gone	tomorrow
boy	field	know	our	talk	world	hair	town
bring	find	large	out	teacher	would	hard	turned
brothers	first	laugh	over	the	write	hello	voice
brown	five	learning	own	their	years	horse	what's
buy	fly	light	paper	there	yellow	hundred	without
by	follow	like	party	these	you	I'll	won't
call	food	listen	people	they	young	I've	words
car	for	little	pictures	think	your	kept	
carry	four	live	play	those	**Grade 2**	knew	
caught	friend	long	please	thought	afraid	leaves	
	friendship	look	pull	three		might	

Decoding skills taught to date: short *a*; short *i*; closed syllables (CVC: short *a, i*); short *o*; short *u*; short *e*; closed syllables (CVC: short *o, u, e*); long *a* (CVC*e*); long *i* (CVC*e*); /k/ spelled *c*; /s/ spelled *c*; long *o* (CVC*e*); long *u* /yo͞o/ (CVC*e*); long *u* /o͞o/ (CVC*e*); long *e* (CVC*e*); consonant *g* (hard *g*); /j/ spelled *g, dge*; blends with *r*; blends with *l*; blends with *s*; final blend *nd*; final blend *ng*; final blend *nk*; final blend *nt*; double final consonants *ll, ss, ff, zz*; consonants *ck*; double consonants (closed syllables); consonant digraph *th*; consonant digraph *sh*; consonant digraph *wh*; consonant digraphs *ch, tch*; consonant digraph *ph*; ending *-s*; ending *-ed* /ed/; ending *-ed* /d/; ending *-ed* /t/; ending *-ing*; ending *-ed*: drop *e*; ending *-ing*: drop *e*; open syllables (CV); contractions *'s, n't*; contractions *'ll, 'd*; contractions *'ve, 're*; endings *-s, -es*; vowel digraphs *ai, ay*; vowel digraphs *ee, ea*; vowel digraphs *oa, ow*; compound words; schwa spelled *a, e, i, o, u*; ending *-ed*: double consonant; ending *-ing*: double consonant; long *i* spelled *igh, ie*; long *i* spelled *i, y*; long *e* spelled *y*; ending *-es*: change *y* to *i*; r-controlled *ar*; r-controlled *or, ore*; r-controlled *er*; r-controlled *ir, ur*; homophones; ending *-er*: double consonant; ending *-est*: double consonant; suffix *-y*; suffix *-ly*; suffix *-ful*; syllable *-tion*; syllable *-ture*; prefix *un-*; prefix *re-*; prefix *over-*; prefix *pre-*; prefix *mis-*; silent consonants *kn, gn*; silent consonants *mb*; silent consonants *wr*; /ô/ spelled *au, aw*; /ô/ spelled *al, a*; /ô/ spelled *o*; /o͞o/ spelled *oo, ou*; /o͞o/ spelled *ew, ue*; /o͞o/ spelled *oo* **From Grade 1:** consonants; short vowels; vowel combination *ou*

Looking for Bigfoot

Hi there! I was in the woods today with Cookie and my dad. We were looking for Bigfoot!

I read about Bigfoot in a book. Do you think he is real?

Cookie does! "Woof! Woof!"

Well, we didn't find Bigfoot, but my dad and I had a good time in the woods!

Cookie, too!

"Woof! Woof!"

We came to a brook. Dad stood still
and looked into the woods.

Dad said, "Shh! No speaking." Cookie
and I looked, too.

We saw birds and trees. We didn't
see Bigfoot.

At night, I listened to the woods. I
could hear the brook and frogs. I didn't
hear Bigfoot.

Dad took out his cookbook and started
to cook dinner.

Mmm! It smelled good!

2

3

A Good Day to Fish

DECODABLE WORDS

Target Skill: /o͝o/ spelled *oo*

book	cook	good	look	woods
brook	fishhook	hook	unhooks	

Previously Taught Skills

and	fish	let's	take	with
bait	go	like	that	wraps
big	home	lots	then	
by	hope	lucky	this	
cannot	I	my	try	
close	ice	now	tug	
Dad	in	on	up	
day	is	out	wait	
eat	it	pull	walk	
feel	it's	say	water	
feels	jabs	sit	will	

SKILLS APPLIED IN WORDS IN STORY: short *a*; short *i*; closed syllables; short *o*; short *u*; long *a* (CVC*e*); long *i* (CVC*e*); /k/ spelled *c*; long *o* (CVC*e*); consonant *g* (hard *g*); blends with *r*; final blend *nd*; double final consonants *ll*; consonants *ck*; consonant digraph *th*; consonant digraph *sh*; ending -*s*; open syllables (CV); contraction '*s*, vowel digraphs *ai*, *ay*; vowel digraphs *ee*, *ea*; compound words; long *i* spelled *i*, *y*; long *e* spelled *y*; prefix *un*-; silent consonants *wr*; /ô/ spelled *al*, *a*; /o͝o/ spelled *oo*   **From Grade 1:** consonants; short vowels; vowel combinations *ou*, *ow*

HIGH-FREQUENCY WORDS

a	be	says	something	to
are	of	some	the	we

© Houghton Mifflin Harcourt Publishing Company

Houghton Mifflin Harcourt

A Good Day to Fish

High-Frequency Words Taught to Date

Grade 1	city	full	loudly	pushed	to	against	mind
a	cold	funny	loved	put	today	ago	morning
about	come	give	make	read	together	air	move
above	could	go	many	ready	too	alone	next
across	country	goes	maybe	right	took	also	other
after	covers	good	me	said	toward	another	outside
again	cried	great	minute	school	try	any	part
all	different	green	more	second	two	anything	pretty
almost	do	ground	most	see	under	behind	really
along	does	grow	mother	seven	until	being	river
always	done	happy	my	shall	use	better	room
and	don't	have	myself	she	very	book	saw
animal	door	he	near	should	walk	care	says
are	down	head	never	show	want	cheer	sky
around	draw	hear	new	sing	warms	children	sleep
away	earth	heard	night	small	was	coming	slowly
baby	eat	help	no	soil	wash	dark	someone
ball	eight	her	noise	some	watch	didn't	something
be	enough	here	nothing	sometimes	water	doing	sound
bear	even	high	now	soon	we	else	stood
beautiful	every	hold	of	sorry	were	ever	store
because	everyone	house	off	starts	what	everything	table
been	eyes	how	old	stories	where	floor	tall
before	fall	I	once	story	who	flower	this
began	family	idea	one	studied	why	found	though
begins	far	into	only	sure	window	front	through
bird	father	is	open	surprised	with	girl	told
blue	few	kinds	or	take	work	gone	tomorrow
both	field	know	our	talk	world	hair	town
boy	find	large	out	teacher	would	hard	turned
bring	first	laugh	over	the	write	hello	voice
brothers	five	learning	own	their	years	horse	what's
brown	fly	light	paper	there	yellow	hundred	without
buy	follow	like	party	these	you	I'll	won't
by	food	listen	people	they	young	I've	words
call	for	little	pictures	think	your	kept	
car	four	live	play	those		knew	
carry	friend	long	please	thought	**Grade 2**	leaves	
caught	friendship	look	pull	three	afraid	might	

Decoding skills taught to date: short *a*; short *i*; closed syllables (CVC: short *a, i*); short *o*; short *u*; short *e*; closed syllables (CVC: short *o, u, e*); long *a* (CVC*e*); long *i* (CVC*e*); /k/ spelled *c*; /s/ spelled *c*; long *o* (CVC*e*); long *u* /y͞o͞o/ (CVC*e*); long *u* /o͞o/ (CVC*e*); long *e* (CVC*e*); consonant *g* (hard *g*); /j/ spelled *g, dge*; blends with *r*, blends with *l*; blends with *s*; final blend *nd*; final blend *ng*; final blend *nk*; final blend *nt*; double final consonants *ll, ss, ff, zz*; consonants *ck*; double consonants (closed syllables); consonant digraph *th*; consonant digraph *sh*; consonant digraph *wh*; consonant digraphs *ch, tch*; consonant digraph *ph*; ending *-s*; ending *-ed* /ed/; ending *-ed* /d/; ending *-ed* /t/; ending *-ing*; ending *-ed*: drop *e*; ending *-ing*: drop *e*; open syllables (CV); contractions *'s, n't*; contractions *'ll, 'd*; contractions *'ve, 're*; endings *-s, -es*; vowel digraphs *ai, ay*; vowel digraphs *ee, ea*; vowel digraphs *oa, ow*; compound words; schwa spelled *a, e, i, o, u*; ending *-ed*: double consonant; ending *-ing*: double consonant; long *i* spelled *igh, ie*; long *i* spelled *i, y*; long *e* spelled *y*; ending *-es*: change *y* to *i*; r-controlled *ar*; r-controlled *or, ore*; r-controlled *er*; r-controlled *ir, ur*; homophones; ending *-er*: double consonant; ending *-est*: double consonant; suffix *-y*; suffix *-ly*; suffix *-ful*; syllable *-tion*; syllable *-ture*; prefix *un-*; prefix *re-*; prefix *over-*; prefix *pre-*; prefix *mis-*; silent consonants *kn, gn*; silent consonants *mb*; silent consonants *wr*; /ô/ spelled *au, aw*; /ô/ spelled *al, a*; /ô/ spelled *o*; /o͞o/ spelled *oo, ou*; /o͞o/ spelled *ew, ue*; /o͞o/ spelled *oo* **From Grade 1:** consonants; short vowels; vowel combinations *ou, ow*

A Good Day to Fish

Dad and I feel it is a good day to fish.
We walk to the brook, and take my lucky fishhook.

I hope that lots of fish are in the brook!

Dad unhooks the fish and wraps it up.
I then pack it in ice.
"Now let's go home and cook,"
Dad says.
"This fish will be good to eat!" I say.

4

1

The brook is close to the woods. Dad jabs bait on my hook. I cannot wait to hook some fish!

We sit by the brook and wait. It feels good to be with my dad.

I feel a tug on my hook. I look. It's a big fish! It's like something out of a book!

I try to pull the fish out of the water.

2

3

My Friends' Houses

DECODABLE WORDS

Target Skill: **possessives with *'s, s'***

bed's	mom's	pie's	weekend's
Hector's	pals'	Trisha's	

Previously Taught Skills

all	filling	I	pals	smells
always	full	in	peach	so
and	fun	is	pie	spend
apple	good	it's	pies	this
bake	has	likes	plan	time
bed	Hector	makes	read	Trisha
best	her	middle	room	under
books	his	mom	row	with
cakes	homes	my	sheets	yum
cookies	house	next	shelves	
desk	houses	on	side	

SKILLS APPLIED IN WORDS IN STORY: short *a*; short *i*; closed syllables; short *o*; short *u*; short *e*; long *a* (CVCe); long *i* (CVCe); /k/ spelled *c*; consonant *g* (hard *g*); blends with *r*; blends with *s*; final blend *nd*; double final consonants *ll*; consonant digraph *th*; consonant digraph *sh*; consonant digraph *ch*; ending *-s*; open syllables (CV); contraction *'s*, endings *-s, -es*; vowel digraphs *ee, ea*; vowel digraph *ow*; compound words; schwa sound; long *i* spelled *ie*; long *i* spelled *y*; r-controlled *or*; r-controlled *er*; /ô/ spelled *al*; /o͞o/ spelled *oo*; possessives with *'s, s'* **From Grade 1:** consonants; short vowels; vowel combination *ou*

HIGH-FREQUENCY WORDS

a	full	of	she	we
are	he	one	the	
even	live	other	to	

 Houghton Mifflin Harcourt.

My Pals' Homes

High-Frequency Words Taught to Date

Grade 1	city	full	loudly	pushed	to	against	mind
a	cold	funny	loved	put	today	ago	morning
about	come	give	make	read	together	air	move
above	could	go	many	ready	too	alone	next
across	country	goes	maybe	right	took	also	other
after	covers	good	me	said	toward	another	outside
again	cried	great	minute	school	try	any	part
all	different	green	more	second	two	anything	pretty
almost	do	ground	most	see	under	behind	really
along	does	grow	mother	seven	until	being	river
always	done	happy	my	shall	use	better	room
and	don't	have	myself	she	very	book	saw
animal	door	he	near	should	walk	care	says
are	down	head	never	show	want	cheer	sky
around	draw	hear	new	sing	warms	children	sleep
away	earth	heard	night	small	was	coming	slowly
baby	eat	help	no	soil	wash	dark	someone
ball	eight	her	noise	some	watch	didn't	something
be	enough	here	nothing	sometimes	water	doing	sound
bear	even	high	now	soon	we	else	stood
beautiful	every	hold	of	sorry	were	ever	store
because	everyone	house	off	starts	what	everything	table
been	eyes	how	old	stories	where	floor	tall
before	fall	I	once	story	who	flower	this
began	family	idea	one	studied	why	found	though
begins	far	into	only	sure	window	front	through
bird	father	is	open	surprised	with	girl	told
blue	few	kinds	or	take	work	gone	tomorrow
both	field	know	our	talk	world	hair	town
boy	find	large	out	teacher	would	hard	turned
bring	first	laugh	over	the	write	hello	voice
brothers	five	learning	own	their	years	horse	what's
brown	fly	light	paper	there	yellow	hundred	without
buy	follow	like	party	these	you	I'll	won't
by	food	listen	people	they	young	I've	words
call	for	little	pictures	think	your	kept	
car	four	live	play	those		knew	
carry	friend	long	please	thought	**Grade 2**	leaves	
caught	friendship	look	pull	three	afraid	might	

Decoding skills taught to date: short *a*; short *i*; closed syllables (CVC: short *a, i*); short *o*; short *u*; short *e*; closed syllables (CVC: short *o, u, e*); long *a* (CVC*e*); long *i* (CVC*e*); /k/ spelled *c*; /s/ spelled *c*; long *o* (CVC*e*); long *u* /y$\overline{oo}$/ (CVC*e*); long *u* /$\overline{oo}$/ (CVC*e*); long *e* (CVC*e*); consonant *g* (hard *g*); /j/ spelled *g, dge*; blends with *r*; blends with *l*; blends with *s*; final blend *nd*; final blend *ng*; final blend *nk*; final blend *nt*; double final consonants *ll, ss, ff, zz*; consonants *ck*; double consonants (closed syllables); consonant digraph *th*; consonant digraph *sh*; consonant digraph *wh*; consonant digraphs *ch, tch*; consonant digraph *ph*; ending *-s*; ending *-ed* /ed/; ending *-ed* /d/; ending *-ed* /t/; ending *-ing*; ending *-ed*: drop *e*; ending *-ing*: drop *e*; open syllables (CV); contractions *'s, n't*; contractions *'ll, 'd*; contractions *'ve, 're*; endings *-s, -es*; vowel digraphs *ai, ay*; vowel digraphs *ee, ea*; vowel digraphs *oa, ow*; compound words; schwa spelled *a, e, i, o, u*; ending *-ed*: double consonant; ending *-ing*: double consonant; long *i* spelled *igh, ie*; long *i* spelled *i, y*; long *e* spelled *y*; ending *-es*: change *y* to *i*; r-controlled *ar*; r-controlled *or, ore*; r-controlled *er*; r-controlled *ir, ur*; homophones; ending *-er*: double consonant; ending *-est*: double consonant; suffix *-y*; suffix *-ly*; suffix *-ful*; syllable *-tion*; syllable *-ture*; prefix *un-*; prefix *re-*; prefix *over-*; prefix *pre-*; prefix *mis-*; silent consonants *kn, gn*; silent consonants *mb*; silent consonants *wr*; /ô/ spelled *au, aw*; /ô/ spelled *al, a*; /ô/ spelled *o*; /$\overline{oo}$/ spelled *oo, ou*; /$\overline{oo}$/ spelled *ew, ue*; /$\overline{oo}$/ spelled *oo*; possessives with *'s, s'* **From Grade 1:** consonants; short vowels; vowel combination *ou*

This weekend's plan is to spend time with Hector and Trisha. So fun!

It's good to live next to my best pals!

My Pals' Homes

Hector and Trisha are my best pals. We all live in a row.

I live in the middle. Hector's house is on one side, and Trisha's house is on the other side.

Hector's room is full of books. He likes to read.

Hector has books on his desk, on the shelves, and on his bed. He even has books under the bed's sheets!

Trisha's mom likes to bake, so her house always smells good. She makes cakes, pies, and cookies!

Her mom's best pie is apple. This pie's filling is peach! Yum!

Look Closely

DECODABLE WORDS

Target Skill: **possessives with 's, s'**

birds'	snake's	tree's
frog's	spiders'	trunk's

Previously Taught Skills

alive	can	is	might	stop
all	closely	it	moving	strong
an	closer	it's	much	that
and	critters	leaves	nest	this
at	eat	let's	nests	tree
bark	egg	like	nuts	trees
bit	few	long	on	trunk
branches	has	look	rabbits	webs
bugs	high	lots	roots	under
but	home	low	seen	
call	in	meal	still	

SKILLS APPLIED IN WORDS IN STORY: short *a*; short *i*; closed syllables; short *o*; short *u*; short *e*; long *a* (CVC*e*); long *i* (CVC*e*); /k/ spelled *c*; long *o* (CVC*e*); consonant *g* (hard *g*); blends with *r*; blends with *l*; blends with *s*; final blend *nd*; final blend *ng*; final blend *nk*; consonant digraph *th*; consonant digraph *ch*; contraction *'s*; ending -*ing*; endings -*s*, -*es*; vowel digraphs *ee*, *ea*; vowel digraph *ow*; schwa sound; long *i* spelled *igh*; r-controlled *ar*; r-controlled *er*, *ur*; ending -*er*: double consonant; /ô/ spelled *al*, *a*; /o͞o/ spelled *ew*; /o͞o/ spelled *oo*; possessives with *'s, s'* **From Grade 1:** consonants; short vowels

HIGH-FREQUENCY WORDS

a	be	many	some	you
animals	before	of	the	
are	have	over	to	

Houghton Mifflin Harcourt.

BOOK 174

High-Frequency Words Taught to Date

Grade 1	city	full	loudly	pushed	to	against	mind
a	cold	funny	loved	put	today	ago	morning
about	come	give	make	read	together	air	move
above	could	go	many	ready	too	alone	next
across	country	goes	maybe	right	took	also	other
after	covers	good	me	said	toward	another	outside
again	cried	great	minute	school	try	any	part
all	different	green	more	second	two	anything	pretty
almost	do	ground	most	see	under	behind	really
along	does	grow	mother	seven	until	being	river
always	done	happy	my	shall	use	better	room
and	don't	have	myself	she	very	book	saw
animal	door	he	near	should	walk	care	says
are	down	head	never	show	want	cheer	sky
around	draw	hear	new	sing	warms	children	sleep
away	earth	heard	night	small	was	coming	slowly
baby	eat	help	no	soil	wash	dark	someone
ball	eight	her	noise	some	watch	didn't	something
be	enough	here	nothing	sometimes	water	doing	sound
bear	even	high	now	soon	we	else	stood
beautiful	every	hold	of	sorry	were	ever	store
because	everyone	house	off	starts	what	everything	table
been	eyes	how	old	stories	where	floor	tall
before	fall	I	once	story	who	flower	this
began	family	idea	one	studied	why	found	though
begins	far	into	only	sure	window	front	through
bird	father	is	open	surprised	with	girl	told
blue	few	kinds	or	take	work	gone	tomorrow
both	field	know	our	talk	world	hair	town
boy	find	large	out	teacher	would	hard	turned
bring	first	laugh	over	the	write	hello	voice
brothers	five	learning	own	their	years	horse	what's
brown	fly	light	paper	there	yellow	hundred	without
buy	follow	like	party	these	you	I'll	won't
by	food	listen	people	they	young	I've	words
call	for	little	pictures	think	your	kept	
car	four	live	play	those		knew	
carry	friend	long	please	thought	*Grade 2*	leaves	
caught	friendship	look	pull	three	afraid	might	

Decoding skills taught to date: short *a*; short *i*; closed syllables (CVC: short *a, i*); short *o*; short *u*; short *e*; closed syllables (CVC: short *o, u, e*); long *a* (CVC*e*); long *i* (CVC*e*); /k/ spelled *c*; /s/ spelled *c*; long *o* (CVC*e*); long *u* /yoo/ (CVC*e*); long *u* /oo/ (CVC*e*); long *e* (CVC*e*); consonant *g* (hard *g*); /j/ spelled *g*, *dge*; blends with *r*; blends with *l*; blends with *s*; final blend *nd*; final blend *ng*; final blend *nk*; final blend *nt*; double final consonants *ll, ss, ff, zz*; consonants *ck*; double consonants (closed syllables); consonant digraph *th*; consonant digraph *sh*; consonant digraph *wh*; consonant digraphs *ch, tch*; consonant digraph *ph*; ending *-s*; ending *-ed* /ed/; ending *-ed* /d/; ending *-ed* /t/; ending *-ing*; ending *-ed*: drop *e*; ending *-ing*: drop *e*; open syllables (CV); contractions *'s, n't*; contractions *'ll, 'd*; contractions *'ve, 're*; endings *-s, -es*; vowel digraphs *ai, ay*; vowel digraphs *ee, ea*; vowel digraphs *oa, ow*; compound words; schwa spelled *a, e, i, o, u*; ending *-ed*: double consonant; ending *-ing*: double consonant; long *i* spelled *igh, ie*; long *i* spelled *i, y*; long *e* spelled *y*; ending *-es*: change *y* to *i*; r-controlled *ar*; r-controlled *or, ore*; r-controlled *er*; r-controlled *ir, ur*; homophones; ending *-er*: double consonant; ending *-est*: double consonant; suffix *-y*; suffix *-ly*; suffix *-ful*; syllable *-tion*; syllable *-ture*; prefix *un-*; prefix *re-*; prefix *over-*; prefix *pre-*; prefix *mis-*; silent consonants *kn, gn*; silent consonants *mb*; silent consonants *wr*; /ô/ spelled *au, aw*; /ô/ spelled *al, a*; /ô/ spelled *o*; /oo/ spelled *oo, ou*; /oo/ spelled *ew, ue*; /oo/ spelled *oo*; possessives with *'s, s'* **From Grade 1:** consonants; short vowels

Look a bit closer. Under the trunk's bark are bugs! Under the tree's roots are rabbits!

This tree might look still, but it's alive and moving!

4

Look Closely

This tree is like many trees you have seen before. It has a trunk, branches, and leaves.

The tree's trunk is strong. The tree's branches are long.

But let's look closer.

1

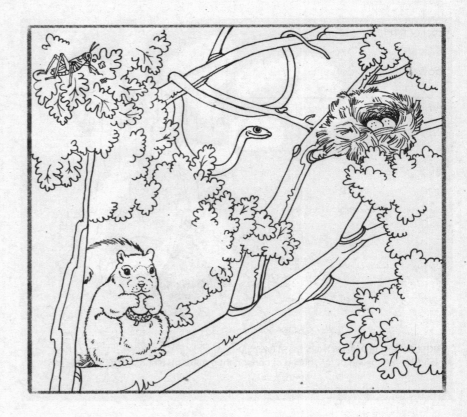

Many animals call the tree home.

Birds' nests are on low branches.

A tree frog's home is on high branches.

Spiders' webs can be all over.

Lots of critters stop at the tree to eat.

Some like to eat the tree's nuts. A few like to eat the tree's leaves.

This snake's meal might be an egg in that nest!

The Flower

DECODABLE WORDS

Target Skill: /ou/ spelled *ou, ow*

bow	down	gown	loud	sound
bowed	flower	how	loudly	tower
clown	flowers	howled	out	wow
crown	frowned	howls	outside	

Previously Taught Skills

a	fix	know	or	the
after	gave	lived	pick	then
ago	go	long	queen	time
all	good	look	queen's	too
and	he	made	Rex	tripped
Beth	her	my	rip	went
day	I	named	she	what
dent	in	nice	shine	while
didn't	is	off	so	
fell	it	on	steps	

SKILLS APPLIED IN WORDS IN STORY: short *a, i*; closed syllables; short *o, e*; long *a, i* (CVC*e*); /k/ spelled *c*; /s/ spelled *c*; consonant *g* (hard *g*); blends with *r*; blends with *l*; blends with *s*; final blend *nd*; final blend *ng*; final blend *nt*; double final consonants *ff, ll*; consonants *ck*; double consonants (closed syllables); consonant digraph *th*; consonant digraph *sh*; consonant digraph *wh*; ending *-s*; ending *-ed* /d/, /t/; open syllables (CV); contraction *n't*; vowel digraph *ay*; long *e* (*e, ee*); vowel digraphs *oa, ow*; compound words; schwa sound; ending *-ed*: double consonant; long *i* spelled *i, y*; r-controlled *or, ore*; r-controlled *er*; suffix *-ly*; silent consonants *kn, gn*; /ô/ spelled *al, a*; /o͞o/ spelled *oo*; /o͝o/ spelled *oo*; possessives with *'s, s'*; /ou/ spelled *ou, ow*   **From Grade 1:** consonants; short vowels

HIGH-FREQUENCY WORDS

have	heard	said	they	want
head	put	someone	to	

© Houghton Mifflin Harcourt Publishing Company

The Flower

High-Frequency Words Taught to Date

Grade 1							
a	city	full	loudly	pushed	to	against	lived
about	cold	funny	loved	put	today	ago	might
above	come	give	make	read	together	air	mind
across	could	go	many	ready	too	alone	morning
after	country	goes	maybe	right	took	also	move
again	covers	good	me	said	toward	another	next
all	cried	great	minute	school	try	any	other
almost	different	green	more	second	two	anything	outside
along	do	ground	most	see	under	behind	part
always	does	grow	mother	seven	until	being	pretty
and	done	happy	my	shall	use	better	really
animal	don't	have	myself	she	very	book	river
are	door	he	near	should	walk	care	room
around	down	head	never	show	want	cheer	saw
away	draw	hear	new	sing	warms	children	says
baby	earth	heard	night	small	was	coming	sky
ball	eat	help	no	soil	wash	dark	sleep
be	eight	her	noise	some	watch	didn't	slowly
bear	enough	here	nothing	sometimes	water	doing	someone
beautiful	even	high	now	soon	we	else	something
because	every	hold	of	sorry	were	ever	sound
been	everyone	house	off	starts	what	everything	stood
before	eyes	how	old	stories	where	floor	store
began	fall	I	once	story	who	flower	table
begins	family	idea	one	studied	why	found	tall
bird	far	into	only	sure	window	front	this
blue	father	is	open	surprised	with	girl	though
both	few	kinds	or	take	work	gone	through
boy	field	know	our	talk	world	hair	told
bring	find	large	out	teacher	would	happened	tomorrow
brothers	first	laugh	over	the	write	hard	town
brown	five	learning	own	their	years	hello	turned
buy	fly	light	paper	there	yellow	horse	voice
by	follow	like	party	these	you	hundred	what's
call	food	listen	people	they	young	I'll	while
car	for	little	pictures	think	your	I've	without
carry	four	live	play	those		kept	won't
caught	friend	long	please	thought	Grade 2	knew	words
	friendship	look	pull	three	afraid	leaves	

Decoding skills taught to date: short *a*; short *i*; closed syllables (CVC: short *a, i*); short *o*; short *u*; short *e*; closed syllables (CVC: short *o, u, e*); long *a* (CVC*e*); long *i* (CVC*e*); /k/ spelled *c*; /s/ spelled *c*; long *o* (CVC*e*); long *u* /yo͞o/ (CVC*e*); long *u* /o͞o/ (CVC*e*); long *e* (CVC*e*); consonant *g* (hard *g*); /j/ spelled *g, dge*; blends with *r*; blends with *l*; blends with *s*; final blend *nd*; final blend *ng*; final blend *nk*; final blend *nt*; double final consonants *ll, ss, ff, zz*; consonants *ck*; double consonants (closed syllables); consonant digraph *th*; consonant digraph *sh*; consonant digraph *wh*; consonant digraphs *ch, tch*; consonant digraph *ph*; ending *-s*; ending *-ed* /ed/; ending *-ed* /d/; ending *-ed* /t/; ending *-ing*; ending *-ed*: drop *e*; ending *-ing*: drop *e*; open syllables (CV); contractions *'s, n't*; contractions *'ll, 'd*; contractions *'ve, 're*; endings *-s, -es*; vowel digraphs *ai, ay*; vowel digraphs *ee, ea*; vowel digraphs *oa, ow*; compound words; schwa spelled *a, e, i, o, u*; endings *-ed, -ing*: double consonant; long *i* spelled *igh, ie*; long *i* spelled *i, y*; long *e* spelled *y*; ending *-es*: change *y* to *i*; r-controlled *ar*; r-controlled *or, ore*; r-controlled *er*; r-controlled *ir, ur*; homophones; endings *-er, -est*: double consonant; suffix *-y*; suffix *-ly*; suffix *-ful*; syllable *-tion*; syllable *-ture*; prefix *un-*; prefix *re-*; prefix *over-*; prefix *pre-*; prefix *mis-*; silent consonants *kn, gn*; silent consonants *mb*; silent consonants *wr*; /ô/ spelled *au, aw*; /ô/ spelled *al, a*; /ô/ spelled *o*; /o͞o/ spelled *oo, ou*; /o͞o/ spelled *ew, ue*; /o͝o/ spelled *oo*; possessives with *'s, s'*; /ou/ spelled *ou, ow* **From Grade 1:** consonants, short vowels

The queen's clown heard the loud howls. He didn't know how to fix her gown or shine her crown.

So the clown bowed and gave a flower to Queen Beth.

"How nice," said the queen. "It is a good day after all."

4

© Houghton Mifflin Harcourt Publishing Company

The Flower

A long time ago, a queen named Beth lived in a tower.

"Wow!" she said. "Look how nice it is outside. I want to go out."

Queen Beth put on her gown and her crown. Then she went down to pick flowers outside.

1

While Queen Beth went down her tower steps, she tripped on her gown. Her crown fell off her head.

"I have a rip in my gown! I have a dent in my crown!" Queen Beth frowned.

Queen Beth howled, "Someone fix my gown! Someone shine my crown!" She howled so loudly!

Rex howled, too. "Bow wow!" What a loud sound they made!

The Wet Ground

DECODABLE WORDS

Target Skill: /ou/ spelled *ou, ow*

around	found	howled	shouted	wow
bounded	frown	loud	snout	
crouched	ground	mound	sound	
down	Hound	out	sprout	

Previously Taught Skills

a	for	it	plop	that's
all	go	Jill	rain	then
and	green	jumped	she	time
anyway	grow	long	sniff	too
at	growing	look	started	up
came	he	made	stop	wanted
can	his	muddy	stopped	wet
didn't	hitting	played	sun	will
falling	I	plip	that	

SKILLS APPLIED IN WORDS IN STORY: short vowels; closed syllables; long *a* (CVC*e*); long *I* (CVC*e*); /k/ spelled *c*; consonant *g* (hard *g*); blends with *r, l, s*; final blends *nd, ng, nt, mp*; double final consonants *ll, ff*; consonant digraphs *th, sh, ch*; ending *-ed* /ed/; ending *-ed* /t/; ending *-ing*; open syllables (CV); contraction *n't*; vowel digraphs *ai, ay*; long *e* (*e, ee*); vowel digraphs *oa, ow*; compound words; endings *-ed, -ing*: double consonant; long *e* spelled *y*; r-controlled *ar, or, ore*; suffix *-y*; /ô/ spelled *al, a*; /o͞o/ spelled *oo, ou, ew, ue*; /o͞o/ spelled *oo*; /ou/ spelled *ou, ow*   **From Grade 1:** consonants

HIGH-FREQUENCY WORDS

could	of	the	very	you
from	onto	to	wanted	
hear	said	used	was	

Houghton Mifflin Harcourt.

/ou/ spelled *ou, ow*

BOOK 176

The Wet Ground

High-Frequency Words Taught to Date

Grade 1	city	full	loudly	pushed	to	against	lived
a	cold	funny	loved	put	today	ago	might
about	come	give	make	read	together	air	mind
above	could	go	many	ready	too	alone	morning
across	country	goes	maybe	right	took	also	move
after	covers	good	me	said	toward	another	next
again	cried	great	minute	school	try	any	other
all	different	green	more	second	two	anything	outside
almost	do	ground	most	see	under	behind	part
along	does	grow	mother	seven	until	being	pretty
always	done	happy	my	shall	use	better	really
and	don't	have	myself	she	very	book	river
animal	door	he	near	should	walk	care	room
are	down	head	never	show	want	cheer	saw
around	draw	hear	new	sing	warms	children	says
away	earth	heard	night	small	was	coming	sky
baby	eat	help	no	soil	wash	dark	sleep
ball	eight	her	noise	some	watch	didn't	slowly
be	enough	here	nothing	sometimes	water	doing	someone
bear	even	high	now	soon	we	else	something
beautiful	every	hold	of	sorry	were	ever	sound
because	everyone	house	off	starts	what	everything	stood
been	eyes	how	old	stories	where	floor	store
before	fall	I	once	story	who	flower	table
began	family	idea	one	studied	why	found	tall
begins	far	into	only	sure	window	front	this
bird	father	is	open	surprised	with	girl	though
blue	few	kinds	or	take	work	gone	through
both	field	know	our	talk	world	hair	told
boy	find	large	out	teacher	would	happened	tomorrow
bring	first	laugh	over	the	write	hard	town
brothers	five	learning	own	their	years	hello	turned
brown	fly	light	paper	there	yellow	horse	voice
buy	follow	like	party	these	you	hundred	what's
by	food	listen	people	they	young	I'll	while
call	for	little	pictures	think	your	I've	without
car	four	live	play	those		kept	won't
carry	friend	long	please	thought	**Grade 2**	knew	words
caught	friendship	look	pull	three	afraid	leaves	

Decoding skills taught to date: short *a*; short *i*; closed syllables (CVC: short *a, i*); short *o*; short *u*; short *e*; closed syllables (CVC: short *o, u, e*); long *a* (CVC*e*); long *i* (CVC*e*); /k/ spelled *c*; /s/ spelled *c*; long *o* (CVC*e*); long *u* /yo͞o/ (CVC*e*); long *u* /o͞o/ (CVC*e*); consonant *g* (hard *g*); /j/ spelled *g, dge*; blends with *r*; blends with *l*; blends with *s*; final blend *nd*; final blend *ng*; final blend *nk*; final blend *nt*; double final consonants *ll, ss, ff, zz*; consonants *ck*; double consonants (closed syllables); consonant digraph *th*; consonant digraph *sh*; consonant digraph *wh*; consonant digraphs *ch, tch*; consonant digraph *ph*; ending -*s*; ending -*ed* /ed/; ending -*ed* /d/; ending -*ed* /t/; ending -*ing*; ending -*ed*: drop *e*; ending -*ing*: drop *e*; open syllables (CV); contractions *'s, n't*; contractions *'ll, 'd*; contractions *'ve, 're*; endings -*s, -es*; vowel digraphs *ai, ay*; vowel digraphs *ee, ea*; vowel digraphs *oa, ow*; compound words; schwa spelled *a, e, i, o, u*; endings -*ed, -ing*: double consonant; long *i* spelled *igh, ie*; long *i* spelled *i, y*; long *e* spelled *y*; ending -*es*: change *y* to *i*; r-controlled *ar*; r-controlled *or, ore*; r-controlled *er*; r-controlled *ir, ur*; homophones; endings -*er, -est*: double consonant; suffix -*y*; suffix -*ly*; suffix -*ful*; syllable -*tion*; syllable -*ture*; prefix *un*-; prefix *re*-; prefix *over*-; prefix *pre*-; prefix *mis*-; silent consonants *kn, gn*; silent consonants *mb*; silent consonants *wr*; /ô/ spelled *au, aw*; /ô/ spelled *al, a*; /ô/ spelled *o*; /o͞o/ spelled *oo, ou*; /o͞o/ spelled *ew, ue*; /o͝o/ spelled *oo*; possessives with *'s, s'*; /ou/ spelled *ou, ow* **From Grade 1:** consonants

The Wet Ground

Plip, plop! Plip, plop!

Jill could hear the sound of rain falling down and hitting the ground. It was very loud. Jill started to frown.

She wanted to go out. Hound wanted to go out, too.

Jill and Hound jumped up, down, and all around. Jill shouted, and Hound howled.

Jill and Hound played for a long time. Then the plip plop sound stopped.

The sun came out!

4

1

The sound of rain didn't stop.

"That's it," said Jill. "I will go out anyway. Hound, you can go out, too."

Jill and Hound bounded out onto the wet, muddy ground.

Hound used his snout to sniff the wet ground. He found a mound.

A green sprout was growing from the mound. Jill crouched down to look at the sprout.

"Wow," Jill said. "The rain made that green sprout grow."

2

3

My Sister's Playdate

DECODABLE WORDS

Target Skill: long *a* in longer words

Amy	babies	escape	playdate	rainbows
Amy's	behave	favor	playing	
awake	crayons	later	playmates	

Previously Taught Skills

a	can't	if	play	the
after	day	is	she's	this
all	draw	lot	sister	three
am	go	me	sister's	watch
and	helping	mom	so	we
as	her	my	stuck	when
bad	home	needs	that	with
be	I	of	that's	wow

SKILLS APPLIED IN WORDS IN STORY: short *a*; short *i*; closed syllables; short *o*; short *u*; short *e*; long *a* (CVCe); /k/ spelled *c*; long *o* (CVCe); consonant *g* (hard *g*); blends with *r*; blends with *l*; blends with *s*; final blend *nd*; consonants *ck*; consonant digraph *th*; consonant digraph *sh*; consonant digraph *wh*; consonant digraph *tch*; ending -*s*; ending -*ing*; open syllables (CV); contractions *'s, n't*; contraction *'ll*, vowel digraphs *ai, ay*; vowel digraph *ee*; vowel digraph *ow*; compound words; schwa sound; long *i* spelled *i, y*; long *e* spelled *y*; ending -*es*: change *y* to *i*; r-controlled *er*; r-controlled *or*; /ô/ spelled *aw*; /ô/ spelled *al, a*; possessives with *'s, s'*; /ou/ spelled *ou, ow*; long *a* in longer words
From Grade 1: consonants; short vowels; long *e* (*e, ee*)

HIGH-FREQUENCY WORDS

always	coming	gives	here	they'll
another	does	have	love	to
are	friends	having	something	wasn't

Houghton Mifflin Harcourt.

My Sister's Playdate

High-Frequency Words Taught to Date

Grade 1							
a	city	full	loudly	pushed	to	against	lived
about	cold	funny	loved	put	today	ago	might
above	come	give	make	read	together	air	mind
across	could	go	many	ready	too	alone	morning
after	country	goes	maybe	right	took	also	move
again	covers	good	me	said	toward	another	next
all	cried	great	minute	school	try	any	other
almost	different	green	more	second	two	anything	outside
along	do	ground	most	see	under	behind	part
always	does	grow	mother	seven	until	being	pretty
and	done	happy	my	shall	use	better	really
animal	don't	have	myself	she	very	book	river
are	door	he	near	should	walk	care	room
around	down	head	never	show	want	cheer	saw
away	draw	hear	new	sing	warms	children	says
baby	earth	heard	night	small	was	coming	sky
ball	eat	help	no	soil	wash	dark	sleep
be	eight	her	noise	some	watch	didn't	slowly
bear	enough	here	nothing	sometimes	water	doing	someone
beautiful	even	high	now	soon	we	else	something
because	every	hold	of	sorry	were	ever	sound
been	everyone	house	off	starts	what	everything	stood
before	eyes	how	old	stories	where	floor	store
began	fall	I	once	story	who	flower	table
begins	family	idea	one	studied	why	found	tall
bird	far	into	only	sure	window	front	this
blue	father	is	open	surprised	with	girl	though
both	few	kinds	or	take	work	gone	through
boy	field	know	our	talk	world	hair	told
bring	find	large	out	teacher	would	happened	tomorrow
brothers	first	laugh	over	the	write	hard	town
brown	five	learning	own	their	years	hello	turned
buy	fly	light	paper	there	yellow	horse	voice
by	follow	like	party	these	you	hundred	what's
call	food	listen	people	they	young	I'll	while
car	for	little	pictures	think	your	I've	without
carry	four	live	play	those	**Grade 2**	kept	woman
caught	friend	long	please	thought	afraid	knew	won't
	friendship	look	pull	three		leaves	words

Decoding skills taught to date: short *a*; short *i*; closed syllables (CVC: short *a, i*); short *o*; short *u*; short *e*; closed syllables (CVC: short *o, u, e*); long *a* (CVC*e*); long *i* (CVC*e*); /k/ spelled *c*; /s/ spelled *c*; long *o* (CVC*e*); long *u* /yōō/ (CVC*e*); long *u* /ōō/ (CVC*e*); long *e* (CVC*e*); consonant *g* (hard *g*); /j/ spelled *g, dge*; blends with *r*; blends with *l*; blends with *s*; final blend *nd*; final blend *ng*; final blend *nk*; final blend *nt*; double final consonants *ll, ss, ff, zz*; consonants *ck*; double consonants (closed syllables); consonant digraph *th*; consonant digraph *sh*; consonant digraph *wh*; consonant digraphs *ch, tch*; consonant digraph *ph*; ending -*s*; ending -*ed* /ed/; ending -*ed* /d/; ending -*ed* /t/; ending -*ing*; ending -*ed*: drop *e*; ending -*ing*: drop *e*; open syllables (CV); contractions '*s, n't*; contractions '*ll, 'd*; contractions '*ve, 're*; endings -*s, -es*; vowel digraphs *ai, ay*; vowel digraphs *ee, ea*; vowel digraphs *oa, ow*; compound words; schwa spelled *a, e, i, o, u*; endings -*ed, -ing*: double consonant; long *i* spelled *igh, ie*; long *i* spelled *i, y*; long *e* spelled *y*; ending -*es*: change *y* to *i*; r-controlled *ar*; r-controlled *or, ore*; r-controlled *er*; r-controlled *ir, ur*; homophones; endings -*er, -est*: double consonant; suffix -*y*; suffix -*ly*; suffix -*ful*; syllable -*tion*; syllable -*ture*; prefix *un*-; prefix *re*-; prefix *over*-; prefix *pre*-; prefix *mis*-; silent consonants *kn, gn*; silent consonants *mb*; silent consonants *wr*; /ô/ spelled *au, aw*; /ô/ spelled *al, a*; /ô/ spelled *o*; /ōō/ spelled *oo, ou*; /ōō/ spelled *ew, ue*; /ōō/ spelled *oo*; possessives with '*s, s'*; /ou/ spelled *ou, ow*; long *a* in longer words   **From Grade 1:** consonants; short vowels; long *e* (*e, ee*)

After all the babies go home, my mom
pays me. Wow!

That wasn't so bad! When does Amy
have another playdate?

My Sister's Playdate

This is my sister Amy. She's having
a playdate later. Three of her friends
are coming to play.

That's a lot of babies! And I can't
escape. I am stuck here all day.

My mom needs a favor, so I am helping her watch Amy's playmates.

I wonder if they'll be awake all day. I wonder if they'll behave.

We have a lot of crayons. We draw a lot of rainbows.

Babies love crayons! Amy is always playing with crayons.

2

3

Making Raisins

© Houghton Mifflin Harcourt Publishing Company

DECODABLE WORDS

Target Skill: long *a* in longer words

amazing	explain	making	remain	taking
baking	flavor	paper	safety	today
became	Kayla	Rachel	stayed	waiting
classmate	layer	raisins	table	

Previously Taught Skills

a	direct	hardest	name	so	towel
all	drain	hi	need	start	try
always	dry	how	next	stems	until
and	each	I	now	step	up
ask	eat	I'll	off	sun	we
bunch	few	important	on	sunlight	will
by	for	in	own	that's	with
can	fresh	is	pick	the	you
check	good	like	place	them	
day	grapes	look	sheet	then	
days	grown	my	single	this	

SKILLS APPLIED IN WORDS IN STORY: short *a, i, o, u, e*; closed syllables; long *a* (CVCe); /k/ spelled *c*; /s/ spelled *c*; consonant *g* (hard *g*); blends with *r, l, s*; final blends *nd, nt, xt*; consonants *ll, ss, ff, ck*; double consonants (closed syllables); consonant digraphs *th, sh, ch*; ending -*ing* (with and without spelling changes); open syllables (CV); contractions '*s, 'll*; endings -*s, es*; ending -*ed* /d/; vowel digraphs *ai, ay, ee, ea, ow*; compound words; schwa sound; long *i* spelled *igh, i, y*; long *e* spelled *y*; long *o* spelled *o*; r-controlled *ar, or, er, ir*; ending -*est*: double consonant; /ô/ spelled *al*; /o͞o/ spelled *ou, ew*; /o͝o/ spelled *oo*; /ou/ spelled *ou, ow*; long *a* in longer words **From Grade 1:** consonants, short vowels, long *e* (*e, ee*); syllable *_le*

HIGH-FREQUENCY WORDS

are	help	of	they	want	your
do	none	our	to	wash	

Houghton Mifflin Harcourt.

Making Raisins

High-Frequency Words Taught to Date

Grade 1							
a	city	full	loudly	pushed	to	against	lived
about	cold	funny	loved	put	today	ago	might
above	come	give	make	read	together	air	mind
across	could	go	many	ready	too	alone	morning
after	country	goes	maybe	right	took	also	move
again	covers	good	me	said	toward	another	next
all	cried	great	minute	school	try	any	other
almost	different	green	more	second	two	anything	outside
along	do	ground	most	see	under	behind	part
always	does	grow	mother	seven	until	being	pretty
and	done	happy	my	shall	use	better	really
animal	don't	have	myself	she	very	book	river
are	door	he	near	should	walk	care	room
around	down	head	never	show	want	cheer	saw
away	draw	hear	new	sing	warms	children	says
baby	earth	heard	night	small	was	coming	sky
ball	eat	help	no	soil	wash	dark	sleep
be	eight	her	noise	some	watch	didn't	slowly
bear	enough	here	nothing	sometimes	water	doing	someone
beautiful	even	high	now	soon	we	else	something
because	every	hold	of	sorry	were	ever	sound
been	everyone	house	off	starts	what	everything	stood
before	eyes	how	old	stories	where	floor	store
began	fall	I	once	story	who	flower	table
begins	family	idea	one	studied	why	found	tall
bird	far	into	only	sure	window	front	this
blue	father	is	open	surprised	with	girl	though
both	few	kinds	or	take	work	gone	through
boy	field	know	our	talk	world	hair	told
bring	find	large	out	teacher	would	happened	tomorrow
brothers	first	laugh	over	the	write	hard	town
brown	five	learning	own	their	years	hello	turned
buy	fly	light	paper	there	yellow	horse	voice
by	follow	like	party	these	you	hundred	what's
call	food	listen	people	they	young	I'll	while
car	for	little	pictures	think	your	I've	without
carry	four	live	play	those		kept	woman
caught	friend	long	please	thought	Grade 2	knew	won't
	friendship	look	pull	three	afraid	leaves	words

Decoding skills taught to date: short *a*; short *i*; closed syllables (CVC: short *a, i*); short *o*; short *u*; short *e*; closed syllables (CVC: short *o, u, e*); long *a* (CVC*e*); long *i* (CVC*e*); /k/ spelled *c*; /s/ spelled *c*; long *o* (CVC*e*); long *u* /yōo/ (CVC*e*); long *u* /ōo/ (CVC*e*); long *e* (CVC*e*); consonant *g* (hard *g*); /j/ spelled *g, dge*; blends with *r*; blends with *l*; blends with *s*; final blend *nd*; final blend *ng*; final blend *nk*; final blend *nt*; double final consonants *ll, ss, ff, zz*; consonants *ck*; double consonants (closed syllables); consonant digraph *th*; consonant digraph *sh*; consonant digraph *wh*; consonant digraphs *ch, tch*; consonant digraph *ph*; ending -*s*; ending -*ed* /ed/; ending -*ed* /d/; ending -*ed* /t/; ending -*ing*; ending -*ed*: drop *e*; ending -*ing*: drop *e*; open syllables (CV); contractions *'s, n't*; contractions *'ll, 'd*; contractions *'ve, 're*; endings -*s, -es*; vowel digraphs *ai, ay*; vowel digraphs *ee, ea*; vowel digraphs *oa, ow*; compound words; schwa spelled *a, e, i, o, u*; endings -*ed,-ing*: double consonant; long *i* spelled *igh, ie*; long *i* spelled *i, y*; long *e* spelled *y*; ending -*es*: change *y* to *i*; r-controlled *ar*; r-controlled *or, ore*; r-controlled *er*; r-controlled *ir, ur*; homophones; endings -*er,-est*: double consonant; suffix -*y*; suffix -*ly*; suffix -*ful*; syllable -*tion*; syllable -*ture*; prefix *un-*; prefix *re-*; prefix *over-*; prefix *pre-*; prefix *mis-*; silent consonants *kn, gn*; silent consonants *mb*; silent consonants *wr*; /ô/ spelled *au, aw*; /ô/ spelled *al, a*; /ô/ spelled *o*; /ōo/ spelled *oo, ou*; /ōo/ spelled *ew, ue*; /ŏo/ spelled *oo*; possessives with *'s, s'*; /ou/ spelled *ou, ow*; long *a* in longer words   **From Grade 1:** consonants; short vowels; long *e* (*e, ee*); syllable _*le*

Raisins! Our grapes stayed in the sun and became raisins!

That's amazing!

The flavor is good! Now you can try making your own raisins.

Kayla and I will eat all of our raisins!

4

Making Raisins

Hi! My name is Rachel. This is my classmate Kayla. Today, we are making raisins.

Do you want to help? I'll explain how! Start by taking a bunch of fresh grapes.

1

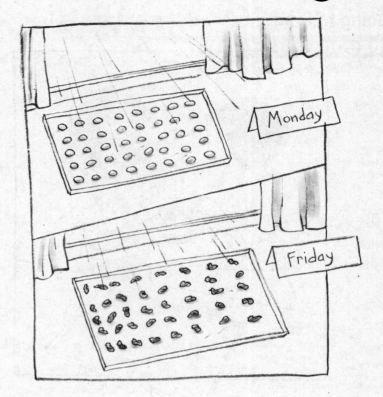

Wash and drain the grapes. Then dry them with a paper towel.

Next, pick off all the stems. None can remain! Safety is important, so always ask a grown up if you need help.

Place the grapes in a single layer on a baking sheet.

Place the baking sheet of grapes on a table in direct sunlight. Now the hardest step: waiting!

The grapes need to remain in the sun for a few days. Check them each day until they look like raisins.

Going to Gran's

© Houghton Mifflin Harcourt Publishing Company

DECODABLE WORDS

Target Skill: long *i* in longer words

bagpipes	kindly	Rylee	turnstile
crying	reptile	showtime	

Previously Taught Skills

a	dance	I'll	Mom	see	thing
am	far	in	my	she	things
and	first	is	next	show	think
at	for	it	now	sign	train
baby	fun	it's	on	sleep	wait
before	go	kind	part	snake	we
best	good	lady	person	so	with
but	Gran's	last	platform	speaks	
cage	happy	like	playing	subway	
can	her	look	read	swipes	
card	home	looks	sad	take	
carry	I		man	say	the

SKILLS APPLIED IN WORDS IN STORY: short *a, i, o, u, e*; CVC syllable pattern; long *a, i, o, e* (CVCe); /k/ spelled *c*; /s/ spelled *c*; /g/ spelled *g*; /j/ spelled *g*; blends with *r, l, s*; final blend *nd, ng, xt*; double consonants (closed syllables); consonant digraphs *th, sh*; base words and endings *-ing, -s*; contractions with *'s, 'll*; vowel digraphs *ai, ay, ee, ea*; vowel digraph *ow*; compound words; schwa sound; long *i* spelled *i, igh, ie*; long *i* spelled *y*; long *e* spelled *y*; *r*-controlled *ar*; *r*-controlled *or, ore*; *r*-controlled *er*; *r*-controlled *ir, ur*; suffix *-y*; suffix *-ly*; silent consonants *gn*; /o͞o/ spelled *oo*; possessives with *'s*; /ou/ spelled *ou, ow*; long *a* in longer words; long *i* in longer words   **From Grade 1:** consonants; short vowels ; long *e* (*e, ee*)

HIGH-FREQUENCY WORDS

are	here	people	to	what
comes	lives	put	today	who
going	of	someone	very	words
have	our	they	wants	

Houghton Mifflin Harcourt

Going to Gran's

happened	kept	move	river	someone	this	voice
hard	knew	next	room	something	though	what's
hello	leaves	other	saw	sound	through	while
horse	lived	outside	says	stood	told	without
hundred	might	part	sky	store	tomorrow	woman
I'll	mind	pretty	sleep	table	town	won't
I've	morning	really	slowly	tall	turned	words

High-Frequency Words Taught to Date

Grade 1	buy	few	house	night	seven	too	
a	by	field	how	no	shall	took	*Grade 2*
about	call	find	I	noise	she	toward	afraid
above	car	first	idea	nothing	should	try	against
across	carry	five	into	now	show	two	ago
after	caught	fly	is	of	sing	under	air
again	city	follow	kinds	off	small	until	alone
all	cold	food	know	old	soil	use	also
almost	come	for	large	once	some	very	another
along	could	four	laugh	one	sometimes	walk	any
always	country	friend	learning	only	soon	want	anything
and	covers	friendship	light	open	sorry	warms	behind
animal	cried	full	like	or	starts	was	being
are	different	funny	listen	our	stories	wash	better
around	do	give	little	out	story	watch	book
away	does	go	live	over	studied	water	care
baby	done	goes	long	own	sure	we	cheer
ball	don't	good	look	paper	surprised	were	children
be	door	great	loudly	party	take	what	coming
bear	down	green	loved	people	talk	where	dark
beautiful	draw	ground	make	pictures	teacher	who	didn't
because	earth	grow	many	play	the	why	doing
been	eat	happy	maybe	please	their	window	else
before	eight	have	me	pull	there	with	ever
began	enough	he	minute	pushed	these	work	everything
begins	even	head	more	put	they	world	floor
bird	every	hear	most	read	think	would	flower
blue	everyone	heard	mother	ready	those	write	found
both	eyes	help	my	right	thought	years	front
boy	fall	her	myself	said	three	yellow	girl
bring	family	here	near	school	to	you	gone
brothers	far	high	never	second	today	young	hair
brown	father	hold	new	see	together	your	

Decoding skills taught to date: short *a*; short *i*; CVC syllable pattern (closed syllables); short *o*; short *u*; short *e*; long *a* (CVCe); long *i* (CVCe); /k/ spelled *c*; /s/ spelled *c*; long *o* (CVCe); long *u* /yoo/ (CVCe); long *u* /oo/ (CVCe); /g/ spelled *g*; /j/ spelled *g*, *dge*; blends with *r*; blends with *l*; blends with *s*; final blend *nd*; final blend *ng*; final blend *nk*; final blend *nt*; double final consonants *ll*, *ss*, *ff*, *zz*; consonants *ck*; double consonants (closed syllables); consonant digraph *th*; consonant digraph *sh*; consonant digraph *wh*; consonant digraphs *ch*, *tch*; consonant digraph *ph*; base words and ending *-s* (no spelling changes); base words and ending *-ed* /ed/ (no spelling changes); base words and ending *-ed* /d/ (no spelling changes); base words and ending *-ed* /t/ (no spelling changes); base words and ending *-ing* (no spelling changes); ending *-ed*: drop *e*; ending *-ing*: drop *e*; CV syllable pattern (open syllables); contractions with *'s* and *n't*; contractions with *'ll* and *'d*; contractions with *'ve* and *'re*; base words and endings *-s*, *-es*; vowel digraphs *ai*, *ay*; vowel digraphs *ee*, *ea*; vowel digraphs *oa*, *ow*; compound words; schwa spelled *a*, *e*, *i*, *o*, *u*; ending *-ed*: double consonant; ending *-ing*: double consonant; long *i* spelled *igh*, *ie*; long *i* spelled *i*, *y*; long *e* spelled *y*; ending *-es*: change *y* to *i*; r-controlled *ar*; r-controlled *or*, *ore*; r-controlled *er*; r-controlled *ir*, *ur*; homophones; ending *-er*: double consonant; ending *-est*: double consonant; suffix *-y*; suffix *-ly*; suffix *-ful*; syllable *-tion*; syllable *-ture*; prefix *un-*; prefix *re-*; prefix *over-*; prefix *pre-*; prefix *mis-*; silent consonants *kn*, *gn*; silent consonants *mb*; silent consonants *wr*; /ô/ spelled *au*, *aw*; /ô/ spelled *al*, *a*; /ô/ spelled *o*; /oo/ spelled *oo*, *ou*; /oo/ spelled *ew*, *ue*; /oo/ spelled *oo*; possessives with *'s*, *s'*; /ou/ spelled *ou*, *ow*; long *a* in longer words; long *i* in longer words **From Grade 1:** short vowels; consonants; long *e* (*e*, *ee*)

But, the best part of our wait is the last thing I see before the train comes. A lady is playing bagpipes. I read a sign with the words "It's Showtime!" I'll say it is! She put on a good show. And, now I can dance!

4

Going to Gran's

I am so happy. Today, Mom, Rylee, and I are going to my Gran's home. She lives kind of far. We have to take the subway. I have fun on the subway. I like to look at the people and the things they carry.

1

First, we go in a turnstile. Mom swipes the card, and in we go. Look at the man with the cage! What is in the cage? It looks like it is a reptile. I think it is a snake. My first fun person is a man with a reptile.

Next, we go on the platform to wait for the train. Who can I see here? I see someone crying. She looks very sad. Her mom speaks kindly to her. She wants the baby to go to sleep.

Jack and Pat

DECODABLE WORDS

Target Skill: long *i* in longer words

alike	fighting	outside	pilot

Previously Taught Skills

a	bike	first	like	same
after	both	games	look	so
along	boys	get	make	switch
always	brown	has	mark	take
and	but	his	not	the
arm	can	if	on	then
at	curls	is	Pat	turns
back	Dad	Jack	plane	up
be	faces	left	play	while
best	fight	leg	rides	with

SKILLS APPLIED IN WORDS IN STORY: short *a*; short *i*; short *o*; short *e*; closed syllables; long *a* (CVC*e*); long *i* (CVC*e*); /k/ spelled *c*; /s/ spelled *c*; /g/ spelled *g* (hard *g*); blends with *r*; blends with *l*; blends with *s*; final blend *nd*; final blend *ng*; final blend *ft*; consonants *ck*; double consonants (closed syllables); consonant digraphs *th, wh, tch*; base words and ending -*s*; base words and ending -*ing*; base words and ending -*es*; open syllables; vowel digraph *ay*; schwa sound; long *i* spelled *igh*; r-controlled *ar, er, ir, ur*; /ô/ spelled *al*; /o͞o/ spelled *oo*; /o͝o/ spelled *oo*; /ou/ spelled *ou, ow*; long *a* in longer words; long *i* in longer words   **From Grade 1:** consonants; short vowels; long *e* (*e, ee*); vowel combination *oy*

HIGH-FREQUENCY WORDS

are	does	pulls	to	wants
brothers	eyes	sometimes	today	you
comes	friends	their	together	
do	nobody	they	want	

© Houghton Mifflin Harcourt Publishing Company

Jack and Pat

High-Frequency Words Taught to Date (continued from inside back cover)

hundred	lived	other	room	someone	tall	town	woman
I'll	might	outside	saw	something	this	turned	won't
I've	mind	part	says	sound	though	voice	words
kept	morning	pretty	sky	stood	through	what's	
knew	move	really	sleep	store	told	while	
leaves	next	river	slowly	table	tomorrow	without	

High-Frequency Words Taught to Date

Grade 1	by	find	idea	now	sing	until	also
a	call	first	into	of	small	use	another
about	car	five	is	off	soil	very	any
above	carry	fly	kinds	old	some	walk	anything
across	caught	follow	know	once	sometimes	want	behind
after	city	food	large	one	soon	warms	being
again	cold	for	laugh	only	sorry	was	better
all	come	four	learning	open	starts	wash	book
almost	could	friend	light	or	stories	watch	care
along	country	friendship	like	our	story	water	cheer
always	covers	full	listen	out	studied	we	children
and	cried	funny	little	over	sure	were	coming
animal	different	give	live	own	surprised	what	dark
are	do	go	long	paper	take	where	didn't
around	does	goes	look	party	talk	who	doing
away	done	good	loudly	people	teacher	why	else
baby	don't	great	loved	pictures	the	window	ever
ball	door	green	make	play	their	with	everything
be	down	ground	many	please	there	work	floor
bear	draw	grow	maybe	pull	these	world	flower
beautiful	earth	happy	me	pushed	they	would	found
because	eat	have	minute	put	think	write	front
been	eight	he	more	read	those	years	girl
before	enough	head	most	ready	thought	yellow	gone
began	even	hear	mother	right	three	you	hair
begins	every	heard	my	said	to	young	happened
bird	everyone	help	myself	school	today	your	hard
blue	eyes	her	near	second	together		hello
both	fall	here	never	see	too	Grade 2	horse
boy	family	high	new	seven	took	afraid	
bring	far	hold	night	shall	toward	against	
brothers	father	house	no	she	try	ago	
brown	few	how	noise	should	two	air	
buy	field	I	nothing	show	under	alone	

Decoding skills taught to date: short *a*; short *i*; CVC syllable pattern (closed syllables); short *o*; short *u*; short *e*; long *a* (CVC*e*); long *i* (CVC*e*); /k/ spelled *c*; /s/ spelled *c*; long *o* (CVC*e*); long *u* /yōō/ (CVC*e*); long *u* /ōō/ (CVC*e*); /g/ spelled *g*; /j/ spelled *g*, *dge*; blends with *r*, blends with *l*, blends with *s*; final blend *nd*; final blend *ng*; final blend *nk*; final blend *nt*; double final consonants *ll*, *ss*, *ff*, *zz*, consonants *ck*; double consonants (closed syllables); consonant digraph *th*; consonant digraph *sh*; consonant digraph *wh*; consonant digraphs *ch*, *tch*; consonant digraph *ph*; base words and ending -*s* (no spelling changes); base words and ending -*ed* /ed/ (no spelling changes); base words and ending -*ed* /d/ (no spelling changes); base words and ending -*ed* /t/ (no spelling changes); base words and ending -*ing* (no spelling changes); ending -*ed*: drop *e*; ending -*ing*: drop *e*; CV syllable pattern (open syllables); contractions with '*s* and *n't*; contractions with '*ll* and '*d*; contractions with '*ve* and '*re*; base words and endings -*s*, -*es*; vowel digraphs *ai*, *ay*; vowel digraphs *ee*, *ea*; vowel digraphs *oa*, *ow*; compound words; schwa spelled *a*, *e*, *i*, *o*, *u*; ending -*ed*: double consonant; ending -*ing*: double consonant; long *i* spelled *igh*, *ie*; long *i* spelled *i*, *y*; long *e* spelled *y*; ending -*es*: change *y* to *i*; r-controlled *ar*; r-controlled *or*, *ore*; r-controlled *er*; r-controlled *ir*, *ur*; homophones; ending -*er*: double consonant; ending -*est*: double consonant; suffix -*y*; suffix -*ly*; suffix -*ful*; syllable -*tion*; syllable -*ture*; prefix *un*-; prefix *re*-; prefix *over*-; prefix *pre*-; prefix *mis*-; silent consonants *kn*, *gn*; silent consonants *mb*; silent consonants *wr*; /ô/ spelled *au*, *aw*; /ô/ spelled *al*, *a*; /ô/ spelled *o*; /ōō/ spelled *oo*, *ou*; /ōō/ spelled *ew*, *ue*; /ŏŏ/ spelled *oo*; possessives with '*s*, *s*'; /ou/ spelled *ou*, *ow*; long *a* in longer words; long *i* in longer words **From Grade 1:** short vowels; consonants; long *e* (*e*, *ee*); vowel combination *oy*

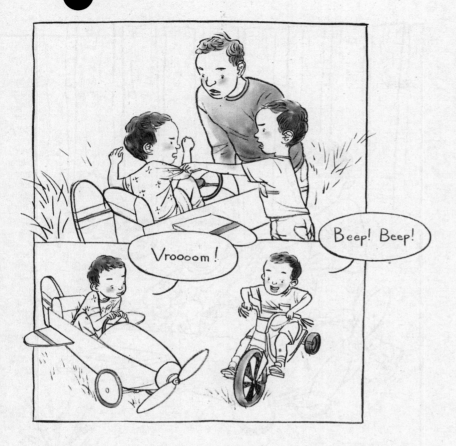

Dad comes outside. "Nobody can be the pilot if you boys do not get along. Take turns."

So, Pat and Jack take turns. Jack is the pilot first while Pat rides the bike. Then the boys switch!

4

Jack and Pat

Jack and Pat are brothers. They look alike. Their faces are alike. They both have brown eyes and the same curls. Jack has a mark on his left arm. Pat does not. Pat has a mark on his left leg.

1

Jack and Pat are best friends, but sometimes they fight. After fighting Jack and Pat always make up. They like to play games together.

Today, Jack and Pat want to play with their plane. Jack wants to be the pilot, but so does Pat. Pat pulls at Jack. Jack pulls back. The boys are fighting.

Join Troy at the Feast

DECODABLE WORDS

Target Skill: /oi/ spelled *oy, oi*

boil	foil	oil	soy
broil	join	soil	Troy
coil	moist	spoil	

Previously Taught Skills

a	eat	holds	plates	this
adds	feast	hot	pot	we
am	food	I	sets	when
and	for	is	so	will
at	garden	meat	start	you
bowl	get	Nan	stove	yum
came	glad	Nan's	take	
can	greens	now	the	
cook	helps	on	them	
don't	his	picked	then	

SKILLS APPLIED IN WORDS IN STORY: short *a, i, o, u, e*; closed syllables; long *a, o* (CVCe); /k/ spelled *c*; consonant *g* (hard *g*); blends with *r, l, s*; final blend *nd*; consonants *ck*; double final consonants *ll*; consonant digraphs *th, wh*; open syllables (CV); contraction *n't*; endings *-s, -ed*; vowel digraphs *ee, ea, ow*; schwa sound; long *i* spelled *i*; r-controlled *ar, or*; /o͞o/ spelled *oo*; /o͝o/ spelled *oo*; possessives with *'s*; /o͞o/ spelled *ou*; /ou/ spelled *ou, ow*; /oi/ spelled *oy, oi*   **From Grade 1:** consonants; short vowels; long *e* (*e, ee*)

HIGH-FREQUENCY WORDS

care	put	says	want
from	puts	to	

Houghton Mifflin Harcourt

BOOK 181

Join Troy at the Feast

High-Frequency Words Taught to Date (continued from inside back cover)

Grade 2

afraid	behind	doing	hair	leaves	pretty	something	tomorrow
against	being	else	happened	lived	really	sound	town
ago	better	ever	hard	might	river	stood	turned
air	book	everything	hello	mind	room	store	voice
alone	care	floor	horse	morning	saw	table	what's
also	cheer	flower	hundred	move	says	tall	while
another	children	found	I'll	next	sky	this	without
any	coming	front	I've	other	sleep	though	woman
anything	dark	girl	kept	outside	slowly	through	won't
	didn't	gone	knew	part	someone	told	words

High-Frequency Words Taught to Date

Grade 1

a	boy	even	grow	look	our	sometimes	under
about	bring	every	happy	loudly	out	soon	until
above	brothers	everyone	have	loved	over	sorry	use
across	brown	eyes	he	make	own	starts	very
after	buy	fall	head	many	paper	stories	walk
again	by	family	hear	maybe	party	story	want
all	call	far	heard	me	people	studied	warms
almost	car	father	help	minute	pictures	sure	was
along	carry	few	her	more	play	surprised	wash
always	caught	field	here	most	please	take	watch
and	city	find	high	mother	pull	talk	water
animal	cold	first	hold	my	pushed	teacher	we
are	come	five	house	myself	put	the	were
around	could	fly	how	near	read	their	what
away	country	follow	I	never	ready	there	where
baby	covers	food	idea	new	right	these	who
ball	cried	for	into	night	said	they	why
be	different	four	is	no	school	think	window
bear	do	friend	kinds	noise	second	those	with
beautiful	does	friendship	know	nothing	see	thought	work
because	don't	full	large	now	seven	three	world
been	door	funny	laugh	of	shall	to	would
before	down	give	learning	off	she	today	write
began	draw	go	light	old	should	together	years
begins	earth	goes	like	once	show	too	yellow
bird	eat	good	listen	one	sing	took	you
blue	eight	great	little	only	small	toward	young
both	enough	green	live	open	soil	try	your
		ground	long	or	some	two	

Decoding skills taught to date: short *a*; short *i*; CVC syllable pattern (closed syllables); short *o*, short *u*; short *e*; long *a* (CVC*e*); long *i* (CVC*e*); /k/ spelled *c*; /s/ spelled *c*; long *o* (CVC*e*); long *u* /yo͞o/ (CVC*e*); long *u* /o͞o/ (CVC*e*); /g/ spelled g; /j/ spelled *g*, *dge*; blends with *r*; blends with *l*; blends with *s*; final blend *nd*; final blend *ng*; final blend *nk*; final blend *nt*; double final consonants *ll*, *ss*, *ff*, *zz*; consonants *ck*; double consonants (closed syllables); consonant digraph *th*; consonant digraph *sh*; consonant digraph *wh*; consonant digraphs *ch*, *tch*; consonant digraph *ph*; base words and ending *-s* (no spelling changes); base words and ending *-ed* /ed/ (no spelling changes); base words and ending *-ed* /d/ (no spelling changes); base words and ending *-ed* /t/ (no spelling changes); base words and ending *-ing* (no spelling changes); ending *-ed*: drop *e*; ending *-ing*: drop *e*; CV syllable pattern (open syllables); contractions with 's and *n't*; contractions with 'll and 'd; contractions with 've and 're; base words and endings *-s*, *-es*; vowel digraphs *ai*, *ay*; vowel digraphs *ee*, *ea*; vowel digraphs *oa*, *ow*; compound words; schwa spelled *a*, *e*, *i*, *o*, *u*; ending *-ed*: double consonant; ending *-ing*: double consonant; long *i* spelled *igh*, *ie*; long *i* spelled *i*, *y*; long *e* spelled *y*; ending *-es*: change *y* to *i*; r-controlled *ar*; r-controlled *or*, *ore*; r-controlled *er*; r-controlled *ir*, *ur*; homophones; ending *-er*: double consonant; ending *-est*: double consonant; suffix *-y*; suffix *-ly*; suffix *-ful*; syllable *-tion*; syllable *-ture*; prefix *un-*; prefix *re-*; prefix *over-*; prefix *pre-*; prefix *mis-*; silent consonants *kn*, *gn*; silent consonants *mb*; silent consonants *wr*; /ô/ spelled *au*, *aw*; /ô/ spelled *al*, *a*; /ô/ spelled *o*; /o͞o/ spelled *oo*, *ou*; /o͞o/ spelled *ew*, *ue*; /o͝o/ spelled *oo*; possessives with 's, s'; /ou/ spelled *ou*, *ow*; long *a* in longer words; long *i* in longer words; /oi/ spelled *oy*, *oi*

From Grade 1: short vowels; consonants; long *e* (*e*, *ee*)

Nan and Troy put the feast on plates. "We can eat the greens and the soy now," says Nan. "We don't want this food to spoil!" Yum, yum! Will you join Troy for the feast?

Join Troy at the Feast

Troy and his Nan start to cook the feast. Troy holds the bowl and Nan adds greens and oil. The greens came from Nan's garden. Troy picked them from the moist soil.

Nan sets a pot on the stove to boil.
Then, Troy adds greens, oil, and soy.
"I am so glad I can join you to cook this
feast, Nan," says Troy.

Nan puts the meat on the foil. When
the stove coil is hot, Troy helps Nan broil
the meat. "Take care, Troy," says Nan.
"The foil can get hot!"

A Toy for Joy

DECODABLE WORDS

Target Skill: /oi/ spelled *oy, oi*

choice	Joy	noise	Roy	toy
join	Joy's	oil	soil	

Previously Taught Skills

a	fixed	made	smiled	went
and	fly	needs	that	wish
at	for	now	then	with
bad	got	on	think	without
bit	had	or	this	you
broke	her	outside	took	
can	high	plane	up	
crashed	I	played	wait	
down	it	rose	waited	
fix	looked	sad	we	

SKILLS APPLIED IN WORDS IN STORY: short *a*, short *i*, short *o*, short *u*, short *e;* closed syllables; long *a* (CVC*e*); long *i* (CVC*e*); /k/ spelled *c*; long *o* (CVC*e*); blends with *r;* blends with *l;* blends with *s;* final blends *nd, nt;* double consonants (closed syllables); consonant digraphs *sh, th;* base words and endings -*s,* -*ed* /ed/, -ed /d/, -ed /t/; r-controlled *or;* long *i* spelled *igh, I, y;* possessives with '*s;* vowel digraphs *ai, ow, ou;* compound words; schwa sound; /o͞o/ spelled *oo*; /oi/ spelled *oy, oi*

HIGH-FREQUENCY WORDS

could	new	she	was
heard	of	the	we
me	said	to	

Houghton Mifflin Harcourt.

A Toy for Joy

High-Frequency Words Taught to Date

Grade 1							
a	city	full	loudly	pushed	to	against	lived
about	cold	funny	loved	put	today	ago	might
above	come	give	make	read	together	air	mind
across	could	go	many	ready	too	alone	morning
after	country	goes	maybe	right	took	also	move
again	covers	good	me	said	toward	another	next
all	cried	great	minute	school	try	any	other
almost	different	green	more	second	two	anything	outside
along	do	ground	most	see	under	behind	part
always	does	grow	mother	seven	until	being	pretty
and	done	happy	my	shall	use	better	really
animal	don't	have	myself	she	very	book	river
are	door	he	near	should	walk	care	room
around	down	head	never	show	want	cheer	saw
away	draw	hear	new	sing	warms	children	says
baby	earth	heard	night	small	was	coming	sky
ball	eat	help	no	soil	wash	dark	sleep
be	eight	her	noise	some	watch	didn't	slowly
bear	enough	here	nothing	sometimes	water	doing	someone
beautiful	even	high	now	soon	we	else	something
because	every	hold	of	sorry	were	ever	sound
been	everyone	house	off	starts	what	everything	stood
before	eyes	how	old	stories	where	floor	store
began	fall	I	once	story	who	flower	table
begins	family	idea	one	studied	why	found	tall
bird	far	into	only	sure	window	front	this
blue	father	is	open	surprised	with	girl	though
both	few	kinds	or	take	work	gone	through
boy	field	know	our	talk	world	hair	told
bring	find	large	out	teacher	would	happened	tomorrow
brothers	first	laugh	over	the	write	hard	town
brown	five	learning	own	their	years	hello	turned
buy	fly	light	paper	there	yellow	horse	voice
by	follow	like	party	these	you	hundred	what's
call	food	listen	people	they	young	I'll	while
car	for	little	pictures	think	your	I've	without
carry	four	live	play	those		kept	woman
caught	friend	long	please	thought	**Grade 2**	knew	won't
	friendship	look	pull	three	afraid	leaves	words

Decoding skills taught to date: short *a*; short *i*; closed syllables (CVC: short *a*, *i*); short *o*; short *u*; short *e*; closed syllables (CVC: short *o*, *u*, *e*); long *a* (CVC*e*); long *i* (CVC*e*); /k/ spelled *c*; /s/ spelled *c*; long *o* (CVC*e*); long *u* /yōō/ (CVC*e*); long *u* /ōō/ (CVC*e*); long *e* (CVC*e*); consonant *g* (hard *g*); /j/ spelled *g*, *dge*; blends with *r*; blends with *l*; blends with *s*; final blend *nd*; final blend *ng*; final blend *nk*; final blend *nt*; double final consonants *ll*, *ss*, *ff*, *zz*; consonants *ck*; double consonants (closed syllables); consonant digraph *th*; consonant digraph *sh*; consonant digraph *wh*; digraphs *ch*, *tch*; consonant digraph *ph*; ending -*s*; ending -*ed* /ed/; ending -*ed* /d/; ending -*ed* /t/; ending -*ing*; ending -*ed*: drop *e*; ending -*ing*: drop *e*; open syllables (CV); contractions *'s*, *n't*; contractions *'ll*, *'d*; contractions *'ve*, *'re*; endings -*s*, -*es*; vowel digraphs *ai*, *ay*; vowel digraphs *ee*, *ea*; vowel digraphs *oa*, *ow*; compound words; schwa spelled *a*, *e*, *i*, *o*, *u*; ending -*ed*: double consonant; ending -*ing*: double consonant; long *i* spelled *igh*, *ie*; long *i* spelled *i*, *y*; long *e* spelled *y*; endings -*es*, -*ed*: change *y* to *i*; r-controlled *ar*; r-controlled *or*, *ore*; r-controlled *er*; r-controlled *ir*, *ur*; homophones; ending -*er*: double consonant; ending -*est*: double consonant; suffix -*y*; suffix -*ly*; suffix -*ful*; syllable -*tion*; syllable -*ture*; prefix *un*-; prefix *re*-; prefix *over*-; prefix *pre*-; prefix *mis*-; silent consonants *kn*, *gn*; silent consonants *mb*; silent consonants *wr*; /ô/ spelled *au*, *aw*; /ô/ spelled *al*, *a*; /ô/ spelled *o*; /ōō/ spelled *oo*, *ou*; /ōō/ spelled *ew*, *ue*; /ŏŏ/ spelled *oo*; possessives with *'s*, *s'*; /ou/ spelled *ou*, *ow*; long *a* in longer words; long *i* in longer words; /oi/ spelled *oy*, *oi*

Roy fixed it. Then Roy took Joy's toy outside. "Join me, Joy!" said Roy. "We can fly this toy plane." The toy plane rose up high. Joy and Roy smiled.

A Toy for Joy

Joy got a new toy plane. She had a choice. She could fly her toy plane now or wait to fly her toy plane with Roy. Joy made her choice. She played with her toy plane without Roy!

Joy's new toy went up high! Then Joy heard a bad noise. The toy plane crashed down on the soil. Joy broke her new toy!

Joy was sad that she broke her toy. "I wish I waited for you to join, Roy." Roy looked at the toy. "I think it needs a bit of oil. I can fix this toy plane!" said Roy.

The Big Oak Tree

BOOK 183

DECODABLE WORDS

Target Skill: long *o* in longer words

almost	mostly	snowed
groaning	Owen	snowstorm

Previously Taught Skills

a	feet	is	mom	shouted	touch
all	for	it	my	snow	tree
and	ground	jumps	not	soon	try
at	had	just	now	spring	wait
aw	hard	last	oak	starting	will
backyard	has	like	off	swing	with
big	her	liked	on	tells	yet
but	high	look	out	ten	
came	house	making	over	that	
can	huge	March	play	then	
day	I	Meg	ran	they	
days	in	melted	rose	time	

SKILLS APPLIED IN WORDS IN STORY: short *a, i, o, u, e*; CVC syllable pattern; long *a* (CVC*e*); long *i* (CVC*e*); long *o* (CVC*e*); long *u* /o͞o/ (CVC*e*); /k/ spelled *c*; /j/ spelled *g*; blends with *r, l, s*; final blends *nd; ng; mp*; double final consonants *ll; ff*; consonants *ck*; double consonants (closed syllables); consonant digraphs *th; sh; ch*; base words and endings *-s; -ed* /ed/; *-ed* /t/; *-ed* /d/; *-ing*; ending *-ed*: drop *e*; vowel digraphs *ai, ay*; *ee, oa, ow*; compound words; schwa sound; long *i* spelled *igh*; *I, y*; r-controlled *ar; or, er*; suffix *-ly*; /ô/ spelled *aw*; *al*; /o͞o/ spelled *oo*; /o͞o/ spelled *oo, ew*; /ou/ spelled *ou, ow*; long *o* in longer words **From Grade 1:** consonants; short vowels

HIGH-FREQUENCY WORDS

again	come	new	she	their	want
are	could	one	the	to	

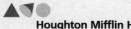

Houghton Mifflin Harcourt

High-Frequency Words Taught to Date *(continued from inside back cover)*

Grade 2

afraid	being	else	happened	might	remember	stood	voice
against	better	ever	hard	mind	river	store	what's
ago	book	everything	hello	money	room	table	while
air	care	floor	horse	morning	saw	tall	without
alone	cheer	flower	hundred	move	says	this	woman
also	children	found	I'll	next	sky	though	won't
another	coming	from	I've	other	sleep	through	words
any	dark	front	kept	outside	slowly	told	
anything	dear	girl	knew	part	someone	tomorrow	
behind	didn't	gone	leaves	pretty	something	town	
	doing	hair	lived	really	sound	turned	

© Houghton Mifflin Harcourt Publishing Company

High-Frequency Words Taught to Date

Grade 1

a	boy	even	grow	look	our	sometimes	under
about	bring	every	happy	loudly	out	soon	until
above	brothers	everyone	have	loved	over	sorry	use
across	brown	eyes	he	make	own	starts	very
after	buy	fall	head	many	paper	stories	walk
again	by	family	hear	maybe	party	story	want
all	call	far	heard	me	people	studied	warms
almost	car	father	help	minute	pictures	sure	was
along	carry	few	her	more	play	surprised	wash
always	caught	field	here	most	please	take	watch
and	city	find	high	mother	pull	talk	water
animal	cold	first	hold	my	pushed	teacher	we
are	come	five	house	myself	put	the	were
around	could	fly	how	near	read	their	what
away	country	follow	I	never	ready	there	where
baby	covers	food	idea	new	right	these	who
ball	cried	for	into	night	said	they	why
be	different	four	is	no	school	think	window
bear	do	friend	kinds	noise	second	those	with
beautiful	does	friendship	know	nothing	see	thought	work
because	done	full	large	now	seven	three	world
been	don't	funny	laugh	of	shall	to	would
before	door	give	learning	off	she	today	write
began	down	go	light	old	should	together	years
begins	draw	goes	like	once	show	too	yellow
bird	earth	good	listen	one	sing	took	you
blue	eat	great	little	only	small	toward	young
both	eight	green	live	open	soil	try	your
	enough	ground	long	or	some	two	

Decoding skills taught to date: short *a*; short *i*; CVC syllable pattern; short *o*; short *u*; short *e*; long *a* (CVC*e*); long *i* (CVC*e*); /k/ spelled *c*; /s/ spelled *c*; long *o* (CVC*e*), long *u* /yoō/ (CVC*e*); long *u* /oō/ (CVC*e*); long *e* (CVC*e*); /g/ spelled *g*; /j/ spelled *g, dge*; blends with *r*, blends with *l*, blends with *s*; final blend *nd*; final blend *ng*; final blend *nk*; final blend *nt*; double final consonants *ll*; double final consonants *ss*; double final consonants *zz*; double final consonants *ff*, consonants *ck*, double consonants (closed syllables); consonant digraph *th*; consonant digraph *sh*; consonant digraph *wh*; consonant digraphs *ch, tch*; consonant digraph *ph*; base words and ending -*s*; base words and ending -*ed* /ed/; base words and ending -*ed* /t/; base words and ending -*ed* /d/; base words and ending -*ng*; ending -*ed*: drop *e*; ending -*ing*: drop *e*; CV syllable pattern (open syllables); contractions with *'s, n't*; contractions with *'ve, 're*; base words and ending -*s, -es*; vowel digraphs *ai, ay*; vowel digraphs *ee, ea*; vowel digraphs *oa, ow*; compound words; schwa sound; ending -*ed*: double consonants; ending -*ing*: double consonants; long *i* spelled *igh, ie*; long *i* spelled *i, y*; long *e* spelled *y*; endings -*es, -ed*: change *y* to *i*; r-controlled *ar*; r-controlled *or, ore*; r-controlled *er*; r-controlled *ir, ur*; homophones; ending -*er*: double consonant; ending -*est*: double consonant; suffix -*y*; suffix -*ly*; suffix -*ful*; syllable -*tion*; syllable -*ture*; prefix *un*-; prefix *re*-; prefix *over*-; prefix *pre*-; prefix *mis*-; silent consonants *kn, gn*; silent consonants *mb*; silent consonants *wr*; /ô/ spelled *au, aw*; /ô/ spelled *al, a*; /ô/ spelled *o*; /oō/ spelled *oo, ew, ue, ou*; /oō/ spelled *oo*; possessives with *'s, s'*; /ou/ spelled *ou, ow*; long *a* in longer words; long *i* in longer words; long *o* in longer words **From Grade 1:** consonants; short vowels

The Big Oak Tree

One March day, the snow had mostly melted. Owen and Meg ran out to try the swing again. Meg jumped on, and she shouted, "Look, look, I can touch the ground! My feet are on the ground!"

Owen and Meg are in a new house. It has a big backyard and a huge oak tree with a swing. Owen and Meg like to swing. Owen can touch the ground.

4

1

Meg can almost touch the ground but not yet. Her mom tells her that one day soon she will, but now it is time to come in. Mom tells Owen and Meg, "A snowstorm is starting." Meg jumps off the swing groaning. "Aw, Mom! I just want to play."

At last the snow came. It snowed for ten days. Snow rose high over the swing, making it hard to swing at all. Meg and Owen liked to play in the snow, but they could not wait for spring and their swing again.

Fishing

BOOK 184

DECODABLE WORDS

Target Skill: long *o* in longer words

boating	going	raincoats	unload
Cody	over	showed	

Previously Taught Skills

a	coming	go	life	ready	they
about	cooler	got	midday	right	time
and	day	great	mile	rods	too
bait	eat	had	needed	sea	up
before	excited	hard	not	silly	vests
better	first	hat	now	six	wet
boat	fish	his	on	so	when
by	fisher	hooks	our	started	with
can	fishing	in	out	stopped	
car	food	it	packed	take	
case	for	kidding	pleased	tell	
caught	get	let's	Pop	then	

SKILLS APPLIED IN WORDS IN STORY: short vowels; closed syllables; long *a, i* (CVC*e*); /k/, /s/ spelled *c*; blends with *r, l, s*; final blends *nd, ng*; double final consonants; CVC closed syllables; consonant digraphs *th, sh, wh*; base words and endings *–s, -ed, -ing*; CV open syllables; contractions *n't, 's*; vowel digraphs *ai, ay, ee, ea, oa, ow, ou*; compound words; schwa sound; long *i* spelled *igh*; long e spelled *y*; *r*-controlled *ar, or, ore, er, ir*; prefix *un-*; vowel combinations *ou, au*; /ô/ spelled *au, o*; /o͞o/ spelled *oo*; /o͞o/ spelled *oo*; long *a, i, o* in longer words   **From Grade 1:** consonants; /z/ spelled *s*

HIGH-FREQUENCY WORDS

are	everyone	never	some	to	were
been	everything	of	something	was	work
began	he	said	the	we	you

Houghton Mifflin Harcourt.

High-Frequency Words Taught to Date *(continued from inside back cover)*

Grade 2

afraid	being	else	happened	might	remember	stood	voice
against	better	ever	hard	mind	river	store	what's
ago	book	everything	hello	money	room	table	while
air	care	floor	horse	morning	saw	tall	without
alone	cheer	flower	hundred	move	says	this	woman
also	children	found	I'll	next	sky	though	won't
another	coming	from	I've	other	sleep	through	words
any	dark	front	kept	outside	slowly	told	
anything	dear	girl	knew	part	someone	tomorrow	
behind	didn't	gone	leaves	pretty	something	town	
	doing	hair	lived	really	sound	turned	

High-Frequency Words Taught to Date

Grade 1

a	brown	far	here	myself	right	those	would
about	buy	father	high	near	said	thought	write
above	by	few	hold	never	school	three	years
across	call	field	house	new	second	to	yellow
after	car	find	how	night	see	today	you
again	carry	first	I	no	seven	together	young
all	caught	five	idea	noise	shall	too	your
almost	city	fly	into	nothing	she	took	
along	cold	follow	is	now	should	toward	
always	come	food	kinds	of	show	try	
and	could	for	know	off	sing	two	
animal	country	four	large	old	small	under	
are	covers	friend	laugh	once	soil	until	
around	cried	friendship	learning	one	some	use	
away	different	full	light	only	sometimes	very	
baby	do	funny	like	open	soon	walk	
ball	does	give	listen	or	sorry	want	
be	done	go	little	our	starts	warms	
bear	don't	goes	live	out	stories	was	
beautiful	door	good	long	over	story	wash	
because	down	great	look	own	studied	watch	
been	draw	green	loudly	paper	sure	water	
before	earth	ground	loved	party	surprised	we	
began	eat	grow	make	people	take	were	
begins	eight	happy	many	pictures	talk	what	
bird	enough	have	maybe	play	teacher	where	
blue	even	he	me	please	the	who	
both	every	head	minute	pull	their	why	
boy	everyone	hear	more	pushed	there	window	
bring	eyes	heard	most	put	these	with	
brothers	fall	help	mother	read	they	work	
	family	her	my	ready	think	world	

Decoding skills taught to date: short *a*; short *i*; CVC syllable pattern; short *o*; short *u*; short *e*; long *a* (CVC*e*); long *i* (CVC*e*); /k/ spelled *c*; /s/ spelled *c*; long *o* (CVC*e*), long *u* /yōō/ (CVC*e*); long *u* /ōō/ (CVC*e*); long *e* (CVC*e*); /g/ spelled *g*; /j/ spelled *g*, *dge*; blends with *r*, blends with *l*, blends with *s*; final blend *nd*; final blend *ng*; final blend *nk*; final blend *nt*; double final consonants *ll*; double final consonants *ss*; double final consonants *zz*; double final consonants *ff*; consonants *ck*, double consonants (closed syllables); consonant digraph *th*; consonant digraph *sh*; consonant digraph *wh*; consonant digraphs *ch*, *tch*; consonant digraph *ph*, base words and ending *-s*; base words and ending *-ed* /ed/; base words and ending *-ed* /t/; base words and ending *-ed* /d/; base words and ending *-ng*; ending *-ed*: drop *e*; ending *-ing*: drop *e*; CV syllable pattern (open syllables); contractions with '*s*, *n't*; contractions with '*ve*, '*re*; base words and endings *-s*, *-es*; vowel digraphs *ai*, *ay*; vowel digraphs *ee*, *ea*; vowel digraphs *oa*, *ow*; compound words; schwa sound; ending *-ed*: double consonants; ending *-ing*: double consonants; long *i* spelled *igh*, *ie*; long *i* spelled *i*, *y*; long *e* spelled *y*; endings *-es*, *-ed*: change *y* to *i*; r-controlled *ar*; r-controlled *or*, *ore*; r-controlled *er*, -r controlled *ir*, *ur*; homophones; ending *-er*: double consonant; ending *-est*: double consonant; suffix *y*; suffix *ly*; suffix *ful*; syllable *-tion*; syllable *-ture*; prefix *un-*; prefix *re-*; prefix *over-*; prefix *pre-*; prefix *mis-*; silent consonants *kn*, *gn*; silent consonants *mb*; silent consonants *wr*; /ô/ spelled *au*, *aw*; /ô/ spelled *al*, *a*; /ô/ spelled *o*; /ōō/ spelled *oo*, *ew*, *ue*, *ou*; /ōō/ spelled *oo*; possessives with '*s*, *s*'; /ou/ spelled *ou*, *ow*; long *a* in longer words; long *i* in longer words; long *o* in longer words **From Grade 1:** consonants; short vowels

Fishing

Pop was not kidding. By midday, Pop and Cody caught six fish. Pop was pleased. He said, "You are a great fisher, Cody. Now let's get the car packed up, so we can tell everyone about our day."

Pop was coming over, and Cody was excited. Cody was going to go fishing with his Pop. Pop had a boat, and they were going to take it out in the sea. Cody had never been boating in the sea before.

4

1

Pop showed up right on time. He had everything they needed for fishing. He had hooks, bait, rods, life vests, a silly hat, a cooler with food, and raincoats in case it got too wet.

When they got to the sea, Pop started the boat. He stopped the boat about a mile out and got the rods ready. Then he began to unload some of the food. Pop said, "We had better eat something first. Fishing is hard work."

A Team Meeting

DECODABLE WORDS

Target Skill: **long *e* in longer words**

copied	fielded	Nicky	really
field	meeting	Nicky's	season

Previously Taught Skills

a	before	had	on	they
after	called	help	play	this
all	class	how	played	throw
and	Coach	if	ran	time
as	didn't	it	rules	understand
at	first	kids	same	up
ball	five	looked	showed	well
baseball	for	Mike	smaller	yay
bases	Friday	next	so	
bat	game	nice	team	
batted	going	older	them	

SKILLS APPLIED IN WORDS IN STORY: short *a*; *i*; CVC syllable pattern; short *o*; *u*; *e*; long *a, i,* (CVC*e*); /k/ spelled *c*; long *u* /ōō/ (CVC*e*); /g/ spelled *g*; blends with *r*; *l*; *s*; final blends *nd*; *ng*; double final consonants *ll, ss*; consonants *ck*; consonant digraphs *th*; *sh*; *ch*; base words and endings *-s*; *-ed* /ed/; *-ed* /t/; *-ed* /d/; *-ing*; CV syllable pattern (open syllables); contraction with *n't*; vowel digraph *ay*; vowel digraphs *ee, ea*; vowel digraphs *oa, ow*; compound words; schwa sound; ending *-ed*: double consonants; long *e* spelled *y*; *r*-controlled *or, ore, ir*; base words and ending *-er*; /ōō/ spelled *oo*; long *a* in longer words; long *o* in longer words; long *e* in longer words **From Grade 1:** consonants; /z/ spelled *s*

HIGH-FREQUENCY WORDS

do	knew	the	was	where
everyone	learn	there	were	who
he	some	to	what	

 Houghton Mifflin Harcourt.

A Team Meeting

High-Frequency Words Taught to Date *(continued from inside back cover)*

everything	hair	kept	move	river	something	through	without
floor	happened	knew	next	room	sound	told	woman
flower	hard	leaves	other	saw	stood	tomorrow	won't
found	hello	lived	outside	says	store	town	words
from	horse	might	part	sky	table	turned	
front	hundred	mind	pretty	sleep	tall	voice	
girl	I'll	money	really	slowly	this	what's	
gone	I've	morning	remember	someone	though	while	

High-Frequency Words Taught to Date

Grade 1

a	brown	far	here	myself	right	those	would
about	buy	father	high	near	said	thought	write
above	by	few	hold	never	school	three	years
across	call	field	house	new	second	to	yellow
after	car	find	how	night	see	today	you
again	carry	first	I	no	seven	together	young
all	caught	five	idea	noise	shall	too	your
almost	city	fly	into	nothing	she	took	
along	cold	follow	is	now	should	toward	**Grade 2**
always	come	food	kinds	of	show	try	afraid
and	could	for	know	off	sing	two	against
animal	country	four	large	old	small	under	ago
are	covers	friend	laugh	once	soil	until	air
around	cried	friendship	learning	one	some	use	alone
away	different	full	light	only	sometimes	very	also
baby	do	funny	like	open	soon	walk	another
ball	does	give	listen	or	sorry	want	any
be	done	go	little	our	starts	warms	anything
bear	don't	goes	live	out	stories	was	behind
beautiful	door	good	long	over	story	wash	being
because	down	great	look	own	studied	watch	better
been	draw	green	loudly	paper	sure	water	book
before	earth	ground	loved	party	surprised	we	care
began	eat	grow	make	people	take	were	cheer
begins	eight	happy	many	pictures	talk	what	children
bird	enough	have	maybe	play	teacher	where	coming
blue	even	he	me	please	the	who	dark
both	every	head	minute	pull	their	why	dear
boy	everyone	hear	more	pushed	there	window	didn't
bring	eyes	heard	most	put	these	with	doing
brothers	fall	help	mother	read	they	work	else
	family	her	my	ready	think	world	ever

Decoding skills taught to date: short *a*; short *i*; CVC syllable pattern; short *o*; short *u*; short *e*; long *a* (CVC*e*); long *i* (CVC*e*); /k/ spelled *c*; /s/ spelled *c*; long *o* (CVC*e*), long *u* /yōō/ (CVC*e*); long *u* /ōō/ (CVC*e*); long *e* (CVC*e*); /g/ spelled *g*; /j/ spelled *g, dge*; blends with *r*; blends with *l*; blends with *s*; final blend *nd*; final blend *ng*; final blend *nk*; final blend *nt*; double final consonants *ll*; double final consonants *ss*; double final consonants *zz*; double final consonants *ff*; consonants *ck*; double consonants (closed syllables); consonant digraph *th*; consonant digraph *sh*; consonant digraph *wh*; consonant digraphs *ch, tch*; consonant digraph *ph*; base words and ending *-s*; base words and ending *-ed* /ed/; base words and ending *-ed* /t/; base words and ending *-ed* /d/; base words and ending *-ng*; ending *-ed*: drop *e*; ending *-ing*: drop *e*; CV syllable pattern (open syllables); contractions with *'s, n't*; contractions with *'ve, 're*; base words and endings *-s, -es*; vowel digraphs *ai, ay*; vowel digraphs *ee, ea*; vowel digraphs *oa, ow*; compound words; schwa sound; ending *-ed*: double consonants; ending *-ing*: double consonants; long *i* spelled *igh, ie*; long *i* spelled *i, y*; long *e* spelled *y*; endings *-es, -ed*: change *y* to *i*; r-controlled *ar*; r-controlled *or, ore*; r-controlled *er*; r-controlled *ir, ur*; homophones; ending *-er*: double consonant; ending *-est*: double consonant; suffix *-y*; suffix *-ly*; suffix *-ful*; syllable *-tion*; syllable *-ture*; prefix *un-*; prefix *re-*; prefix *over-*; prefix *pre-*; prefix *mis-*; silent consonants *kn, gn*; silent consonants *mb*; silent consonants *wr*; /ô/ spelled *au, aw*; /ô/ spelled *al, a*; /ô/ spelled *o*; /ōō/ spelled *oo, ew, ue, ou*; /ōō/ spelled *oo*; possessives with *'s, s'*; /ou/ spelled *ou, ow*; long *a* in longer words; long *i* in longer words; long *o* in longer words; long *e* in longer words **From Grade 1:** consonants; short vowels

For the first time this season, Mike and Nicky's team looked as if they knew what to do. They fielded, they batted, and they ran the bases well. Yay, team! Nice going!

A Team Meeting

Mike and Nicky were on the same baseball team. There were kids on the team who didn't really understand the rules, so Coach called a team meeting.

All the kids on the team showed up on Friday after class. They had a game at five, so Coach had a meeting before the game. He had some older kids there to help the team learn some rules.

The older kids ran the bases. They showed how to bat. They played the field and showed everyone how and where to throw the ball. After the older kids played, the smaller kids copied them. Next it was time to play.

Wake Up, Edie

BOOK 186

DECODABLE WORDS

Target Skill: long *e* in longer words

already	Edie	Kathleen	oversleep	ready	sweetie
dreaming	Edie's	needed	quickly	sleeping	thirty

Previously Taught Skills

a	dressed	her	me	so	when
and	feel	home	meet	still	woke
as	for	if	Mom	swim	you
at	get	in	name	they	
be	go	is	no	think	
big	going	it	on	time	
bus	good	job	rubbed	up	
calling	got	late	rushed	wake	
car	green	like	sat	we	
coach	had	make	she	well	
don't	hands	makes	six	will	

SKILLS APPLIED IN WORDS IN STORY: short *a*; short *i*; short *o*; short *u*; short *e*; closed syllables; long *a* (CVC*e*); long *i* (CVC*e*); /k/ spelled *c*; long *o* (CVC*e*); blends with *r*; blends with *l*; blends with *s*; final blend *nd*; final blend *nk*; double final consonants *ll*; double final consonants *ss*; double consonants (closed syllables); consonant digraph *th*; consonant digraph *sh*; consonant digraph *wh*; consonant digraph *ch*; base words and ending -*s*; base words and ending -*ed* /ed/; base words and ending -*ed* /t/; base words and ending -*ed* /d/; base words and ending -*ing*; CV syllable patterns (open syllables); contraction with *n't,* vowel digraphs *ee, ea*; vowel digraph *oa*; compound words; schwa sound; base words and ending -*ed*: final consonants *ss, ll*; long *i* spelled *l*; long *e* spelled *y*; r-controlled *ar*; r-controlled *er*; r-controlled *or*; /o͞o/ spelled *ou*; /o͞o/ spelled *oo*; long *o* in longer words; long *e* in longer words **From Grade 1:** consonants; short vowels; long *e* (*e, ee*)

HIGH-FREQUENCY WORDS

are	could	have	said	was
boy	day	into	the	
clothes	eyes	oh	to	

Houghton Mifflin Harcourt

Wake Up, Edie

High-Frequency Words Taught to Date (continued from inside back cover)

everything	hair	kept	move	river	something	through	without
floor	happened	knew	next	room	sound	told	woman
flower	hard	leaves	other	saw	stood	tomorrow	won't
found	hello	lived	outside	says	store	town	words
from	horse	might	part	sky	table	turned	
front	hundred	mind	pretty	sleep	tall	voice	
girl	I'll	money	really	slowly	this	what's	
gone	I've	morning	remember	someone	though	while	

High-Frequency Words Taught to Date

Grade 1

a	brown	far	here	myself	right	those	would
about	buy	father	high	near	said	thought	write
above	by	few	hold	new	school	three	years
across	call	field	house	night	second	to	yellow
after	car	find	how	no	see	today	you
again	carry	first	I	noise	seven	together	young
all	caught	five	idea	nothing	shall	too	your
almost	city	fly	into	now	she	took	
along	cold	follow	is	of	should	toward	**Grade 2**
always	come	food	kinds	off	show	try	afraid
and	could	for	know	old	sing	two	against
animal	country	four	large	once	small	under	ago
are	covers	friend	laugh	one	soil	until	air
around	cried	friendship	learning	only	some	use	alone
away	different	full	light	open	sometimes	very	also
baby	do	funny	like	or	soon	walk	another
ball	does	give	listen	our	sorry	want	any
be	done	go	little	out	starts	warms	anything
bear	don't	goes	live	over	stories	was	behind
beautiful	door	good	long	own	story	wash	being
because	down	great	look	paper	studied	watch	better
been	draw	green	loudly	party	sure	water	book
before	earth	ground	loved	people	surprised	we	care
began	eat	grow	make	pictures	take	were	cheer
begins	eight	happy	many	play	talk	what	children
bird	enough	have	maybe	please	teacher	where	coming
blue	even	he	me	pull	the	who	dark
both	every	head	minute	pushed	their	why	dear
boy	everyone	hear	more	put	there	window	didn't
bring	eyes	heard	most	read	these	with	doing
brothers	family	help	mother	ready	they	work	else
	fall	her	my		think	world	ever

Decoding skills taught to date: short *a*; short *i*; CVC syllable pattern; short *o*; short *u*; short *e*; long *a* (CVC*e*); long *i* (CVC*e*); /k/ spelled *c*; /s/ spelled *c*; long *o* (CVC*e*), long *u* /yōō/ (CVC*e*); long *u* /ōō/ (CVC*e*); long *e* (CVC*e*); /g/ spelled *g*; /j/ spelled *g, dge*; blends with *r*; blends with *l*; blends with *s*; final blend *nd*; final blend *ng*; final blend *nk*; final blend *nt*; double final consonants *ll*; double final consonants *ss*; double final consonants *zz*; double final consonants *ff*; consonants *ck*; double consonants (closed syllables); consonant digraph *th*; consonant digraph *sh*; consonant digraph *wh*; consonant digraphs *ch, tch*; consonant digraph *ph*; base words and ending -*s*; base words and ending -*ed* /ed/; base words and ending -*ed* /t/; base words and ending -*ed* /d/; base words and ending -*ng*; ending -*ed*: drop *e*; ending -*ing*: drop *e*; CV syllable pattern (open syllables); contractions with '*s, n't*; contractions with '*ve, 're*; base words and ending -*s, -es*; vowel digraphs *ai, ay*; vowel digraphs *ee, ea*; vowel digraphs *oa, ow*; compound words; schwa sound; ending -*ed*: double consonants; ending -*ing*: double consonants; long *i* spelled *igh, ie*; long *i* spelled *i, y*; long *e* spelled *y*; endings -*es, -ed*: change *y* to *i*; r-controlled *ar*; r-controlled *or, ore*; r-controlled *er*; r-controlled *ir, ur*; homophones; ending -*er*: double consonant; ending -*est*: double consonant; suffix -*y*; suffix -*ly*; suffix -*ful*; syllable -*tion*; syllable -*ture*; prefix *un*-; prefix *re*-; prefix *over*-; prefix *pre*-; prefix *mis*-; silent consonants *kn, gn*; silent consonants *mb*; silent consonants *wr*; /ô/ spelled *au, aw*; /ô/ spelled *al, a*; /ô/ spelled *o*; /ōō/ spelled *oo, ew, ue, ou*; /ŏŏ/ spelled *oo*; possessives with '*s, s*'; /ou/ spelled *ou, ow*; long *a* in longer words; long *i* in longer words; long *o* in longer words; long *e* in longer words **From Grade 1:** consonants; short vowels; long *e* (*e, ee*)

Edie dressed quickly, and she was ready on time. She said to her mom as they got into the car, "Boy, I don't like to oversleep. It makes me feel so rushed."

"I think we will make it on time. Good job, Edie," Mom said.

4

Wake Up, Edie

It was a big day in the Green home. Edie had a swim meet to go to, and she needed to get up at six.

Edie was dreaming and sleeping well, when she woke up to her mom calling her name.

1

"Edie, it is late! It is six thirty. You are going to be late for the meet, Sweetie."

Edie rubbed her eyes and sat up quickly. "Oh, no! Coach Kathleen said we have to be on time for the bus!"

2

Mom already had Edie's clothes in her hands, and she said if Edie got dressed quickly, they could still make it to the bus.

3

Mable and Twinkles

DECODABLE WORDS

Target Skill: syllable _le

beagle	circles	little	settles	twinkled
bubbles	gentle	Mable	stumbles	Twinkles
bundle	giggle	maple	twinkle	wrinkles

Previously Taught Skills

and	funny	is	not	then
big	got	it	now	this
blows	had	jump	out	tree
by	has	jumps	pile	until
came	her	leaves	play	what
can	him	likes	pup	when
chases	home	loves	runs	will
dad	how	make	saw	with
dog	if	name	so	you
down	in	new	that	

SKILLS APPLIED IN WORDS IN STORY: short *a*; short *i*; CVC syllable pattern (closed syllables); short *o*; short *u*; short *e*; long *a* (CVC*e*); long *i* (CVC*e*); /k/ spelled *c*; long *o* (CVC*e*); /g/ spelled *g*; blends with *l*; blends with *s*; final blends *nd, mp*; double final consonants *ll*; double consonants (closed syllables); consonant digraph *ch*, consonant digraph *th*; consonant digraph *wh*; base words and ending -*s*; base words and ending -*ed* /d/; long *i* spelled *y*; long *e* spelled *y*; *r*-controlled -*er*; CV syllable pattern (open syllables); vowel digraphs *ee, ea*; vowel digraph *ow;* /ô/ spelled *aw*; /ōō/ spelled *ou, ew*; /ou/ spelled *ou*; syllable _le

HIGH-FREQUENCY WORDS

a	eyes	of	today
be	have	the	was
does	he	to	would

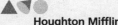

Mable and Twinkles

High-Frequency Words Taught to Date *(continued from inside back cover)*

Grade 2							
afraid	being	else	happened	might	remember	stood	voice
against	better	ever	hard	mind	river	store	what's
ago	book	everything	hello	money	room	table	while
air	care	floor	horse	morning	saw	tall	without
alone	cheer	flower	hundred	move	says	this	woman
also	children	found	I'll	next	sky	though	won't
another	coming	from	I've	other	sleep	through	words
any	dark	front	kept	outside	slowly	told	
anything	dear	girl	knew	part	someone	tomorrow	
behind	didn't	gone	leaves	pretty	something	town	
	doing	hair	lived	really	sound	turned	

High-Frequency Words Taught to Date

Grade 1							
a	boy	even	grow	look	our	sometimes	under
about	bring	every	happy	loudly	out	soon	until
above	brothers	everyone	have	loved	over	sorry	use
across	brown	eyes	he	make	own	starts	very
after	buy	fall	head	many	paper	stories	walk
again	by	family	hear	maybe	party	story	want
all	call	far	heard	me	people	studied	warms
almost	car	father	help	minute	pictures	sure	was
along	carry	few	her	more	play	surprised	wash
always	caught	field	here	most	please	take	watch
and	city	find	high	mother	pull	talk	water
animal	cold	first	hold	my	pushed	teacher	we
are	come	five	house	myself	put	the	were
around	could	fly	how	near	read	their	what
away	country	follow	I	never	ready	there	where
baby	covers	food	idea	new	right	these	who
ball	cried	for	into	night	said	they	why
be	different	four	is	no	school	think	window
bear	do	friend	kinds	noise	second	those	with
beautiful	does	friendship	know	nothing	see	thought	work
because	done	full	large	now	seven	three	world
been	don't	funny	laugh	of	shall	to	would
before	door	give	learning	off	she	today	write
began	down	go	light	old	should	together	years
begins	draw	goes	like	once	show	too	yellow
bird	earth	good	listen	one	sing	took	you
blue	eat	great	little	only	small	toward	young
both	eight	green	live	open	soil	try	your
	enough	ground	long	or	some	two	

Decoding skills taught to date: short *a*; short *i*; closed syllables (CVC: short *a, i*); short *o*; short *u*; short *e*; closed syllables (CVC: short *o, e*); long *a* (CVC*e*); long *i* (CVC*e*); /k/ spelled *c*; /s/ spelled *c*; long *o* (CVC*e*); long *u* /yōō/ (CVC*e*); long *u* /ōō/ (CVC*e*); long *e* (CVC*e*); consonant *g* (hard *g*); /j/ spelled *g, dge*; blends with *r*; blends with *l*; blends with *s*; final blend *nd*; final blend *ng*; final blend *nk*; final blend *nt*; double final consonants *ll, ss, ff, zz*; consonants *ck*; double consonants (closed syllables); consonant digraph *th*; consonant digraph *sh*; consonant digraph *wh*; consonant digraphs *ch, tch*; consonant digraph *ph*; ending *-s*; ending *-ed* /ed/; ending *-ed* /d/; ending *-ed* /t/; ending *-ing*; ending *-ed*: drop *e*; ending *-ing*: drop *e*; open syllables (CV); contractions *'s, n't*; contractions *'ll, 'd*; contractions *'ve, 're*; endings *-s, -es*; vowel digraphs *ai, ay*; vowel digraphs *ee, ea*; vowel digraphs *oa, ow*; compound words; schwa spelled *a, e, i, o, u*; ending *-ed*: double consonant; ending *-ing*: double consonant; long *i* spelled *igh, ie*; long *i* spelled *i, y*; long *e* spelled *y*; endings *-es, -ed*: change *y* to *i*; *r*-controlled *ar*; *r*-controlled *or, ore*; *r*-controlled *er*; *r*-controlled *ir, ur*; homophones; ending *-er*: double consonant; ending *-est*: double consonant; suffix *-y*; suffix *-ly*; suffix *-ful*; syllable *-tion*; syllable *-ture*; prefix *un-*; prefix *re-*; prefix *over-*; prefix *pre-*; prefix *mis-*; silent consonants *kn, gn*; silent consonants *mb*; silent consonants *wr*; /ô/ spelled *au, aw*; /ô/ spelled *al, a*; /ô/ spelled *o*; /ōō/ spelled *oo, ou*; /ōō/ spelled *ew, ue*; /ōō/ spelled *oo*; possessives with *'s, s'*; /ou/ spelled *ou, ow*; long *a* in longer words; long *i* in longer words; long *o* in longer words; long *e* in longer words; syllable *_le*

Mable and Twinkles

Today dad came home with a new little bundle. It is a beagle pup! This pup does not have eyes that twinkle. This pup has little wrinkles. What will Twinkles and Mable name the new pup?

Mable loves Twinkles. Twinkles is her dog. Twinkles is a beagle, and he came home in a little bundle. Mable had to be gentle. Twinkles was so little! If you saw him, you would giggle. He had eyes that twinkled! That is how he got the name Twinkles.

4

1

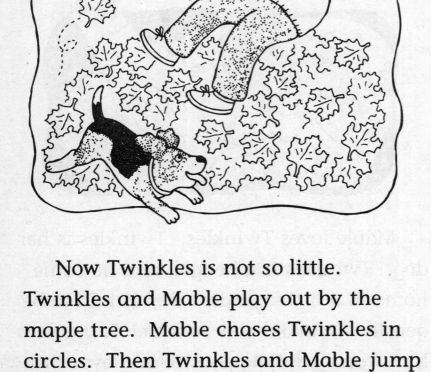

Now Twinkles is not so little.
Twinkles and Mable play out by the
maple tree. Mable chases Twinkles in
circles. Then Twinkles and Mable jump
in a big pile of maple leaves.

Twinkles is funny. He can make
Mable giggle. Twinkles likes it when
Mable blows bubbles. When Mable blows
bubbles, Twinkles jumps and runs in
circles. Twinkles runs until he stumbles.
Then he settles down.

In The Middle of the Woods

DECODABLE WORDS

Target Skill: syllable _le

apples	bundles	little	paddle	turtle
bottles	circle	maple	paddled	twinkle
brambles	eagle	middle	settled	
bundle	kettle	noodles	struggle	

Previously Taught Skills

a	dropped	looked	saw	took
all	fire	made	sharp	trees
an	food	many	sky	trip
and	for	Mom	spot	under
at	from	needed	stars	up
before	had	never	stayed	watched
best	heated	nice	stone	well
camping	held	night	stream	went
can	I	on	tent	with
dinner	in	our	then	woods
down	it	pitched	things	
drank	like	plants	thorns	

SKILLS APPLIED IN WORDS IN STORY: short *a, i, o, u, e*; long *a, i* (CVCe); /k/ spelled *c*; blends with *r, l, s*; final blends *nd, nk, nt*; double final consonants *ll*; consonant digraphs *th, sh, tch*; base words and endings –*s, -ed* /ed/, *-ed* /d/, *-ing*; vowel digraphs *ay, ee, ea, ow*; schwa sound; long *e* spelled *y*; long *i* spelled *igh, I, y*; r-controlled *ar, or, ore, er, ur*; /ô/ spelled *aw*; /o͞o/ spelled *oo*; /ou/ spelled *ou*; /o͝o/ spelled *oo*; syllable _le

HIGH-FREQUENCY WORDS

are	of	the	very	water
away	some	to	was	we

Houghton Mifflin Harcourt.

In the Middle of the Woods

High-Frequency Words Taught to Date *(continued from inside back cover)*

Grade 2

afraid	being	else	happened	might	remember	stood	voice	
against	better	ever	hard	mind	river	store	what's	
ago	book	everything	hello	money	room	table	while	
air	care	floor	horse	morning	saw	tall	without	
alone	cheer	flower	hundred	move	says	this	woman	
also	children	found	I'll	next	sky	though	won't	
another	coming	from	I've	other	sleep	through	words	
any	dark	front	kept	outside	slowly	told		
anything	dear	girl	knew	part	someone	tomorrow		
behind	didn't	gone	leaves	pretty	something	town		
	doing	hair	lived	really	sound	turned		

High-Frequency Words Taught to Date

Grade 1

a	bring	everyone	he	many	party	studied	was
about	brothers	eyes	head	maybe	people	sure	wash
above	brown	fall	hear	me	pictures	surprised	watch
across	buy	family	heard	minute	play	take	water
after	by	far	help	more	please	talk	we
again	call	father	her	most	pull	teacher	were
all	car	few	here	mother	pushed	the	what
almost	carry	field	high	my	put	their	where
along	caught	find	hold	myself	read	there	who
always	city	first	house	near	ready	these	why
and	cold	five	how	never	right	they	window
animal	come	fly	I	new	said	think	with
are	could	follow	idea	night	school	those	work
around	country	food	into	no	second	thought	world
away	covers	for	is	noise	see	three	would
baby	cried	four	kinds	nothing	seven	to	write
ball	different	friend	know	now	shall	today	years
be	do	friendship	large	of	she	together	yellow
bear	does	full	laugh	off	should	too	you
beautiful	done	funny	learning	old	show	took	young
because	don't	give	light	once	sing	toward	your
been	door	go	like	one	small	try	
before	down	goes	listen	only	soil	two	
began	draw	good	little	open	some	under	
begins	earth	great	live	or	sometimes	until	
bird	eat	green	long	our	soon	use	
blue	eight	ground	look	out	sorry	very	
both	enough	grow	loudly	over	starts	walk	
boy	even	happy	loved	own	stories	want	
	every	have	make	paper	story	warms	

Decoding skills taught to date: short *a*; short *i*; closed syllables (CVC: short *a, i*); short *o*; short *u*; short *e*; closed syllables (CVC: short *o, u, e*); long *a* (CVC*e*); long *i* (CVC*e*); /k/ spelled *c*; /s/ spelled *c*; long *o* (CVC*e*); long *u* /yo͞o/ (CVC*e*); long *u* /o͞o/ (CVC*e*); long *e* (CVC*e*); consonant *g* (hard *g*); /j/ spelled *g, dge*; blends with *r*; blends with *l*; blends with *s*; final blend *nd*; final blend *ng*; final blend *nk*; final blend *nt*; double final consonants *ll, ss, ff, zz*; consonants *ck*; double consonants (closed syllables); consonant digraph *th*; consonant digraph *sh*; consonant digraph *wh*; consonant digraphs *ch, tch*; consonant digraph *ph*; ending *-s*; ending *-ed* /ed/; ending *-ed* /d/; ending *-ed* /t/; ending *-ing*; ending *-ed*: drop *e*; ending *-ing*: drop *e*; open syllables (CV); contractions *'s, n't*; contractions *'ll, 'd*; contractions *'ve, 're*; endings *-s, -es*; vowel digraphs *ai, ay*; vowel digraphs *ee, ea*; vowel digraphs *oa, ow*; compound words; schwa spelled *a, e, i, o, u*; ending *-ed*: double consonant; ending *-ing*: double consonant; long *i* spelled *igh, ie*; long *i* spelled *i, y*; long *e* spelled *y*; endings *-es, -ed*: change *y* to *i*; r-controlled *ar*; r-controlled *or, ore*; r-controlled *er*; r-controlled *ir, ur*; homophones; ending *-er*: double consonant; ending *-est*: double consonant; suffix *-y*; suffix *-ly*; suffix *-ful*; syllable *-tion*; syllable *-ture*; prefix *un-*; prefix *re-*; prefix *over-*; prefix *pre-*; prefix *mis-*; silent consonants *kn, gn*; silent consonants *mb*; silent consonants *wr*; /ô/ spelled *au, aw*; /ô/ spelled *al, a*; /ô/ spelled *o*; /o͞o/ spelled *oo, ou*; /o͞o/ spelled *ew, ue*; /o͞o/ spelled *oo*; possessives with *'s, s'*; /ou/ spelled *ou, ow*; long *a* in longer words; long *i* in longer words; long *o* in longer words; long *e* in longer words; syllable *_le*

In the Middle of the Woods

At night, we made a fire in a stone circle. Mom heated up a kettle. We had noodles for dinner and drank water from bottles. Then we looked up in the sky and watched the stars twinkle.

We went on a camping trip to the woods. We took a bundle of things we needed. We had food like apples and noodles. We had many bottles of water, too.

We settled in a nice spot. It was under some maple trees. We dropped our bundles and pitched the tent. We stayed away from brambles. Brambles are plants with sharp thorns!

We went for a paddle down the stream. I had never held a paddle before. It was a little struggle. Mom can paddle very well! We saw an eagle and a turtle. The turtle paddled best of all!